AMERICAN TRAITOR

AMERICAN TRAITOR

General James Wilkinson's Betrayal of the Republic and Escape from Justice

HOWARD W. COX

Georgetown University Press / Washington, DC

The publisher is not responsible for third-party websites or their content. URL links were active at time of publication.

Library of Congress Cataloging-in-Publication Data

Names: Cox, Howard W., author.
Title: American traitor : General James Wilkinson's betrayal of the republic and escape from justice / Howard W. Cox.
Description: Washington, DC : Georgetown University Press, [2023] | Includes bibliographical references and index.
Identifiers: LCCN 2022026973 (print) | LCCN 2022026974 (ebook) | ISBN 9781647123420 (hardcover) | ISBN 9781647123413 (ebook)
Subjects: LCSH: Wilkinson, James, 1757-1825. | Generals—United States—Biography. | Spies—United States—Biography. | Espionage—United States—History—18th century. | Espionage—United States—History—19th century. | United States—History, Military—To 1900. | United States—History—1783-1815. | LCGFT: Biographies.
Classification: LCC E353.1.W6 C79 2023 (print) | LCC E353.1.W6 (ebook) | DDC 355.0092 [B]--dc23/eng/20220708
LC record available at https://lccn.loc.gov/2022026973
LC ebook record available at https://lccn.loc.gov/2022026974

∞ This paper meets the requirements of ANSI/NISO Z39.48-1992 (Permanence of Paper).

24 23   9 8 7 6 5 4 3 2 First printing

Printed in the United States of America

Cover design by Amanda Hudson, Faceout Studio
Interior design by Paul Hotvedt

CONTENTS

ILLUSTRATIONS

ACKNOWLEDGMENTS

Throughout my forty-year career as an attorney, criminal investigator, and intelligence officer for the federal government, I have maintained my love of history, which has allowed me to place modern issues within their historical context. As I conducted criminal investigations of contract fraud and official misconduct, I became interested in identifying historical patterns that have repeated throughout our nation's history and suggest repeated failures in the oversight of federal officials and programs. The character and activities of James Wilkinson repeatedly stand out.

This work is an attempt to examine Wilkinson's criminal deeds and also examine the numerous oversight mechanisms that existed in the early republic which failed to bring misconduct by its highest-ranking military officer to justice. I thank many of the people and organizations that enabled me to complete the task of researching and writing this book. Though I commenced research before the onslaught of the COVID-19 pandemic, many libraries were subsequently closed to researchers when COVID-19 lockdowns were put in place. However, many library staffs continued to work throughout the pandemic and accepted research requests. In this regard I would thank the research staffs of the National Archives and Records Administration, the Filson Historical Society, the William L. Clements Library of the University of Michigan, the University of Chicago Library, and the Historical Society of Pennsylvania for their gracious assistance in responding to my requests.

I thank the archival staff of Heritage Frederick, the Historical Society of Frederick County Maryland. The staff was able to identify a reasonably complete copy of the transcript of the 1811 Wilkinson court-martial as well as assist me in identifying the sites of many of the events that occurred in Frederick during the conduct of the trial. Shaun Butcher, who was on the board of directors of Heritage Frederick, was also kind enough to host a YouTube presentation that I prepared on the court-martial. I also thank Mary Mannix of the Maryland Room of the Frederick County Public Library for sharing her encyclopedic knowledge of the history of Frederick. Furthermore, the research staff of the Chicago History Museum was of immense assistance in identifying relevant materials regarding Wilkinson's papers. The research staff of the Madison Room of the Library of Congress was of great help in identifying translated copies of materials from the Spanish archives relating to Wilkinson's relationship with Spain.

Several persons who were of great assistance in the writing of the manuscript are also deserving of thanks. Don McKeon was kind enough to assist me in editing my proposal and introduced me to the staff of Georgetown University Press. Edward Allan, a retired Army Judge Advocate General's Corps colonel, was kind enough to review the manuscript and provide insights on the military justice process. My editor, Don Jacobs at Georgetown University Press, was my advocate in getting the book published and was both insightful and patient in helping me navigate through the complexities of the editorial process.

Finally, I thank my wife, Sharon W. Cox, for her love and support throughout this process. During our more than forty years of marriage she has supported my love of history and has accompanied me on tours of historic sights and battlefields throughout the United States and Europe. My favorite memory was during the height of a sweltering South Carolina summer, when she walked with me through an obscure Revolutionary War battlefield even though she was seven months pregnant.

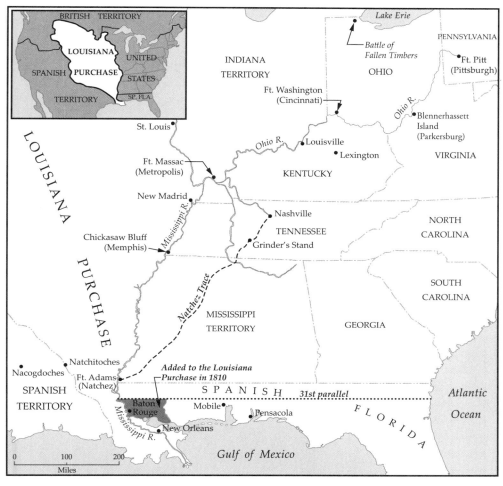

United States and Spanish Territory, 1789–1805

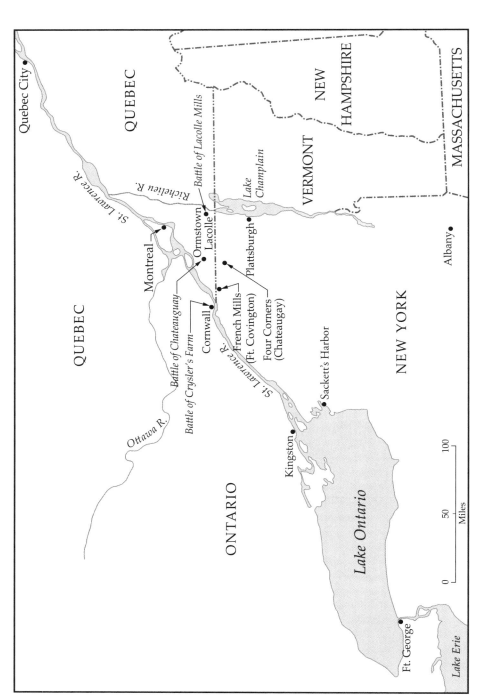

The United States' St. Lawrence River Campaign, 1813

INTRODUCTION

In character, he can only be compared to Benedict Arnold, though he entirely lacked Arnold's ability and brilliant courage. He had no conscience and no scruples; he had not the slightest idea of the meaning of the word honor; he betrayed his trust from the basest motives, and he was too inefficient to make his betrayal effective. He was treacherous to the Union while it was being formed and after it had been formed; and his crime was aggravated by the sordid meanness of his motives, for he eagerly sought opportunities to barter his own infamy for money. In all our history, there is never a more despicable character.
—Theodore Roosevelt, *Winning of the West*

On Christmas evening of December 1776, James Wilkinson, a nineteen-year-old Continental Army lieutenant from Frederick County, Maryland, stood on the banks of the Delaware River. While awaiting his turn to board the Durham boats that would carry General George Washington and the remnants of the Continental Army in a surprise attack on Hessian forces in Trenton, Wilkinson could look back on his short military career with a degree of well-deserved pride.

In the space of eighteen short months Wilkinson had had an amazingly active career. He left his medical practice in Maryland in the fall of 1775 to be one of the first persons to answer the call for volunteers for the Continental Army in Boston. As an educated gentleman, a rarity in the Continental Army, Wilkinson was appointed as an officer and quickly assigned to the staffs of several important generals. Joining General Benedict Arnold in his stubborn 1776 retreat from Canada, Wilkinson was one of the last American soldiers to leave Canadian soil. After

1

obeying Arnold's order to shoot his horse rather than let it fall into British hands, Wilkinson returned to the army's Northern Department, where he left Arnold and joined the staff of General Horatio Gates, a more senior officer. Directed by Gates to carry dispatches to General Washington, who was retreating across New Jersey into Pennsylvania, Wilkinson joined General Charles Lee, Washington's second in command, while Lee spent the night with a prostitute, away from his troops, at a home in Basking Ridge, New Jersey. Wilkinson, present when a British commando raid surprised Lee and captured him in his nightshirt, narrowly escaped capture by hiding up a chimney. Wilkinson eventually met Washington at McConkey's Ferry on the Delaware River and informed Washington that Gates, his new second in command, had deserted the army on the eve of the attack. Wilkinson joined the troops on their crossing of the river as a staff officer and was present for the subsequent American victories at Trenton and Princeton.

Unfortunately, this would be the last honorable service Wilkinson was to render to the United States during his forty-year career of "service." From this point forward Wilkinson betrayed virtually everyone he served for, with, or near as he rose to the highest ranks of the US Army.

Because of his longevity of service with the army (1775–1815), Wilkinson was in a unique position to directly interface with almost every American president from George Washington to Zachary Taylor. He served with or commanded every major American military figure in the first half-century of the American army's existence, from the Revolution to the War of 1812, betraying each one in turn when a better opportunity arose for wealth or advancement. Throughout his career he consistently sought intrigue and avoided combat, and every major military campaign he commanded ended in disaster or defeat. He remains the highest-ranking federal official ever charged with being an agent of a foreign government and was one of the best-paid spies in American history, earning in today's value over $1 million in payments from Spain. As the commanding general of the US Army, he betrayed the Lewis and Clark expedition to his Spanish masters, providing the Spanish with information that could have allowed them to kill or capture the expedition. He worked for President Thomas Jefferson and at the same time conspired with Jefferson's enemy, Aaron Burr, in a conspiracy against Jefferson and the American government. True to form, he eventually betrayed Burr to Jefferson and served as Jefferson's chief witness in the treason trials against Burr.

One of the enduring mysteries of the history of the new republic is how Wilkinson could remain in command of the army for more than fifteen years. His paid relationship with the Spanish government was widely suspected by numerous public officials and repeatedly reported in press articles throughout his service as a general officer. Many future leaders, such as Andrew Jackson and Winfield Scott, widely and publicly denounced him. Prior to his election as president, James Monroe stated to Thomas Jefferson that he would rather be shot than take a government position where he would have to serve under Wilkinson's orders. Numerous congressional investigations and military justice proceedings widely documented his improper relationship with Spain as well as his responsibility for causing, through peacetime incompetence and neglect, the loss of over one-quarter of the American army by death and desertion. Furthermore, Wilkinson's military combat record was deplorable. He regularly avoided combat, except to duel with personal enemies and former commanders. There are only two recorded campaigns where he actually commanded federal troops in combat. In one, he actively sought to undercut his commander so that he could replace him. In the other, he was soundly and repeatedly defeated by inferior Canadian forces, resulting, once again, in his relief from command and court-martial.

Since his death, Wilkinson has been dismissed by most historians as an inept and blusterous buffoon.[1] Yet, while many have condemned him, most have not sought to assess the true damage he caused to American interests through military incompetence, greed, or deliberate treachery.[2] And, despite their dismissal of Wilkinson's actions, many historians have relied on Wilkinson's memoirs as a reliable source of early republic military history, at least regarding historic events where neither Wilkinson nor an enemy is a central player in the narrative. Given Wilkinson's proven propensity for overstatement, misrepresentation, and forgery, any historical reliance on Wilkinson's recollections is misplaced unless facts can be independently verified through other sources.[3]

This biography is the first examination of Wilkinson's life to focus on the inability and unwillingness of the federal government to investigate criminal misconduct committed by a senior federal official. The investigations of Wilkinson resulted in the first judicial examination of concepts such as executive privilege and the role of the president in criminal investigations. As demonstrated by our nation's response to the events surrounding the January 6, 2021, attack on the US Capitol Building, the federal government is still struggling to determine the appropriate manner for investigating senior official misconduct. The tools that are available to us today—congressional oversight and the criminal justice system—proved to be inadequate to find and address Wilkinson's misdeeds. An understanding of why they failed can provide a valuable insight into their effectiveness today.

Despite a pattern of treason, betrayal, and incompetence, Wilkinson was repeatedly chosen by Washington, Adams, Hamilton, Jefferson, and Madison to remain in command of the American army. Some, such as Washington, Adams, and Hamilton, likely selected and retained Wilkinson out of a failure to understand the full scope of his incompetence and treachery. Others, such as Madison, re-tained Wilkinson only after an unsuccessful attempt to court-martial him, and re-moved him only when a better generation of American military officers was finally available to take command. One, Thomas Jefferson, likely chose to retain Wilkin-son in an attempt to gather damning evidence against Jefferson's mortal enemy, Aaron Burr. Jefferson tolerated treason, incompetence, and other unconscionable acts by his army commander since Wilkinson was willing to implicate Burr in an improbable scheme to separate the western states from the United States and lead them in an attack on Spanish Mexico. Ultimately, Wilkinson's treachery toward all would be partially exposed at Burr's conspiracy trials and would undermine Jefferson's efforts against Burr as well. But Jefferson remained loyal to his chosen general, to the lasting detriment of the American army and nation.

This book examines James Wilkinson's rise through the ranks to eventually command the American army despite the complete absence of his having any meaningful military skills or accomplishments. It examines his corrupt relation-ship with the government contractors who jeopardized military campaigns and resulted in one of the greatest peacetime disasters ever to befall the US military. It examines Wilkinson's role as a spy for a foreign power and his successful use of espionage tools to avoid detection. This book also establishes that Wilkinson used his position as commanding general to provide critical intelligence to another country in a manner that frustrated American military and political interests and placed American lives at risk. It explores Wilkinson's role in numerous conspira-cies that nearly fractured the young American republic and assesses the failure of these military leaders, numerous Founding Fathers, and Congress to hold Wilkin-son accountable for his various crimes against the nation.

1

YOUNG DOCTOR WILKINSON
GOES TO WAR

1757–1776

> With one voice and a rising vote, scribes of every persuasion denounce
> Wilkinson. Venal, cowardly, treacherous, a bribe taker from Spain, a traitor
> to the United States, faithless in all relations, public and private, he stands
> in the pillory besides Benedict Arnold.
> —Thomas E. Watson, *The Life and Times of Thomas Jefferson*

Stoakely Manor, a stately home on Hunting Creek, was located on the east
bank of the Patuxent River in Calvert County, Maryland. Since its founding
in the colony in 1650, Calvert County had been a center of the tobacco culture
that predominated the early Maryland landscape. Tobacco fields, harvested and
cured by enslaved persons and indentured servants, produced hogsheads of tobacco, the principal currency of the colony. By the mid-1700s Stoakely Manor,
built by James Wilkinson's grandfather Joseph Wilkinson, was the family's primary
residence. While Wilkinson's father's (also Joseph) marriage to Elizabeth Heighe,
a wealthy resident of nearby Prince George's County, provided some economic
relief, it could not offset the poor management of the plantation and the expense
of a growing family. James was born in 1757, the second child of the marriage,
following an elder brother (Joseph once again). By 1764 Wilkinson's father, only
thirty-three, was in poor health and bordering on death and bankruptcy. According to Wilkinson, Joseph provided his second son with a meager legacy. Joseph's
will directed that, following the custom of primogeniture, the bulk of his estate
went to his firstborn son. James inherited nothing and was given only a piece of
advice by his father on his deathbed: "My son, if you ever put up with an insult,
I will disinherit you."[1]

Shortly after Joseph's death the estate was broken up to avoid bankruptcy. Wilkinson's mother took charge of her second son and, through a private tutor, provided for a solid classical education befitting a member of the Maryland plantation class. James's first experience away from home took place when he and his brother were sent to be inoculated against smallpox in Baltimore when he was thirteen years old. Since the remnant of the Wilkinson estate was the responsibility of Wilkinson's older brother, a career in medicine was chosen for the young teenager. Wilkinson was apprenticed out to Dr. John Bond, a relative and veteran of the French and Indian War. According to Wilkinson, in addition to medicine he was thrilled with Bond's tales of military glory, which served as an early inspiration for a military, and not a medical, career.[2]

In 1774 Wilkinson was sent to Philadelphia and enrolled in the first medical school in the colonies. The school, part of the College of Philadelphia, was the result of the collaboration between two medical giants of early American medicine, Dr. John Morgan and Dr. William Shippen Jr.[3] Founded in 1764, the school provided a three-year course of learning in anatomy, pharmacology, and chemistry. The seventeen-year-old student reveled in his introduction to Philadelphia society, which was far removed from his sheltered plantation upbringing. Wilkinson stated that he sought to cultivate relationships with society women of his own age and avoided "libertinism and profligate dissipation." Wilkinson hinted that his classmates might have dallied with prostitutes and that by avoiding such liaisons he was subjected to sarcasm. Wilkinson also stated that he was distracted by the military drills of the Royal Irish Regiment that was stationed in Philadelphia at the time.[4]

Less than two years into his studies, Wilkinson concluded that he had sufficient training to begin his own practice of medicine. He left Philadelphia and opened a practice in Monocacy, Maryland, in Frederick County.[5] At the time, Monocacy had been settled by German immigrants from Pennsylvania, many of whom spoke no English. The reason behind Wilkinson's choice of Monocacy as the location for his practice remains a mystery. Monocacy was significantly removed from his home county of Calvert and from the colony's municipal centers of Baltimore, Annapolis, and Frederick Town. It was a rural area filled with few people, an unusual location for the practice of medicine, particularly for someone who spoke no German and was a stranger to the area.

It soon became apparent that Wilkinson's study of medicine was driven by his family's wishes and not his own. The growing tensions between colonial governments and their British overlords were rapidly consuming many aspects of daily life and were particularly prevalent in Philadelphia during Wilkinson's school years. The Boston Tea Party occurred shortly before Wilkinson started school,

and many local communities, including Philadelphia and Frederick County, be-
gan protests in support of Boston and in opposition to the oppressive Intolerable
Acts passed by Great Britain in response to the tea protests. The First Continental
Congress, convened in Philadelphia in September 1774 a few blocks from Wilkinson's medical school, soon became the center of colonial opposition to British rule.
Wilkinson's arrival in Monocacy in April 1775 was greeted with news of the first
outbreak of violence between Minutemen and British troops at Lexington and
Concord.[6] In many locations, including Frederick County, local militias began to
form and drill in anticipation of an armed response to British oppression.

Wilkinson decided to commence drilling with a local militia unit, and though
all armed forces need medical personnel, Wilkinson sought out a role as a line
soldier and not as a medical surgeon. He had several militia units from which
to choose, and his selection reflected his goal of using military service for social
advancement. Two militia units had been formed in Frederick Town, the biggest
city in western Maryland and a few short miles from Monocacy.[7] These units,
comprised of backwoodsmen and riflemen, were among the first to answer their
colony's call for volunteers to join the Continental Army in the summer of 1775.[8]
However, rather than choosing to enlist with these nearby units, Wilkinson chose
to drill with another Frederick County militia unit located in Georgetown, on
the banks of the Potomac River and more than thirty miles from Monocacy.[9] The
unit, commanded by Thomas Richardson, a wealthy tobacco merchant and business partner of George Washington, was chosen by Wilkinson undoubtedly for the
opportunity it offered to cultivate relationships likely to advance his social status.
While Wilkinson chose to drill once a week with this unit, he did not accompany
them when they were called to join the Continental Army that summer. Instead,
Wilkinson proceeded on his own to Boston and arrived in September 1775.[10]

Wilkinson's failure to remain with any of the Frederick County units was most
likely the result of his inability to obtain a position in these units as a commissioned officer. At that time militia units elected their own officers, so as an educated but unknown newcomer Wilkinson was unable to get elected by either a
group of Frederick backwoodsmen or Georgetown socialites. Wilkinson instead
proceeded at his own expense to Boston, in the hope of obtaining a commission
based on his upbringing, education, and ability to charm superiors who would be
looking for officer candidates. He arrived in September and joined a rifle corps
as an enlisted volunteer in a unit commanded by Colonel William Thompson of
Pennsylvania.[11]

Wilkinson arrived in Boston after the Battle of Bunker Hill, when British
forces still controlled the city of Boston and its harbor and Washington's forces
surrounded the city. Washington was in the process of fortifying his defensive

position around the city and raising and training a professional army from a collection of local militia units raised throughout the colonies. Wilkinson was involved in the fortification of Dorchester Heights, overlooking Boston Harbor, and following the successful emplacement of artillery there the British evacuated Boston in March 1776.[12]

Having served as an enlisted volunteer for six months, at the time of the British evacuation of Boston, Wilkinson obtained a commission from Washington as a captain in Colonel James Reed's Third New Hampshire Regiment.[13] Throughout the fall and spring Washington sought to create a professional officer corps for the Continental Army, and since real military experience was limited to aging French and Indian War veterans and expatriated former British army officers, Washington looked for men who had intelligence, education, and breeding who could serve as an effective officer corps. In a practice common for the time, Wilkinson's commission was backdated to September 1775, the date of his first arrival in the army. Because Wilkinson was an educated man of letters, he did not immediately join his line unit but was instead assigned to the staff of one of Washington's most important generals, Nathaniel Greene of Rhode Island. Wilkinson later accompanied Greene and the rest of the army as they moved from Boston to the defense of New York City.[14]

Upon arriving in New York, Wilkinson chose to leave Greene's staff and assume the command of his assigned company, a close-knit group of New Hampshire men under the longtime leadership of their elected commander, Lieutenant Thomas Grover, a man old enough to be Wilkinson's father. Grover, a veteran of Roger's Rangers during the French and Indian War, had raised his New Hampshire company at the beginning of the Revolution and had participated at the Battle of Bunker Hill. Wilkinson stated that despite Grover's qualifications, Washington had selected himself to command the unit because Grover's "want of education" precluded him from promotion to captain.[15] Taking command under these circumstances would have been difficult for an experienced leader, let alone a novice soldier one month after his nineteenth birthday. Grover would have been rightfully resentful that his contributions had not been appreciated and that a teenaged southern "gentleman," a total stranger to his men and a military novice, had been selected to command the men that he had raised. Wilkinson could have chosen a tactful way to recognize these sensitivities in assuming command, but instead he chose the role of military martinet.

At the first mustering of troops under Wilkinson's command, Wilkinson's men failed to move, and Lieutenant Grover approached Captain Wilkinson to ask what he was doing. Wilkinson responded by placing Grover under arrest for mutiny and directed him to return to his quarters. Wilkinson then proceeded to lecture the troops about his right of command and stated that he would renew his order and if it was not obeyed, he would proceed to "run the man nearest to me through the body, and would proceed on from right to left, so long as they continued refractory and my strength would support me."[16] With this bravura performance of military authority Wilkinson obtained the obedience of his company. Not satisfied with merely obtaining compliance, Wilkinson immediately proceeded to prefer court-martial charges against Grover. By seeking to court-martial his first subordinate after giving his first order as a commander, Wilkinson demonstrated a willingness to use the military justice process to enforce his will. He continued to demonstrate his willingness to use and abuse the military justice process for his own ends throughout his career. Wilkinson maintained that he was commended by Washington for his rapid response to a perceived resistance to his orders.[17] Grover was court-martialed and convicted but received a minor penalty when he apologized for his lack of prompt obedience. He rejoined the unit when Wilkinson moved on to another assignment.

While Washington anticipated a British invasion of New York City sometime soon, he also realized that Continental forces in Canada were in critical need of reinforcement.[18] Following the unsuccessful assault on the walls of Quebec on New Year's Eve 1775, the remaining American forces, under the command of the wounded Colonel Benedict Arnold, maintained a loose siege around the city. Hunger, disease, winter exposure, and expiration of enlistments had reduced American strength at Quebec to barely 700 soldiers. General David Wooster, in overall command of the Continentals in Canada, had additional troops in Montreal that were sent to reinforce Arnold at Quebec, but most of the troops had succumbed to the outbreak of smallpox that was ravishing the American command.[19] In order to maintain the slim American presence in Canada, on April 21 Washington chose to reinforce the Continental forces with units from his army in New York City. Washington hoped these reinforcements would reach Canada before the expected arrival of British reinforcements. On April 29 Wilkinson's regiment, along with three others, were dispatched to Canada as reinforcements under the command of Brigadier General John Sullivan.[20]

Unfortunately, the reinforcements sent by Washington were too little and arrived too late. British reinforcements of 10,000 men, under the command of Major General John Burgoyne, were spotted off the mouth of the St. Lawrence River at the beginning of May. American general Wooster was replaced by Major General John Thomas, who could do nothing to prevent the Canadian garrison, under command of Major General Sir Guy Carleton, from breaking through the American siege lines.[21] Thomas and the shattered American command retreated up the St. Lawrence River to Sorel, a town at the confluence of the St. Lawrence and Richelieu Rivers. Since the promised American reinforcements were expected to descend the Richelieu to the St. Lawrence, Thomas chose Sorel as the best place to await their arrival.

Wilkinson and the American reinforcements under Sullivan reached the American lines at Sorel on May 22. At this point Wilkinson maintained that he was without orders, so on his own authority he took the 86 men under his command and set out to reinforce a detachment under Arnold, which was located near Montreal.[22] While awaiting Arnold's return to camp, Wilkinson composed a letter to General Greene on May 24, one typical of the theatrical style that would dominate most of his future communications and memoirs. In the letter he accurately set forth the lack of troops, food, and ammunition that was confronting the American force but grossly overstated the immediate danger facing his unit. He ended the letter with a florid conclusion: "But the morning dawns—that morn, big with the fate of a few, a handful of brave fellows. I shall do my part—but remember, if I fall, I am sacrificed. May God bless you equal to your merits—*Vale!*"[23]

Until this time in his military career Wilkinson had been a volunteer enlistee and then a company grade officer, performing tasks assigned to him by his superiors. From this point on in his memoirs Wilkinson exhibits a pattern of exaggeration involving the dangers he faced and the importance of his personal actions on subsequent military events. By his own later admission, Wilkinson's dire warning to Greene was based on rumor and significantly overstated the tactical threat.[24] The closest British troops were over three days away and posed no immediate danger.[25]

Around this time, Arnold approached Wilkinson and asked him to serve as an aide-de-camp. Wilkinson quickly left his line command and agreed to join Arnold's military family.[26] Wilkinson's command of troops in action had lasted fewer than sixty days, involved no combat, and would be his only command experience during the Revolution. The remainder of Wilkinson's Revolutionary military career was spent in a series of political intrigues, staff assignments, and recruiting duty and not in command of troops on maneuver, let alone in combat. Having briefly served on the staff of other army generals, Wilkinson viewed a staff assignment with a celebrity like Benedict Arnold as a path to rapid advancement without actually having to be in command.

Wilkinson's time with Arnold's family was also relatively short, and his observations of Arnold in his 1816 memoirs were colored by his later betrayal of Arnold as well as by the general hostility toward Arnold's 1780 treason. Arnold had received permission from the visiting congressional delegation to seize local provisions to supply his troops. Arnold offered payment for the seized goods, but had the owners refused to accept the American invoice, the goods were to be seized. Wilkinson

was dispatched by Arnold to conduct some seizures, but Wilkinson balked at forcing local merchants to surrender supplies. Wilkinson asked Arnold to be excused
from this duty, and Arnold agreed, stating that Wilkinson was "more nice than
wise."[27] Wilkinson was then directed by Arnold to bring dispatches from Montreal
down the St. Lawrence to General John Sullivan, encamped at Sorel. Before reaching Sorel, Wilkinson encountered British troops, indicating that Sorel had fallen
and that Sullivan had either been captured or was withdrawing up the Richelieu
River toward New York. Wilkinson promptly reversed course and headed back
toward Montreal to warn Arnold that the British troops were fourteen miles from
Montreal. As a theatrical flourish, Wilkinson wrote that at one point he had to
commandeer a canoe at sword point in order to cross the St. Lawrence. Wilkinson
was then dispatched by Arnold to find Sullivan on the Richelieu and obtain from
him a covering force that would allow Arnold to safely withdraw from Montreal
and unite with Sullivan on the Richelieu. Wilkinson later claimed that this action saved "Arnold and the entire Montreal garrison from the grasp of Sir Guy
Carleton."[28]

Wilkinson proceeded overland to the Richelieu, located Sullivan, and informed
him of Arnold's request for a covering force.[29] Sullivan directed Wilkinson to
locate the army's rear guard and direct the commander of the guard to detach a
covering force for Arnold. Wilkinson met Colonel Anthony Wayne, who agreed
to provide a cover for Arnold's withdrawal. By June 18, Arnold had united with
Sullivan's force and together they moved up the Richelieu to Saint Jean, the last
major Canadian town before the New York border. Wilkinson remained with
Arnold on the shore while the American forces withdrew by wagon and boat toward New York and Lake Champlain. According to Wilkinson, Arnold vainly insisted on being the last American to leave Canada. Arnold shot his horse, directed
Wilkinson to do the same to his own horse, and then was the last man aboard the
last boat to leave.[30] The American invasion of Canada, which had begun thirteen
months before, when Arnold attacked Saint Jean, had ended in dismal failure.

With the remnants of the American army temporarily located on Isle aux Noix
near Lake Champlain, Arnold and Wilkinson were sent south to Albany to confer
with General Philip Schuyler on plans for the defense of the Northern Department. There they encountered Major General Horatio Gates, who had recently
been appointed to command the American army in Canada. Unfortunately for
Gates, by the time he arrived in Albany the American army was no longer in Canada. Gates and Schuyler appealed to Congress for additional guidance on who was
now in command of the army, given its withdrawal. When Congress finally decided that Gates would be subordinate to Schuyler as the department commander,
Gates and Schuyler initially worked cooperatively to address the expected British

invasion. Gates, Schuyler, and Arnold then traveled north to view the army, which had retreated to the French and Indian War encampment at Crown Point. The generals held a council of war and agreed that Crown Point should be abandoned and that the army should retreat to Fort Ticonderoga, fifteen miles further up Lake Champlain. For a time Arnold and Wilkinson remained at Crown Point to supervise the withdrawal.[31]

While at Crown Point, Wilkinson attempted to conduct a patrol to capture a British reconnaissance party that was exploring American lines. Wilkinson proposed a patrol with 50 men and boats that would proceed under cover of darkness to a location near the British lines; the patrol would hide among creeks and inlets along the shore and await the approach of a British scouting party, then overpower the British, take prisoners, and return to Crown Point. Although Arnold supported the plan, Wilkinson stated that the Pennsylvania troops chosen to conduct the patrol balked at his leadership. Though Wilkinson claimed that their objections were because he was not from Pennsylvania, it is more likely that the troops objected due to Wilkinson's complete lack of combat experience. The patrol was instead led by Pennsylvania captain James Wilson, who eventually led the patrol into being ambushed and captured by a superior British force.[32]

Wilkinson further expressed his indignation regarding another American patrol launched at the same time. Lieutenant Benjamin Whitcomb of New Hampshire led a patrol into the same area that Wilkinson had proposed to lead his patrol, and Whitcomb's mission was also to seize prisoners for interrogation. Unfortunately, this patrol also was discovered by the British, and Whitcomb and his men scattered into the woods to avoid capture. Whitcomb, a skilled woodsman, evaded capture for several days even though British troops passed within six feet of his position. When the British patrols were called off, Whitcomb decided to proceed on his mission alone rather than returning to Crown Point. He positioned himself along a major trail from Saint Jean and awaited an opportunity. It is unclear how Whitcomb, alone and behind enemy lines, could have expected to capture a prisoner for interrogation and bring that person back to Crown Point. However, shortly after taking up his position, Whitcomb observed British brigadier Patrick Gordon, the commander of the Twenty-Ninth Regiment of Foot and of the First Brigade of the British invading force, riding alone along the trail. Rather than capture Gordon, Whitcomb shot him in the chest. Although Gordon was able to escape to Saint Jean, he subsequently died of his wound. Whitcomb also evaded capture and returned to American lines.[33]

British reaction to the ambush was one of outrage. Under the customs of war at the time, the deliberate targeting of officers in combat was viewed as improper. While officers were expected to expose themselves and lead conspicuously by example, it was considered to be improper to deliberately target officers in combat. The ambush and slaying of Gordon were viewed as tantamount to murder and led to a significant hardening of British attitudes toward the Americans. Carleton issued a reward for Whitcomb's capture, dead or alive.[34]

American reaction was also initially harsh. Wilkinson called the shooting an "abominable outrage on the customs of war and the laws of humanity" and said that "men of sensibility and honor did not conceal their abhorrence of its perpetrator."[35] Wilkinson also speculated that robbery may have been Whitcomb's motive. Washington condemned the action as an assassination that was "highly unbecoming the character of a Soldier and a Gentleman."[36] However, as Wilkinson noted, the "temper of the times" was causing attitudes to change.[37] Fifteen months later American troops were directed to target British officers at the Battles of Saratoga, with devastating effect. American forces under Colonel Daniel Morgan, Major Henry Dearborn, and now Captain Benjamin Whitcomb deliberately targeted and killed another British general and decimated the British officer corps.[38]

Wilkinson, having completed his duties at Crown Point, repaired with the army to Fort Ticonderoga. The stone fortress on the western side of Lake Champlain had been built by the French as Fort Carillon during the French and Indian War. Since 1759 the fort had been under British control and had fallen into significant disrepair. At the beginning of the Revolution, Benedict Arnold and Ethan Allen had seized the fort and its artillery without firing a shot. Despite its state of disrepair, the fort was the strongest fortification on Lake Champlain and, when properly commanded, was thought to be an impossible obstacle to any British force moving up the lake.

While stationed at Fort Ticonderoga, Wilkinson became involved in his first command intrigue. Though Benedict Arnold would prove to be the finest American combat leader in 1776 and 1777, Arnold had the unfortunate habit of developing a coterie of bitter enemies who later launched a series of personal attacks that would distract him from his command responsibilities. In Canada, Arnold had taken several steps, with congressional approval, to requisition or seize goods from local Canadians in order to support the army. A group of officers with questionable loyalty to the American cause began to make a series of allegations that Arnold had seized goods for his personal use and fortune. Tired of complaints by disgruntled subordinates, Arnold directed the court-martial at Fort Ticonderoga of the most prominent voice, Colonel Moses Hazen, for insubordination and mishandling of supplies.[39] When the court rejected the testimony of Arnold's primary witness against Hazen, Arnold proceeded to attack the members of the court itself. The members, all junior officers to Arnold, then demanded that court-martial charges be brought against Arnold and that Arnold be immediately arrested.[40]

Gates, as the superior officer on the scene, finally put a stop to the military justice theater and dissolved the military court. As he explained in his letter to Congress, Gates was forced to act dictatorially because Arnold, who was also busy building a fleet on Lake Champlain to repel the British invasion, was too valuable to be consumed any further in the contretemps.[41]

While Wilkinson had no role in these proceedings, in his memoirs he condemned Arnold as being guilty of misappropriation and engaged in a long condemnation of abuses in the military justice process. As examples of this abuse, he identified his own courts-martial, the exoneration of Arnold by Gates, and the failure of military justice proceedings that he had recommended against several of his enemies over the course of his career.[42] Wilkinson's 1816 condemnation of Arnold was obviously the product of his subsequent betrayal of Arnold and reflective of the general disdain of popular opinion against Arnold following his 1780 treason. However, contrary to his memoirs, Wilkinson's contemporary observations about Arnold at the time of the 1776 proceedings are strikingly at odds with his memoir's portrayal. In an August 5 letter to Captain Richard Varick, an aide to General Schuyler, Wilkinson stated that attacks against Arnold's character had been "villainous" and that he had "always found Him, the intrepid, generous friendly, upright Honest Man."[43]

However, by the time of Hazen's court-martial, Wilkinson had already shifted his allegiance to General Gates. On July 20 Wilkinson transferred from Arnold's to Gates's staff and was promoted to brigade major (an adjutant or chief of staff for the brigade commander who was typically a brigadier general). The switch from Arnold to Gates was amicable and reflected Wilkinson's belief that advancement was more likely through Gates, the possible future head of the Northern Department, rather than remaining with Arnold. Wilkinson's demonstrated aversion to combat would also be satisfied through this move. In his short time with Arnold, Wilkinson had repeatedly been exposed to close contact with British forces. Arnold was an aggressive commander who led from the front, and his aides were expected to be near enemy fire as well. In the summer of 1776 Arnold was busy building a fleet of ships on Lake Champlain and he clearly intended to lead these ships against a superior British fleet. A promotion to serve under a general who led from the rear, which would also place Wilkinson in a rear echelon position, was likely a driving motivator for Wilkinson.

By this point in his army career Wilkinson had served ninety days as a captain. The first thirty days were spent in commanding his company's movement from New York to Canada and in court-martialing his first subordinate. The last sixty days were spent as a staff aide to Arnold, assisting him in supervising the withdrawal of American troops from Canada to Fort Ticonderoga. Wilkinson had yet to demonstrate that he had the range of capabilities that warranted further promotion. At the time of Wilkinson's promotion to brigade major, Gates was still operating under the mistaken belief that he would be commanding the Northern Department and would need a full staff. However, shortly after Wilkinson accepted the transfer and promotion, Gates learned that Congress had selected Schuyler to command the Northern Department, meaning Gates would no longer need a staff. Arrangements were made to transfer Wilkinson to the staff of Brigadier General Arthur St. Clair, who was in command of the forces located at Fort Ticonderoga. St. Clair, a former British officer, had served honorably with the American army in Quebec. Wilkinson's time with St. Clair would eventually be cut short when Wilkinson, along with a good portion of the troops at Fort Ticonderoga, was stricken with typhoid fever.[44]

Large bodies of troops were highly susceptible to the infectious diseases that rapidly spread through troops housed in close confinement with poor sanitation. Smallpox, measles, and dysentery ran rampant in the Continental Army, effects that were exacerbated by the fact that the cause of these maladies was often unknown and cures had yet to be discovered. (Inoculation against smallpox was still considered to be controversial by some medical professionals at the time of the Revolution.[45]) Typhoid, a bacterium spread through unsanitary conditions, had affected armies for thousands of years, and colonial medicine was limited to treatment by isolation and the administration of vinegar. Typhoid began to affect the troops at Fort Ticonderoga in August, and by October Wilkinson and others were evacuated to Albany for treatment and recovery. Wilkinson stated that he was treated by Albany patroon families such as the Van Rensselaers and the Schuylers, where he gradually recovered.[46]

While he was recovering in Albany, the British advance up Lake Champlain proceeded as far as Crown Point. On October 11, Arnold's fleet confronted the superior British fleet at the Battle of Valcour Island. After a valiant fight, Arnold's ships were either sunk or driven toward Fort Ticonderoga.[47] However, the delay caused by the need to build and equip a superior opposing fleet caused the British advance to halt at Crown Point and eventually withdraw to Canada for the winter.

October brought an end to the 1776 campaigns of the Northern Department but Continental woes in the mid-Atlantic region continued to mount. By December 8, Washington and the steadily diminishing troops under his command had fled New York and New Jersey and crossed the Delaware River into Pennsylvania. Upon his entry into Pennsylvania, Washington had fewer than 4,000 troops under his command. Desertions, disease, the failure of the New Jersey militia to turn out in response to Governor William Livingston's call, and the expiration of many of his troops' enlistments had steadily reduced Washington's force to a shadow of the army that had welcomed independence in July. Washington recognized that if he was going to maintain an effective adversary to the British he would have to consolidate his scattered forces. Following the Northern Department's campaign, Washington sent orders to Schuyler to send reinforcements. In early December Schuyler dispatched Gates with 800 troops, including Wilkinson, to rendezvous with Washington's retreating army. Washington also directed his second in command, Major General Charles Lee, to leave Westchester County in New York with his 7,000 troops and join him in Pennsylvania.

Charles Lee, one of the more eccentric figures of the early Revolution, was born in England as the son of a colonel in the British Army; his career as a soldier was preordained. In 1747 Lee's father purchased a commission for him in his father's own regiment. In 1755 Lee served with Braddock, Washington, and Gates at the Battle of the Monongahela, where he avoided Braddock's unfortunate fate. After the battle Lee purchased a captain's commission and was present for Abercrombie's failed assault on Fort Carillon in 1758, and he later participated in the 1759 British invasion of Canada. During his assignment in Albany, Lee, like many British officers, immersed himself in Indian culture and "married" the daughter of a Seneca chief, who bore him twin sons.[48] Following the fall of Canada, Lee was promoted to major and served against Spanish forces in Portugal under the command of Brigadier John Burgoyne. Following the war Lee retired on half-pay as a lieutenant colonel and served for a time as a major general in the Polish army against the Turks. In 1773 Lee returned to America and purchased an estate in Virginia. He socialized with colonial radicals who supported colonial opposition to British oppression such as Samuel Adams, Benjamin Franklin, and Richard Henry Lee. When hostilities between Britain and America broke out in 1775, Lee resigned his British commission and offered his services to the Continental Congress.

With an overwhelming sense of entitlement, Lee expected to be named commander of the Continental Army and actively lobbied for the position. As the most senior former British officer to extend his services to the US Congress, and with a significant record of commanding troops in combat in America and Europe, Lee expected Congress to respect his demonstrated talents and place him in command. He was greatly disappointed and resentful of losing out to Washington, whom he viewed as a military inferior.[49] In April, on his way to his new assignment as the commander of the Southern Department, Lee became the second most senior general in the army, just below Washington.[50]

After receiving undue credit for the successful defense of Charleston, Lee was recalled to assist Washington in the defense of New York City. Upon arrival, Lee commenced to criticize Congress and Washington for insisting on staying in

Manhattan.[51] Lee favored withdrawing from the island to avoid being trapped there and proposed mounting a defense from either New York or New Jersey, away from the city. But Congress insisted on a defense of the island, and a significant number of Continental troops committed to its defense were subsequently captured when the British assaulted and took Fort Washington.[52] When Washington finally withdrew the bulk of the army, he foolishly split it into three sections. One section of 2,000 troops under Washington's command would defend the New Jersey shore of the Hudson River from the recently renamed Fort Lee. Another 3,000 troops would guard the Hudson Highlands, to prevent a British movement up the Hudson River. The remaining 7,500 troops, under Lee, would remain in Westchester County to guard against a British movement toward New England.

When Howe's forces captured Fort Washington and its entire garrison, British general Lord Cornwallis scaled Palisade's Cliffs on the New Jersey side of the Hudson and put the garrison at Fort Lee to flight. Seeing his prediction about the ill-considered defense of Manhattan come true, Lee became more vocal in his criticism of Washington's tactics and strategy. Upon the receipt of what Lee termed a "suggestion" from Washington to join Washington's men in New Jersey, Lee promptly ignored the request. As Washington retreated across New Jersey toward the Delaware River, his calls for Lee to join him became steadily more frantic. Lee responded with several excuses, some valid and some seeking to establish his independence from Washington as well as his eligibility to replace Washington as the commander in chief.

Lee commenced his campaign to replace Washington by seeking to suborn Washington's staff and by criticizing Washington among Lee's allies in Congress. Lee was also likely sharing similar sentiments with his former fellow British officer Horatio Gates, which is why on December 13, Wilkinson arrived at Lee's quarters in Basking Ridge, New Jersey. Finally recovered from his bout with typhoid fever, Wilkinson had returned to duty in Albany in the beginning of December. During his recovery his brigade had been disbanded, so he returned to serve in a staff position with Gates. In early December Schuyler had received an order to reinforce Washington and chose to send Gates and 800 troops from Albany. By December 12 Gates and his reinforcements had reached central New Jersey. Though it was widely known that Washington had left New Jersey four days before, Gates and his reinforcements were closer to Lee than to Washington across the river. Wilkinson was dispatched by Gates, ostensibly to find and obtain directions on how to join their forces. Rather than cross the Delaware where he knew Washington was located, Wilkinson chose to seek out General Lee at his headquarters on the New Jersey side of the river.[53] Likely he was carrying communications from Gates that were part of an ongoing dialogue between Lee and Gates, commiserating on Washington's failing leadership, and Gates may also have intended, like Lee, to disobey Washington's orders and join up with Lee in the hopes of forming a nucleus of a new command independent of Washington.

On the evening of December 12, Lee chose an overnight accommodation at Widow White's Tavern, an isolated inn in Basking Ridge three miles from his troops. Lee was accompanied only by one aide, two French volunteer officers, and fifteen members of his personal guard. His selection of this remote location, away from his men, may have been driven by the need for privacy in his tryst with a prostitute.[54] By the time Wilkinson appeared at 4:00 a.m. the prostitute was gone and Wilkinson was brought before Lee, who was still in bed. Wilkinson later stated that he presented Lee with the letter from Gates to Washington, then curled up by the fire and awaited the dawn.[55]

The following morning, Lee arose and composed a letter to Gates. In the letter he attacked Washington repeatedly, observing that "a certain great man is damnably deficient."[56] He gave the letter to Wilkinson to deliver to Gates, then proceeded to breakfast with his staff and Wilkinson. According to his memoirs, Wilkinson arose from the breakfast table, looked out the window, and cried out, "Here, Sir, are the British Cavalry. *Where*, replied the General, who had signed the letter in an instant" (emphasis in original). Wilkinson responded, "Around the house."[57]

Lee's dalliance away from his troops had come to the attention of a detachment of the Sixteenth Regiment of Light Dragoons under the command of Lieutenant Colonel William Harcourt, who was serving with Cornwallis and the British Army stationed in New Jersey between Lee's and Washington's locations. Hearing rumors of Lee's approach to the British rear, Harcourt volunteered to lead a scouting party to find the exact location of Lee's troops. A group of thirty-two dragoons was chosen, including Coronet Banastre Tarleton, who would go on to notoriety in the southern campaign of 1780–81.[58] Harcourt and his well-mounted dragoons headed northeast toward Lee's encampment and, aided by a group of New Jersey Loyalists, learned that Lee was housed in an inn, away from his troops. Tarleton then captured a messenger from Lee and, by threatening him with death, obtained Lee's precise location. Harcourt decided to immediately storm the inn and capture Lee.

Lee's small guard force immediately scattered upon sighting the charging dragoons. The British troops surrounded the inn and began firing into the inn, demanding Lee's surrender. Inside the inn were Lee, Wilkinson, Lee's aide Major William Bradford, and the two French volunteer officers. All but Lee and Wilkinson returned fire, and when Harcourt threated to burn the house down if Lee did not surrender, the firing stopped. One of the French officers sought to escape but was wounded and captured at sword point. Lee chose to surrender and appeared at the door with Bradford, who had been slightly wounded. Since Lee was still in his night clothes, Bradford offered to go back into the house and retrieve Lee's hat and cloak. After fetching Lee's clothing, Bradford escaped, and the British mounted Lee on Wilkinson's horse and carried him off to British lines.[59]

Wilkinson's role in the affair did not inspire confidence. Other than Lee, he was the only soldier present who did not return fire, even though he was armed with two pistols and was the only Continental officer present who was not wounded or captured. While Wilkinson does not mention this fact in his memoirs, historians have reported that he was hiding in the inn's chimney when the British surrender offer was delivered.[60] Staying well hidden in the inn, Wilkinson awaited the departure of the British raiders before he sought out General Sullivan, who now commanded Lee's forces. After finding Sullivan and informing him of Lee's capture, Wilkinson returned to Gates. Within two days of the capture, the forces under Sullivan and Gates were able to join Washington in Pennsylvania.

On the day of Lee's capture the Continental Congress, concerned that Cornwallis might continue his campaign and capture Philadelphia, moved to Baltimore. With the scattered elements of the Continental Army finally reunited in Pennsylvania and additional militia elements from Pennsylvania and New Jersey arriving, Washington decided to reorganize the structure of the Continental Army. Arnold was dispatched to New England to organize a defense against General Henry Clinton, who had recently seized Newport, Rhode Island. New brigades were restructured, and St. Clair was given a brigade to command. Wilkinson, as St. Clair's former brigade major, was assigned to St. Clair's brigade as a staff officer.[61] Washington then began to devise his daring plan for a Christmas night assault across the Delaware River into Trenton.

Gates, as the senior major general present, should have been working to assist Washington in reorganizing the army and planning for the Trenton assault. However, Gates had his own ideas about how the war should be fought and who should lead the troops. Gates believed that rather than continuing to confront the British, Washington and the army should concede New Jersey and Philadelphia to the British and retreat to lines behind the Susquehanna River, seventy miles away. Unable to convince Washington to adopt his plan, Gates feigned illness and, with Washington's permission, departed for Philadelphia.[62] On December 23, two days before the assault on Trenton was supposed to be launched, Gates informed Wilkinson that he intended to go to Baltimore and asked Wilkinson to accompany him as far as Philadelphia.

Wilkinson, as St. Clair's brigade major, should have been assisting St. Clair in preparing the brigade for its role in the assault. Instead of facing combat, Wilkinson asked St. Clair's permission to accompany Gates to Philadelphia. St. Clair approved with the admonishment, "[I] have no objection, if he did not think it interested my honour, at that time, to remain with the brigade."[63] On the eve of a critical assault designed to keep the Revolution alive, Wilkinson believed it was more appropriate for him to accompany Gates on his quest to undermine Washington than to accompany his brigade into combat. However, according to Wilkinson's memoirs, St. Clair's remonstration about honor caused Wilkinson to reconsider his trip with Gates. When he informed Gates on December 24 that he had changed his mind, Gates caused him to vacillate yet again. As they departed for Philadelphia, Gates explained his ultimate plan to Wilkinson, that he intended to travel first to Philadelphia and then to Baltimore to petition Congress to support his alternate plan for a defensive line along the Susquehanna.[64] When they arrived in Philadelphia, Wilkinson apparently wavered again and decided to return to St. Clair's command. Gates then prepared a letter to Washington explaining his course of action and asked Wilkinson to deliver it. Wilkinson left Gates in Philadelphia and finally caught up with Washington and the army on Christmas evening, just as they were preparing to carry out Washington's daring plan to cross the ice-choked Delaware River at McConkey's Ferry.

Colonel John Glover and his regiment of boatmen from Marblehead, Massachusetts, were responsible for loading troops, supplies, horses, and artillery into the Durham boats that were usually used to haul iron along the Delaware. The crossing, in the dark of Christmas night, was also conducted in the middle of a storm that brought wind, rain, hail, snow, and sleet. While the crossing was under the immediate control of Colonel Henry Knox, Washington remained nearby to closely monitor the movement. Washington's nervous state was exposed when Wilkinson arrived that evening with the letter from Gates. (The letter itself has never been found.) According to Wilkinson, when he tried to hand him Gates's letter, Washington exploded: "'What a time is this to hand me letters!' I answered that I had been charged with it by General Gates. 'By General Gates! Where is he?' I left him this morning in Philadelphia. 'What was he doing there?' I understood him that he was on his way to Congress. He earnestly repeated 'On his way to Congress!' then broke the seal, and I made my bow and joined General St. Clair on the bank of the river."[65]

This exchange, if accurate, clearly establishes that Gates's trip to Congress in Baltimore was without Washington's knowledge and permission. (Gates's most recent biographer asserts that sickness was the real reason for Gates being absent from the battle at Trenton. He also rejects Wilkinson's version of the ferry-side conversation with Washington as coming from a wholly unreliable witness and bitter enemy of Gates.[66]) Gates's absence from the assault, based on feigned illness, was tantamount to desertion in the face of the enemy. Similarly, his travel to Baltimore and appeal to Congress, over Washington's head and without Washington's permission, was a major breach of military protocol and ethics. Yet Gates strangely avoided any adverse consequences for his actions. Because Gates had powerful congressional allies, Washington may have thought that a charge of desertion might cause further dissension in Congress and within the army.

Wilkinson retreated to his staff position with St. Clair's brigade, which crossed the river and headed eight miles along the riverbank to Trenton. Once again Wilkinson did not command troops but only served as a messenger between St. Clair and other commanders. The American attack proceeded in two columns and soon overwhelmed the Hessian garrison with the deployment of seven batteries of artillery that fired down the streets of Trenton. American infantry stormed the Hessian artillery as it attempted counter battery fire and captured several guns. When St. Clair's column captured its objective, Wilkinson was dispatched to bring the good news to Washington. According to Wilkinson, he arrived just as Washington was accepting the sword of Hessian commander Colonel Johann Rall, who had been mortally wounded earlier in the attack. When he approached, Washington took Wilkinson's hand and exclaimed, "Major Wilkinson, this is a glorious day for our country."[67]

It was a glorious day indeed. The lopsided victory was clearly demonstrated in the casualty count. American losses were 4 men wounded, 2 killed in action, and 1 frozen to death. Hessian losses were 22 killed, 83 wounded, and 896 captured.[68] Hundreds of muskets, six cannon, numerous ammunition wagons, fifteen stands of colors, and a Hessian music corps completed the score of the American victory. Following a council of war with his officers, Washington decided that there was a great likelihood that the British in Princeton would counterattack and the safest course of action would be to withdraw the army back across the Delaware. Following another difficult winter crossing, Washington successfully withdrew the army, including the Hessian prisoners, by the end of the day.

The following week Washington again crossed the Delaware and evaded a British force sent to crush him in Trenton. After slipping around the British force in a daring night march, Washington proceeded to Princeton, where his force assaulted the rear of the oncoming British force. Part of the battle was fought on the campus of the college that would eventually become Princeton University and involved the shelling of Nassau Hall by Continental artillery captain Alexander Hamilton.[69] (Legend has it that Hamilton may have assaulted the building with a particular vengeance after having unsuccessfully applied for admission to Princeton.) One of the shells is believed to have destroyed a portrait of King George II that hung in the building.[70] The British subsequently fled the town, having suffered over 450 casualties.

Wilkinson related another incident of the shelling of the college. According to his memoirs, he was riding by the college while it was being shelled by a single cannon under the command of an officer. One of the cannonballs ricocheted and nearly killed Wilkinson and his horse.[71] Wilkinson did not name the officer in his memoirs, but historians have surmised that the friendly fire incident may have been caused by the guns being fired by Hamilton.[72]

While some of Washington's officers wanted to press on to seize the British depot at Brunswick, Washington instead wisely chose to withdraw to winter quarters in Morristown, New Jersey. Washington recognized that he had accomplished much in the week following Christmas but that his most important responsibility was keeping the Continental Army intact.[73] Washington and his newly revitalized army suffered through the first of many miserable winters in Morristown.

2

THE "MILITARY GENIUS" OF
THE NORTHERN ARMY

1777

[He] attained the rank of brigadier general in the Continental Army
through an unabashed campaign of lying, cheating, double crossing,
and backstabbing.
—G. J. O'Toole, *Honorable Treachery*

Following his alleged near miss from Hamilton's cannon at Princeton, Wilkinson accompanied Washington and the Continental Army as they repaired to winter quarters in Morristown. Washington chose to reorganize and revise the army in anticipation of a renewed spring campaign. As part of the reorganization, he directed Colonel Nathaniel Gist to raise a regiment of rangers to be deployed against Cherokee Indians, who were believed to be allied with the British. The new regiment, raised from Maryland and Virginia, needed new officers, and Washington offered the nineteen-year-old Wilkinson a promotion to lieutenant colonel in the new regiment. While Wilkinson was initially grateful for the rapid promotion, he subsequently balked at active service in a ranger regiment on the frontier. He approached Washington with the suggestion that a man of his refinement might not fit in with the "harmony of the corps" and requested a reassignment to another unit. Washington replied that ranger units needed officers of Wilkinson's refinement to "remedy the defects of lax discipline and polite manners." Despite Washington's urging, Wilkinson persisted in his insistence of an assignment to a more genteel unit and was eventually allowed to be transferred to a new regiment being raised by Colonel Thomas Hartley, another veteran of the ill-fated Canadian expedition. Wilkinson accepted this assignment and proceeded to Maryland to assist in recruitment.[1]

Within ninety days Wilkinson had completed his recruitment duties and returned to Philadelphia, where his new regiment was to be headquartered. There he renewed his acquaintance with General Horatio Gates, who had conveniently avoided any combat role under Washington during the Trenton-Princeton campaign. Rather than serving with Washington in revitalizing the army, Gates was busy lobbying the Continental Congress to supplant General Philip Schuyler as the commander of the Northern Department. Without clearly resolving the command situation between Schuyler and Gates, Congress directed Gates to assume command at Fort Ticonderoga and allowed him to select General Arthur St. Clair as his second in command. Seeking to avoid an active combat command, Wilkinson again solicited a staff appointment with Gates. Wilkinson's offer was accepted by Gates with two conditions: he would have to obtain Washington's approval and he would have to accept demotion to the rank of major. Wilkinson couched his appeal to Washington by stating that he was more familiar with the topography of the Northern Department and that the northern theater was most likely to see active operations in the near future. Evidence shows Washington was clearly piqued at Wilkinson's inability to make up his mind: "I would to God, gentlemen could for once know their own minds; I have been endeavoring to form a register of the army, but with so many caprices, that I fear it will be impossible; but if you have a mind to resign, you have my permission."[2] With Washington's permission in hand, Major Wilkinson accompanied Gates and arrived in Albany in April. (In his memoirs Wilkinson sought to use this volunteered demotion as proof that he was not always avariciously seeking promotions.)

Prior to his departure from Philadelphia, Wilkinson commenced the courtship of Ann "Nancy" Biddle, a spinster fourteen years his senior. The Biddles of Philadelphia were a well-established Quaker family with solid connections to Pennsylvania's revolutionary government. Wilkinson may have met Nancy during his Philadelphia medical school years but commenced his courtship in earnest during his 1777 stay in the city. Their marriage in November 1778 lasted twenty-nine years and produced five sons, two of whom followed their father into a military career, and three daughters. Despite Wilkinson's repeated history of betrayals throughout his career, there is no evidence that he was anything but faithful to Nancy.[3] However, though he was apparently devoted to her, there are few mentions of his wife in the three volumes of his memoirs.[4] She loyally followed him to frontier posts and assignments in Pittsburgh, Cincinnati, St. Louis, Louisville, Natchez, Frederick Town, New Orleans, and Havana, Cuba, and Wilkinson's attempts to provide a stylish lifestyle for his socially conscious wife was one of the sources of his perpetual economic distress.

Wilkinson's representation to Washington that the Northern Department would be the scene of the greatest action in 1777 proved to be accurate. While Washington was leading the Continental Army in a series of unsuccessful actions to keep the British from reaching Philadelphia, the northern campaign under Schuyler and Gates proved to have the greatest effect on the cause of the Revolution. Sir Guy Carleton's 1776 invasion from Canada to Lake Champlain was tactically sound but was eventually frustrated by General Benedict Arnold's series of delaying actions, culminating in the Battle of Valcour Island in October and, with winter approaching, Carleton being forced to retire back to Canada. British strategists sought to repeat the effort in 1777, with some additional improvements. According to this plan, once again, a combined column of British regulars, Hessian mercenaries, American Loyalists, Canadian militia, and Indian irregulars would attack from Canada, travel up Lake Champlain, and cross over to the Hudson River with the goal of eventually seizing Albany and the Hudson River valley toward New York City. To divide American attention, a second smaller detachment would be sent to Albany via Lake Ontario and the Mohawk River valley. A third column would proceed up the Hudson River valley from New York City to Albany. The three columns would converge at Albany and sever New York and the New England states from the mid-Atlantic and southern states.

This plan was particularly espoused by British lieutenant general John Burgoyne, a wealthy British socialite, playwright, and member of Parliament. Burgoyne, affectionately known to his troops as "Gentleman Johnny," was also a distinguished soldier, having fought in the War of the Austrian Succession (1740–48) and the Seven Years' War (1756–63) in Europe as well as serving with British troops at Boston and in Canada during the Revolution.[5] Burgoyne urged the three-part invasion plan, with himself serving as the commanding officer of the main thrust from Canada. Lord George Germain endorsed the plan to King George III, who approved the plan as well as Burgoyne's command of the expedition.[6]

Unfortunately, strategic planning by the British for military operations in the colonies was often plagued by poor communications, political strife, and jealous military personalities. Though a three-part plan was clearly envisioned by Burgoyne, and apparently endorsed by the king, Germain failed to convey this direction to General Sir William Howe, who would be responsible for the military strike up the Hudson River. Howe had previously communicated to Germain that his priority in 1777 was the seizure of the rebel capital at Philadelphia. Germain failed to provide to Howe adequate direction to support Burgoyne, which allowed Howe to lead his forces away from Albany toward the Chesapeake Bay and Philadelphia. He also failed to inform Burgoyne about Howe's stated intention to attack Philadelphia instead of Albany. Unaware of the fact that he would not be meeting Howe's army in Albany, Burgoyne arrived in Quebec in May 1777 and commenced his campaign.

Confronting Burgoyne was the Continental Army's Northern Department under the divided command of Major General Philip Schuyler and Major General Horatio Gates. Schuyler was a wealthy Albany Dutch patroon and had technically been in command of the American troops in Canada in 1775 and 1776. However, because of health reasons, Schuyler never left New York and allowed actual command in Canada to become the responsibility of a succession of subordinate commanders. While a superb logistician, Schuyler had the unfortunate habit of irritating both Congress and the New England states, especially those responsible for providing most of the troops that would fight under his command.

New Englanders preferred a commander more to their liking and settled on Major General Horatio Gates as their favorite son. Gates was a former British army major who had served and was wounded under General Edward Braddock during the disastrous western Pennsylvania campaign of 1755. Gates subsequently sold his commission and moved to Virginia, where he took up farming. Following the battles of Lexington and Concord in the spring of 1775, he approached Washington and offered his services. Recognizing Gates's administrative skills, Washington appointed Gates as the first adjutant general of the Continental Army, at the rank of brigadier general. As one of the few officers in the army with prior British military experience, Gates could have served as a valuable senior officer. However, two significant factors would lead to his eventual marginalization and downfall. First, while Gates was a veteran of the British Army, much of his service was in a support role and not as a combat commander. Gates repeatedly oversold his British military experience to his congressional supporters, portraying himself as a senior military commander with skills that were superior to those of other officers, including Washington. Throughout his career as a combat commander Gates repeatedly demonstrated his deficiencies as a military leader. Second, Gates, like Wilkinson, was drawn into several intrigues that were designed to undermine senior commanders and advance his own career at their expense. Over the course of his career Gates developed alliances with malcontents such as Wilkinson, General Charles Lee, General Thomas Conway, General Thomas Mifflin, and Major John Armstrong, all of which were designed to embarrass or remove Washington and other senior officers aligned with him.

The two generals reached an uneasy agreement whereby Schuyler would be in overall command and Gates would exercise command in the area around Fort Ticonderoga. However, rather than assuming direct command, Gates traveled to Philadelphia to lobby Congress for Schuyler's removal and delegated command at Fort Ticonderoga to Major General Arthur St. Clair, with Wilkinson again serving on St. Clair's staff.[7] At the time, Fort Ticonderoga was considered to be an impregnable fortress and was expected to be a major impediment to Burgoyne's campaign up Lake Champlain. St. Clair accepted this vision of impregnability and ignored advice regarding a major vulnerability: overlooking the southern walls of the fort was a promontory known as Mount Defiance. Artillery placed on this hill could dominate the fort and its immediate environs. Despite the warning provided to Gates and St. Clair in 1776 regarding this vulnerability, no effort was made to fortify the hill.[8]

On June 30, three days after departing from Canada, Burgoyne and his army arrived at Ticonderoga and immediately recognized the tactical value of placing artillery on Defiance. By July 5 St. Clair belatedly noted his tenuous position when British troops were seen erecting an artillery battery there. (Burgoyne's deputy, Major General William Phillips, stated, "Where a goat can go, a man can go. And where a man can go, he can drag a gun."[9]) St. Clair directed an immediate withdrawal, which was accomplished by early the following morning. St. Clair saved the more than 2,000 troops who had escaped certain capture at Fort Ticonderoga, but the loss of the "impregnable" fort and its artillery and supplies demanded immediate accountability.[10] At the time of the fort's demise, Gates was in Philadelphia, stirring up his New England congressional supporters to place the blame for the defeat on Schuyler and St. Clair. On August 10 Schuyler was informed by the president of the Continental Congress that he and St. Clair were relieved of command and would face courts-martial for the loss of the fort. Schuyler was also informed that he would be replaced by Gates as the commander of the Northern Department.[11] (Even Wilkinson agreed that Schuyler was unfairly denied appropriate credit for his efforts in the Saratoga campaign, prior to Gates's arrival. With typical self-pity, Wilkinson stated, "The calumnies daily invented and industriously circulated against Generals Schuyler and St. Clair, exceeded all precedent, and stood unrivalled until the flood-gates of slander were opened against myself."[12])

Gates subsequently sought to claim exclusive credit for the success of the subsequent Battles of Saratoga and the entire Saratoga campaign, though many Continental officers who served at the time and scholars since believe that a good portion of Burgoyne's eventual loss can be attributed to Schuyler's delaying actions before Gates's arrival on August 19.[13] Burgoyne left Canada on June 27 with 9,500 men. As a result of Schuyler's efforts, all of which were accomplished before Gates took command, Burgoyne's invasion was in serious trouble by mid-August. More than 20 percent of his original force had been lost as casualties, through desertion, or from the need to garrison Fort Ticonderoga and other posts on the supply route from Canada. Most of the Indian allies had left Burgoyne's force when the expedition failed to provide adequate opportunities for plunder. Foraging for supplies proved to be hazardous, as more and more New York and New England militias gathered to ambush foraging parties and support the American cause. Progress was much slower than anticipated and, with barely two months left in the fighting season, Burgoyne had yet to reach the Hudson River. Rather than repeat Carleton's ignominious retreat to Canada, Burgoyne desperately sought to reach Albany and link up with Howe's force, which he still believed was moving up from New York City. Unfortunately, by the beginning of August Burgoyne had belatedly learned that Howe was not coming. On August 3 Burgoyne received a letter, dated July 17, from Howe informing him that he and the bulk of his forces in New York City were on their way to fight Washington and capture Philadelphia. If Washington were to abandon Philadelphia and flee north, Howe would pursue him and would then be able to support Burgoyne. Burgoyne was informed that in the event Washington failed to move, General Sir Henry Clinton would remain in New York City with a reduced force and "act as occurrences may direct. Putnam is in the highlands with 4,000 men. Success be ever with you."[14] Howe also informed Burgoyne that Washington had sent 2,500 men to reinforce Schuyler.

Howe's letter, written on a tiny note hidden inside a quill pen (the eighteenth-century version of covert communications), was devastating news that Burgoyne chose not to immediately share with his subordinates. (Another copy of the July 17 letter was hidden in a hollow silver ball, the size of a bullet, and transmitted through another messenger. The messenger, when captured by Continental forces, was observed swallowing the bullet. The captors administered an emetic to the messenger, which caused him to disgorge the bullet. When he swallowed the bullet a second time, he was threatened with disembowelment if he did not dislodge the ball a second time. The ball and message were then successfully retrieved. The messenger was then court-martialed and hanged as a spy.[15]) Germain's failure to communicate and coordinate the two active British armies in North America left Burgoyne with only one choice: force his way through the growing American opposition and seize Albany for his winter headquarters. (The third force in Burgoyne's plan, a mixed command of British regulars, American loyalists, and Indian irregulars, was turned back at Fort Stanwix in western New York and never made it to the rendezvous in Albany.)

Upon his arrival at the Northern Army, Gates assumed command of a steadily growing force. Recruitment efforts in New York and New England, spurred by accounts of Burgoyne-inspired Indian atrocities, slowly brought Gates's force to almost 10,000 Continentals and militias by the end of the first week of September.

In addition to troops brought in from western New York by Benedict Arnold, Gates was joined by forces from Vermont under the command of Major General Benjamin Lincoln.

The growing collection of seasoned Continental soldiers and untrained militias required a capable leadership team able to turn them into an effective fighting force. Unlike Washington's army, which had fought, and mostly lost, in 1776 and 1777 under the direction of a capable leader and a reasonably skilled group of subordinate commanders working together, Gates's army had never fought as an army and his subordinate commanders were a mixed group, at best. Most were relatively new general officers who had never commanded large bodies of troops in combat. The most experienced officer available was Arnold, who had repeatedly demonstrated his ability to command in adverse conditions, to motivate Continental and militia soldiers, and to think and act aggressively at the tactical level. Furthermore, during the 1776 Lake Champlain campaign, Arnold had been able to work effectively with both Schuyler and Gates. Unfortunately, he had also demonstrated a prickly preoccupation with military rank and recognition, which attracted numerous complaints, most of them groundless, from far less capable subordinates.

Gates's subsequent actions leading up to the Battles of Saratoga demonstrated both his strengths and weaknesses as an army commander. On the positive side, his demonstrated capability to administer a military force was on full display. Between his arrival on August 19 and the Battle of Freeman's Farm on September 19, Gates's army grew from 4,000 to almost 9,000 troops.[16] These troops had to be housed, clothed, fed, and armed in a military camp that had to be built virtually from scratch and in the face of an advancing British force. Building on the exceptional administrative efforts demonstrated by his predecessor, Gates was able to ensure that his growing army had adequate supplies to operate as an effective fighting force.[17]

However, though capably bringing an army together as an effective combat command, Gates quickly demonstrated his inadequacy as a military leader. Prior to the Battle of Freeman's Farm, Gates had never led a sizable level of troops in combat and his British military experience was limited by his inability to purchase a higher-ranking military commission. He had served valiantly in several actions but never commanded troops in a grade above major and, though he was able to use this service to obtain a general officer's commission in the Continental Army, during his two years of service with the army he had never commanded troops in combat. Gates's service was limited to his role as Washington's adjutant general, avoiding combat at Trenton-Princeton and politically maneuvering around Schuyler to gain control of the Northern Department.

A wise but inexperienced combat commander would normally rely on the advice of more experienced subordinates and seek to surround himself with capable staff officers. Unfortunately, Gates did neither. Rather than recognizing Arnold for the military asset he was, Gates treated Arnold as a threat, first to be ignored and then to be discredited and discarded. Gates chose to rely on Wilkinson, his principal staff officer whom he referred to as "Wilky," not because of his skill or experience but because of his demonstrated sycophancy and willingness to create a false narrative about Gates's military brilliance.[18]

Command relations started well. Gates divided the army into two wings, with Arnold in charge of the brigades of Generals Enoch Poor and Ebenezer Learned and Colonel Daniel Morgan's rifle corps, including Major Henry Dearborn's light infantry. The remaining brigades of Generals John Glover, John Patterson, and John Nixon formed the other wing, under the command of Gates. Gates determined that the current location of the army at Stillwell, New York, did not provide an appropriate ground for the defensive battle he envisioned. Having little faith in the ability of American troops to withstand a determined British bayonet assault, Gates was determined to fight behind fortifications constructed at a suitably sound location. Scouting parties were sent out toward the British lines to find an appropriate location.

The sight chosen was an elevated location known as Bemis Heights and Wilkinson claimed that he had selected the location.[19] However, though this claim has been accepted by some historians, it is highly unlikely. In his two years of Continental service Wilkinson had never led troops in combat, had never conducted scouting operations, and had never chosen any tactical site for any kind of action. The site was most likely chosen by Gates's chief engineer, Colonel Tadeusz Kosciuszko, Wilkinson's tentmate, who was then tasked with the job of building the defensive fortifications. Kosciuszko's fortifications were only partially completed by the time of the first clash with Burgoyne on September 19.

At some point before the first battle, relations between Arnold and Gates began to deteriorate over trivial matters. Following Schuyler's departure, Arnold agreed to take some of Schuyler's aides into his official "family." Gates viewed their presence on Arnold's staff as proof that Arnold's loyalties were to Schuyler, which planted a seed of distrust in Gates's already suspicious mind. Arnold believed that Wilkinson was the "designing villain" in fanning the flames of tension between the two.[20] While Wilkinson and Arnold had served well together the previous year during the retreat from Canada, Wilkinson probably saw an opportunity to ingratiate himself further with Gates by provoking an argument with Arnold and then siding with Gates. On September 10 Arnold took further umbrage to Wilkinson's move to countermand orders he had given regarding the distribution of certain troops. Arnold argued that Wilkinson's action had placed him "in the ridiculous light of presuming to give orders I had no right to do and having them publicly contradicted."[21] While Gates promised to correct Wilkinson's slight, he never did, thereby increasing the tension between them.

In addition to this petty bickering, Gates and Arnold began to disagree about the stance to be taken by the Northern Army. Gates favored a defensive posture, allowing the army to remain behind fortifications built to withstand British attacks. Arnold was, as always, an advocate for aggressive action and pushed for probing attacks on the advancing British. He remained concerned that if the Americans stayed behind their fortifications, they would be driven out by superior British artillery. The tension, fanned by Wilkinson, resulted in Arnold's exclusion from Gates's staff meetings prior to the battle.[22] With no other credible senior commander in attendance, Gates increasingly relied on his own poorly informed counsel, leavened by the advice provided by Wilkinson, his twenty-year-old adjutant with no combat experience and his own agenda to pursue.

In his memoirs Wilkinson claimed that a few days prior to the battle he had volunteered to lead a reconnaissance mission to determine if Burgoyne was on the move. According to Wilkinson's account, he was given a unit of 150 men to lead on the scout, including a unit of riflemen under Lieutenant John Hardin, and was able to report back to Gates that Burgoyne was on the move.[23] Wilkinson notes that in 1791 Hardin was murdered by Indians when he approached them to parley under a flag of truce. Wilkinson's praise of Hardin in his memoirs may have been an attempt to deflect yet another charge of misconduct that had recently been made against him. In 1812 Humphry Marshall, a creditor and enemy of Wilkinson, speculated that Wilkinson viewed Hardin as a rival for command of the army in 1791, surmising that Wilkinson had tipped off the Indians and thus was responsible for Hardin's murder.[24]

The Battle of Freeman's Farm began as a classic meeting engagement between two forces. Having crossed to the west bank of the Hudson River a few days prior, Burgoyne commenced his movement to Albany by dividing his army into three columns. The eastern column of 3,011 mostly Hessian troops under Major General Friedrich von Riedesel proceeded along a road that paralleled the Hudson River. A central column of 1,598 British troops under Brigadier James Hamilton moved south in a position toward the center of the suspected Continental fortification. A third column of 3,011 troops under the command of Brigadier Simon Fraser comprised a mixture of British troops and Hessian Jaegers. Burgoyne chose to accompany Hamilton and the center column in order to maintain control of all three advances.[25]

An understanding of the response of the American forces to the British movement on their left requires an understanding of the portrayal of the role of Benedict

Arnold by contemporary chroniclers, such as Wilkinson, and by later historians. Arnold's treachery in September 1780, when he sought to surrender the American post at West Point and defect to the British side, was widely regarded as the worst possible betrayal of the Revolution. Arnold's subsequent actions after this betrayal, such as in leading British troops against American forces in Virginia and Connecticut, added to the sense of outrage by his former comrades in arms. Even though Burgoyne himself credited Arnold with the leadership that led to his defeat, most early historians denied any credit to Arnold and some, like Wilkinson, tried to write him out of the narrative entirely.[26] As a result of this perfidy, Arnold was immediately cast as the consummate villain, a reputation that would persist for generations to come. Today even Arnold's role at Saratoga, three years before his treachery, remains subject to controversy among historians of the period.[27]

Wilkinson's *Memoirs of My Own Times*, published in 1816, clearly adhere to the viewpoint that was popular at the time, denying Arnold virtually any credit for his contributions at the Battles of Saratoga. But Wilkinson's view of Arnold deserves a particularly skeptical treatment. Wilkinson clearly viewed the publication of his memoirs as a way to settle old scores with those who either opposed him or dared to accuse him of the treachery that he was actually committing. Wilkinson's memoirs are filled with gross distortions, if not outright fabrications, of his own role and contributions as well as with vituperative assaults on his many enemies. Arnold, who had attacked Wilkinson as a lackey of Gates, was clearly a ripe target for Wilkinson's poison pen, particularly after Arnold had died and few veterans were willing to rise to Arnold's defense. Furthermore, the more Wilkinson attacked Arnold, the more attention would be indirectly drawn to Arnold's treason and away from the continuing suspicions of Wilkinson's own collaboration with Spain.

Gates's headquarters at Bemis Heights was located at the Woolworth House, well behind the front line of fortifications.[28] When it became apparent that some form of movement was taking place near Freeman's Farm, well to the front of the American left, Arnold immediately requested permission to advance his troops. In addition to reflecting his aggressive spirit and desire not to be trapped inside the fortifications, Arnold was concerned that Kosciuszko had not yet completed the fortifications on Arnold's side of the line.[29] Gates initially resisted any advance from the fortifications but finally agreed to allow Arnold to send a small detachment forward to scout the area around Freeman's Farm. Arnold knew that Daniel Morgan's rifle corps possessed the best troops to accomplish this work, and he ordered them, accompanied by Major Henry Dearborn's light infantry, to advance to contact. Shortly after noon, Morgan's troops encountered the advancing British forces and opened fire. The remainder of the day was a pattern of confusion with sides advancing and retreating in an uncoordinated piecemeal fashion. The British were shocked by the high number of officer casualties caused by the deliberate targeting of Morgan's riflemen firing from trees. Finally, a contingent of Hessians and supporting artillery from the British river column arrived on the American right flank, bringing the British number to 3,500 engaged and eventually forcing the Americans' withdrawal to Bemis Heights.[30]

By traditional standards the British had "won" the battle because, at the end of the day, they controlled the field. It was a hollow victory at best. The British had sustained over 600 casualties, representing 10 percent of the British troops engaged and far more than the Americans' 350 casualties. Furthermore, the control of the field proved to be an ephemeral standard of success and Burgoyne realized that without support from Clinton in New York City, a further advance would be impossible.

The American failure to decisively win the battle must fall squarely on Gates's shoulders. The slow and piecemeal commitment of additional troops was clearly caused by Gates's refusal to exercise proper control over the engagement taking place far in front of his headquarters location. Gates directed that Arnold and all other general officers, plus even aides like Wilkinson, had to remain within the lines of the Bemis Heights fortification. The eventual commitment of almost one-third of the American forces present at Bemis Heights clearly required the closer presence of a skilled general officer to direct the actions of the diverse American units that were gradually appearing at Freeman's Farm. Gates, who had never commanded a large body of troops in combat, did not recognize this need and stubbornly refused all requests to provide closer control.

The leading advocate for closer control was Arnold. In all his previous campaigns he had pushed for aggressive action and led from the front, espousing a style of leadership that was designed to inspire and direct untrained American troops against an experienced enemy. At the New Year's Eve assault on the walls of Quebec, Arnold led from the front and suffered a grievous leg wound. At Valcour Island, Arnold and his ship were in the heat of the battle and suffered accordingly. Considering that most of the engaged American forces were coming from the wing under his command, and considering the growing size of the American troop commitment, it was impossible to believe that Arnold would not have sought to be present at the most critical location of the growing battle.

Wilkinson's memoirs contain one of the most detailed contemporary accounts regarding the struggle between Arnold and Gates for control at the front. According to Wilkinson, following the commitment of Morgan's corps, Wilkinson, in violation of Gates's orders, rode forward to observe the action.[31] Wilkinson arrived as Morgan's men were recoiling from the arrival of Fraser's reinforcements to their left. According to Wilkinson, he found Morgan in tears, attempting to alert his troops using a turkey call. It is not clear from Wilkinson's memoirs whether Morgan's tears were from frustration or rage, but it is hard to imagine a backwoodsman like Morgan, who had withstood 499 punishment lashes as a British waggoneer and who had led his troops both on the grueling march through Maine and in an assault into the walled city of Quebec in a blizzard, crying in a time of crisis. Since Morgan was an ally of Arnold, this observation may have been pure invention. Morgan died in 1802 and could not rebut Wilkinson's denigrating remarks. After allegedly stiffening Morgan's spirits, Wilkinson claimed he returned to Gates and recommended the commitment of more troops. Based on Wilkinson's recommendation, Gates agreed to commit more of Arnold's troops.

By Wilkinson's account no general officer was on the field until the evening, when General Learned was ordered out. At the same time, Wilkinson reported that Gates and Arnold were present when Colonel Morgan Lewis, deputy quartermaster general, appeared and informed them about the undecisive progress of the action. According to Wilkinson, Arnold exclaimed, "by G-d I will soon put an end to it," and galloped off to assume control at the front. Lewis advised Gates that Arnold's presence might cause some "rash act of mischief," and Gates directed Wilkinson to pursue Arnold and order him back to camp. Arnold reluctantly complied with the order.[32]

If Wilkinson's account is to be believed, then for the entire day Arnold stood idly by, in camp and two miles from the action, while his entire division was committed piecemeal without his direct involvement. If Wilkinson is to be believed, when Gates finally allowed a general officer's onsite supervision, Arnold dispatched General Learned, one of his least experienced brigade commanders, to take control instead of himself. Arnold's presence, or absence, on the field has been the subject of significant historical debate.[33] It must be noted that when Wilkinson published his memoirs in 1816, denying Arnold's presence, many of the surviving participants of the battle did not dispute Wilkinson's account. It must also be noted that this silence may have been caused by a hesitancy to be drawn into a dispute with Wilkinson in the defense of the actions of a known traitor and not by their agreement with Wilkinson not giving any credit to Arnold.

Despite Wilkinson's memoirs, the most likely explanation is that Arnold, acting true to form, snuck on to the field like Wilkinson, in direct defiance of Gates's orders. To whatever degree he exercised control, it was out of Gates's sight and clearly without Gates's approval, thus constrained in its effectiveness. The one time Arnold sought to exercise greater control of his troops that day in Gates's presence, he was recalled by Wilkinson at Gates's direction. Both Gates and Wilkinson had a motive after the Battle of Freeman's Farm to deny any credit to Arnold in the fear that his style of warfare would be compared to Gates's timorous leadership. This fear of comparison led to the open schism between the two that commenced shortly after the battle.

Immediately following the battle, Gates, aided by Wilkinson, commenced a series of actions that were calculated to cause the prickly Arnold to explode in a way that would allow Gates to be rid of the subordinate who was most likely to outshine him. On September 21, in his report of the battle to John Hancock, president of the Continental Congress, Gates pointedly failed to mention that all the troops engaged in the battle belonged to Arnold. Wilkinson then deliberately exacerbated the problem the following day by issuing orders removing Morgan and Dearborn from Arnold's command and assigning them to Gates's headquarters.[34] Upon receipt of this second slight, Arnold directly confronted Gates about the series of perceived insults to his honor and accomplishments. A furious argument that ensued was a discredit to both officers, which ended in Gates informing Arnold that, with General Benjamin Lincoln returning to the army, Gates no longer had need of Arnold's services. Arnold left the meeting in an Achilles-like huff and sought permission from Gates to depart the army and report to Congress. While he eventually received this permission, senior officers in the army circulated a petition urging Arnold to remain.[35] Sensing that another clash with the British was imminent, Arnold chose to remain in the camp without a command in the hopes that there would be a role for him to play in the coming battle.

Arnold clearly suspected that someone was denouncing him to Gates behind his back, calling that person a "designing villain."[36] Undoubtedly, that person was Wilkinson. In discussing Arnold in a letter written to St. Clair describing the action, Wilkinson remarked that "General Gates despises a certain pompous little fellow as much as you can."[37] In another letter to St. Clair, written on the morning of the Battle of Bemis Heights, Wilkinson remarked that "General Gates and Arnold have differed beyond reconciliation. As I, too, have a quarrel with the little man, I will not expose his conduct."[38]

In the absence of any movement by the American lines, Burgoyne commenced to fortify his location around Freeman's Farm and hoped that Clinton would dispatch a relief force up the Hudson in order to catch Gates between two British armies. While Clinton did send a small force up the Hudson, he intended it more as a distraction than a relief. His distraction captured a few Continental forts around West Point, moved a distance up the Hudson River, then returned to New York City. As September turned to October, Burgoyne faced the slow starvation of his army. Continental forces had severed his supply line to Canada, many foraging expeditions had failed to find enough food and forage, and his troop strength continued to decline from desertions and captures. By October 7 Burgoyne's force had been reduced to fewer than 7,000 effectives.[39] Conversely, Gates's army continued to grow to over 13,000, as 3,000 more militia and a contingent of Oneida Indians arrived to supplement his force.[40] Burgoyne held a series of councils of war with his senior staff and devised a desperate course of action. The plan was that on October 7 a portion of the army, approximately 2,000 strong, would conduct a reconnaissance in force toward the left flank of the Continental line. If a weakness in the Americans' position was found, a general attack would be launched the following day, with the goal of breaking through the American lines and heading for Albany. If no weakness was found, the army would commence a retreat to a previous camp to the north, on the east side of the Hudson.[41]

The Battle of Bemis Heights commenced in a similar manner to the Battle of Freeman's Farm: at noon on October 7 the British force, accompanied by all the senior leadership of the army, proceeded toward the left of the Continental line. According to Wilkinson, he discovered this movement and reported it to Gates, who ordered Morgan's corps to probe the British advance. The Continental left was now commanded directly by Gates, with more than 5,000 men in twenty regiments. Major General Benjamin Lincoln commanded the more than 6,000 troops of the right wing of the army. Most of these troops played no role in the battle, and neither Gates nor Lincoln left the Bemis Heights fortifications at any point during the battle. Pursuant to the orders delivered by Wilkinson, Morgan moved forward and sought to flank the right of the British column. The brigades of Generals Learned and Enoch Poor, along with the militia brigade of General Abraham Ten Broeck, were deployed to halt the front of the British column. When the flank assault of Morgan began, the British were outnumbered two to one and commenced a retreat to the two large redoubts constructed at their camp near Freeman's Farm.

At this point of the battle, aggressive leadership was needed to drive the British from their fortifications and put the entire army to flight. None of the American generals on the scene had any experience in leading thousands of troops in an attack, and Gates again remained at his headquarters two miles behind the scene of the action, apparently incapable of seizing the moment and taking control.[42] Arnold, who was present with Gates and lacking a command, saw the leadership gap and mounted his horse and headed for the front. Once again Gates directed a subordinate aide, Major John Armstrong Jr, to recall Arnold, but the aide was unable to catch him.[43] Arnold rushed to the left front, where he met Morgan and Dearborn in their attack on the far right of the British line under the command of Brigadier Simon Fraser. Fraser, in full uniform and mounted on a horse, was attempting to rally his troops and presented a conspicuous target for Morgan's riflemen. A few well-placed shots were directed at Fraser, who fell mortally wounded, causing the collapse of his rally. Arnold then rushed to the head of the American forces to their right, on the other side of the battlefield, and led them in a futile attack against the Balcarres Redoubt. Following this repulse, Arnold again went back to the American left side of the battlefield and led an assault by Morgan, Dearborn, and Learned on the Breymann Redoubt. This time the British fortification was overwhelmed when Arnold, on horseback, led a charge through the back opening of the redoubt. In the final moments of the charge Arnold was shot in the same leg in which he had been wounded in the assault on Quebec.[44]

The wound resulted in the end of Arnold's career as a combat commander for the Americans. His shattered leg required months of treatment and he played no further role in the affairs of the Northern Army. In reward for his services at Saratoga, Congress elevated Arnold's seniority to major general (over the five other generals who had previously been promoted before him). Lincoln played no role in the action of October 7 and remained inside the lines for the entire engagement. On October 8 Lincoln led part of his right wing on an exploration of the British lines to his front and he, too, suffered a grievous leg wound, removing him from any further role in the Northern Army.

Despite Arnold's conspicuous gallantry, which has been recognized by most historians and by Burgoyne himself as a leading cause of the victory, Wilkinson's memoirs sought to deny any credit to Arnold and instead to accumulate as much credit as possible for himself. While graciously stating that he "would not offer injustice even to a traitor," Wilkinson went on to do just that.[45] According to Wilkinson, Arnold was drinking freely prior to the assault and "acted exceedingly rash and intemperate; he exposed himself with great folly and temerity."[46] Wilkinson charged that in his drunken battle rage, Arnold accidently struck one of Dearborn's officers with his sword and narrowly missed being shot by that officer. Wilkinson concluded, "It is certain, that he neither rendered service, nor deserved credit on that day, and the wound he received alone saved him being overwhelmed, by the torrent of General Gates's good fortune and popularity."[47] Not content in simply denying Arnold credit, Wilkinson also claimed that he, not Arnold, personally directed Learned in the conduct of the final crucial assault on the Breymann Redoubt.[48]

Arnold's official status at the Battle of Bemis Heights remains a subject of continuing historical debate. Many historians have adopted some of Wilkinson's conclusion in asserting that Arnold's inspired leadership was performed without the formal role of command.[49] However, in a new history of the battle, Kevin Weddle notes the unreliability of Wilkinson's written account and asserts that between the battles of Freeman's Farm and Bemis Heights, Gates and Arnold were reconciled. Finding no official record that Arnold was relieved of his command of the left wing after Freeman's Farm, Weddle concludes that Arnold was acting as the official left-wing commander at Bemis Heights.[50]

Following the battle, Gates was concerned that he should receive full credit for the victory. On October 12 he prepared a letter to Hancock and Congress, describing the American victory and even commending the "gallant major general Arnold."[51] (Arnold's grave wound had removed him as an immediate threat to Gates.) As he had in his communiqué regarding the Battle of Freeman's Farm, Gates deliberately did not communicate the results to Washington and sent his notice only to Congress. It is possible that Gates at this time was again thinking that he could supplant Washington as the senior general of the army. If Congress were to compare Gates's two victories with Washington's defeats around Philadelphia, Gates's allies in Congress could push for a change in command.

By the end of the day of the battle, Burgoyne realized the staggering number of casualties his forces had endured. More than half of the reconnaissance force was killed, wounded, or missing, including one of his senior generals and thirty other officers. By comparison, American casualties were relatively light: 30 killed and 100 wounded.[52] When Gates failed to renew the offensive on October 8, Burgoyne ordered a withdrawal, commencing that evening. Abandoning his hospital and the more than 400 sick and wounded to American care, Burgoyne proceeded four miles to the north and reunited with Riedesel and the left wing of the army. His immediate goal was Fort Edward, less than twenty-five miles from Freeman's Farm, but weather, lack of provisions, desertions, captures, and exhaustion slowed the withdrawal to a crawl. (Burgoyne did have enough time to burn Philip Schuyler's home in Saratoga as the army passed through.)

Gates commenced his pursuit on October 10 and, in one of his few calls for an attack, the next day directed an assault on what he thought was a lightly guarded section of the British rear guard. Unfortunately, Gates had failed to properly reconnoiter both the location of the attack and the strength of the British force. Just as the attack was commencing, General John Glover encountered a British deserter, who informed him that the British had not withdrawn and that Gates's force was headed for a heavily fortified section of the main British line. Glover immediately dispatched a message to Gates, who called off the attack.[53]

Wilkinson's memoirs tell a different story, with him once again cast as the hero: that he led a reconnaissance of the front on the morning of the battle and discovered that the British had not withdrawn. Recognizing that Gates's order would send the American forces into a trap, Wilkinson, by his own authority, valiantly halted the advance and then rode back to Gates and convinced him to cancel the attack.[54]

This was only one of the many representations of Wilkinson's bravura performance during the battle. According to his self-congratulatory memoirs,

Wilkinson sought to claim an outsize personal role for the victory at Bemis Heights. The twenty-year-old lieutenant colonel, who had never commanded troops in battle, claimed credit for being the first to discover Burgoyne's movement,[55] for being the first to discover the purpose behind Burgoyne's movement,[56] for directing the deployment of Poor's and Learned's brigades in the attack at Bemis Heights,[57] for saving the life of the wounded commander of the British grenadiers,[58] and for canceling Gates's ill-considered assault on the retreating British.[59]

By October 12 the less-than-aggressive Gates had surrounded Burgoyne well short of Fort Edward. On October 13 Burgoyne held a council of war that concluded that surrender was his only option. A drummer was dispatched to the American lines with a message requesting a truce and a meeting for the following day, to discuss a "matter of high moment." Gates agreed to both requests.[60]

In the subsequent negotiations Wilkinson assumed a predominant role. On October 14, at the agreed on time, a British drummer beat the chamade, a signal for the commencement of a parley. A British major came forward and was greeted by Wilkinson; he was then blindfolded and escorted to Gates, where he presented Burgoyne's request for a cessation of hostilities and a commencement of negotiation of terms for surrender. Gates responded with a breach of protocol by presenting the British major with Gates's proposed terms of surrender. (Even Wilkinson recognized that protocol required Burgoyne to propose terms and Gates to respond. Wilkinson even gently chastised Gates for ceding the momentum of the negotiations to Burgoyne. Gates responded, "Wilky, you are right again; but it is done, and we must make the most of it; I shall be content to get the arms out of their hands."[61]) Over the next two days back-and-forth negotiations took place, with Wilkinson serving as the primary American negotiator. At one point in the negotiations Wilkinson met personally with Burgoyne and his senior staff. According to Wilkinson, Gates played virtually no role in these negotiations, except to endorse the terms that Wilkinson had negotiated.[62]

Much of the delay was caused by Burgoyne stalling for time. During the negotiations a courier had arrived, carrying news that a British relief force, dispatched by General Clinton from New York City, was approaching. Burgoyne then chose to prolong negotiations with petty objections, in the hopes that Clinton's force would arrive. In reality, no relief force was even close. Following the seizure of the forts around West Point, Clinton dispatched 2,000 troops under Major General John Vaughn to proceed up the Hudson by boat in the direction of Albany. At the time of the negotiations, Vaughn's boats were able to navigate the Hudson only as far as Livingston Manor, sixty miles short of Albany. Any further movement would have required overland travel through rebel-held territory, an unlikely occurrence given the overwhelming presence of American militia. Clinton directed Vaughn to withdraw on October 22.[63]

According to Wilkinson, he alone broke the deadlock by convincing Gates to accept the British proposal to call the surrender a "convention" rather than a "capitulation."[64] With this face-saving alteration the convention was signed on October 16. It required the British and German troops to surrender their arms and march under American guard to Boston, where they would be transported to Great Britain with the understanding that they would not serve again in North America.[65]

When the convention was sent to Congress for ratification, Congress recognized a major loophole that had escaped the attention of Wilkinson and Gates. The convention prohibited Burgoyne's troops from serving again in North America. It did not prevent Great Britain from swapping and replacing those troops with other British forces stationed elsewhere. As a result of this belated awakening, Congress refused to ratify the convention. The so-called Convention Army was neither repatriated nor exchanged until the war ended in 1783. The mixed force of British and Hessian prisoners was eventually sent to the Albemarle Barracks, a prisoner-of-war camp constructed in Charlottesville, Virginia, safely distant from British efforts to free them. When British troops under Colonel Banastre Tarleton got too close to Charlottesville in 1781, the prisoners were moved again to prison camps in Winchester, Virginia; Frederick, Maryland; and Lancaster, Pennsylvania. During their movements from New York to Massachusetts to Virginia to Maryland and finally to Pennsylvania, many of the prisoners died, escaped, or deserted and joined the American economy as farmers and tradesmen.[66]

At the surrender ceremony on October 17, Wilkinson formally introduced Burgoyne to Gates (though Gates needed no introduction; the two officers had served in the same regiment of the British Army in 1745[67]). According to Wilkinson, Burgoyne remarked, "The fortune of war, General Gates, has made me your prisoner," to which Gates obsequiously replied, "I shall always be ready to bear testimony that it has not been through any fault of your excellency."[68] If the British catastrophe at Saratoga was not Burgoyne's fault, it also was not the result of superior leadership by Gates. From the outset of the campaign Burgoyne had arrogantly underestimated the difficulty of force projection from Canada to Albany. Since he was present during Carleton's failed 1776 campaign, Burgoyne had firsthand knowledge of the logistical and tactical challenges the British would face. Despite this knowledge, coupled with the fact that he would not have to confront American forces until he reached Fort Ticonderoga, Burgoyne did not enter New York until July, giving him only three to four months of good weather to accomplish his seizure of Albany. Although the bloodless seizure of the "impregnable"

Fort Ticonderoga was a major accomplishment, the remainder of the campaign was spent marching and countermarching through the New York wilderness until his fateful arrival at Saratoga. Burgoyne also underestimated the skill by which General Schuyler would, like Arnold the year before, mount an effective delaying action at every step of his path. Burgoyne also underestimated the skill and determination shown by the American militia at Bennington, Freeman's Farm, and Bemis Heights in the defense of their land. As stated by Henry Dearborn, "we . . . had Something more at Stake than fighting for six Pence Pr Day."[69]

If, contrary to Gates's view, much of Burgoyne's loss was indeed caused by his own mistakes, those mistakes were not materially exploited by Gates's strategic or tactical actions. A significant amount of Gates's efforts in 1777 were spent in political machinations to overthrow Schuyler from command of the army, not in building an effective fighting force. Gates was also the beneficiary of the recruiting efforts of others, which allowed him to have the overwhelming advantage of superior numbers in battle. During the Battle of Freeman's Farm, Gates failed to exercise any meaningful control of the battle and allowed it to grow in a piecemeal fashion and without any tactical plan. Given Gates's avowed defensive attitude, had he truly been in control at Freeman's Farm, American forces would have remained within the Bemis Heights fortifications and been able to withstand a British assault. Instead, Gates allowed the American forces to slowly leak out of the fortifications to confront a growing British force on the field, two miles from the American fortifications.

The Battle of Freeman's Farm developed through his indecisive leadership and therefore resulted in an indecisive conclusion. Gates, working with Wilkinson, subsequently proceeded to cause an unnecessary fight with Arnold, his most talented subordinate, leading to recriminations that adversely affected the morale and leadership of the entire army. At the Battle of Bemis Heights, Gates again endorsed a gradual engagement in front of the American fortifications and then failed to provide any meaningful control of the forces engaged, particularly when the British commenced their withdrawal. If Wilkinson is to be believed, he, without any direction from Gates, directed the final American attack on the British redoubts. Such a claim is a gross distortion of the facts. Arnold's actions on the field clearly rebut Wilkinson's attempt to seize the glory and were the inspired leadership that captured the day. Gates was, once again, merely a witness to what most historians agree is the decisive battle of the Revolution. As a result of the American victory, France agreed to formally enter the war and support the Americans through the joint victory at Yorktown in 1781.[70] Gates's one attempt at aggressive action during the pursuit of Burgoyne's retreating force was conducted without any meaningful reconnaissance and could have resulted in a significant defeat.

Following the surrender on October 17, Gates commenced his next campaign: the seizure of the control of the entire Continental Army from Washington. Gates had repeatedly demonstrated a willingness to seek out disaffected army officers and members of Congress and use their dissatisfaction to further advance his career in the army. In 1776 Gates had formed a common bond with General Charles Lee in seeking to undercut Washington's leadership. That attempt failed due to Lee's untimely capture by the British Army. Gates avoided combat at Trenton and Princeton while he lobbied Congress for Washington's removal. In 1777 Gates again worked to use his congressional allies to remove Schuyler and give to himself command of the Northern Army. Now, with the victory at Saratoga in hand, Gates commenced his next move to replace Washington.

Gates was required to promptly report the results of Burgoyne's surrender to his superiors. As he had done following Freeman's Farm and Bemis Heights, Gates chose to communicate to John Hancock as the president of Congress and to conspicuously insult Washington by refusing to directly communicate with him. Gates chose Wilkinson, his loyal subordinate, as his messenger. Under military protocol of the time, the officer who was chosen to carry the news of a military triumph would receive an honorary, or brevet, promotion. On October 18, Wilkinson was dispatched to Congress with Gates's official report of the final surrender. In his report to Congress, Gates provided the following view of Wilkinson's role in the campaign: "I desire to be permitted to recommend this gallant officer, in the warmest manner, to Congress; and intreat that he may be continued in his present office with the brevet rank of a brigadier-general. The honorable Congress will believe me when I assure them, that from the beginning of this contest I have (not) met with a more promising military genius than Colonel Wilkinson, and *whose services have been of the last importance to this army*" (emphasis in original).[71] With Gates's full support, Wilkinson commenced his journey to Congress, where he would perform in a starring role in the intrigue known as the Conway Cabal.

3

———

WILKINSON AND THE CONWAY CABAL

1777–1782

To attempt sowing dissentions amongst the principal officers of the army,
and rendering them odious to each other, by false suggestions and forgeries,
is in my opinion a crime of the first magnitude; it involves with it all the
consequences of positive treason.
—General Horatio Gates to General George Washington,
on James Wilkinson

During the fifteen months that Wilkinson and Gates had been working together, they had developed an almost father-and-son relationship. Wilkinson had betrayed Arnold, his former mentor, to solidify his relationship with Gates; he was rewarded for his loyalty with Gates's support for a promotion which, if granted, would make the twenty-year-old Wilkinson the youngest general in the Continental Army. Gates demonstrated his faith in Wilky by allowing him to negotiate the terms of the Saratoga Convention and to relay the terms of that convention to Congress. Unfortunately, the relationship between the two men did not survive the trip. Their mutual failings of honor and character were on display before all of Congress and the officer corps of the Continental Army, and within a few short months both saw their hopes for advancement dissipate into recriminations, accusations, and a series of duels.

Wilkinson spent almost twenty days completing his journey from Albany to York Town, Pennsylvania, where Congress was temporarily located after being driven out of Philadelphia by Sir William Howe's victorious force. The slow pace of Wilkinson's journey was part of a pattern he followed throughout his career whenever he was required to report to the capital on important business. Wilkinson established his own deliberate pace, seemingly oblivious to the importance of his mission or the wishes of his superiors. (During the same period, Colonel Alexander Hamilton would journey from York Town to Albany in only five days.) According to Wilkinson, his journey of three hundred miles got off to a slow start on October 20 due to his recovery from a bout of colic.[1] Strong storms along the way caused flooding and required him to seek shelter until the storms passed, though Wilkinson's journey provided an opportunity for romance and political intrigue that was responsible for the greatest portion of the delay. By October 24 Wilkinson had reached Easton, Pennsylvania, where he spent a few days pursuing his courtship of Nancy Biddle. Wilkinson then stopped in Reading, Pennsylvania, where he was entertained by General Thomas Mifflin.[2] At the time Mifflin was serving as quartermaster general of the Continental Army and was facing a good deal of criticism from Washington and others regarding the quartermaster department's failure to supply the army. As a result, Mifflin had suffered a serious falling out with Washington and was becoming one of the primary critics of George Washington's leadership.

It is not clear whether their Reading meeting occurred by chance, or if Wilkinson had been directed by Gates to meet with Mifflin to exchange information regarding their mutual desire to eliminate Washington as the head of the Continental Army. By mid-October 1777 Washington was facing one of his greatest challenges to remain in command as the result of his defeats at Brandywine and Germantown and the loss of Philadelphia and the ignominy of having his political masters in the Continental Congress forced into fleeing to another city. Congress was also in the process of creating a full-time organization, the Board of War, to provide greater control and oversight over the Continental Army. Though the charter for the board was still in a state of development, Washington was concerned that members of the board chosen by Congress were outspoken critics, both military and civilian, of his leadership. Congress further snubbed Washington by pointedly refusing to consult with him on those selections. Washington was also concerned that if the charter of the board was drawn too broadly, he would be subordinate to the board in all decisions related to the strategic and tactical operations of the Continental Army.

Following his midday meeting with Mifflin, Wilkinson accepted an invitation to a "potluck" supper with Major General William Alexander, also known as Lord Stirling (due to his claim to a Scottish peerage). Stirling had a reputation for heavy drinking and, following the dinner, Wilkinson engaged in a celebration with Stirling and two of his aides, Major James Monroe and Major William McWilliams. After Stirling retired for the evening, Wilkinson and McWilliams, perhaps suffering the effects of too much alcohol, began trading gossip about the Continental Army. Wilkinson foolishly betrayed Gates by disclosing the substance of a confidential communication recently sent to Gates by one of Washington's more outspoken critics, Brigadier General Thomas Conway. Conway, a colonel of the Irish Brigade of the French Army, had been recruited by Silas Deane in Paris to come to the United States and work for the American cause. Upon his arrival in the United States in 1777, Conway, like many foreign officers, was given a brigadier general's commission and served under Washington at the Battle of Germantown. At some point following that battle Conway had written a letter to Gates, congratulating him for the victory at Saratoga. It is unclear whether Conway and Gates had had a previous relationship, but, according to Wilkinson in his tipsy disclosure, Conway felt comfortable enough in his relationship with Gates to include in his letter the following condemnation of Washington: "Heaven has been determined to Save your Country; Or a Weak General and Bad Counsellors would have ruined it."[3] According to Wilkinson's later defense of his disclosure of this remark, Gates believed that the Conway letter, while private, was not meant to be treated as a secret.[4] Gates therefore read the letter, with its condemnation of Washington, to members of his staff, undoubtedly to demonstrate the dissatisfaction within the officer corps and the need for Gates to assume overall command from Washington. Following his intemperate disclosure to McWilliams, Wilkinson stumbled off to bed and did not think further of the night's discussion.

Major McWilliams was a loyal subordinate of Lord Stirling, who was in turn a loyal subordinate of Washington. On the following day, when Wilkinson finally departed Reading for York Town, McWilliams shared the Conway communication with Stirling. Stirling, who detested Conway and was aware of the dissension among some disaffected Continental Army officers regarding Washington's leadership, decided to inform Washington of the Conway letter. On November 3 he sent a letter to Washington describing the "wicked duplicity" of Conway's letter, noting that Wilkinson had been the source of the information.[5]

Historians continue to debate about the scope and breadth of the Conway Cabal. Whether it was truly a broad-ranging conspiracy among numerous officers and members of Congress acting in concert to remove Washington or merely the growing discontent among a diverse group of individuals, it cannot be denied that at this point in the Revolution, Washington was facing a daunting crisis in maintaining control over the army. The fall and winter of 1777–78 Washington had been defeated repeatedly on the battlefield, the capital of the United States was abandoned to the British, and the army suffered numerous logistical failures at the encampment at Valley Forge. When this dismal record was compared with Gates's victory at Saratoga, an argument could have been made by all but Washington's staunchest defenders that the time was ripe for a change in leadership. Horatio Gates was certainly prepared to address this perceived leadership gap by promoting his own cause and by seeking support from congressional admirers who had placed him in control of the Northern Army in July. Furthermore, to advance his cause it was natural for him to identify other disaffected army leaders and establish a common bond with them on the need to bring fresh leadership to the Continental Army. However, because of Washington's adept handling of the crisis, the correspondence degenerated into a morass of mendacity and finger-pointing and led to the collapse of the cabal.

While tactical brilliance on the battlefield has never been viewed as one of Washington's strengths, Washington demonstrated an amazing ability to both weather military, logistical, and political storms throughout the eight years of the conflict and persevere in keeping the army together and committed to the goal of independence. At no time in the Revolution was that skill better displayed than in his response to the Conway Cabal. Washington had always respected and deferred to the civilian political leadership of Congress, but by the summer and fall of 1777 tensions with Congress stemming from numerous factors had risen to new levels. Many of the initial leaders of the Continental Congress, who had led the cause of independence and issued the Declaration of Independence, had left Congress and had been replaced with persons of lesser talent and commitment. As Washington's army amassed a series of military failures, some members of Congress, those who had no military skill or experience with which to judge the difficulties the army faced, sought to exert greater control over the strategic and tactical course of the war.

In addition to providing funding and general oversight over the Continental Army, one way Congress sought to exert greater control was through the selection of general officers who met their approval, battlefield accomplishments notwithstanding. Gates's selection to command the Northern Army was the most egregious example of this form of political control and interference. By his own choice Washington played no role in Gates's selection and thereby created a dangerous precedent: Congress directing Gates without input from Washington, and Gates's freedom to ignore Washington. Recognizing that Gates would welcome Congress's greater role in military decisions, Congress decided to improve its ability to run the war by reorganizing the Board of War and empowering it with greater control over all Continental Army operations. With this new structure in place Washington recognized that, rather than reporting to members of Congress, he might be reporting to the nonelected leadership of the board, many of whom were his rivals and who could direct the operational control of the Continental Army.

By the time of the surrender of Saratoga, Washington became aware of his mistake in ceding control of the Northern Army to Congress and Gates. Gates had ignored Washington and reported the victories directly to Congress. Similarly, at the time of Stirling's November 3 warning about Conway, Gates was snubbing

Washington by having Wilkinson deliver the report of the convention's features to Congress, deliberately ignoring Washington. Washington now decided to take several steps to reestablish his overall control of the entire Continental Army.

First, following the surrender of Burgoyne's forces, Washington recognized that there was no longer a British threat in the Northern Department. Though most of the militias in the Northern Army disbanded after Saratoga, Gates retained a significant portion of the Continental Line, much of which had been sent to him as reinforcements by Washington. Since Washington was still skirmishing with British troops outside Philadelphia, on October 30 Washington dispatched a trusted aide, Lieutenant Colonel Alexander Hamilton, to Albany to direct the return of some of these forces. Unlike Wilkinson, Hamilton proceeded with alacrity to Albany and on November 5 presented Gates with Washington's demand for the return of troops. Gates probably bristled at the brash request of the twenty-two-year-old Hamilton and sought to avoid compliance with the request, citing the alleged threat to the Northern Department posed by British troops stationed in New York City.[6] When Hamilton insisted on the dispatch of two brigades, Gates agreed to send only General John Patterson's brigade. Hamilton immediately recognized that Gates was sending his weakest brigade, and he insisted on more troops, with which Gates begrudgingly complied.[7]

Washington next set his sights on Thomas Conway. When Conway was recruited as a colonel from the French Army, he had been promised that no subordinate officer in the French Army would be promoted over him in the Continental Army. In September 1777, Baron Johann de Kalb, a lieutenant colonel in the French Army, was promoted to major general in the Continental Army, leading Conway to protest loudly to Washington and Congress about being denied a promotion to major general.[8] By this time Washington was greatly concerned about the way Congress was granting promotions, particularly those affecting the senior ranks. Political quotas and connections, as well as rank in a foreign army, seemed to be the primary criteria for congressional promotions.[9] Proven battlefield commanders like Benedict Arnold had been passed over by Congress, creating a crisis in morale. Washington decided to oppose further meritless promotions by making an example of Conway, and Stirling's letter provided the perfect opportunity to demonstrate that Conway was unworthy of higher command.

Recognizing that his knowledge of the offensive communication was based on quadruple hearsay, Washington chose not to directly confront Conway even though, as his commanding officer, Washington had the right to do so. (The actual letter itself was never produced by either Conway or Gates during the entire controversy. It is believed that Gates returned it to Conway at some point in late January 1778.) Instead, on November 5, Washington sent a simple note to

Conway: "Sir: A letter which I received last Night, contained the following paragraph. In a letter from General Conway to General Gates he says—'Heaven has been determined to save your Country; or a weak General and Bad Counselors would have ruined it.' I am Sir Yr Hble Srvt."[10]

The note contained no direct accusation but placed Conway in a considerable bind. Since Conway knew the actual content of the letter to Gates, he was left to wonder how much more of his criticism about Washington had been made known to Washington. He was also concerned about the source of the information. Had he been exposed by Gates, a supposed ally in the effort to remove Washington? If not, was someone on Gates's staff responsible for the leak? Not knowing the answer to these questions, Conway responded to Washington immediately to see whether he could learn more about what Washington knew. In a rambling manner Conway set forth his admiration for Washington, qualified by the fact that Washington was often influenced by persons who were not his equal. He admitted that he had shared these concerns with Generals Gates and Mifflin but that he had never used the phrase "weak general." He went on to say that correspondence between generals in all armies is encouraged and that he would approve of General Gates releasing the letter to Washington. He also noted that Washington's aides had previously attributed things to him which he had never said.[11] Conway then commenced a search to determine how his sentiments had ended up in Washington's hands.

Following his inebriated indiscretion with Major McWilliams on October 24, Wilkinson proceeded to York Town to meet with the Continental Congress and deliver his dispatches from Gates, completely oblivious to the alarm he had caused with Stirling. Citing weather delays, Wilkinson took another week to travel from Reading to York Town, a distance of less than sixty miles. On October 31 he arrived in York Town and sought an opportunity to present his dispatches and to defend the terms of the convention to members of Congress. He made a formal presentation before Congress on November 3 and anxiously awaited Congress's action on his brevet promotion to brigadier general.[12] The following day he wrote Gates, observing that Gates's failure to formally notify Washington about the convention had been publicly noted and setting forth his concern that in the three days since his presentation, he had not learned whether Congress had acted on his promotion.[13]

While the prevailing military tradition was to reward the bearer of good news of a military triumph with a brevet or temporary promotion, Congress's actions had been uneven. Following General Stark's victory at Bennington, Schuyler had dispatched Major Henry Brockholst Livingston to Congress with the good news and a recommendation for a brevet promotion to lieutenant colonel for Livingston. Congress refused to grant the request. Following the victory at Freeman's Farm,

Gates dispatched Major Robert Troup to Congress with the news of the victory and sought Troup's promotion to lieutenant colonel. Feeling generous, shortly before Wilkinson's arrival Congress approved the promotion of Troup and the delayed promotion of Livingston. Gates's recommendation of a two-step promotion for the "military genius" of a twenty-year-old aide who had never led troops in combat was likely to cause concern in Congress and resentment among other officers with more distinguished records. Nevertheless, in due course Congress adopted Gates's language regarding the military genius and approved Wilkinson's brevet promotion to brigadier general.[14]

Having received what he called his "unsolicited promotion," Wilkinson traveled around Pennsylvania showing off his new rank and status.[15] First he traveled from York Town to Reading, where he socialized with members of the Biddle family, his soon-to-be in-laws. From Reading he made his way to White Marsh to pay his respects to Washington and meet with other members of the Continental Army and parade his new rank in front of other officers who had spent many months in hard and unsuccessful combat but would not be rewarded with a promotion based on that sacrifice. The twenty-year-old general with no command or combat experience was once again oblivious to the effect his promotion and presence had on the officer corps. While in White Marsh, Wilkinson was approached by General Conway, a person whom Wilkinson claimed he had never previously met, who asked Wilkinson if he had seen the letter referenced by Washington and if the letter contained the criticism cited by Washington. Wilkinson dissembled and told Conway that he recalled the letter but did not think it contained the phrase stated by Conway. Conway replied that he had the right to state his opinions and that the criticism attributed to him was justified.[16] Of course, Wilkinson did not share with Conway the fact that Wilkinson's own conversation with Stirling's staff might have been the source of the leak. Wilkinson remained in Pennsylvania for a few weeks more, visiting friends and courting Nancy before departing for Albany and reporting back to Gates on December 8.[17]

During Wilkinson's absence from the Northern Army, events surrounding Gates's future with the army accelerated rapidly. In addition to his fight with Hamilton over reinforcements to Washington, Gates worked with his congressional allies to be named the president of the newly reconstituted Board of War, perhaps putting him in a position as Washington's superior. While the previous members of the board had all been congressional delegates, the new board was composed of civilians and two major generals, Gates and Mifflin, both of whom were allowed to keep their Continental Army ranks.

However, Gates's delight in the appointment to his new position was offset by the growing furor over the Conway correspondence. On November 28 Mifflin wrote to Gates and warned him that Washington was aware of Conway's correspondence with Gates, stating that Conway's expressed sentiments were just but that they should not have been shared by Gates with members of his military family. Mifflin urged Gates to "take care of your *generosity and frank disposition*; they cannot injure yourself but may injure some of your best friends" (emphasis in original).[18] When Gates received the letter on December 3 he immediately wrote Conway in an attempt to find out exactly what item of correspondence had caused the excitement. In the letter he referred to Mifflin as "our worthy friend" and stated, "It is of the greatest importance, that I should detect the person who has been guilty of that act of infidelity; I cannot trace him out, unless I have your assistance."[19] If Wilkinson's memoirs are to be believed, Gates had shared the Conway correspondence freely with numerous members of his staff.[20] Gates therefore had to identify which of these staffers had deliberately or inadvertently conveyed the correspondence to Washington.

This series of letters displays several important facts. While some historians have doubted whether the Conway Cabal was a true conspiracy to remove Washington, the Gates-Mifflin-Conway correspondence of November and December has all the hallmarks of persons acting in concert, that is, a classic conspiracy. The three members are in clear communication with each other; they share a common theme of criticism of their commander in chief; they urge caution that their communications have been compromised; and they urge a hunt for the person who has betrayed them.

The correspondence also displays that Gates knew the initial Conway correspondence existed and did indeed contain a criticism of Washington. Gates's subsequent correspondence with Washington, where he first sought, with Wilkinson's aid, to frame an innocent person for the leak then later deny the existence of the criticism as a forgery, demonstrates a clear lack of honesty, honor, and integrity by a general at the highest level of the Continental Army.

Less than a week after Gates's promise of a leak hunt, the inadvertent leaker returned to Gates and was immediately brought into Gates's hut. Wilkinson would later claim that the first time he learned that he was suspected as being the source of the leak was in February 1778, when he received a letter from Lord Stirling dated January 6, 1778, identifying him as the source of the allegations forwarded to Washington.[21] If Wilkinson's memoirs are to be believed, at their December reunion Gates never directed any of the focus of his leak hunt on Wilkinson. Instead, Gates encouraged Wilkinson to help him create a narrative that would falsely implicate Alexander Hamilton as the source of the leak.

According to Wilkinson, upon his arrival in Albany he immediately met with Gates. At this time Gates supposedly never questioned Wilkinson regarding his possible role in the leak. Instead, Gates shared with Wilkinson his theory that the

Conway correspondence had been stolen by Hamilton during his November visit to Gates. Gates speculated that Hamilton had been alone in Gates's closet during some period of his visit, had searched his office and found the Conway letter, then communicated it to Washington. This manufactured tale would deflect the attention from Gates's correspondence with Conway and focus it on the thievery by a senior member of Washington's own staff.

In addition to implicating Washington in trafficking in stolen documents, the tale had the additional benefit of providing revenge on Hamilton, who had humiliated Gates in the argument over sending reinforcements to Washington. (Wilkinson quotes Gates as saying, "He had adopted a plan, which would *compel* General Washington to give him [Hamilton] up, and that the receiver and the thief would be alike disgraced" [emphasis in original].[22]) Wilkinson allegedly sought to temper this attack on both Washington and Hamilton by proposing a more innocent explanation, observing that a different Gates aide, the newly promoted Colonel Robert Troup, was a close friend of Hamilton. Since Troup was among the people with whom Gates had shared the Conway letter, Wilkinson suggested that perhaps Troup had inadvertently shared the correspondence with Hamilton, who then provided it to Washington.[23] According to Wilkinson, Gates rejected this approach and insisted on framing Hamilton as the culprit.[24]

In his letter to Washington, written on the day of his meeting with Wilkinson, Gates posed as an innocent victim filled with righteous indignation because his correspondence had been stolen. Stating plainly that no member of his staff was under suspicion for having leaked the correspondence, Gates requested that Washington provide him with the source of the original allegation involving Conway. To demonstrate his allegiance to his new congressional overseers as the newly appointed president of the Board of War, Gates informed Washington that he was sending a copy of his response to Washington to the president of Congress, "so that Congress may, in concert with your excellency, obtain as soon as possible a discovery, which so deeply affects the safety of the states. Crimes of that magnitude ought not to remain unpunished."[25]

This ill-conceived letter illustrates several matters affecting Gates at the time. In his "leak investigation," which exonerated all his immediate staff, Gates either never questioned Wilkinson about being the source of the leak or Wilkinson deliberately lied to Gates and denied any role in the affair. Furthermore, by telling Washington that he was informing Congress about the matter and inviting their inquiry as well, Gates was signaling to Washington that he suspected that Washington or a member of his staff would be implicated in any inquiry and that he did not trust Washington to conduct an inquiry that was likely to implicate himself or his staff.

It seems clear that Gates did not suspect Wilkinson and indeed trusted him to participate in his effort to falsely frame Hamilton, to embarrass Washington, and to elevate the entire affair to Congress. Gates was clearly signaling to Washington that he would be pursuing this matter on Congress's behalf as the new president of the Board of War. It was also during this time in Albany that Gates and Wilkinson discussed Wilkinson's future role. Because Gates believed that they had worked so well together in the past, Gates and Wilkinson agreed that as a newly promoted general, Wilkinson would continue to serve Gates as the secretary to the Board of War.[26]

Wilkinson's appointment as secretary to the board represented the high-water mark of his Revolutionary career. From this point forward Wilkinson would be caught in a series of lies, charges, and countercharges made by himself or Gates which would, within four months, result in his loss of promotion, lead to more than one duel with Gates, and remove him from any further active role in the Continental Army.

Following the army's reorganization in October, Congress and the board took several steps that caused a growing sense of distress for Washington. Of the new congressionally appointed members, Mifflin and Gates were clearly opposed to him, and when the board attempted to define its jurisdiction and role in the oversight of the Continental Army, Congress promoted Conway to major general and the first inspector general of the Continental Army.[27] Washington had opposed Conway's promotion as another example of rewarding underperforming foreign-born officers at the expense of proven military leaders. Washington was critical of Conway's performance at the Battle of Germantown and objected to his promotion over twenty other brigadiers with more seniority.[28] Despite Washington's stated criticism to Congress regarding Conway, as well as his veiled threat to resign over Conway's promotion, Congress proceeded with Conway's promotion and gave him broad but vaguely worded powers as inspector general. Washington learned of Conway's promotion when Conway suddenly appeared in January at the army's encampment at Valley Forge, intent on exerting his new position. Washington greeted Conway politely and coolly, then promptly ignored him, causing Conway to write a letter of complaint to his superiors. In the letter Conway stated that his frosty reception at Valley Forge was caused by Washington's reaction to the controversy surrounding Conway's letter to Gates.[29]

Having temporarily stalled Conway, Washington once again turned his attention to Gates. Knowing that Wilkinson, Gates's aide in the Northern Army, and now Gates's newly appointed secretary at the Board of War, was the source of the disclosure of the Conway correspondence, Washington was incredulous at the receipt of Gates's December 8 letter. Gates's assurances (that he had conducted a full review of his staff and exonerated them from any responsibility) and his attempt to place the blame on Hamilton and Washington was belied by Washington's actual knowledge of Wilkinson's involvement. Washington knew that Gates was either deliberately lying or had been fooled by Wilkinson's denials. Furthermore, Washington knew that Gates was seeking to escalate the fight by forwarding his correspondence to Congress. In a sternly worded reply to Gates, also sent to Congress, Washington identified Wilkinson's conversation with Stirling's staff as his source of information. Washington then went on to state that he had merely forwarded the information to Conway to "shew that gentleman that I was not unapprised of his intriguing disposition." Washington went on to disclose to Gates, for the first time, that the Marquis de la Fayette had approached Conway and had been shown a copy of the letter. Washington stated that until this matter was brought to his attention, he was not aware that Gates and Conway had exchanged confidential *letters* about Washington. Washington concluded that he originally believed that Wilkinson had deliberately mentioned the correspondence on orders from Gates to alert Washington to Conway's mischief. Washington dryly concluded that "in this, as in other matters of late, I have found myself mistaken."[30]

Washington apparently shared with Stirling Gates's December 8 letter, where Gates exonerated any member of his staff as the source of the leak. Stirling was also aware of Wilkinson's November meeting with Conway, when Wilkinson had obliquely denied knowledge of the wording of Gates's letter. To further expose the mendacity of Gates's assurance and Wilkinson's denial, Stirling wrote Wilkinson directly on January 6. In the letter Stirling stated that it was impossible to believe that Wilkinson had denied the conversation. He politely asked Wilkinson to confirm the fact that Conway had asked about the wording of the original letter and confirm the wording of the letter. He also asked Wilkinson to provide him with a copy of the letter. In his memoirs Wilkinson claimed that this was the first time he became aware that he had been implicated in the Conway affair.[31] In his February 4 reply Wilkinson informed Stirling that his only recollection was of a social day, where conversation became "general, unreserved and copious." For this reason, Wilkinson stated that he could not remember particulars but that "in the course of social intercourse, when the mind is relaxed and the heart is unguarded, the observations may have elapsed which have not since occurred to me." He went on to state that he could not recall the particulars of the contents of the letter. He concluded by taking great exception to the fact that Stirling was asking him to provide a copy of a private letter. "I may have been indiscreet, my Lord, but be assured I am not dishonorable."[32]

Wilkinson's expressed inability to recall a critical conversation from ninety days before is belied by the fact that, in his memoirs of the event forty years later, he was able to recall details with amazing precision. The most benign excuse for his bad memory of the event could be the fact that liquor flowed freely throughout the evening in question. As one of his biographers observes, "Wilkinson was always quickest to come to his own defense when he was most in the wrong."[33]

However, by the beginning of February, the need to dodge Stirling's request was the least of Wilkinson's worries. In a series of letters sent to Washington and Congress in late December, virtually the entire general officer corps of the Continental Line protested the recent series of unjustified promotions.[34] These officers were amazed that Congress could recognize and reward officers for military talent when all their fellow officers, their commander in chief included, had failed to recognize that talent themselves. Worthy officers were being passed over in favor of "persons whose inexperience promises but little, and whose want of firmness may be discovered at a time fatal to the Liberties of this country—Our duty as soldiers and citizens oblige us to inform Congress that we see signs of the dissolution of this Army, that fill us with horror." The letter concluded with a request for Congress to appoint someone to examine their grievance, review recent promotions, and regulate the process to ensure that all future promotions were based on demonstrated merit only. While the letter did not mention Wilkinson or Conway by name, it was clearly targeted at the recent promotions granted to these two unworthy officers. The immature twenty-year-old Wilkinson had clearly underestimated the impact of his ostentatious display of his recent promotion before Washington's officers.

Following his December meeting with Gates in Albany, when they had plotted the accusation of thievery against Hamilton and discussed Wilkinson's future role as secretary to the board, Wilkinson was sent on a series of inspections of military posts in western New York. He arrived back in Albany on February 4, discovered and responded to Stirling's letter of January 6, and received the official notification of his January appointment as secretary to the board. (At least one member of Congress informed Washington that Wilkinson's appointment to the board was intended to remove the "just causes of complaint" that had been raised regarding his promotion. The letter goes on to state that if Wilkinson did not accept the assignment, Congress would be justified in "taking effectual Measures to remedy the evils resulting therefrom."[35]) During this time Wilkinson apparently had no communication with Gates, who had arrived in York Town on January 19 to assume his new duties as board president. In blissful ignorance that a massive change in his relationship with Gates was taking place, Wilkinson departed Albany on February 12 for York Town and arrived in Lancaster on February 21 to discover that his military career was in shambles.

Gates was apparently shocked upon the receipt of Washington's January 4 letter, outing Wilkinson as the source of the Conway controversy. Whether that shock was caused by his sudden awakening to Wilkinson's duplicity in denying any role in the affair or by the realization that his scheme with Wilkinson to frame Hamilton was doomed to failure, Gates decided to create a set of "alternative facts" that would preserve his innocence in any scheme with Conway and Mifflin and would deflect Washington's attention from Gates toward Wilkinson. On January 23, from his new headquarters in York Town, Gates responded to Washington's letter with his newest defense: the offending Conway statement was a forgery created by Wilkinson! Gates characterized Conway's original letter as Conway's candid observations of the state of the army after Germantown. Gates now denied that it contained any reference to the "weakness" of any general or mentioned "bad counsellor." Gates characterized the letter as "perfectly harmless" and continued to defend Conway. However, Gates did not offer to provide Washington with the best evidence of the letter's contents: a copy of the letter itself. Gates informed Washington that the release of the letter would create "anxiety and jealousy" in the breast of respectable officers. "Honour forbids it, and patriotism demands that I should return the letter into the hands of the writer. I will do it; but at the same time, I declare, that the paragraph conveyed to your excellency as a genuine part of it, was in words as well as in substance a wicked forgery."[36]

Gates went on to explain that his December 8 letter, in which he accused some unnamed person of theft, was designed to defend the honor of his staff and cause an inquiry that would lead to the discovery of the person who was stealing confidential communications, thereby placing the integrity of the army at risk. Gates informed Washington that he had hidden the true purpose of his letter from Wilkinson and that Wilkinson had suggested blaming Troup and Hamilton for the leak. Gates stated that he refused to countenance this aspersion against these officers. He now felt that it was important for Washington to know what Wilkinson had suggested. Gates then added an additional cause for concern regarding his aide, which merited his disclosure of Wilkinson's attempt to frame Hamilton:

> It will enable your excellency to judge whether or not he [Wilkinson] would scruple to make such a forgery as that which he now stands charged with, and ought to be exemplarily punished. To attempt sowing dissentions amongst the principal officers of the army, and rendering them odious to each other, by false suggestions and forgeries, is in my opinion a crime of the first magnitude; it involves with it all the consequences of positive treason.[37]

This would be the first, but not the last, time Wilkinson would be accused of forgery and treason, but it may be the only time Wilkinson was unfairly accused.

Washington refused to accept this latest mendacious finger-pointing from Gates. In his February 9 reply he dismissed the claim of forgery as a recent fabrication by Gates. Washington observed that if the offending paragraph was not in the original correspondence in Gates's possession, Gates would have said so in his first reply to Washington and Conway would have taken the same position in his original reply to Washington as well. Washington expressed his dismay at the recent manufacture of the forgery defense: "After making the most earnest pursuit of the author of the supposed treachery, without saying a word about the truth or falsehood of the passage; your letter of the 23rd Ulto; to my great surprize, proclaims it 'in words as well as in substance a wicked forgery.'" Washington went on to rebut Gates's concern that release of the letter would cause anxiety and jealousy. He instead asserted that, considering the current controversy, refusal to release the letter would cause anxiety and jealousy even more so. Washington observed that Conway had admitted to showing the letter to certain officers and that Gates himself had admitted that the letter had been seen by members of Congress and other officers. Washington was at a loss as to how Gates could freely share criticisms of the army with Congress and certain officers but not share those same concerns with the commander in chief. In response to Gates's continuing support of Conway in his final letter, Washington then proceeded with a sarcastic attack on Conway as an "adapt in Military Science." If Conway in his letter to Gates was critical of the army's tactics under Washington's command, Washington wondered why such "rich treasures of knowledge and experience," so freely provided to Gates, had never been presented by Conway during numerous councils of war with the army's leadership. He concluded by ridiculing Gates's continued defense of Conway.[38]

Washington's February 9 letter had a devastating effect on Gates. Recognizing that Washington was not backing away from his condemnation of Conway and his insistence that Gates was knowingly involved in communications with Conway that were, at a minimum, disloyal, intemperate, and unwise, Gates felt compelled to respond. In a February 19 letter he abandoned support for Conway and assured Washington that the original letter from Conway was the only communications they had ever shared prior to the current controversy. Shifting from his previous postures of innocent victim and mendacious accuser, Gates moved on to obsequiousness: "I Solemnly declare that I am of no Faction; & if any of my Letters taken aggregately, or by paragraphs, convey any meaning, which under any construction is Offensive to your Excellency; that was by no means the intention of the Writer; after this; I cannot believe Your Excellency will either suffer your own suspicions, or the prejudices of others, to induce you to Spend another moment upon this Subject."[39] In a final letter back to Gates on the affair, Washington then agreed to end the matter by "burying them hereafter in silence, and, as far as future events will permit, oblivion."[40]

Gates's decision to walk away from Conway and the fight with Washington may have been affected by his failed attempt to exert operational control over the conduct of the war. As the new board president, Gates had decided to direct another invasion of Canada outside of Washington's operational control. The "interruption into Canada" would involve 2,500 men and seek to exploit Burgoyne's defeat.[41] Gates selected Washington's young protégé the Marquis de la Fayette to command the winter campaign. The folly of a winter invasion into Canada soon became apparent as weather and logistical nightmares prevented an army from even being formed. This failure, combined with Gates's fight with Washington and the neutering of Conway's inspector general position, soon demonstrated the overall failure of the board as a command authority over Washington, eventually leading to the collapse of the Conway Cabal.

Shortly after Gates's surrender to Washington, other members of the cabal were eliminated. In July 1778 Colonel John Cadwallader, a friend of Washington, accused Conway of cowardice at the Battle of Germantown. A duel was fought and Cadwallader shot Conway in the mouth.[42] When informed that the wound was not fatal, Cadwallader supposedly said, "I've stopped the damn rascal's tongue anyhow."[43] Shortly thereafter Conway resigned his commission and returned to France. At the same time, Mifflin sought to leave the board and obtain a field command but was denied that opportunity by Washington, who cited the fact that such an assignment would be viewed as an insult to officers who had spent the winter at their posts, doing their duty. Mifflin submitted his resignation from the army in August 1778, which was accepted by Congress six months later.[44]

Wilkinson was unaware of Gates's increasingly desperate communications with Washington until he arrived in Lancaster on February 21 and began receiving curious communications from army officers about the dispute. Wilkinson received an odd note from Colonel Robert Troup that stated, "Your generous Conduct at Albany, in endeavoring to fix Genl. Gates's Suspicions on me, will be duly remembered."[45] While Wilkinson and Gates had plotted to implicate Troup and Hamilton at their December 8 meeting, Gates's subsequent letter to Washington did not name either Troup or Hamilton. Wilkinson now knew that much had transpired during his absence on the New York frontier. From this note and other sources in Lancaster, Wilkinson deduced that he had been accused by Gates as being the source of the Conway leak. Rather than seeking a meeting with his former benefactor, who was only twenty-five miles away in York Town, to gain a better understanding of the facts, Wilkinson wrote a letter to Gates in which he expressed outrage that Gates had besmirched his honor and demanded satisfaction.[46] In his reply of the same day Gates stated that he was prepared to provide Wilkinson with any satisfaction he required. He also provided Wilkinson with an extract from Washington's correspondence that identified Wilkinson as being the source of the leak to Lord Stirling. Gates ended his note with an expression of incredulity at Wilkinson's conduct: "After reading the whole of the above extract, I am astonished if you really gave Major McWilliams such information how you could *intimate* to me, that it was *possible* Colonel Troup had conversed with Colonel Hamilton upon the subject of General Gates's letter" (emphasis in original).[47]

Following the receipt of Gates's reply, Wilkinson snuck into York Town after dark to avoid detection.[48] He sought out his old comrade, Captain Benjamin Stoddert, and asked him to serve as his second in delivering a formal challenge of a duel to Gates. (Despite Washington's general disapproval of duels among officers and its prohibition under the Articles of War, duels were somewhat common among officers during the Revolution, and punishment for dueling was relatively light.[49]) Stoddert refused the request and told Wilkinson that he was running headlong to destruction. Having been rejected by Stoddert, Wilkinson was able to convince Colonel Burgess Ball to serve as his second and to deliver the challenge. Wilkinson demanded that Gates meet him on the field of honor the following morning. Ball delivered the note, and a time for meeting was agreed to behind the English church in York Town, with pistols serving as the chosen weapon. Wilkinson arrived first and was surprised to see Stoddert in attendance. According to Wilkinson, Stoddert brought a message from Gates, requesting a meeting before the start of the duel. Wilkinson stepped outside and was greeted by Gates with "tenderness, but manifest embarrassment." According to Wilkinson, Gates supposedly exclaimed, "*I* injure you, it is impossible, I should as soon think of injuring my own child" (emphasis in original).[50] All was quickly forgiven, and it was agreed that Wilkinson would report for duty as secretary to the board. (Wilkinson's portrayal of a remorseful Gates was published in Wilkinson's memoirs in 1816, ten years after Gates's death. Gates left no record of his side of the meeting.)

Arriving at the board, Wilkinson found Gates acting coolly toward him, despite Gates's alleged fawning apology of a few days before. In a subsequent conversation with James Craik, Washington's close friend and personal physician, Wilkinson learned for the first time about the objections filed by Continental Line officers regarding his promotion. Acting honorably for one of the few times in his career, Wilkinson recognized that his position as a general was untenable and resigned his general's commission on March 6.[51] Wilkinson believed that when he resigned his general's position, he still retained his rank and position as a lieutenant colonel. However, he never again held a military position during the Revolution.[52] He then traveled to Lancaster to stay with his fiancé and her family for two weeks.

With Wilkinson's departure from the general officer ranks, Washington could concentrate on the army's spring campaign. However, he decided to take an action that was sure to provoke further strife between Gates and his new board secretary. In mid-March he reached out to Wilkinson and invited him to dine at his camp. At the dinner meeting, Wilkinson started with a lie by again denying any role in providing information about Conway to Stirling or his staff. Brushing aside Wilkinson's denials, Washington informed him that it was important for Wilkinson to be aware of the exact nature of the allegations that Gates had made against him. He then provided Wilkinson with an opportunity to review all the correspondence between Gates and Washington regarding the Conway matter. From this correspondence Wilkinson learned for the first time that Gates, in order to get out of the trap that he had unintentionally set for himself, had accused Wilkinson of forgery and treason as well as being the instigator for the false allegations against Troup and Hamilton.[53] Upon leaving his dinner with Washington, Wilkinson realized that he could no longer serve with Gates on the board, and on March 29 he submitted his resignation to Congress from that position, citing the treachery and falsehoods that he had detected about Gates.[54] Congress accepted his resignation but returned the letter to him as "being improper to remain on the files of Congress."[55] Wilkinson was replaced as board secretary by the slandered Robert Troup. Wilkinson's memoirs strangely halt at this point and pick up thirty-eight years later.

Wilkinson spent the remainder of the spring and summer preparing for his November 1778 nuptials to Nancy Biddle in Philadelphia. He made a brief trip to Boston in the summer to meet with British general Phillips, who was on parole in that city, awaiting exchange for a suitable Continental Army general. Phillips was distressed at the treatment of the Convention Army and Wilkinson sought to provide insights to him on Congress's actions in not approving the release of Burgoyne's troops.[56]

In August 1778 Wilkinson had a final confrontation with Gates at the court-martial of General Arthur St. Clair in White Plains, New York. Both Wilkinson and Gates had agreed to be witnesses for St. Clair in his court-martial for the loss of Fort Ticonderoga, and when the two former colleagues met, Gates made an unfavorable remark about Wilkinson's conduct at their duel in York Town. Wilkinson took exception to the slight and challenged Gates to another duel. Colonel Tadeusz Kosciuszko agreed to serve as Gates's second and Wilkinson was represented by John Barker Church, a son-in-law of Phillip Schuler. (Church had married Angelica Schuyler in 1777. A wealthy merchant, he would also fight a duel with Aaron Burr in 1799. Neither party was injured in the duel.)

The duel was held on September 4, and this time it actually took place. Each party fired three times and each time either missed or suffered a misfire before both sides agreed that honor was satisfied. (It is ironic to note that on one of the few times Wilkinson is ever recorded as having fired a weapon in anger, the target was his former commander, and he missed.) Gates agreed to state that Wilkinson had acted honorably at their previous duel. However, the truce between the parties soon fell apart. Kosciuszko, on Gates's behalf, agreed to sign a statement confirming Gates's acknowledgment of Wilkinson's honorable conduct in York Town but refused to provide it to Church until Church issued a similar statement that Gates, too, had acted honorably. Wilkinson refused to provide such a statement, calling Gates a rascal and a coward, and he challenged Gates to yet another duel. The comic opera continued when the parties all arrived at the St. Clair court-martial at the same time and the seconds drew swords and commenced fighting in the courtroom. The event ended with the seconds retreating without harm when guards were called. The duelists departed, never to meet again, and St. Clair was acquitted of any misconduct for the abandonment of Fort Ticonderoga.[57]

Gates resigned from the board in November 1778 but continued to extoll his military prowess arising from his victory at Saratoga. Following Benjamin Lincoln's surrender at Charleston in May 1780, Gates, relying on his steady congressional support, was appointed commander of the Southern Department and sent south to stem the British invasion of the Carolinas. In August 1780 Gates was defeated and routed at the Battle of Camden, one of the worst Continental defeats in the war. Gates fled the scene without any attempt to rally his troops and stopped only after he was 180 miles away from the scene of the debacle.[58] He was relieved from command but his congressional supporters refused to convene a court of inquiry into his conduct and Gates continued to vex Washington as a participant in the Newburgh Conspiracy of 1783.[59]

In November 1778 Wilkinson married Nancy Biddle in an Episcopalian ceremony in Philadelphia. For her apostasy to her Quaker faith Nancy was "read out" of the Society of Friends the following month. Using the Biddle family connections, Wilkinson began to court the social and political elite of Philadelphia. Around the time of their wedding, the Wilkinsons purchased Trevose, a Loyalist estate in Bucks County confiscated by the Pennsylvania government, at a deep discount. At Trevose, Wilkinson acquired a tasted for fine living that became his chosen lifestyle throughout his subsequent career. He hosted lavish balls, joined the Freemasons, and traveled around Philadelphia in a horse-drawn carriage with footmen.[60] It soon became apparent that he would need another form of employment to maintain this extravagance. Perhaps at the urging of his Biddle in-laws, Wilkinson sought a quasi-commercial enterprise that would allow him to capitalize on his military background and landed on the civilian position of clothier-general of the Continental Army in July 1779. In his memoirs Wilkinson stated that he accepted the position for a number of reasons: to demonstrate that he still had the public's confidence, to allow him to associate with his military friends, and to continue to participate in the war effort.[61] He did not state the two reasons that were probably the primary driving factors: the job paid an annual salary of $5,000 and it would allow him to exploit his military connections into a future commercial enterprise.

The Continental Army's clothing department, like all other logistical offices of the Continental Army, was in a state of shambles in 1779. Washington desired to reform the functioning of the clothing department of the army, which reported directly to the Board of War. Washington was particularly critical of the repeated failures of Wilkinson's predecessor, George Measam, to procure adequate clothing, blankets, and shoes for the army. He insisted that as clothier-general Measam's place was with the army in the field, and when Measam failed to comply Washington complained that he was required to act as his own clothier-general.[62] Congress had addressed Measam's failure by accepting his resignation and reestablishing the position as a salaried appointment, not one based on commissions. Following Measam's resignation, Congress offered the position to two persons, both of whom declined because the annual salary of $5,000 was deemed insufficient. Wilkinson was the third choice and he accepted on July 24, 1779.[63]

Given Wilkinson's total lack of business experience and his clouded military experience, it is difficult to accept how anyone thought that Wilkinson could succeed in his new position. Wilkinson had never run a business, had never commanded a large body of troops, and had never run any kind of an organization. In all likelihood the Biddle brothers-in-law, who worked in the Quartermaster Department, convinced Wilkinson to apply for the position and hoped to use it for the continued expansion of their private business dealings.

Washington's reaction to Wilkinson's appointment has not been recorded, but within a few months Washington was once again complaining that he was serving as his own clothier-general. Rather than deploying in the field at army headquarters, as Washington repeatedly directed, Wilkinson preferred the refined comforts provided by his estate at Trevose and at the Biddle residence in Philadelphia. Rather than clothing the troops, Wilkinson much preferred organizing dances in Philadelphia with names like "Burgoyne's Surrender" and "Clinton's Retreat."[64] In one of the few times Wilkinson joined Washington's headquarters in the field, he served as the dancing master at a ball for Washington's officers in Morristown.[65] Responding to Washington's criticism, Congress cut Wilkinson's salary in half, prompting Wilkinson's resignation from the position in March 1781. In a remarkable display of honesty that was never again repeated, Wilkinson noted in his resignation letter, "I should be wanting in Personal Candour and in Public Justice if I did not profess that I find my Mercantile knowledge, *on thorough examination*, inadequate to the Just Conduct of the Clothing Department, under the proposed establishment" (emphasis in original).[66]

Unemployed again, Wilkinson fell back on his Biddle connections and friendship with Joseph Reed to establish himself in Pennsylvania politics. Through Reed's influence he was appointed a general in the Pennsylvania State Militia, but with Washington's October 1781 victory at Yorktown, the purpose of the militia was superfluous and Wilkinson changed course to politics. In October 1781 Wilkinson was elected as a representative to the Pennsylvania State Assembly and reelected in 1782. However, by this time the financial burdens of Trevose and the lifestyle to which he had become accustomed overwhelmed his limited finances. Furthermore, Nancy had borne him two sons, John in 1780 and James in 1783, further straining the family's finances.

The Biddles had invested heavily in land warrants in an area of western Virginia that would eventually become the commonwealth of Kentucky. The new land seemed to hold the promise of a new beginning, and in the fall of 1783 Wilkinson left Nancy to manage the sale of Trevose and headed off to Kentucky and the Spanish Conspiracy.

4

AGENT 13 AND THE SPANISH
CONSPIRACY

1783–1791

I am obliged to dissemble. This makes me extremely desirous of resorting
to some contrivance that will put me in a position, in which I flatter myself
to be able to profess myself publicly the vassal of his Catholic Majesty, and
therefore to claim his protection, in whatever public or private measures
I may devise to promote the interest of the Crown.
—James Wilkinson to Spanish governor Esteban Miro, 1790

The Kentucky that Wilkinson encountered in late 1783 was at the edge of the American wilderness. Though the British Royal Proclamation of 1763 had discouraged migration west of the Allegheny Mountains, settlers continued to ignore the restriction and increasingly sought cheap land for settlement and investment. One major obstacle to settlement was the presence of Indian tribes that actively resisted encroachment on their ancestral lands. In 1768 Great Britain and Iroquois Nation leaders had signed the Treaty of Fort Stanwix, whereby the Iroquois ceded the territory south of the Ohio River to British control. Unfortunately for the British, they failed to recognize that the Iroquois did not control those lands, and other tribes, such as the Shawnees and Cherokees, were in actual control of Kentucky and would continue to violently oppose white encroachment.[1]

Ten years before Wilkinson's arrival, settlers could reach Kentucky through two primary routes. The first, constructed during the French and Indian War, was a rudimentary road network leading to Fort Pitt (modern-day Pittsburgh), giving eastern settlers access to the Ohio River valley. From there keelboats and flatboats provided access to primitive settlements at Louisville, at the Falls of the Ohio, and at Lexington near the Kentucky River. The second was via the Wilderness Road, an overland trail blazed by Daniel Boone and used by settlers from southern states like North Carolina.[2] In 1775 Boone established the settlement of Boonesborough on the Kentucky River, providing a link to the Ohio.[3] (Boone, a survivor of Braddock's ill-fated 1755 assault on French Fort Duquesne, later also established a settlement on the Missouri River, which Wilkinson, in his 1804 "reflection" to Spain, urged the Spanish to eradicate.) By the time Wilkinson landed in the area, Kentucky was part of Virginia and Kentucky settlers were displaying a growing sense of resentment toward the faraway commonwealth government in Richmond.

While Kentucky presented a source of open and fertile land, its remoteness from eastern markets produced a serious economic challenge. Manufactured goods such as clothing, furniture, and farm equipment that could not be produced locally had to be imported from the eastern states. Given the poor road networks that existed, most of these goods had to be sent down the Ohio River, making them extremely expensive to purchase. Most Kentucky farms produced either corn- or tobacco-related products and, once their immediate subsistence needs had been met, many Kentucky farmers and merchants realized that eastern markets were beyond their reach using these rudimentary networks. The most economically viable way to sell their products was to ship them by keelboat or flatboat down the Kentucky, Ohio, and Mississippi Rivers to markets in Spanish New Orleans.

Though Spain had been a cobelligerent with the American colonies during the Revolution, Spain's main interest was the recovery of Spanish lands in Florida previously lost to Great Britain and not in the establishment of an independent American nation. The Treaty of Paris had ceded British navigation rights along the Mississippi to the United States, but Spain did not recognize this transfer and in 1784 shut New Orleans to American shipping.[4] American goods passing through New Orleans were subject to confiscation by Spanish authorities, and American traders were subject to arrest.[5] The growing American presence along the Ohio and the Mississippi was viewed as a threat to Spain's holdings along the Mississippi, and Spain initiated a policy to frustrate American trade and settlements along the river. In Kentucky, growing resentment of eastern political interests was further inflamed by the Jay-Guardoqui Treaty of 1786 by which the United States surrendered navigation rights on the Mississippi for twenty-five years in return for enhanced trading rights with Spain and its Caribbean possessions. Fortunately for Kentucky farmers, Congress refused to ratify the treaty.

Wilkinson's arrival in late 1783 found a Kentucky beset with constant Indian raids, ignored by commonwealth powers in Richmond, manipulated by national authorities in Philadelphia and New York, and choked from access to the sea by Spain. Empowered by Biddle family finances, Wilkinson embarked on three projects to establish himself in his new home. The first was in land speculation. Wilkinson commenced purchasing land for himself and his Biddle relations, eventually accumulating thousands of acres for resale to subsequent settlers. His second was to open a store in Lexington, the second such establishment in the settlement, to sell household and farm goods imported from the east. His third was the construction of a mansion in Lexington to house Nancy and his sons in as much opulence as the Kentucky frontier could accommodate. As a Revolutionary War general and local businessman of note, known for his extravagant entertainment of neighbors, Wilkinson soon became attached to portions of the growing Kentucky political elite.[6] Among his early colleagues was Harry Innes, who would later serve as Wilkinson's personal attorney and go on to be named Kentucky's first federal judge; Benjamin Sebastian, a local attorney, businessman, and future state court judge; and John Brown, who would go on to serve as one of Kentucky's first senators in Congress. All four men became enmeshed in a series of actions known as the Spanish Conspiracy.

As Kentucky grew in population and isolation from the east, local politicians began to debate the status of the country. In 1784 most land west of the Alleghenies and south of the Ohio River was considered to belong to the territory of eastern states. However, as the West's population grew, its residents sought a more independent status. The Northwest Ordinance of 1787 provided an orderly way for territories north of the Ohio to eventually move into statehood, but eastern state attachment to lands south of the Ohio proved to be more difficult to sever. Beginning in December 1784, Kentucky residents commenced a series of conventions to determine their future status within or apart from Virginia and the United States. Among the options that were debated were the establishment of a new state that was separate and distinct from Virginia, total secession as an independent commonwealth from the nascent United States, or some form of dependent-state status with Spain that would provide access to New Orleans. The Spanish Conspiracy included the factions that wanted to sever Kentucky from the United States and establish some form of linkage with Spain.

In 1785 Wilkinson was elected to one of the Kentucky conventions that debated the area's future status and he became directly involved in the ongoing struggle. On a national level, the Kentucky debate was eclipsed by the realization that the Articles of Confederation were inadequate and needed to be replaced by a constitution that would better apportion responsibilities between the states and the national government. As the national debate continued, Wilkinson's mercantile interests were increasingly compromised by Spain's stranglehold on the Mississippi. To avoid economic ruin Wilkinson conceived a bold plan to circumvent the Spanish trade prohibition by directly approaching the Spanish authorities in

New Orleans and proposing a trade relationship that would be acceptable and profitable to both sides. Wilkinson prepared a cargo for trade in New Orleans and in April 1787 departed Kentucky by river, heading for New Orleans.[7]

The contents of this first cargo, reflective of the goods that were available in Kentucky, included flour, bacon, butter, tobacco, and may have included enslaved persons for sale in New Orleans.[8] Slavery was present in New Orleans from the time of the city's founding by the French and, having grown up in a plantation culture, Wilkinson had no aversion to slavery or slave-trading. By the time of this first trip down the Mississippi, Kentucky already had almost ten thousand enslaved persons living within its borders and the purchase and sale of enslaved persons was clearly part of its economic culture. As set forth in the sale proposal presented to Spanish authorities upon his arrival in New Orleans, Wilkinson described his cargo as follows: "I humbly propose that I may be permitted to transmit to an Agent in this City in Negroes, live Stock, tobacco, Flour, Bacon, Lard, butter, Cheese tallow, Apples the amount of fifty or sixty thousand Dollars, cost of Kentucky, which articles may be sold on my account, and the proceeds held by his Excellency the Governor, as a pledge for my good conduct until the issue of our plans is known, or I have fixed my residence in Louisiana."[9]

After receiving permission to pass from the Spanish garrisons at St. Louis and Natchez, Wilkinson arrived in New Orleans on July 2 and immediately sought an introduction to the governing Spanish officials. New Orleans was a thriving city of over five thousand inhabitants, a multicultural mix of Spanish, French, Cajun, and Creole cultures. Since its founding in 1718, New Orleans and Louisiana had been a French possession, but France's defeat in the French and Indian War resulted in the loss of the city and territory to Spain through the 1763 Treaty of Paris. Shortly after his arrival, Wilkinson arranged a meeting with Spanish governor Esteban Miro and immediately sought to charm the governor into accepting a personal proposal.

Because of Spain's trade embargo with the United States, Miro was not fully aware of the status of the western American states and possible filibustering activity emerging from the area. (In the eighteenth century a filibusterer, derived from a combination of the Spanish word *filibustero* and the Dutch word *freebooter*, was a foreign national engaged in an illegal insurrection against another country. Most American filibustering activity was directed against Spanish holdings in North and Central America.) While Wilkinson and others had previously provided Spanish officials with hints of possible filibustering activities against Spanish Louisiana by George Rogers Clark, Miro was desirous of learning about the threat to Spain by western territories of the United States. Wilkinson's so-called First Memorial to

Miro offered to fill this intelligence gap as well as provide Miro with an opportunity for personal enrichment.

In this first communication Wilkinson renounced his American citizenship and swore allegiance to Spain: "Having these principles, and holding to this opinion, I hope that no one can say of me with justice that I break any law of nature or of nations, or of conscience or of honor, in transferring my allegiance, from the United States to his Catholic Majesty."[10] While some of Wilkinson's biographers have suggested that this vow was only a commercial accommodation and not a true oath of allegiance to Spain, the plain language in Wilkinson's usually overblown prose and the accompanying advice that was clearly targeted to benefit Spanish interests at the expense of the United States can only be viewed as a formal relinquishment of loyalty by a former American general officer.[11] Such a conclusion is also supported by the fact that Wilkinson and his Spanish allies sought to hide this oath of allegiance from subsequent scrutiny by American officials. (Some other well-known Americans did swear fealty to Spain as part of commercial accommodations, including a young Andrew Jackson, who took such an oath in 1789 to establish a trade relationship between Nashville and the Spanish settlement in Natchez. Unlike Wilkinson, however, Jackson detested the "Dons" and there is no proof that as a military officer or president he ever compromised American interests on their behalf.[12])

In addition to his vow of allegiance to "his Catholic Majesty," Wilkinson provided valuable political and economic intelligence to his new Spanish master. Wilkinson described the dissatisfaction of western residents with the East Coast–centric actions of the state and national governments and suggested that discontent was so great that independence from the eastern governments was seriously being considered. He predicted that once independence was declared, the western territories would seek to align themselves with Spanish New Orleans and if their overture was rejected, Kentuckians would look to ally with Great Britain and seize New Orleans by force. Wilkinson advised the Spanish that to avoid this outcome they should enter into an economic relationship with western interests to form a barrier against future encroachment on Spanish territory. Doing so would encourage western settlers to declare independence from the United States and seek an alliance with Spain. However, rather than a blanket release of its stranglehold on the Mississippi, Wilkinson urged the Spanish to maintain its blockade but discreetly grant trading privileges to a few Kentucky agents who would work with Spain to separate the western territories into a Spanish alliance. Of course, Wilkinson would be preeminent among these privileged agents: "I will therefore only observe that I shall be ready to give my feeble assistance at all times, and that

I am persuaded the negotiation may be so conducted to secure to Spain every advantage she can wish from the connection without involving her with any dispute with the United States."[13]

To further protect Spain from American encroachment, Wilkinson advised the Spanish authorities to erect a military fortification on the Mississippi just below its junction with the Ohio. Such a fort would enable the Spanish to extract greater concessions from western settlers seeking access to the Mississippi. Spain did follow this advice and erected a fortification at New Madrid on the west bank of the Mississippi, near the mouth of the Ohio. Wilkinson also advised the Spanish to encourage settlement in Spanish territory, dependent on a settler's sworn allegiance to Spain. To make emigration more palatable to Americans, he urged the Spanish to encourage freedom of religion in these settlements and encouraged all religious worship and civil government be conducted in the English language. Wilkinson proposed that upon his return to Kentucky he would actively seek to encourage independence and alliance with Spain:

> When I return to Kentucky . . . I shall forthwith proceed though with cautious deliberation to exert my political weight and influence to familiarize and recommend to the Body of People among whom I live those views which constitute the design of my present voyage. . . , and I will engage constantly to transmit to his Excellency the Governor by trusty Couriers . . . a particular representation of every measure which I may adopt in this important business, as well as every proceeding of Congress interesting to our views and the effects either may produce on the subject.[14]

Finally, in return for his oath of allegiance, his willingness to work for the separation of the western territories and promote their alliance with Spain, and in anticipation of his own emigration to Louisiana, Wilkinson requested permission to sell his cargo for the sum of $60,000. Most important, he requested that the Spanish keep his proposal secret: "I have committed secrets of an important nature, such as would, were they divulged destroy my Fame and Fortune forever. But I feel the strongest confidence in your silence and discretion and if the plan should eventually be rejected by the Court, I must rely on the candor and high honor of a dignified Minister to bury these communications into eternal oblivion."[15]

Wilkinson would get his wish. The First Memorial remained hidden in Spanish archives until it was discovered by Charles Gayarre in the 1850s. Gayarre, a Louisiana attorney and politician, had been commissioned by the Louisiana legislature to prepare an official history of Louisiana. While researching his multi-volume *History of Louisiana*, Gayarre traveled to Spain and was the first American historian to access some of the Wilkinson-related correspondence resting in the

Spanish archives. Gayarre's work was the first confirmation of the true nature of Wilkinson's dealings with Spain.

To further conceal his ongoing role of service to Spain, Wilkinson and Miro agreed on a complex "dictionary" cypher code to be used in future communications, substituting a number for a word.[16] The number was determined by identifying a particular dictionary, then identifying a specific page and a specific word on that page. The page number and the number of the word on the page was then substituted for the word to be encrypted. Wilkinson and his Spanish handlers also devised an elaborate set of numbers to refer to persons or places that were not found in the dictionary. Miro's report to Madrid on the discussions with Wilkinson bore the number "Dispatch 13," and in later communications Wilkinson was referred to as "Agent 13" to avoid disclosing his true name.[17]

While formal approval of the agreement required the endorsement of the Spanish government in Madrid, Miro approved the agreement the day after it was presented. Trade goods from Kentucky, including enslaved persons, totaling $30,000 would be allowed into New Orleans, with the proceeds being held in the Spanish treasury in New Orleans until Madrid's approval was obtained. (Miro also used this trade agreement to supplement his meager government salary.[18]) In his endorsement of Wilkinson's proposal, Miro also suggested that Madrid should grant Wilkinson a reward on top of the privilege of duty-free trade. Wilkinson also obtained a $3,000 loan against future proceeds from Spanish *intendant* Martin Navarro.

Wilkinson's First Memorial, while disloyal to the interests of the United States, was not precisely a crime against the United States. The crime of treason against the United States was not set forth in the Articles of Confederation that were in effect in 1787. Furthermore, as was eventually demonstrated during the Burr trials in 1807, when treason was described as a crime in the Constitution of 1789, Wilkinson's offer to serve as a Spanish agent in dismembering the United States still did not rise to the federal definition of treason: providing aid and comfort to a country at war with the United States or making war against the United States. Eventually many other western politicians would swear allegiance to Spain to gain a commercial advantage or actively sought to go on the Spanish payroll in return for supporting a severance of the western states into an alliance with Spain. At the commencement of his relationship with Spain, Wilkinson was a private individual who offered to use his private status in lobbying the nascent Kentucky politicians to align with Spain; the relationship would only become criminal later under military law, when Wilkinson accepted Spanish gold to commit espionage while serving as an army officer (after reaffirming his oath of allegiance to the United States as part of his army commission in 1791). However, as the political climate matured and evolved toward the establishment of Kentucky as an independent state within the United States, Wilkinson and his other Spanish conspirators had every reason to deny and hide their previous dalliance with severance and alliance with Spain, not to mention their receipt of Spanish pensions. The need for secrecy became particularly acute when some of the conspirators continued to work for a Spanish alliance after Kentucky statehood, because doing so would have required the secession of Kentucky and other western states from the union. (Kentucky was admitted as the fifteenth state in the union in 1792 and the prime members of the conspiracy, including Wilkinson, Innes, Sebastian, and Brown, subsequently faced significant scrutiny for their paid affiliation with Spain.)

Believing that he had established a monopoly over Kentucky trade through New Orleans, Wilkinson chose to return to Louisville by sea. Leaving New Orleans on September 19, he transited through several Spanish Caribbean ports before arriving in Charleston, South Carolina, in November, then departed immediately for Richmond, where the Virginia legislature was debating the ratification of the Constitution. Wilkinson, who joined Patrick Henry in lobbying against ratification, believed that a weak central government would provide him with greater flexibility in establishing Kentucky trading rights on the Mississippi. He departed Richmond and arrived back in Louisville on February 24, 1788, in an ostentatious carriage with liveried enslaved persons serving as outriders.[19]

Nancy was grateful for his return. Two weeks before his arrival she had written to her father in Philadelphia regarding her discomfort in raising two small children alone on the edge of the frontier, and longing for "a Neighbor that had been brought up tenderly as I have myself, how much it would lighten & enliven the tedious Hours of absence."[20] She went on to describe a nagging illness that confined her to her room and asked her father to send needed items like molasses, shoes, and pins that would make life in the wilderness somewhat more tolerable. Her devotion to her husband is obvious throughout the letter and provides an insight on why, despite her longing for a refined environment, she willingly followed her husband to a variety of primitive assignments. Her devotion to Wilkinson combined with her desire for a more refined lifestyle also helps explain Wilkinson's continuous need for money to sustain an opulent standard of living that was beyond his ability to provide through honest commerce and government service.

Upon his return to Kentucky, Wilkinson commenced two activities, trade and political espionage, to solidify his new relationship with the Spanish. He first worked with his business partners to prepare another shipment of goods to be shipped for sale in New Orleans. Barely a week after his return a fleet of twenty-five boats, crewed by 150 boatmen, commenced a journey back to New Orleans. To Nancy's relief, Wilkinson did not accompany the fleet and instead left it under the direction of two of his partners, Isaac Dunn and Philip Nolan. Upon their arrival in New Orleans, Dunn and Nolan entered a relationship with Daniel Clark Sr., a local merchant and agent, who would be responsible for the sale of the goods. (Clark ran a trading firm in New Orleans with his nephew, named Daniel Clark Jr.) On this trip Dunn and Nolan delivered a cyphered communication from Wilkinson, advising the Spanish on the current state of political affairs in Kentucky. Wilkinson assured Miro that he would use his best efforts in the ongoing Kentucky conventions to advance Spain's interest in severing Kentucky from both Virginia and the union and aligning it with Spain. In passing on Wilkinson's intelligence to Madrid, Miro displayed a complete understanding of the true nature of Wilkinson's flexible loyalty: "Although his candor, and the information which I have sought from many who have known him well, seem to assure us that he is working in good earnest, yet I am aware that it may be possible that his intention is to enrich himself at our expense, by inflating us with hopes and promises which he knows to be in vain. Nevertheless, I have determined to humor him on this occasion."[21]

In order to make his trade relationship with New Orleans truly profitable, Wilkinson directed Dunn and Nolan to use the proceeds from their first delivery to purchase and ship a return cargo from New Orleans upriver to Louisville. A two-way trading relationship would be doubly profitable and provide Kentucky residents with easier access to Spanish and other goods imported into New Orleans. Miro approved the shipment of trade goods worth over $18,000, a sum that reflected almost all the profits from the first voyage.[22] Upriver commerce on the Mississippi at this time was exceedingly rare and most downriver commerce using flatboats and keelboats was intended for one-way transport. Upon arrival in New Orleans the boats were either sold or broken up for lumber, and most crews either signed on to oceangoing vessels or returned to Kentucky over hazardous trails through potentially hostile Indian country. A return cargo-laden voyage would require skill in either polling or sailing a vessel against the strong current of the Mississippi, and, unfortunately for Wilkinson, the crew chosen by Dunn and Nolan were not up to the task and the entire return cargo was lost in bad weather.[23]

The next few months saw increasing difficulties for Wilkinson. In November 1788, having been elected to the latest convention to determine the future of Kentucky, Wilkinson presented a repackaged version of his Spanish memorial. While downplaying Spanish vassalage as part of his proposal, Wilkinson and other Spanish conspirators strongly urged the convention to consider the benefits of establishing a relationship with Spain apart from its relationship with the United States. In making his case for a relationship with Spain, Wilkinson may have overplayed his hand and created the appearance that he actually was a paid agent of Spain. In December, Arthur St. Clair, Wilkinson's former commander and now governor of the Northwest Territory, expressed his concern in a letter to Wilkinson's business partner:

> I am much grieved to hear that there are strong dispositions on the part of the people of Kentucky to break off their connection with the United States, and that our friend Wilkinson is at the head of this affair. Such a consummation would involve the United States in the greatest difficulties and would completely ruin this country. Should there be any foundation for these reports, for God's sake, make use of your influence to detach Wilkinson from that party.[24]

Further concerns were raised by Kentucky Federalist Thomas Marshall, father of future Supreme Court Chief Justice John Marshall. The elder Marshall had moved from Virginia to Kentucky at the same time as Wilkinson and was a strong supporter of Kentucky statehood. Marshall was also an original investor in Wilkinson's business, and though he was a significant creditor, he became dismayed at the thrust of Wilkinson's position at the November convention and expressed his concern about Wilkinson in a letter to George Washington, who was about to enter office as the first president of the United States under the new constitution.[25]

Though he made little progress in furthering the interests of Spain at the convention, Wilkinson presented a falsely positive picture of his actions to Miro. In addition to overstating his progress, he also alerted Miro to a potential encroachment on Spanish territory by British settlers from Canada. Wilkinson claimed credit for frustrating the settlement by tricking the head of the British effort into believing that he was being targeted by assassins hired by Wilkinson.[26] On his business relationship with Spain, Wilkinson had mixed success. In November 1788 the Spanish Crown formally approved the trade relationship with Wilkinson but extended the same privileges to others who were willing to immigrate to Louisiana. Furthermore, the Crown approved American trade through New Orleans upon the payment of a tariff but without a pledge of emigration.[27]

Wilkinson's business continued to deteriorate through 1789. The absence of a Spanish monopoly, the difficulty in establishing two-way trade, an ostentatious lifestyle, and poor business acumen all contributed to a personal and professional financial crisis. To improve his financial situation Wilkinson returned to New Orleans in June 1789 to redefine his relationship with the Spanish. Upon arrival he was greeted with the devastating news that Isaac Dunn, one of his primary business partners, had committed suicide in Philadelphia.[28] Dunn's suicide, caused in part by his despair over the business's dismal finances, placed the entire enterprise in even greater peril. Wilkinson took up residence with Miro and over a three-month period devised a "Second Memorial" to realign his affiliation with Spain.

In the new memorial Wilkinson informed Miro that the recently ratified United States Constitution had significantly dampened the secession inclination of western settlers. While still keeping hopes for secession alive, Wilkinson urged the Spanish to encourage the immigration of western settlers into Spanish territory. Wilkinson recommended that "pensions and rewards" should be paid to influential western citizens based on their "influence, ability, or services rendered" and that Spanish bribes of $20,000–$30,000 be liberally spread throughout western settlements beyond Kentucky. Wilkinson then decried the Crown's directive allowing open commerce to New Orleans upon the payment of a tariff alone, and he flatly stated that this policy undercut his efforts to effect secession.[29]

Wilkinson urged the Spanish to fortify the Mississippi to project an aura of power on the Lower Mississippi. He also recommended that New Orleans be declared an open port, allowing western goods to be traded freely with other nations and not restricted to Spanish ships trading in ports controlled by Spain.[30] He urged that arms be stockpiled in Natchez, which would enable Spain to arm western settlements when they declared their independence from the United States.[31]

These representations were merely a preamble to the true purpose of his memorial: a request to be placed directly on the Spanish payroll. Wilkinson set forth the financial and professional sacrifices he had made to support Spain and pleaded for a reward for his efforts: "I flatter myself that the solemn obligations which I owe to my wife and three small children will justify the petition which I now submit to the munificence of His Majesty for some settlement upon me that will compensate for the actual sacrifices I have made, and safeguard me against any misfortune I might suffer from the resentment of the United States, where my property lies." Wilkinson also falsely asserted that in the service of his Spanish masters he had declined "honors and awards" from both Great Britain and the United States. Wilkinson told Miro that he would not provide proof of these offers, "for fear of being considered an exaggerator." Wilkinson did not quote an exact price for his continuing service, leaving such a determination to "the justice and goodness of His Majesty." However, because he was a military man, Wilkinson suggested that a commission in the Spanish Army might be the best way to recognize his talents. To seal the bargain, Wilkinson asked for a $7,000 advance on his future salary, an increase in the amount of tobacco that he would be allowed to sell in New Orleans, and a request that Miro limit the number of Spanish officials who were aware of his financial dealings with Spain: "If this circumstance were to transpire it would shortly be brought to the attention of Congress and by exciting the jealousies of this body I would remain exposed to great embarrassments indeed."[32]

The day after Wilkinson delivered his memorial he provided Miro with a list of twenty-two western officials also to be placed on the Spanish payroll, along with a suggested amount that should be paid to each person. Included on the list were future federal judge Harry Innes, future Kentucky Court of Appeals judge Benjamin Sebastian, and member of Congress John Brown. In addition to these known conspirators, Wilkinson suggested the recruitment of other westerners, such as Thomas and Humphry Marshall and Isaac Shelby, the future first governor of Kentucky.[33]

Wilkinson departed New Orleans with his $7,000 advance and a promise that Miro would petition Madrid for formal approval to place Wilkinson on the Spanish payroll.[34] Upon his arrival in Kentucky, Wilkinson sold his properties in Lexington and moved his business and his wife and family to Louisville, a more central location for the river trade. Even with the cash advance from Miro, however, Wilkinson's financial straits remained dire. In 1787 he had netted a mere $377 from his New Orleans trade and, though trade in 1788 was more profitable, his profit in 1789 declined to a paltry $49.[35] Wilkinson was beset by creditors and found an increasingly hostile reaction to his lobbying on behalf of Spain. In early January 1790 he warned Miro that he was increasingly required to lie about their relationship:

> I am justified in saying that Congress strongly suspects my connection with you, and that it spies my movements in this section of the country. . . . My situation is mortally painful, because, whilst I abhor all duplicity, I am obliged to dissemble. This makes me extremely desirous of resorting to some contrivance that will put me in a position, in which I flatter myself to be able to profess myself publicly the vassal of his Catholic Majesty, and therefore to claim his protection, in whatever public or private measures I may devise to promote the interest of the Crown.[36]

It is not likely that Wilkinson ever intended to give up his status as a covert agent for Spain. He knew that his most lucrative course of action was to continue serving in a clandestine role for Spain while still seeking to make his fortune as an American businessman and leading citizen of Kentucky. Wilkinson's January message to Miro was primarily intended to incentivize Miro to obtain Madrid's approval of his Spanish pension.

Miro had no interest in Wilkinson rolling back his American cover and revealing his Spanish affiliation. In his reply to Wilkinson, Miro stated, "I much regret that General Washington and Congress suspect your connection with me, but it does not appear to me opportune that you declare yourself a Spaniard, for the reasons you state. I am of the opinion that this idea of yours is not convenient, and that, on the contrary, it might have prejudicial results. Therefore, continue to dissemble and to work as you promise."[37]

True to his word, Miro petitioned Antonio Valdes, the Spanish minister for the Americas in Madrid, to place Wilkinson on the Spanish payroll.[38] (Approval of the pension would not be obtained until 1792.) Miro reported that while sentiments of secession were declining in the western settlements, Wilkinson was still worth $2,000 per year to monitor western American settlements. However, because he did not fully trust Wilkinson, Miro recommended that Benjamin Sebastian also be placed on the Spanish payroll to "enlighten me on the conduct of Wilkinson, and on what we have to expect from the plans of said brigadier-general."[39]

Miro's actions are a classic example of an intelligence officer seeking to keep the actions of his agent under control. While it appears that Miro actually liked Wilkinson, he never let his personal affection interfere with the hard realities of running an agent in a covert environment. Miro, and most of the other Spanish handlers responsible for running Wilkinson, never believed that Wilkinson's actions were driven by anything other than ego and greed. Wilkinson had not been recruited by Spain; he was a "walk-in" opportunist who had presented the Spanish authorities with an opportunity to gain an insight into the political and economic motivations of the growing American presence on the borders with Spanish territory along the Mississippi River. Wilkinson was controlled by stroking his insatiable ego and by payments from the Spanish treasury. Despite his oath of vassalage, none of Wilkinson's Spanish handlers ever believed in his true loyalty to Spain (or to the United States); they knew his future actions on Spain's behalf would always be motivated by greed. Throughout this dual relationship, Wilkinson's Spanish handlers consistently exercised better judgment and a better understanding of Wilkinson's true motivations than any of his future American superiors.

Despite the repeated influx of Spanish cash, Wilkinson's business continued to deteriorate, and his creditors steadily increased their demands for repayment. As 1790 progressed, Wilkinson was drawn into another growing domestic concern of the western settlers. White settlements west of the Alleghenies had increased throughout the 1780s, and clashes with resident Indian tribes worsened. Tribes continued to receive aid and encouragement from British forces that had not withdrawn from American territory after the Revolution, and most tribal resistance arose from being forced from their ancestral lands. The Shawnee and Miami tribes in the Northwest Territory were the most virulent in their armed opposition along the Ohio River valley. In the fall of 1790, after negotiations with the tribes had failed, Northwest Territory governor Arthur St. Clair turned to military force to drive the hostile tribes away from the growing white settlements.

Unfortunately, the status of the federal army in 1790 was deplorable. Under the Articles of Confederation the army had been reduced to a mere shadow of the force that had compelled the British surrender at Yorktown, with a single under-strength infantry regiment being all that remained of the Continental Army. This tiny force was then scattered over several frontier posts and was completely ineffectual to perform even basic military functions.

For example, in 1786 the post commander at Fort McIntosh on the Ohio River wanted to convene a general court-martial to address rampant desertions at the fort. Under the Articles of War thirteen officers were needed to sit on such a court, which had the power to impose the death penalty for desertion. Unfortunately, at that time there were fewer than forty officers in the entire army and it was impossible to bring almost half of the entire officer corps of the army together to form a court. The frustrated commander addressed the problem by conducting summary trials and executions in violation of the law.[40]

Any military campaign against Indian tribes required the small regular army to be reinforced by militia troops raised from affected local states, including Kentucky. The quality of these troops, as well as their training and equipment, was highly questionable. Just prior to the first expedition against the tribes, Kentucky territorial secretary Winthrop Sargent warned Governor St. Clair, regarding the inadequacy of the local militia, that "it appears to me from the past Conduct of the Kentucky militia that they will absolutely take themselves off—We know how their Officers are appointed & from repeated Experiments how little Dependence can be placed on them."[41]

The first expedition was to be under the command of brevet Brigadier General Josiah Harmar, thirty-seven, who had served loyally under George Washington during the Revolution. Unfortunately, by 1790 Harmar was suspected by Henry Knox, the newly appointed secretary of war, as being addicted to the bottle. Knox wrote to Harmar, "It has been reported, and under circumstances which appear to have gained pretty extensive credit on the frontiers, that you are apt to indulge yourself to excess in a convivial Glass." In the same letter Knox warned Harmar that if the expedition failed "for the want of arrangements or the possession or exercise of any of those great qualities of the mind which a general ought to possess, it will be unfortunate—But if it fails, or is even supposed to fail by any fatal indulgences, your reputation will be forever blasted."[42] Despite the noted concerns about inadequate troops and an inebriated commander, Harmar was allowed to launch this punitive expedition toward the tribes on the Maumee River on September 30, using a force of 330 regulars and 1,100 Pennsylvania and Kentucky militia. Three weeks later the shattered remnants of Harmar's force straggled back to Fort Washington at Cincinnati, having been soundly defeated by a strong coalition of native tribes. President Washington was enraged by Harmar's failure. "I expected *little* from the moment I heard he was a drunkard. I expected *less* as soon as I heard that on this account no confidence was reposed in him by the people of the Western Country—And I gave up *all hope* of Success, as soon as I heard that there were disputes with him about command" (emphasis in original).[43] (Harmar would be cleared of any charge of misconduct by a subsequent court of inquiry.[44])

Wilkinson had avoided taking a role in Harmar's failed campaign. However, with Harmar's defeat, the Kentucky militia was reconstituted under the command of General Charles Scott, fifty-one, a Revolutionary War general and veteran of Braddock's failed 1755 expedition. Scott had refused to serve under Harmar and thereby avoided any taint from that defeat. In December 1790 Virginia governor Beverley Randolph appointed Scott to head up the Kentucky militia, and Scott subsequently appointed Wilkinson, his neighbor and friend, as a militia lieutenant colonel. Wilkinson immediately contacted his Spanish handlers and assured them that his new position "tends only to increase my power which will always be employed under your direction for the interest and honor of the King."[45] Scott was directed to cooperate with Governor St. Clair, who in March 1791 was also appointed by President Washington as federal army commander, in mounting another punitive expedition against the Indians. While St. Clair was enlisting and training the newly expanded federal army, at Washington's direction Scott was mounting a series of raids into the Ohio country to keep the tribes off balance.

Scott launched his first raid on May 24, targeting Indian settlements along the Wabash River. On June 1 the force assaulted a lightly defended Indian village, with Wilkinson leading a small group of mounted troops against part of the encampment. This was Wilkinson's first experience in commanding troops in combat, and by all accounts he performed well and suffered no casualties against a few defenseless Indians.[46] The following day Wilkinson commanded a force of 300 troops on a raid at an Indian village at Tippecanoe, where he was unopposed in burning the deserted village. (Twenty years later Tippecanoe would be the sight of a major battle involving General William Henry Harrison against the tribes in the Northwest.[47]) Scott and Wilkinson returned to Kentucky, having suffered only 5 wounded.

As a result of the success of the raid, Wilkinson was directed to command a second raid against another Wabash River village in August. The brief skirmish resulted in 6 Indian and 2 militia deaths, followed by the troops burning the village and the surrounding fields of crops. Wilkinson returned to Kentucky and filed a bloated report for St. Clair, overstating the meager results that had been obtained through his first and only independent command.[48] Wilkinson caused a copy of this report to be forwarded to Philadelphia, where it was brought to the attention of Secretary of War Knox and President Washington, who responded by formally commending Wilkinson for his "zeal, perseverance, and good conduct."[49]

Having received a modest endorsement of his first military success, Wilkinson chose to abandon his career as an unsuccessful merchant and pursue his first love: military glory. In response to the Harmar expedition's demise, Congress had chosen to expand the regular army with a new infantry regiment, and Wilkinson submitted an appeal to Knox to be named the new commander of the regiment.

> It is my wish to be employed in some station in which I may be able to employ and apply my information, and my small abilities to the public advantage, and my own honor. In short, permit me to say, with a frankness becoming a soldier, that I feel a strong desire to enter once more upon the stage of military life, and that if you can favor me with some appointment, consistent with my former rank, I will not disappoint your expectations or injure the service; but will ever cherish the warmest sense of gratitude to your attention.[50]

Wilkinson later told one of his creditors that his decision to seek active federal service was driven by a desire for "bread and fame."[51] Not leaving anything to chance, Wilkinson included mention of some important political contacts who would support his quest for a commission, such as Harry Innes, one of Wilkinson's Spanish Conspiracy cronies and a newly appointed federal judge in Kentucky. On September 30, 1791, Innes contacted Secretary of State Thomas Jefferson to endorse Wilkinson's petition for a commission.[52] Meanwhile, Wilkinson's several detractors cautioned Washington against such an appointment. Humphry Marshall, a creditor of Wilkinson and a rising voice in Kentucky politics, wrote to Washington to provide a backhanded endorsement of Wilkinson's commission: "I considered Wilkinson well qualified for a commission. . . . I considered him dangerous to the quiet of Kentucky, perhaps to her safety. If the commission does not secure his fidelity, it will at least place him under control, in the midst of faithful officers, whose vigilance will render him harmless, if not honest."[53]

Washington's decision to approve Wilkinson's appointment as a lieutenant colonel in command of the Second Infantry Regiment remains a mystery. Washington knew that Wilkinson had no real combat experience during the Revolution and that he had only served in a series of staff positions; it caused a major uprising among combat generals when he was proposed by Gates for a brevet promotion to brigadier general. Wilkinson was forced to resign that position following the exposure of Wilkinson's drunken role in the Conway Cabal. His subsequent service as civilian clothier-general to the army was a failure, again resulting in dismissal.

His recent militia service in Kentucky, leading raids on defenseless Indian camps, though well publicized, in no way qualified him for command of a regular infantry regiment. Yet Wilkinson had the advantage of being from Kentucky, an important source of militia recruits and supplies for the Indian campaigns, and his appointment to the regular forces might assist in the integration of those militias into operations with the regular army. Despite his lack of qualifications and the warnings of his Spanish connections, Washington offered Wilkinson a lieutenant colonel's commission and command of the new infantry regiment in October 1791.[54]

Ironically, Wilkinson's lieutenant colonel slot was first offered to Major John Doughty, who declined the appointment. In 1790 Doughty, a Revolutionary War friend of Wilkinson's, commanded an army expedition to explore the construction of a federal road between Kentucky and New Orleans. Wilkinson learned of the expedition and determined that such a route would propose a threat to his Mississippi River trade route. Wilkinson alerted Miro to the expedition and recommended that Miro encourage Creek Indians to attack Doughty's party.[55] Doughty's party was attacked and sustained several casualties. Doughty returned to Kentucky, mission unaccomplished.[56]

As a result of either his usual aversion to combat or the ongoing negotiations regarding his federal commission, Wilkinson missed the next armed foray against the tribes in the Northwest. (As a result of personality clashes with St. Clair, General Scott had refused to accompany the expedition.[57]) Arthur St. Clair, who had recently been dual-hatted as territorial governor and army commander, foolishly succumbed to pressure from Knox and Washington to mount an immediate campaign against the tribes before the new levy of federal troops had been adequately trained and supplied. On October 1 the army departed Fort Washington and headed once again for the Indian villages along the Wabash River. St. Clair, fifty-five, suffered from repeated attacks of gout that left him unable to ride a horse, and he delegated much of the command responsibility to his deputy, Brigadier General Richard Butler. The expedition commenced with almost 2,000 troops, but disease and desertions slowly whittled the force down to less than 1,500 effectives and more than 200 camp followers (wives, children, suttlers, and prostitutes). This army of untrained regulars, six-month levies, and poorly led militia slowly moved north, while the tribes in the Northwest, inspired by Wilkinson's August raid into coalescing into a combined fighting force, gathered to meet them. Indian leaders such as Blue Jacket (Shawnee) and Little Turtle (Miami) eventually brought together more than a thousand warriors to shadow St. Clair's movements.[58] The tribes present included Delawares, Shawnees, Kickapoos, Miamis, Wyandots, Ottawas, Ojibwas, Potawatomis, Conoys, Nanticokes, Mohawks, Creeks, and

Cherokees.[59] Oblivious to the Indians' presence, St. Clair had sent a significant portion of this semi-trained force to hunt down army deserters.

On November 4, St. Clair's remaining force was destroyed by a surprise attack. With St. Clair wounded and Butler killed, the panicked remnants of the army and camp followers scattered. Without any meaningful order they desperately sought the closest American fortification at Fort Jefferson, twenty-nine miles away. Upon arrival at the post the remaining officer corps learned of the staggering losses. Thirty-seven officers and 593 enlisted soldiers were either killed or missing, with another 32 officers and 252 enlisted soldiers wounded. At least thirty female camp followers were killed outright, with many more women and children taken prisoner by the victorious tribes. The battle resulted in the worst defeat ever suffered by the American army in the history of all the Indian wars.

On the day following St. Clair's massacre, in blissful ignorance of the destruction of the American army on the banks of the Wabash, Wilkinson accepted his commission as lieutenant colonel and commander of the Second Infantry Regiment. He also swore an oath of allegiance to the United States and commenced his career as a double agent for Spain.

5

RETURN TO THE FRONTIER ARMY

1792–1796

A vile assassin . . . that worst of all bad men.
—General Anthony Wayne

The news of St. Clair's Wabash debacle took more than a month to reach President Washington in Philadelphia. According to Tobias Lear, Washington's private secretary, in mid-December 1791 a mud-splattered messenger arrived while Washington was hosting a dinner. Washington excused himself from his guests, read the message, and returned to the table with his composure intact. However, once the dinner guests had departed, Washington's fabled temper exploded:

> It's all over. St. Clair's defeated-routed, the officers all nearly killed. . . . Here, yes, here on this very spot I took leave of him. . . . You have your instructions, I said from the Secretary of War. I . . . will add but one word—beware of a surprise! You know how the Indians fight us. . . . He went off with that as my last solemn warning. . . . And yet!! To suffer that army to be cut to pieces, hacked, butchered, tomahawked by a surprise—the very thing I guarded him against!! Oh God, Oh God, he is worse than a murderer! How can he answer to his country? The blood of the slain is upon him—the curse of widows and orphans—the curse of Heaven.[1]

Once Washington regained his composure he told Lear that his comments must not leave the room. "General St. Clair shall have justice. . . . I will receive him without prejudice, he shall have full justice."

The "justice" administered to St. Clair was leavened with a healthy dose of whitewash and finger-pointing to avoid any meaningful accountability regarding Washington and his administration. At first St. Clair sought the traditional remedy for a military misadventure—the convening of a court of inquiry under the Articles of War. St. Clair formally requested such a proceeding on March 26,

1792, but his request was rejected by Washington two days later. Since St. Clair was the senior general of the army and a significant portion of the army's officer corps had been wiped out at the Wabash battle, not enough officers of rank existed to sit on a court of inquiry.[2] As Washington and his cabinet struggled to find a way to address the failure, Congress unexpectedly intervened. After the First Congress was convened in 1789, a question arose regarding its authority to conduct oversight of the functions of the executive branch. In a March 1792 debate on the floor of the House of Representatives during the Second Congress, Representative John Vining of Delaware raised a novel proposal: since the Constitution gave the House the authority to impeach executive branch officials for misconduct, it must also have provided the House with the authority to conduct investigations of misconduct that could lead to impeachment. When a motion before the House to request Washington to investigate failed, the House voted 44–10 to conduct its first oversight hearing.[3]

The House investigation got off to a promising start. A special panel of representatives was appointed to conduct the investigation; its first order of business was to demand that the War Department provide all relevant records. Washington convened a meeting of his cabinet to consider the propriety of responding to the committee's request. Following the meeting, Washington concluded that it would be appropriate to furnish the House with relevant documents but that the administration could refuse to disclose documents it believed would "harm the public good."[4] (This is the first consideration of the concept of executive privilege. The principle would be further explored in 1807 in relation to Wilkinson's correspondence with President Jefferson about Aaron Burr.) Despite this hopeful start, the committee's proceedings quickly dissolved into disrepute. Many of the senior officials who bore some degree of culpability for the debacle did not want their names linked to the largest military disaster in the history of the new republic. St. Clair, seeking to avoid blame and spin a narrative that would place culpability elsewhere, traveled to Philadelphia and submitted to the committee documents showing the onerous directions provided to him by Secretary of War Henry Knox and demonstrating the failed logistical support provided to his army by Knox and Quartermaster General Samuel Hodgdon. Knox and Treasury Secretary Alexander Hamilton were also desirous of a less than full examination of the failure of the support provided to the army by contractor William Duer. Duer, a contractor who provided questionable supplies to the army following the Revolution, served as assistant treasury secretary under Hamilton and was soon to be sentenced to debtor's prison for financial misdeeds. Duer spent the rest of his life in prison and died in 1799. A preliminary committee report was issued in May 1792 that criticized Knox, Hodgdon, and Duer but exonerated St. Clair from any responsibility.[5] The issuance of a final report was delayed until the meeting of the second session of Congress in November 1792.

During the interim Washington took several corrective actions and demanded and received St. Clair's resignation as commander of the army, although St. Clair would continue to serve as governor of the Northwest Territory. Hodgdon was also forced to resign. When the returning House took up the report, Knox and Hodgdon submitted significant documentation defending their conduct. A revised report prepared in February 1793 still blamed Knox and Duer and cleared St. Clair, but it did not recommend any action against any government official. The full House eventually voted to abolish the committee without taking any action on the report.[6] (The records gathered by the House investigation have since disappeared.) A limited precedent had been established, but meaningful congressional oversight of the military affairs of the executive branch would have to await another day.

Washington was nevertheless able to exploit the Wabash massacre in a positive way. As the oversight hearings had shown, St. Clair's initiative was significantly hampered by the way the government had responded to the need to quickly call up more troops. Following the disbanding of the Continental Army after the Revolution, the standing regular army of the United States had been reduced to a shadow force. In 1789 the regular army consisted of only 700 soldiers and 44 officers. Congress viewed a standing army to be fiscally unsound and contrary to republican principles, but this shadow force was expected to protect the frontier from Indian raids, defend against encroachments by neighboring Spanish and British territories, and man all coastal fortifications.[7] Should a greater force be necessary, the War Department was expected to rely on short-term levies of local militias.

This idyllic view of the viability of the American yeomanry as a meaningful deterrent soon failed in the response to the escalating Indian violence occurring in the Northwest Territory. In April 1790 Congress expanded the regular army to 1,216 soldiers to provide additional troops to support General Harmar's ill-fated expedition (and, to pay for the increase, simultaneously cut in half a soldier's wage).[8] Unfortunately, the War Department was unable to recruit, train, and support a competent regular army and militia force in time to support Harmar's October 1790 offensive, resulting in the first massacre of an American army in the wilderness of the Northwest Territory. A subsequent congressional investigation showed that St. Clair was afflicted with similar shortsightedness during his failed expedition the following year. In March 1791 congressional authority was granted to recruit a second regiment of regular soldiers, raising the total regular strength level to 2,128.[9] However, St. Clair again repeated Harmar's mistake of succumbing to War Department pressure to mount a quick campaign with raw recruits before his new force was adequately recruited, trained, and supplied.

Following St. Clair's dismal failures, Washington and Knox decided to create and maintain a professional military force to confront the continuing hostilities. Meanwhile, Jefferson, true to his antimilitary proclivity, hoped that the massacre would not be used as an excuse to expand the regular forces—and, despite overwhelming proof of the militias' inadequacy, he clung to the belief that local militias were the proper military response.[10] In March 1792 Congress approved another expansion of the regular army to 5,168 men. This new force would consist of a cavalry arm and an entire regiment of riflemen, and soldier's pay would be increased. The total cost of the package was $1,026,477.05, almost double the earlier estimate for the 1792 military budget.[11] Washington realized that he would face an additional challenge in finding a capable commander for this expanded force, soon to be known as the Legion of the United States. His search for a general brought Wilkinson back into the national spotlight.

Wilkinson had lost no time in using his new position as an American army officer and Spanish double agent to put his financial affairs in order. To stave off creditors he sold property in Frankfort, Kentucky, which eventually was acquired by the commonwealth government to be the capital of the new state. However, Wilkinson recognized that he would never be able to pay off his creditors and support the extravagant lifestyle to which he had become accustomed on his meager annual salary of $600 as a lieutenant colonel. The real value from his commission would be in capitalizing on his new position with his Spanish masters.

The ink was barely dry on his federal oath of office when Wilkinson reached out to Spanish governor Miro to tout his enhanced value to Spain. Wilkinson speculated that with General Butler's death at the Wabash and General St. Clair's imminent removal from command, he was most likely to be given command of the entire US Army. To protect their secret relationship, Wilkinson urged Miro to place further communications in cipher. Wilkinson also asked Miro about the status of his Spanish pension and urged that future communications be sent through Wilkinson's chosen cut-outs, Judge Harry Innes in Kentucky or Clement Biddle, Wilkinson's brother-in-law in Philadelphia.[12] Baron Hector de Carondolet replaced Miro as governor of Spanish Louisiana at the end of December 1791. As Wilkinson's new handler, Carondolet was able to provide Wilkinson with the news he had been hoping for, writing in February 1792 that the Spanish Crown had approved Wilkinson's $2,000 per year "secret pension," backdated to January 1789. Carondolet also informed Wilkinson that $4,000 of this sum was immediately available.[13]

Upon receipt of the good news from Carondolet, Wilkinson dispatched Michel Lacassange, one of his creditors, to retrieve his $4,000 payment. Lacassange took payment from Carondolet, deducted the amount owned to him by Wilkinson, and remitted the remaining $2,600 to Wilkinson in November 1792. Wilkinson would send his first espionage report to Spain as an American double agent the following month.

As Wilkinson's correspondence with Miro showed, Wilkinson was no sooner on the US Army rolls than he commenced his campaign to obtain the spot of commanding general. His immediate goal was to demonstrate to Washington and Knox that he could command troops on the frontier and help rebuild St. Clair's shattered command. He reported to take command of Fort Washington in January 1792 and immediately launched an expedition to recover the remains of the dead at the scene of St. Clair's defeat. On February 1 this force reached the snow-covered battlefield and found a scene of unspeakable horror. More than six hundred bodies, many scalped and mutilated by Indians or eaten by wild animals, lay spread over the frozen ground. Pits were dug to bury the dead who could be found and a search was commenced to find any of the artillery that had been abandoned after the battle. Only one cannon was located; the rest were presumed to have been carried away or lost in the snow. Upon the completion of this grisly task, Wilkinson returned to Fort Washington on February 5.[14]

Once back at the fort, Wilkinson was confronted by the need to instill discipline on a demoralized command. Most of the troops at Fort Washington were either new recruits or survivors of St. Clair's broken force. Few officers remained after the massacre, and the troops suffered from drunkenness, a typical problem of troops in remote locations in winter. Wilkinson responded with stern discipline and military justice proceedings, a lesson learned from his brief stint in command of federal troops in the spring of 1776. When this approach proved inadequate to quell disturbances, Wilkinson authorized summary punishment. Officers were directed to roam the fort and the nearby town of Cincinnati at odd hours, and anyone caught intoxicated would be subjected to an immediate punishment of fifty lashes.

A lack of clarity regarding this order soon brought Wilkinson into contact with a promising new junior officer, nineteen-year-old Ensign William Henry Harrison. Two days after the promulgation of the order, when Harrison encountered a civilian army artificer in a drunken state, he immediately commenced the proscribed lashing and, for good measure, administered ten lashes to a different civilian artificer who had the temerity to intervene. The whipped artificers complained to Wilkinson, properly stating that they were not subject to military discipline. Wilkinson immediately clarified the order to apply only to active duty soldiers and reprimanded Harrison for overstepping. However, the artificers were not satisfied and filed a civil suit against Harrison. Wilkinson refused to allow the local sheriff to serve papers on Harrison and railed against civil authorities seeking to become involved in matters of military discipline. Wilkinson thought such suits infected the artificers and soldiers with a sort of "licentious freedom, incompatible with their respective Stations, tending to the subversion of discipline, destructive to those principles of subordination with out which an army cannot exist, and of consequence pregnant with anarchy and disorder."[15] The acting territorial governor eventually supported Wilkinson and the matter was quietly dropped. Harrison was ordered to escort Mrs. Wilkinson back east to Philadelphia, thereby removing him from the reach of the local courts.

In May 1792 Washington sought to send a message of peace to the warring tribes that were still threatening the northwest frontier. Major Alexander Trueman of the regulars and Colonel John Hardin of the Kentucky militia were selected by Knox to carry his messages to the hostile tribes. The two officers reported to Wilkinson on May 19, then set off into the wilderness. Both messengers were soon killed by Indians. (Humphry Marshall, a creditor and enemy of Wilkinson, speculated in 1812 that Wilkinson viewed Hardin as a rival for command and had the two officers killed.[16])

As it became increasingly clear to Washington that St. Clair could not remain in command of the army, he commenced a search for a new commanding general. On March 9, 1792, Washington convened a meeting of his cabinet to discuss possible candidates. Washington's and Jefferson's notes from the meeting contain a detailed evaluation of the available men.[17] Washington's intention was to evaluate the relative merits of all available former general officers from the Continental Army. Since St. Clair and Harmar were obviously out of consideration and Butler was dead, the list was mostly comprised of aging Revolutionary War veterans. After weighing the relative merits of the available candidates, the selection was narrowed to two finalists: Brevet Major General Anthony Wayne and Wilkinson. Washington observed that Wayne, forty-seven, had a reputation for being more active and enterprising than judicious or cautious and was believed to be susceptible to flattery and getting in scrapes. Apparently Washington was also unfamiliar with Wayne's reputation for sobriety. Jefferson's observation was more blunt: Wayne was brave and nothing else. While successful in leading an attack on the British fort at Stony Point, New York, on another occasion Wayne ran "his head against a wall where success was both impossible and useless."

The cabinet discussion accurately encapsulated both Wayne's personality and his military career. Wayne had attracted several nicknames during the Revolution, the most popular being "Mad Anthony" (mostly used behind his back), a reference to either his temper or his tendency to rush headlong at the enemy. Another was "Dandy Tony," a reference to his fondness for women and fancy dress.[18] Wayne had raised a Pennsylvania militia unit in 1775, then entered Continental service and served with Arnold and Wilkinson on the long retreat from Canada in 1776. Appointed a brigadier general in February 1777, Wayne served under Washington at the Battle of Brandywine. Shortly after the battle, his command was caught by surprise in a night attack by British troops, leading to the Paoli Massacre. Wayne went on to play a leading role at the Battle of Monmouth in 1778 and brilliantly stormed and captured the British fort at Stony Point, New York, in 1779. In 1781 Wayne rashly led his command into a trap set by Lord Cornwallis in the Virginia Tidewater, narrowly escaping capture and the destruction of his command. Following the British surrender at Yorktown, Wayne was sent south to deal with the remnants of the British Army around Savannah, Georgia, and was breveted to the rank of major general in September 1783. Following the war Wayne left the army and tried managing a rice plantation that was awarded to him by the grateful citizens of Georgia. Financial and marital difficulties soon followed, and Wayne turned to politics. At the time of Washington's search for a new commander, Wayne was serving in Congress as a representative from Georgia but was soon to be expelled from his seat for election fraud.[19]

Washington first approached Wayne, through Knox, to see whether Wayne would accept a subordinate position in the new army. Wayne rejected any position below commanding general, leading Washington to relent and formally propose to the Senate Wayne's appointment as commander and major general on April 9, 1792.[20] The same nomination appointed Wilkinson as brigadier general under Wayne.

Washington's consideration of Wilkinson for the commanding general's position was troubling. Washington's notes from the March cabinet meeting mark Wilkinson as being "lively, sensible, pompous and ambitious" but that little could be said of his career as an officer. Washington also noted that Wilkinson was only a brigadier general by brevet and had held that rank for a short period of time. Jefferson's notes had a more ominous overtone: Wilkinson was "brave, enterprising to excess, but [had] many unapprovable points in his character." Jefferson never elaborated on what those "unapprovable" points were. Wilkinson's lack of meaningful combat experience and his deplorable record during the Revolution, which should have debarred him for consideration for his initial lieutenant colonel's slot, were even more disqualifying for a position as a general officer. Of all the candidates on the list, Wilkinson was the least qualified in terms of experience. His only positive qualifications over the other candidates were his age (at thirty-four the youngest under consideration), that he had some familiarity with the military situation in the Northwest Territory, and that he came from Kentucky. Although he quickly accepted the new position, Wilkinson was outraged that he had not been appointed commander and immediately commenced an escalating campaign to undermine, remove, and replace Wayne as the commander of the Legion by whatever means necessary.

At first Wilkinson appeared to Wayne to be a loyal subordinate, an appearance that was probably possible because Wayne was busy raising and training the Legion's force at Legionville outside of Pittsburgh and Wilkinson was three hundred miles away, commanding troops at forts further down the Ohio River. To sustain his campaign into the heart of the Indian confederacy, St. Clair had constructed a series of forts that stretched from Fort Washington at Cincinnati to Fort Jefferson, eighty miles to the north. Maintaining the Ohio forts was a logistical nightmare: in addition to bad roads that were subject to flooding and winter snow, Indian raids on the supply convoys were a common occurrence. Furthermore, Wilkinson understood that the few troops available to him were incapable of mounting any kind of offensive operation. On February 13, 1792, Wilkinson issued an order that "positively prohibits the Commanding Officers of Garrisons, leaving the walls of their respective fortresses, beyond musket shot, on any pretense."[21] The precarious nature of Wilkinson's tenuous hold on the frontier continued through the remainder of 1792 and into 1793. Only the appearance of Wayne's fully trained and staffed force would change the balance of power on the frontier.

Considering the need for men that were healthy, sober, and ready for deployment, the quality of Wilkinson's troops was dismal. The officer corps, decimated by the Harmar and St. Clair massacres, was particularly deplorable and junior officers were either political appointees or green recruits. In September 1792 Wilkinson observed, "Generally speaking, the officers of our late Army, possessing genius, talents, education, or enterprise, have pushed their fortunes and found such Establishments in the world as forbid their retaining the Sword, and of consequence . . . the Beasts & Blockheads only remain for our choice to the exclusion of men of science, pride, principle and polite education."[22] A few months later Wayne passed on a similar Wilkinson assessment to Knox: "General Wilkinson writes me that he had not a single officer of rank, to assist, or countenance him in introducing discipline among the troops—that out of three Majors, one is so extremely illiterate as scarcely to write his own name; another is charged with insanity—and another is a confirmed sot."[23]

In addition to poor troop quality, geographical challenges, and the threat from Indian raids, Wilkinson and Wayne also had to confront the challenge of working within the army's failed system of contracting for logistical support. The Continental Army's struggle to obtain needed armaments was exacerbated by a supply system that repeatedly failed. With the passage of the Constitution in 1789, military supply responsibilities were split between the Department of War and the Department of the Treasury. War Department contracting was controlled by the quartermaster general, a civilian official who reported to the secretary of war and not to the local military commander. Treasury contracting was assigned to the Purveyor of Public Supplies, which would procure supplies and then deposit them into arsenals and magazines under the control of the War Department's quartermaster general. The system was designed to provide a series of internal controls over the contracting system but it proved totally inadequate to meet the needs of the expeditions under Harmar, St. Clair, and Wayne.[24]

Further complicating supply problems was the role of the government contractors selected to provide food and forage for the expeditions and to transport them to the frontier outposts. The supply contract for the expeditions was awarded to the firm of Elliott and Williams. Robert Elliott was the brother of a British army officer stationed in Canada who was active in British efforts to cause Indian unrest against the United States; Eli Williams was the brother of Revolutionary War general Otho Williams. Their company, one of the largest private employers on the western frontier, was somehow able to avoid blame in the postmortems conducted of the Harmar and St. Clair debacles. But their questionable relationship with Wilkinson and their failure to support Wayne figured prominently in the ensuing campaign.

Wilkinson's effective management of the Ohio forts was recognized by officials in Philadelphia and by Wayne. In July 1792 Secretary Knox recommended to Washington that Wilkinson be named adjutant and inspector general of the army.[25] (The appointment was never made.) The next month, Knox informed Washington that Wilkinson was a "great acquisition to the public."[26] The same month Wayne informed Knox that "it would be a species of injustice were it concealed that Brigadier General Wilkinson has afforded the greatest satisfaction by his conduct which he has evinced the most indefatigable industry and zeal to promote the good of the service."[27] These comments were then mirrored by Washington, who observed that Wilkinson "has displayed great zeal and ability for the public weal since he came into Service—His conduct carries strong marks of attention, activity, and Spirit, and I wish him to know the favorable light in which it is viewed."[28]

Despite this praise, Wilkinson's military career stagnated until Wayne and the Legion were strong enough to mount offensive operations. The arrival in mid-1792 of Wilkinson's first payment from Spain, combined with the promise of actually receiving an annual pension, inspired Wilkinson into active espionage as Agent 13. Meanwhile, his new role in the American army increased his value to his Spanish handlers. In July 1792, Manuel Gayoso de Lemos, the Spanish commander at Natchez, observed Wilkinson's worth and decried the delay in obtaining the Crown's approval of his pension.[29]

In December 1792 Wilkinson wrote again to Carondolet. Renewing his commitment to serve Spain, Wilkinson urged the Spanish to take advantage of the fact that he was working for "an incompetent Secretary of War" and "an ignorant commander in chief" (Wayne). He repeated his solicitation for a commission in the Spanish Army to satisfy his passion for military fame but left it open to Carondolet to determine whether he would be of greater service by remaining an undercover agent of Spain. Wilkinson also provided Carondolet with an assessment on the relative capabilities of American forces. While he urged Carondolet to strengthen Spanish defenses on the Mississippi to deter American encroachments, he stated that Spain had nothing to fear from the United States, observing that the country was divided in sectional discord, which "renders the whole [nation] weak and contemptible, [and] the occasion is favorable to Spain and you know how to improve it." He described the United States as a "contemptible Union."[30] At the same time Wilkinson reached out to Gayoso to inquire whether his new American general officer's rank would be transferrable to the Spanish Army, and whether his Spanish pension could be paid directly to his wife and sons.[31] This document was classic espionage: it provided an assessment from a high-ranking federal official of the current military and political posture of the United States as it might affect an enemy's interests, and it revealed actionable intelligence on United States intentions and urged an enemy to build defenses that would be used against federal troops that might encroach on the enemy's territory.

At the same time, Wilkinson commenced a series of steps to assist Spain in repelling filibusterers targeting Spain through US territory. In Europe tensions were rising between newly republican France and the Bourbon Monarchy of Spain. King Louis XVI was beheaded in January 1793 and the Girondist regime that came into power was committed to spreading French revolutionary principles throughout the world. In the spring of 1793 Edmond-Charles Genet, "Citizen Genet," was named minister to the United States. Genet no sooner had arrived than he commenced recruiting privateers to attack British shipping and filibusterers to attack Spanish Louisiana. One of the takers was Revolutionary War hero George Rogers Clark. During the Revolution, Clark had led a series of expeditions and attacks on British outposts in the future Northwest Territory, and his success enabled the United States to claim these territories as part of the 1783 peace treaty with Great Britain. Unfortunately, Clark's postwar activities left him destitute and an alcoholic. To regain some of his former glory and restore his lost fortune, Clark accepted Genet's offer of a commission as a major general and commander of the French Revolutionary Legion on the Mississippi.

Clark sought to capitalize on the animosity toward Spain's control of the Mississippi in the western states, especially in Kentucky and Tennessee. Clark proposed to recruit and supply an army that would travel down the Mississippi River and wrest control of the river and New Orleans from the Spanish. Washington quickly and formally voiced his disapproval of the matter. Knox sent out secret orders to Major Thomas Doyle, the commander of Fort Massac, the newly constructed American fort on the lower Ohio River, authorizing Doyle to use any means necessary to stop the movement of the filibusterers on the Ohio, including by force.[32] By early 1794 the Revolutionary Legion of the Mississippi was no more. The construction of Fort Massac provided another opportunity for Wilkinson to earn his Spanish pension but because the fort would be the closest federal installation to Spanish territory on the Mississippi, in June 1794 he alerted the Spanish to the fort's construction and urged them to build their own forts to counter the federal presence. In response to Wilkinson's warning, Carondolet proceeded to construct Spanish installations at New Madrid in 1794 and Chickasaw Bluffs in 1795.[33]

The end of the Clark filibuster expedition gave Wilkinson an opportunity to capitalize on its demise. As early as December 1792 Wilkinson had alerted his Spanish handlers on the commencement of the recruitment of troops by Clark. When the filibuster failed in 1794, Wilkinson falsely claimed credit for its collapse and sought payment from Spain for his efforts. He even had the temerity to seek reimbursement of the $8,640 that he had allegedly expended to break up the expedition and asked that his pension be increased to $4,000 per year. Wilkinson urged Carondolet to forward funds for him to use to bribe state officials as well as 16 army officers who would be susceptible to receiving cash in support of Spain over the United States. Fearing that his Spanish handlers would choke at this sum, Wilkinson assured them, "Do not believe me avaricious as the sensation never found a place in my bosom. Constant in my attachments, ardent in my affections, and an enthusiast in the cause I espoused, my character is reversed."[34] Carondolet did not agree to the increased pension, but he did agree to pay Wilkinson $12,000 in reimbursement for Clark-related expenses and back payments on Wilkinson's pension. The amount would be shipped to Wilkinson from New Orleans via cash couriers in two installments of $6,000 each.[35]

The subsequent events to deliver the cash almost led to Wilkinson's exposure as Agent 13. The first shipment of cash was placed under the care of Harry Owen, a Wilkinson associate. The silver coin was hidden in barrels in New Orleans and shipped by boat up the Mississippi. Owen got as far as the Ohio River, where he was murdered by the crew of the boat. The Spanish crew divided the currency among themselves and sought to flee back to Spanish territory. In December three of the murderers were apprehended by civil authorities in Kentucky and sent to Frankfort for trial. Fortunately for Wilkinson, their initial appearance was before federal judge Harry Innes, Wilkinson's earlier coconspirator. Recognizing the threat the trio posed to himself and Wilkinson, Innes alerted Wilkinson and had the prisoners shipped to Fort Washington. Wilkinson quickly determined that the murderers should be tried by the Spanish and dispatched the criminals, under military escort, to the Spanish fort at New Madrid. However, before reaching Spanish territory they were intercepted by Major Doyle at the newly constructed Fort Massac. Despite displaying a pass signed by Wilkinson, Doyle insisted on questioning the culprits and because no one at Fort Massac spoke Spanish, Doyle sent a message to New Madrid (in Spanish territory), seeking an interpreter. Recognizing the importance of maintaining Wilkinson's cover, Thomas Power, a confidential aide to Carondelet, was sent to Fort Massac to serve as interpreter. Power carefully interpreted their answers to ensure that the cover of Agent 13 was maintained. Doyle, suspicious of the validity of the cover story, refused to release the culprits and had them sent to Louisville for trial. They again appeared before Judge Innes, who ruled that there was inadequate evidence for trial. The three were returned to Spanish territory and, to ensure passage through Fort Massac, Wilkinson recalled Doyle to Fort Washington, where he faced court-martial for ignoring Wilkinson's pass.[36]

The second payment of $6,000 to Wilkinson traveled a more circuitous route. The money was shipped to an entrusted courier in Charleston, South Carolina, who then proceeded overland to Pittsburgh and arrived in Cincinnati in April 1795. Of the original $6,000 amount, Wilkinson informed the Spanish that he received only $2,500.[37]

While the peripatetic movement of the murderous boatmen enabled Wilkinson to avoid detection as Agent 13, he still needed to be paid for his espionage. In July 1795 Gayoso assured Wilkinson of the payment of the promised $12,000. Furthermore, he promised an additional $9,640 if Wilkinson activated a new version of the Spanish Conspiracy. Since western states such as Kentucky and Tennessee still felt ignored by the federal government in Philadelphia and were suffering from the Spanish stranglehold on the Mississippi, Gayoso urged Wilkinson to approach western leaders and encourage them to align with Spain and sever ties to the United States. Gayoso was willing to meet with some of the former Spanish conspirators and offered them the same pension amount that was being paid to Wilkinson. Carondelet also dangled in front of Wilkinson that he could play a role in the founding of this western country similar to the one Washington had played in the founding of the United States. Carondelet informed his superiors that Wilkinson had assured him that he would keep Carondelet fully apprised of any federal troop movements.[38] In order to safely communicate these plans and transfer the money, Thomas Power was chosen by Carondelet to be the courier. In June 1796 Power had the money packed in sugar and coffee barrels and accompanied the barrels on their delivery to Wilkinson in Cincinnati.[39]

The Spanish authorities viewed Wilkinson's purchased loyalty with great skepticism. Gayoso, commandant at Natchez, warned Carondolet that Wilkinson could not be trusted. He observed that Wilkinson might be inclined to sell out Spanish interests in order to ingratiate himself with his American superiors. He also expressed concerns about the difficulty of using Power as a courier of messages and money.[40]

Wilkinson realized that he needed to create a cover story regarding his receipt of his new Spanish fortune. In September 1796 he informed Carondolet of the cover story he would create to account for his newly acquired wealth: "If I am questioned by Washington on my arrival in Philadelphia, I will avow a mercantile connection with New Orleans since [1788] and in which I still remain interested. . . . I will deny receiving a dollar by [Thomas] Power and I will add that a balance is still due me. To circumstantiate this assertion I will cause the faithful Philip Nolan now with me to make an account in form with a letter of advice dated New Orleans last autumn." For good measure Wilkinson added that he would seek to suppress American military actions, disgrace Major General Wayne, and seek to replace Wayne as the commander of the American army unless he was directed by Carondolet to do otherwise. Wilkinson urged the utmost secrecy in his Spanish correspondence: "I have often requested and I again entreat that my name never be mentioned or written and I hope that my correspondence may be placed beyond the reach of treachery or intrigue."[41]

In this remarkable document Wilkinson set forth the defense that he would manufacture, enhance, and boldly assert throughout numerous military, judicial, and congressional proceedings for the next twenty years. His cover story was supported over time by statements of perjury, the use of forged documents, and the production of corroborating false evidence provided by his Spanish handlers. The success of Wilkinson's cover story is one of the best examples of successful espionage tradecraft in American history.

Wilkinson's vow to destroy and replace Wayne was the latest skirmish in his four-year battle against his commander. An initial geographic separation between Wilkinson and Wayne in 1792 reduced the opportunity for Wilkinson's mischief, and Wayne's training and movement of the Legion in May 1793 from its initial camp at Legionville to its new camp, Hobson's Choice, located outside Cincinnati ended the separation. Wilkinson commenced a multilevel attack on Wayne, intending to cause Wayne's removal and replacement by Wilkinson.

The first piece of the attack was to undermine Wayne's authority among the newly recruited officer corps and divide the Legion into two camps, one supporting Wayne and the other Wilkinson. Wilkinson quietly castigated Wayne to a select group of officers that included Major Thomas Cushing, Captain Isaac Guion, and Captain William Clark. (Clark, the brother of George Rogers Clark, later served as Meriwether Lewis's co-commander on the famous exploration of the Louisiana Purchase.) Wayne vowed to not repeat the mistakes of Harmer and St. Clair in being rushed into a campaign against the Indian confederacy, leaving Wilkinson to spin this caution as Wayne being incompetent and cowardly. Officers who remained loyal to Wayne were targeted by Wilkinson for court-martial and possible dismissal from the service on a series of specious charges. The vigilant Doyle, who had intercepted the Spanish boatmen, believed that he was being targeted for a court-martial not because he had ignored Wilkinson's orders but because he chose to remain loyal to Wayne. Similarly, Captain John Armstrong was brought up on specious charges by Wilkinson, and although he was acquitted at his court-martial, Armstrong resigned his commission in disgust.[42] Though he was initially unaware of Wilkinson's perfidy, Wayne played into Wilkinson's hands due to his harsh temper and dictatorial demeanor. Wayne's actions were designed to instill a spirit of discipline into the Legion, but Wilkinson characterized him as a cruel and unthinking martinet.[43] Wayne soon noticed a pattern of officer disobedience affecting the Legion, and many of the disobedient officers, such as Cushing and Guion, came from the Wilkinson camp.[44]

The second prong of Wilkinson's attack was to cause Wayne's offensive against the Indians to fail, surmising that Washington would then have no choice but to appoint Wilkinson to command the next offensive. When the Legion finally moved into the Ohio backcountry in October 1793, Wayne noted the repeated failure of the provisioning contractor, Elliott and Williams, to provide needed food and forage. The initial bickering was caused by a dispute over the terms of the contract related to the cost of transporting the goods.[45] As a result of the contract dispute, Wayne and the Legion found inadequate supplies to sustain a further campaign when they reached Fort Jefferson in November 1793. Wayne soon began to suspect a more sinister motive for the contractor's failure beyond simple greed: a deliberate conspiracy by the contractor to fail to perform, causing the campaign to fail.[46] Wilkinson's role in this conspiracy would become evident in the following months, leading Wayne to eventually accuse Wilkinson of being the cause of the contractor's recalcitrance. Wilkinson retaliated by alleging that Wayne was engaging in speculation and fraud with Legion suppliers.[47] (Inexplicably, despite Wayne's concerns and violent protests, the Elliott and Williams contract was renewed and no new provisioning contractor was hired until 1795.) Supply problems and the onset of winter caused Wayne to halt the Legion's advance and entrench for the winter at newly constructed Fort Greenville, north of Fort Jefferson.

The Legion's winter halt gave Wilkinson an opportunity to pursue his previous line of attack against Wayne, and the bickering between rival cliques of officers again commenced in full swing. Cushing picked an argument with Wayne's adjutant, resulting in court-martial charges against Cushing. When he was acquitted in January 1794, Cushing became the subject of a civil suit in Cincinnati by former Captain John Armstrong, who also had been forced out of the Legion by Wilkinson. Armstrong sought redress against Cushing for stains against his character and he used the filing of the suit to warn Wayne that "there are characters under your command, and I fear one near your person, who are placed as spies on your conduct ready to communicate in a secret manner to the Supreme Authority, any and every inadvertency which at an unguarded moment might and does happen with all men." Armstrong added, "A most scurrilous piece was some time since penned in camp & forwarded to the printer, who was wise enough to return it."[48] Cushing was arrested by civil authorities and remained in jail until after the Battle of Fallen Timbers, joining Isaac Guion, another Wilkinson ally, who was also in jail on civil charges and missed the campaign.

Armstrong warned Wayne about a surreptitious campaign by Wilkinson to spread rumors about Wayne's supposed incompetence in the local press. In an anonymous posting under the name "Army Wretched," Wilkinson sent a letter to a Cincinnati newspaper, condemning Wayne for drunkenness, incompetence, wastefulness, and favoritism toward "his pimps and parasites."[49] In addition to these anonymous calumnies, Wilkinson maligned Wayne's honor to Kentucky politicians, stating that Wayne's mismanagement of the campaign was leaving the frontier open to Indian depredations and hoping they would communicate their concerns to Congress, Washington, and Knox in Philadelphia.

Wilkinson's increasingly open campaign to undercut Wayne eventually reached Washington and Knox. In April 1794 Knox assured Wayne that he still had the president's full support; Knox naively believed that these allegations would die "of their own imbecility."[50] This was the first instance of Knox and Washington failing to understand and properly address the cancerous effect that Wilkinson's actions had on Wayne and the Legion. While they did not know about Wilkinson's parallel traitorous relationship with Spain, as former officers they should have understood the harm that could be caused by an increasingly vocal and disloyal subordinate. Instead of removing Wilkinson, a two-year pattern of ignoring the problem had begun. They hoped it would simply go away and allow them to avoid the political complications of dealing with the squabble.

Wilkinson's malicious comments—including starting one rumor among the Kentucky militia that they would not be paid because Wayne had stolen the money—came to the attention of Wilkinson's former Kentucky militia commander, General Charles Scott, whose militia would be needed as an important component of the upcoming offensive. Scott's prior military record was far superior to Wilkinson's and, unlike Wilkinson, he had actually commanded troops in combat during the Revolution. As commander of the Fifth Virginia Regiment of the Continental Line, Scott had fought at the Battles of Trenton, Princeton, Brandywine, and Germantown. As a brigadier general he fought at the Battle of Monmouth and was later breveted to major general. Dispatched south in 1780 to assist General Benjamin Lincoln in the defense of Charleston, Scott arrived just in time to be surrendered into captivity with the rest of Lincoln's force in May 1780. He was eventually paroled and exchanged for British Lord Rawdon. Scott went on to serve as governor of Kentucky in 1808. Because of local press accounts of Wayne's supposed failings, Scott decided to visit the Legion at Fort Greenville.[51] Scott subsequently published a glowing account of Wayne's leadership, which caused Wilkinson to condemn Scott as "a fool, a poltroon and a scoundrel."[52] Wilkinson's condemnation of his old friend Scott may also have been driven by fears that Scott would be appointed over Wilkinson as second in command of the Legion.

By April 1794 Wilkinson's campaign to delay a foray north became more open and direct. On April 15 he wrote to Robert Elliott to urge the contractor to slow the delivery of supplies to the Legion and, for obvious reasons, to keep their communications confidential. He wrote, "I beg of you, and do expect, that no Person whatever will see my letters to you."[53] He assured the contractor that Wayne's threats to hold them accountable for nonperformance were merely bluster. While no direct evidence has been established showing that Wilkinson received any remuneration from Elliott for encouraging poor performance and thereby increasing contractor profits, such a possibility cannot be dismissed. As was seen in his relationship with Spain and other government contractors, Wilkinson took every opportunity to monetize his fraudulent and traitorous behavior.

Wayne's frustration with the failure of Elliott and Williams and Wilkinson's apparent role in the failure caused Wayne to directly confront Wilkinson for the first time in May 1794. In response, Wilkinson demanded that Wayne convene a court of inquiry regarding Wilkinson's relationship with the contractor.[54] Simultaneously, Wilkinson surreptitiously lodged the first in a series of complaints with Knox against Wayne. Knox shared these grievances with Washington but also shared Wayne's suspicions about Wilkinson being the cause of the contractor problems.[55] However, aside from Knox's hand-wringing and statements urging the two generals to get along, neither Knox nor Washington did anything to address the increasing open warfare between the two senior generals. Knox spurned Wilkinson's request for a court of inquiry, obtusely stating that the request was informal and could not be addressed on the eve of the campaign.[56] Unfortunately, Knox and Washington chose not to share Wilkinson's charges with Wayne at this time. While Wayne was gradually learning of the betrayal of his second in command, he continued preparations for the campaign in complete ignorance of the depths of Wilkinson's chicanery.

Amid all this bickering, the need for the prompt movement of the Legion into the Ohio backcountry was reaching a critical point. The federal government had long believed that the continuing Indian attacks in the Northwest Territory were encouraged and supported by British forces in Canada. Under the 1783 Treaty of Paris, which ended the Revolutionary War, Britain was required to relinquish a series of forts in the Northwest Territory, primarily Forts Detroit and Michilimackinac. Yet, despite the agreement, Britain maintained these two forts and used them as a base of supply for hostile Indian tribes in their attacks against US forts and settlements. As relations among France, Great Britain, and the United States deteriorated, Britain chose to double down on its incursions into the Northwest. In February 1794 Guy Carleton, now Lord Dorchester and the governor of Lower Canada, met with Indian leaders in Quebec and assured them that Britain would support their increased hostilities against the United States. In April, John Graves Simcoe, the governor of Upper Canada, was directed to construct a new fort in Ohio, Fort Miami, directly in the path of the Legion's advance. From this location British troops would be able to supply the Indian confederacy, and perhaps directly confront the Legion. Simcoe commenced construction of Fort Miami at the falls of the Maumee River, seventy miles south of Detroit and deep within the Northwest Territory.[57] Simcoe met with Indian leaders at the new fort and assured them that the fort was being built for their support and protection against the United States. (Britain's aggressive policy continued until the signing of the Jay Treaty in November 1794, when Britain finally agreed to evacuate British forts in Michigan, New York, Ohio, and Vermont.)

Relying on the promise of British support, the Shawnee leader Blue Jacket commenced offensive operations against the Legion's advance. In June he assembled a force of twelve hundred from among the Shawnee, Ottawa, Potawatomie, and Ojibwa tribes and led an attack on the Legion outpost at Fort Recovery, which had been constructed at the site of the St. Clair massacre. Accompanying Blue Jacket were fourteen British troops under the command of Captain Matthew Elliott, brother of Robert Elliott, Wayne's nonperforming supply contractor.[58] Other than successfully intercepting a supply convoy, the Indian attack against the fort was a complete failure: the Indian force suffered heavy casualties and withdrew back to their camp near Fort Miami, then solicited more active British support in the form of British redcoats and artillery for a new offensive. However, despite the aggressive wishes of Governor Simcoe and Indian agent Alexander McKee, British military support was denied at this time.[59]

In June, following the failure of negotiations with the Indian confederacy, Knox sent the orders Wayne had been waiting for: he urged Wayne to commence his campaign and authorized Wayne to dislodge the British from the illicit Fort Miami if it was convenient to do so.[60] Upon the arrival of General Scott and 1,500 members of the Kentucky militia, Wayne set off from Fort Greenville on July 28. The Legion comprised approximately 2,000 soldiers, with Wilkinson in command of the First and Third sub-legions of the right wing and Lieutenant Colonel John F. Hamtramck in command of the Second and Fourth sub-legions of the left wing. Scott was in command of approximately 720 mounted volunteers. Confirming Wilkinson's fears, Wayne also reorganized the Legion's chain of command, putting Scott in the position of second in command. Wilkinson formally protested this slight to Wayne, but his complaint was ignored.[61] Lack of adequate supplies, swamps, and the possibility of Indian raids on supply convoys reduced the Legion's advance to a crawl. The immediate goal was to reach an Indian encampment at Grand Glaize, a meeting point for the confederacy on the Maumee River. Adhering to Washington's warning to avoid an Indian surprise attack, the Legion constructed a fortified camp at every overnight stop.

At one such stop on August 2, at a location named Fort Adams, Wayne retired to his tent in midafternoon to rest. Suddenly, a large beech tree fell on the tent, almost crushing Wayne asleep on the cot. Wayne was knocked unconscious and suffered a severely bruised leg and ankle, but he quickly recovered and insisted on moving forward. Wayne later became convinced that the tree was deliberately felled by Wilkinson supporters attempting to murder him. Historians have debated whether the fallen tree incident was indeed a murder attempt by Wilkinson; no direct evidence has ever surfaced linking Wilkinson to the fallen tree, but the likelihood cannot be dismissed.[62]

In seeking to establish a criminal act rather than an accident, investigators examine the presence of three factors: motive, means, and opportunity. In this scenario Wilkinson met all three bars, with the most powerful being motive. Wilkinson's growing campaign against Wayne had so far been unsuccessful. If Wayne were to succeed in the present campaign, which was about to arrive at the main Indian encampment, Wilkinson's opportunity to seize command and win an important victory would be lost. Wilkinson had clearly demonstrated no scruples in his treasonous relationship with Spain and would probably have had no moral qualms about murdering an enemy to accomplish his personal goals. A disgruntled officer who was attracted to the Wilkinson camp in the rivalry against Wayne would have provided the means. Were he able to recruit such an assassin, it would not have been the first time he used this technique. In 1788 Wilkinson bragged to Governor Miro that he had scared off a Canadian filibustering expedition against Spanish territory by hiring an assassin to threaten the leader of the expedition.[63] Now the opportunity presented itself because Wayne was surrounded by Wilkinson and his acolytes, all of whom would be present throughout the campaign.

However, a broad daylight attack on the Legion commander in the middle of a Legion encampment might have been too much of an overt act, even for Wilkinson. As will be seen, over the course of his career several curious deaths took place involving Wilkinson rivals or persons who could have implicated Wilkinson in betrayal and other nefarious deeds. In the absence of compelling evidence of Wilkinson's direct involvement, however, some historians rely on little more than mere speculation, insisting that because Wilkinson was a bad man, any bad thing that happened in his vicinity or inured to his benefit must have been his doing.[64]

Wayne moved on from Fort Adams, heading for the Indian encampment at Grand Glaize. Unbeknownst to him, Wayne was benefiting from a recent split in the Indian chain of command. Prior Indian victories had been under the joint leadership of Shawnee war chief Blue Jacket and Miami war chief Little Turtle. By the time of the unsuccessful attack on Fort Recovery, however, Little Turtle and his Miami warriors had withdrawn from joint operations, believing that Blue Jacket was relying too heavily on British promises of support.[65] Wayne would thus confront only a portion of the Indian confederation, led by Blue Jacket and British Indian agent Alexander McKee. On August 8 Wayne reached the site of the now-abandoned Indian encampment at Grand Glaize, located at the confluence of the Auglaize and Maumee Rivers, and built Fort Defiance, a name chosen by General Scott, who proclaimed, "I defy the English, Indians and all the devils in hell to take it."[66] The Legion rested at Defiance for a short period of time while Wayne recovered from a recurring attack of gout.

Wayne next chose to move the Legion down the Maumee River toward the British Fort Miami. Lieutenant Colonel Richard England, commander of the British troops at Fort Detroit, chose to heed Indian requests for additional British troops and ordered Major William Campbell to take command of Fort Miami, with a reinforcement of fifty additional redcoats from Detroit as well as a detachment of Queen's Rangers and a squad of Royal Artillery. The British reinforcements arrived on August 9. Wayne and the Legion reached the vicinity of Fort Miami on August 18 and commenced building Fort Deposit and reconnoitering the surrounding territory.

Legion scouts reported that a sizable contingent of Indians was positioned in a large copse of fallen trees approximately two miles south of Fort Miami. Between 1,100 and 1,200 warriors from among the Shawnee, Wyandotte, Delaware, Potawatomi, Ottawa, and Chippewa tribes eventually gathered there. Despite the promise of British aid, almost 10 percent of the force lacked firearms.[67] Also present was a contingent of Canadian militia.

On the morning of August 20 Wayne launched the Legion's attack. Wilkinson commanded the right wing of the Legion, closest to the Maumee. Hamtramck's left wing was ordered to attack the fallen line of trees directly, while Wilkinson's right wing would move toward the trees from the river. The assault would be Wilkinson's first exposure to command of federal troops in combat, and his performance on this battlefield was mixed. While Wayne was later complimentary of Wilkinson in post-battle dispatches to Knox and Washington, during the battle he reprimanded Wilkinson for his lack of attention to his command. Wilkinson had left his troops to see whether he could view the trading post of British Indian agent Alexander McKee. When he spied the trading post he went to report his sighting to Wayne. According to General Scott, Wayne "cursed him, and told him to go to his post."[68] Wilkinson returned to his position in the company of Wayne's aide, Henry DeButts, who was undoubtedly told by Wayne to keep an eye on Wilkinson. Eventually Wayne got his troops aligned and, after repelling one Indian attack, ordered a bayonet charge into the woods, supported by mounted Kentucky militia. The Indians soon broke and retreated for the safety of Fort Miami, only to find the gates of the fort closed and the British garrison ignoring their pleas for help. In disgust the Indians dispersed into the surrounding wilderness.

The entire engagement lasted less than ninety minutes. Legion casualties were relatively light: 26 killed and 87 wounded. Scott reported that his militia had suffered an additional 20 men either killed or wounded. Indian losses were estimated to be 19 killed with a similar number wounded. Canadian militia reported an additional 5 killed, with others wounded and taken prisoner. Wayne rested his command for the remainder of the day, but on the following day he rode with some of his command staff to the gates of Fort Miami. A British officer rode out from the fort and asked to see Wayne, and upon meeting presented a letter from Major Campbell, the fort's commander. The letter described the major's surprise at being surrounded by US troops and demanded to know the purpose of the incursion on a fort belonging to His Majesty, the King of Great Britain. Wayne delayed an answer until the Kentucky militia finished burning the British trading post outside of the fort and then mocked the temerity of the British demand.[69]

Campbell and Wayne both recognized that they were playing a dangerous game, but ultimately both displayed amazing forbearance. While Lord Dorchester and Governor Simcoe were encouraging hostile Indian actions against the Americans, Campbell knew that he had received no formal orders to commence open hostilities between Britain and the United States. Similarly, Wayne had received broad orders that allowed him to attack Fort Miami, but he recognized that such an attack might have significant adverse consequences regarding American and British relations. Wayne also knew that he did not have enough artillery to breach the fort, nor enough supplies to commence a siege. Campbell and Wayne were also probably aware that American and British diplomats were in the process of negotiating the removal of the British forts and that hostilities at one of the contested forts would probably not aid the successful conclusion of the negotiations. Both sides engaged in further written saber-rattling for two more days, then Wayne wisely withdrew his force to Fort Deposit on August 23.

While a relatively small event in terms of the number of troops engaged and the casualties suffered, the Battle of Fallen Timbers had broad repercussions for further American settlement in the Northwest Territory. With the defeat of the Indian confederacy and the tribes' realization that British help would not be materializing, negotiations commenced, ultimately resulting in Wayne's production of the Treaty of Greenville in August 1795. The treaty resulted in the relinquishment of Indian claims to Ohio Territory, paving the way for greater American settlement and Ohio's entry into the union as a state in 1803. It also moved the center of conflict further west, to Indiana and Illinois, where William Henry Harrison and Tecumseh, veterans of the Battle of Fallen Timbers, eventually met in a series of actions that evolved into the War of 1812.[70]

Immediately following the battle, Wayne led the Legion back to Fort Defiance for refit and resupply. Wayne was not happy with the reappearance of Wilkinson ally Cushing, and he refused to place Cushing in a position of responsibility. On September 14 the Legion left Fort Defiance and headed for the villages of the Miami tribe, located at the juncture of the St. Marie and St. Joseph Rivers where they form the Miami River, arriving there on September 18. Wayne commenced the construction of a new fort, eventually named Fort Wayne and placed Hamtramck in command of the fort with three hundred troops. Wayne led the rest of the Legion force to winter quarters at Fort Greenville, arriving there on November 2.

Shortly after the battle, the conflict between Wayne and his disloyal subordinate resumed. On August 28 Wayne had sent a report to Knox on the success at Fallen Timbers and complimented Wilkinson for setting a brave example to the troops.[71] Wilkinson's pen was even faster. On August 24 Wilkinson's own letter to Kentucky senator John Brown, another Spanish conspirator, belittled the victory as a minor skirmish and accused Wayne of overstating the results of the battle.[72] He also falsely accused Wayne of ignoring his wounded men and failing to supply them properly. Wilkinson repeated these misrepresentations the following month in a series of letters to federal judge and fellow conspirator Innes.

By October 1794 Washington was aware of Wilkinson's prolonged effort to remove Wayne. In a letter to Edmond Randolph, Washington expressed his knowledge of Wilkinson's actions and observed that such attacks often "recoil upon the authors."[73] However, despite his knowledge of this disloyalty, Washington did nothing to address Wilkinson's misconduct or even alert Wayne to the false charges Wilkinson was circulating behind his back. Washington's failure to act is inexplicable.

By December, Knox was coordinating communications with Washington and Hamilton regarding Wilkinson's vague charges against Wayne that had begun the previous July. Knox informed Wilkinson on December 5 that his charges were too vague for action but if he wanted to request a court of inquiry and provide specifics, Washington would direct Wayne to hold such an inquest.[74] Knox also informed Wilkinson that he would pass forward Wilkinson's allegations to Wayne. On the same date Knox sent several letters to Wayne, urging him to get along with Wilkinson and to find some way to reach an acceptable compromise.[75] He then proceeded to destroy any hope of reaching such a compromise by revealing to Wayne the charges filed by Wilkinson the previous July, which were supported by an affidavit of the late contractor Robert Elliott (who had been killed by Indians during a supply run to support the Legion). Knox ordered Wayne to convene a court of inquiry if Wilkinson renewed his request, then closed out his correspondence by informing Wayne that he was resigning his position as secretary of war and wished Wayne the best of luck on dealing with his yet unnamed successor.

These letters are a sordid example of Knox's executive cowardice. Anyone even slightly familiar with Wilkinson's character would have understood that no compromise could be reached when dealing with such a treacherous person. Furthermore, the disclosure to Wayne of the disloyal communications between Wilkinson and Knox were sure to enrage "Mad Anthony." Knowing that a crisis of leadership had been present for months within the Legion, and repeatedly failing to address it, was mismanagement by Knox of the grossest form. He compounded this failure by dumping the matter into the laps of the antagonists and walking away, leaving the matter to his successor to resolve.

Wayne exploded upon receipt of Knox's letters. On January 29, 1795, Wayne wrote to Knox, calling Wilkinson a "vile assassin." He accused Wilkinson of being both a British agent and in league with the Spanish, conspiring with Democrats of Kentucky to dismember the union. Once peace was established with the Indians, Wayne wrote, "no consideration would induce me to remain a single hour longer in the service should that worst of all bad men belong to it."[76] Wayne concluded that the fallen tree incident was indeed an attempt at premeditated murder by Wilkinson.

Evidence that Wilkinson was also secretly providing aid to the British is intriguing but inconclusive. Given his known serial betrayal of numerous superiors and colleagues and his double agent status with Spain, it is entirely possible that Wilkinson was also aiding the British, either to further their cause or bring about the failure of Wayne's campaign and his own elevation to replace him.[77] Communications among British officials such as Governor Simcoe and Colonel England, the commander of Detroit, indicate that Wilkinson did carry on some kind of communication with them during the Fallen Timbers campaign.[78]

Upon his receipt of Knox's "Why can't we all get along" missive, Wilkinson appears to have decided to pursue two seemingly contradictory approaches. In a public response to Knox, Wilkinson assured him that he would seek an accommodation with Wayne. Yet on the following day, in a private communication to Knox, Wilkinson revealed the depths of his ill feelings toward Wayne.[79]

For the immediate future it was in the best interests of all parties to avoid a further public squabble. Following the success of the military campaign, Congress was once again demonstrating its shortsightedness by actively considering a reduction in the size of the army, including a reduction in the number of general officers, and a public fight between the army's two top generals could end up costing one or both a position in a downsized army. To protect his interests, Wilkinson began to quietly work with the Jeffersonian party by circulating the idea that a large standing army was not needed to counter Indian raids on the frontier.[80] Wilkinson proposed that local militias would suffice and that he alone had demonstrated skill in commanding militias during the recent Indian campaign. This had direct appeal to Jeffersonians, who objected to a standing army as being unnecessarily expensive and a danger to civil liberties.

With few responsibilities being assigned to Wilkinson by Wayne in 1795, Wilkinson was free to concentrate on his espionage activities while Wayne concentrated on completing negotiations with the Indian tribes that resulted in the signing of the Treaty of Greenville in August. This treaty was one of three successfully negotiated in 1795 that would have a significant impact on Wilkinson and the United States. The second, Jay's Treaty, had caused the British to evacuate the forts that had been contested since the end of the Revolutionary War. This treaty, ratified by the Senate in August after a lengthy struggle between the Hamilton and Jefferson parties over relations with Britain, resulted in increasing tensions between the United States and Great Britain for the next ten years. However, the British withdrawal from the northern forts allowed the United States to focus instead on international issues with France and Spain. The third, the Treaty of San Lorenzo, was signed by the United States and Spain in October. Negotiated by Thomas Pinckney, this treaty accomplished two important matters critical to the western states and territories: it established for the United States a right of navigation on the Mississippi River and opened New Orleans for unrestricted access to trade, and it fixed the border between the United States and Spanish Florida at the 31st parallel north, with Spain relinquishing its claim to portions of Mississippi, Alabama, and Tennessee and agreeing to stop selling arms to Choctaw and Chickasaw Indians.

Wayne's new superior, Timothy Pickering, the new secretary of war, had served as quartermaster general during the Revolution and was first appointed to Washington's cabinet as postmaster general. Pickering's tenure as secretary of war lasted less than a year, however, when he was moved to the position of secretary of state to replace Edmond Randolph. Other than forwarding to Washington the Knox-Wilkinson correspondence of December and January and politely commiserating with Wayne, Pickering took no role in addressing the existing tensions between the two men.[81] However, on April 15, 1795, Pickering sent two letters to Wayne. In the public one Pickering informed Wayne that he had read Wilkinson's charges against him and that he appreciated Wayne's comments but that no further comments appeared necessary. In his private letter Pickering assured Wayne that the president had seen all the sordid communications between Wayne, Wilkinson, and Knox, and that, considering Wayne's victory at Fallen Timbers and the successful negotiation of Jay's Treaty, Wilkinson's scheme to remove Wayne was over: "The development by your letters . . . has presented and confirmed ideas of a certain character *which have destroyed all confidence in him*. This declaration will suggest many thoughts and conclusions, such as you would wish to entertain, & which are too obvious to require to be noted" (emphasis in original).[82] However, though Pickering likely was familiar with the effect Wilkinson's disloyalty would have on the chain of command (having served on the Board of War in 1777 during the Conway Cabal affair), other than suggesting that Wayne entertain "thoughts and conclusions" about Wilkinson, Pickering took no further action.

With the Treaty of Greenville completed, Wayne retrained his focus on Wilkinson and began to examine Wilkinson's rumored paid relationship with Spain. He noticed that Thomas Power, a representative of the Spanish governor and secret Wilkinson messenger and cash courier, was a frequent visitor of Wilkinson. Wayne's scrutiny led Wilkinson to warn Power in November 1795 that he could no longer see Power because Wayne had stated publicly that Power was "a spy for the British, a spy for the Spanish and a spy for some body else."[83]

Wayne now determined to head home to Pennsylvania for the first time in years. Hesitant to leave Wilkinson in command of the Legion, Wayne obtained guidance from Pickering to ensure that Wilkinson would be limited to a caretaker's role in his absence.[84] Wayne called Wilkinson to Fort Greenville and informed him of the restrictions that would be placed on his authority then departed for Philadelphia and arrived there in February 1796. Wilkinson promptly ignored

Wayne's directive and issued a general order to the Legion to "maintain a Uniform System of Subordination and discipline through all Ranks, without Partiality, Prejudice, Favor or Affection," directly implying that such a system had not been in effect under Wayne.[85] While Wayne traveled to Philadelphia, Pickering resigned his position as secretary of war to become secretary of state and Washington replaced Pickering with James McHenry. McHenry, a physician by background, had served in a variety of staff positions during the Revolutionary War and then after the war was involved in Maryland politics. McHenry accepted the secretary of war position after it had been declined by several other candidates. Fort McHenry, of "Star-Spangled Banner" fame in Baltimore harbor, is named after him.

Wayne arrived in Philadelphia in time to participate in the latest congressional debate about downsizing the army. Driven by the Jeffersonians' shortsightedness and antimilitary proclivities, the House voted in April 1796 to reduce the army's authorized strength to 2,000 and to eliminate all general officer positions except for one brigadier general, thereby effectively demoting both Wayne and Wilkinson. The Federalists knew that Wayne would resign rather than accept a demotion, thereby leaving Wilkinson in command of the shrunken army; Wayne vowed to take the fight to the Senate. Major Thomas Cushing, Wilkinson's loyal ally, was also in Philadelphia and wrote a newspaper article alleging that the administration was actively blocking a court of inquiry into Wayne's alleged inadequacies.[86] The Senate, however, supported retaining Wayne as a major general, and a compromise was reached. In June Congress agreed to downsize the army and abolish the Legion as an organization but retain Wayne as a major general and Wilkinson as a brigadier.

In the spring and summer of 1796 Wilkinson worked to perfect a way to communicate with and receive payment from his Spanish masters and to eliminate and replace Wayne as the commander of the army. Wilkinson realized that actions taken to achieve the first goal had to be carefully hidden to prevent it from being used against him in his second goal to remove Wayne. His success at both is a tribute to his use of espionage tradecraft and his ability to trick and manipulate Washington, McHenry, and others.

Prior to his return to the West, in a letter dated May 25 Wayne received instructions from McHenry that Washington had received intelligence that certain foreign emissaries, including Thomas Power, were scouting out US installations in the West and seeking to encourage western states to secede from the union and join forces with a foreign power. These agents were traveling the Ohio River from Pittsburgh down to the Mississippi and into Spanish territory in New Orleans. Wayne was directed to intercept and arrest the group and seize their papers but to act discreetly so as not to alert other conspirators.[87] While the letter did not directly implicate Wilkinson, Wayne quickly drew the conclusion that Wilkinson was conspiring with agents of Spain. He left Philadelphia soon thereafter with the intention of locking down the rivers of communication with Spain and gathering additional information to establish that Wilkinson was a Spanish pensioner. On June 23 Wayne arrived in Pittsburgh and learned that Power had just left the city after publicly proclaiming that Wilkinson would soon assume command of the army. Wayne departed Pittsburgh and arrived at Fort Washington on July 5. He also learned that all three of the alleged spies had recently visited Wilkinson with stacks of documents and that all of them were now headed down the Mississippi. Wayne immediately left Fort Washington for Fort Greenville, where he relieved Wilkinson of command. Before departing from Fort Greenville, Wilkinson reached out to his handler, Gayoso, and urged greater caution in their dealings: "For the love of God, my friend, enjoin great secrecy and caution in all our concerns; never suffer my name to be written or spoken. The suspicion of Washington is wide awake."[88]

Despite these suspicions and his previous support of Wayne, Washington inexplicably chose to lend credence to Wilkinson's continuing charges of Wayne's misconduct and commenced the process of convening a military justice inquiry about Wayne. Since 1794 Wilkinson and his band of officers had been repeating charges of Wayne's mismanagement during the Fallen Timbers campaign in newspapers and in correspondence with prominent Jeffersonians and Kentucky politicians such as Senator John Brown.[89] Washington had repeatedly ignored these charges. In April 1795, Pickering had assured Wayne that the administration had lost all confidence in Wilkinson and would not be proceeding with a court of inquiry or court-martial. Since that time, Wayne had served honorably in negotiating the Treaty of Greenville, while Wilkinson had sulked in a position of idleness, continually repeating the rejected charges against Wayne to his Kentucky cronies and Jeffersonian supporters.

Washington, as the ultimate convening authority of military justice proceedings, could have refrained from lending credence to the allegations of a disgruntled subordinate and suspected traitor. He could have continued to support his loyal subordinate Wayne and refused to give into whatever congressional pressure Wilkinson sought to apply. But Washington had a history of succumbing to political pressure when it came to the convening of military justice proceedings. During the Revolution, he had given in to political pressure brought by Pennsylvania officials in their animus against Benedict Arnold. In an exercise of realpolitik to placate disgruntled Pennsylvania politicians, Washington chose to sacrifice Arnold by convening a court-martial for a few minor charges. Arnold's resulting conviction and sentence of reprimand was the final act that drove him into the arms of the British.

Perhaps Washington thought that a public court-martial and likely acquittal of Wayne would end the matter permanently or serve as a precursor for a court-martial of Wilkinson. If so, he was being extremely naive. As demonstrated by his correspondence with his Spanish handlers, Wilkinson would never have been satisfied with anything short of Wayne's removal and replacement by himself. Furthermore, Washington underestimated the devastating impact the suggestion of charges would have on Wayne, his most successful military commander: Wayne would be forced to defend himself against specious charges brought by a disloyal subordinate who was also likely a paid agent of Spain. Washington knew of the history of Wilkinson's insubordination and strongly suspected his improper relationship with Spain. Washington's choice to lend credence to even minor allegations by Wilkinson must have had a devastating effect on Wayne's morale and health.

Washington began by seeking to obtain the support of his cabinet for a court-martial of Wayne but was confronted by the problem he addressed five years earlier with St. Clair: how do you court-martial the senior general of the army? On July 1 Washington wrote McHenry and asked him to address how officers would be chosen to sit on such a proceeding involving the two top officers of the army. On July 4 McHenry solicited the advice of Alexander Hamilton.[90] Hamilton replied on July 15, recommending against a court-martial but supporting a court of inquiry in which both Wilkinson and Wayne would present evidence before a board of officers and the results of the fact-finding would be sent to the president for appropriate action. Hamilton urged McHenry to "avoid the imputation of evading the inquiry and protecting a favourite."[91] McHenry also solicited the opinion of other senior officials including Secretary of State Pickering, Attorney General Charles Lee, and Supreme Court Justice Samuel Chase, and at the same time extended to Wayne a courtesy that had been denied to Wayne by Knox: he let him know that Wilkinson was still pressing his charges and that Washington was contemplating either a court of inquiry or court-martial. He urged Wayne to "conciliate the good will and confidence of your officers of every rank; even those who have shewn themselves your personal enemies."[92]

Wayne was devastated by the content of McHenry's letter but grateful that he was being given an early warning of Wilkinson's renewed campaign. In his July 28 response, Wayne thanked McHenry for the warning and observed, "It however does not require any great degree of penetration to discover the real Object of the Malignant and groveling charges exhibited by that worst of all bad men, to whom I feel myself as much superior in every Virtue—as Heaven is to Hell."[93]

The course of action open to Wayne over the next few months was clear: he would continue performing his primary duty of accepting the surrender of British posts throughout the Northwest Territory and he would increase his efforts to prove that Wilkinson was a Spanish pensioner. Shortly after arriving at Fort Greenville, Wayne learned that Power had recently left Wilkinson on his way to return to Spanish territory. Wayne promptly reported this visit to McHenry as well as the fact that another of the suspected spies had also been visiting Wilkinson in June.[94] In August, Power was intercepted by a federal patrol on the Ohio River as he was making his way upriver for a delivery to Wilkinson. After a cursory examination by the patrol, Power was allowed to continue upriver to make his delivery to Wilkinson: $9,000 in Spanish cash and documents. Wayne later reported to McHenry that he was chagrined that Power had slipped through his dragnet and that in June and August, Power had met with Wilkinson and Senator John Brown to foment Wayne's removal from command and to support the separation of the western states from the union. He also informed McHenry that, to explain his newfound wealth, Wilkinson was now using a cover story of receiving late payment from Spain for previous commercial transactions.[95]

Having been relieved by Wayne, Wilkinson started his long journey back to Philadelphia, where he hoped that his physical presence and lobbying efforts would encourage Washington to commence military justice proceedings against Wayne. Wilkinson traveled by barge with his wife up the Ohio River and arrived in Pittsburgh in October. At the time he also received the devastating news that John, his eldest son, had died while attending school in Philadelphia. Wilkinson then traveled to Philadelphia, arriving in November and immediately commencing his lobbying campaign against Wayne.

On November 20 Attorney General Charles Lee opined to McHenry that the president, as commander in chief, had both the authority to convene a court-martial of any subordinate officer, including the most senior commander of the army, and the authority to convene a court of inquiry, in accordance with the Articles of War, regarding the actions of any subordinate officer, with or without the consent of the officer.[96] By mid-December 1796 the stage had thus been set for Washington to either direct a court of inquiry regarding Wilkinson's two-year-old charges against Wayne or to begin the process of court-martial of Wayne. While Wayne was hoping to intercept Power or some other Spanish courier in the act of carrying evidence of Wilkinson's collusion with the Spanish, he had yet to catch such a person in the act. However, the expected clash between Wayne and Wilkinson never took place. On December 15 Wayne suffered a bout of stomach pains while visiting a military installation at Presque Isle, Pennsylvania, and suddenly died at the age of fifty-one.

Wayne's untimely death was extremely fortuitous for Wilkinson. He would no longer have to lobby for Wayne's removal or rely on the vagaries of a military justice proceeding to establish grounds for Wayne's removal. Furthermore, to the extent that anyone was investigating allegations of Wilkinson's Spanish pension, with Wayne's passing no one in a position of authority would continue asking questions. Other than tasking Wayne with examining the travels of Power and other suspected Spanish agents and providing an oral warning to surveyor Andrew Ellicott to keep an eye on Wilkinson, Washington took no action to investigate what appeared to be credible allegations of espionage and treason by a senior army official and a renewed attempt by Spain to lure away the western states. Washington would let the matter die with the passing of Wayne and the end of his presidential administration three months later.

Was Wayne's untimely demise a mere stroke of good luck for Wilkinson, or were darker forces at work? One historian has alleged that Wayne's death might have been caused by Wilkinson.[97] Using a motive, means, and opportunity analysis, the historian alleges that Wilkinson was responsible: his motive to kill Wayne had only increased since the August 1794 tree incident, especially since Wayne was the only federal official actively investigating Wilkinson's misconduct; and the means would be poison, based on Wilkinson's medical knowledge and training. But the opportunity is questionable since Wilkinson would have to operate through an intermediary assassin because he was hundreds of miles away in Philadelphia at the time of Wayne's death. A forensic analysis of Wayne's remains today might detect some form of poison, but the available evidence of murder is scant.

Likely because his term was expiring in March 1797, Washington took no act that would stop Wilkinson from assuming the vacant commanding general's position. Legislation passed on the first day of the new Congress eliminated the position of major general, leaving Wilkinson as the ranking officer but at his current rank of brigadier general. Wilkinson later represented to President Adams that in January 1797 he had met with McHenry, asking whether, despite Wayne's death, Wilkinson should still press for a court of inquiry to clear his name. McHenry assured him that no such action would be necessary.[98] The meeting suggests that Wilkinson pressured McHenry and Adams into a compromise—Wilkinson would not continue to press for a court of inquiry if Adams and McHenry agreed to leave Wilkinson in command of the army. Whether by agreement or coercion, Adams and McHenry agreed to the compromise and Adams was sworn in as president on March 4, 1797, with Wilkinson in attendance as the commanding general of the US Army.

6

LAST MAN STANDING
1797–1805

He made intrigue a trade and treason a profession.
—David Leon Chandler, *The Jefferson Conspiracies*

As a result of the legislation passed in 1796, the army that Wilkinson commanded was to undergo significant change. Despite the Jeffersonians' desire to convert the army into little more than an armed constabulary, the new law recognized that a regular army would be needed to man outposts in the West and on the border, to monitor potentially hostile Indian tribes, and to patrol possible hostilities with Spain and Great Britain at the border. In the absence of actual hostilities, the army would be reduced in size by one-third and reorganized into a different structure. The legislation ended the Legion of the United States and established a structure based on regiments under the command of Wilkinson, with the rank of brigadier general. Secretary McHenry commenced a series of regulatory changes to improve the structure of the army and to prevent Wilkinson from turning the army into a personal fiefdom.[1] Wilkinson wasted little time in undermining this attempt at control by commencing a practice of communicating directly with the president without going through the secretary of war. During Wilkinson's fifteen-year tenure as the commanding general of the army he would serve under seven different war secretaries. Given the continuous turnover in the position, Wilkinson had little trouble in vitiating and circumventing most secretarial attempts at control.

Wilkinson's elevation to command of the army also affected his relations with his Spanish handlers, many of whom were suspicious of his loyalty and concerned with the circuitous route that had to be taken to communicate with him. In June 1795 Gayoso shared his suspicions of Wilkinson with Carondolet.[2] Carondolet

shared some of these concerns, but he continued to have faith in Wilkinson's purchased loyalty, which he felt would be driven by Wilkinson's overwhelming vanity.
Following Wilkinson's September 1796 declaration to Carondolet, to create a
cover story regarding his payments from Spain, in April 1797 Wilkinson was informed that his annual pension would be doubled to $4,000 per year.[3] Carondolet
was understandably surprised the following month when he was informed that his
paid agent was planning to move quickly to enforce the terms of the Treaty of San
Lorenzo and insist on the timely release of Spanish forts on the eastern side of the
Mississippi. Carondolet wanted to delay the handover in the hope that Wilkinson
and other US officials on Spain's payroll would be able to reinvigorate the Spanish
Conspiracy, undo the treaty, and realign the allegiance of the western states and
territories. Carondolet directed Thomas Power to meet with Wilkinson to determine his true purpose and "discover, with your natural penetration, the General's
dispositions. I doubt that a person of his character would prefer, through vanity,
the advantage of commanding the army of the Atlantic states, to that of being the
founder, the liberator, in fine, the Washington of the western states."[4] Power was
given the authority to spend up to $100,000 to use in recruiting other western
officials to abandon the United States and align with Spain.

Despite Carondolet's dreams, Power discovered on his way north from New
Orleans that by giving Americans the full right of access to the Mississippi River
and the port of New Orleans, Spain had removed the principal reason for the
western states' discontent. Formerly reliable Spanish pensioners such as Benjamin
Sebastian informed Power that realignment was no longer a popular idea. By
August, Power had reached Detroit, where he expected to meet with Wilkinson.
However, Wilkinson, having noted the shift in public sentiment, chose to distance himself from his Spanish contacts. When Power arrived, Wilkinson was
on an inspection tour of Fort Michilimackinac in northern Michigan and had
directed the detention of Power in Detroit until his return. When they did meet
in September, Power described Wilkinson greeting him "coolly." Wilkinson believed that because of Spanish imprudence, his cover as an agent of Spain had been
blown. He stated that Carondolet's dream of separating the western states was a
"chimerical project" and that Spain's concessions in the Treaty of San Lorenzo
had undermined all of Wilkinson's work on Spain's behalf during the previous
ten years. Wilkinson informed Power that he was destroying his cyphers and that
his "duty and honor" no longer permitted him to work for Spain. Not surprisingly, Wilkinson's "duty and honor" did not prohibit him from asking Power
when the remainder of the outstanding balance on his Spanish pension would
be paid. Wilkinson then had Power sent back to Spanish territory under military
escort.[5]

Power's December 1797 letter to Carondolet detailed a complete description of the order of battle of the new American military establishment under Wilkinson. He provided details on the makeup of each regiment, including all current duty stations and commanders, and observed that the officers were "deficient of those qualities which adorn a good soldier, except fierceness, and are overwhelmed in ignorance, and in most base vices."[6] This valuable intelligence on the current state of the American army could only have come from Wilkinson, its commander.

Power's visit to Wilkinson and other western notables also came to the attention of Andrew Ellicott, a noted astronomer and surveyor who had previously served his nation by plotting out the boundaries of the newly established District of Columbia. Based on this valuable service, Washington picked Ellicott to be the head of the survey team establishing the new boundary between Spanish Florida and the United States.

In addition to providing the United States with free passage on the Mississippi River, the Treaty of San Lorenzo adjusted the boundary between the United States and Spanish Florida, establishing the southern boundary of the United States at the 31st parallel south of Natchez, and required that Spain relinquish territory to the United States, including forts at Natchez and Chickasaw Bluffs (later Memphis, Tennessee). Based on Ellicott's previous work, Washington picked him to head up the American delegation of a joint American-Spanish surveying team that would mark the new border. However, prior to his departure from Philadelphia, Ellicott was given a curious and secret side mission by Washington. Because Washington knew that Ellicott would be interfacing with Spanish authorities and with Wilkinson, who would be assuming command of the surrendered Spanish posts, Washington orally tasked Ellicott with reporting any suspicious activity between Spain and Wilkinson.[7]

Washington's direction to Ellicott was the second "investigation" directed into Wilkinson's supposed relationship with Spain. It was indicative of the sad state of counterintelligence operations being conducted under the Washington and Adams administrations. In the spring of 1796, rumors of Wilkinson's illicit dealings with Spain had caused the Washington administration to commence two inquires. In the first, Secretary of War McHenry warned Anthony Wayne that Thomas Power and other known Spanish agents were contacting officials in the western states and to report any suspicious conduct by these persons. Wayne subsequently focused on the fact that each of the named Spanish officials had met with Wilkinson, and he unsuccessfully sought to apprehend them. Wayne expressed dismay at the fact that Power had eluded his dragnet and he continued to investigate Wilkinson's supposed illicit relations with Spain up to the time of his death. Even though Wayne reported to McHenry that Power had repeatedly met with Wilkinson,

Wayne's inquiry into Wilkinson died with him. No further action was taken by anyone in Washington's administration to further determine if the commanding general of the US Army was a paid agent of Spain.

The second inquiry, launched simultaneously, was to task Ellicott with the responsibility of reporting any suspicious contacts between Spain and Wilkinson. Though Ellicott was a diligent and excellent surveyor, he proved to be a poor choice as a spy hunter. He did uncover certain hints of an untoward relationship between Spanish agents and Wilkinson, but his reports were ignored by his superiors in Philadelphia. Furthermore, despite evidence of Wilkinson's improper relationship with Spain, Ellicott would continue to naively trust him, and Wilkinson in turn repaid this trust by repeatedly undermining Ellicott and his staff and by viciously attacking Ellicott's character when Ellicott's warnings came to the attention of Wilkinson's superiors.

Ellicott first met Wilkinson in Pittsburgh in October 1796 on his journey west to commence the border survey. Wilkinson graciously offered Ellicott the use of a government barge, which would allow Ellicott to travel in style down the Ohio and Mississippi. Ellicott was accompanied on this journey by Phillip Nolan, a close Wilkinson associate, Spanish courier, and money launderer. Ellicott and Nolan eventually became close friends, providing Wilkinson with a window onto Ellicott's activities.[8] When Ellicott arrived in Chickasaw Bluffs and Natchez, he detected Spanish unwillingness to promptly surrender the military posts as well as its hesitancy to participate in the joint surveying activity. At some point Ellicott was introduced to Power, who had been appointed as a Spanish representative to the surveying team. Eventually Ellicott learned of Power's 1797 trip to the western states and its true purpose: to recruit allies for the separation of Kentucky. In June 1797, Ellicott sent a report to Secretary of State Pickering, alerting him to the true purpose of Power's trip and reporting that Wilkinson would be the first person that Power would meet.[9] This report, coupled with the 1796 warning provided by Wayne to McHenry regarding other Wilkinson-Power meetings, should have provided more than sufficient evidence to Secretary of State Pickering, Secretary of War McHenry, and Presidents Washington and Adams that Wilkinson may have had an improper and ongoing relationship with a Spanish agent. Rather than directing a further inquiry, they chose to do nothing.[10]

Ellicott's next warning to Pickering regarding Wilkinson's paid relationship with Spain was less opaque than his June report. On November 14, 1797, Ellicott's second report specifically alleged that he had received information demonstrating that Wilkinson, Senator John Brown, and Judge Benjamin Sebastian were all Spanish pensioners and that Power had been commissioned by the Spanish government to carry payments and communications in cypher to them as part of a plot to detach Kentucky and Tennessee and align them with Spain. Ellicott also alleged that Wilkinson was preparing to lead a body of troops in an invasion of Spanish New Mexico, where he would be involved in the creation of a new empire.[11] While not disclosed in the report, the source of this damning information to Ellicott was Power himself, abetted by Wilkinson's former business partner Daniel Clark Jr.

Power was apparently bitter over his cool reception by Wilkinson in September, and when he returned to New Orleans he sought out Clark. Clark family members were reputed to be Spanish citizens with major commercial investments in New Orleans. Daniel Clark Sr. was a business partner of Wilkinson's from his early trading days in New Orleans. By 1797 the trading business was being run by nephew Daniel Jr., who apparently thought that his future would lie with the United States rather than with Spain. Clark Jr. sought Ellicott's endorsement to be named US consul in New Orleans and wanted to prove his loyalty to his new country by providing damaging evidence against the Spanish conspirators.[12]

Wilkinson immediately recognized the threat this new communication posed to his position. While Ellicott might prove to be a naive messenger, the sources of his message could have proved damning. Clark's business dealings in New Orleans and knowledge of the true nature of Wilkinson's business dealings with Spain put him in a perfect position to expose the falsity of Wilkinson's cover story regarding his pension payments from Spain. To defend against this new threat, Wilkinson chose to reach out directly to President Adams.

In late December 1797 Wilkinson arranged to have Miami Indian chief Little Turtle make a formal visit to Adams in Philadelphia. Wilkinson simultaneously had Little Turtle deliver a letter to Adams in which Wilkinson bemoaned the calumnies that had been heaped on him in return for his loyal service to his country: "To justify to our Country & to the World, your protection of me at the moment, when numerous & powerful Enemies were combined to destroy me, by implications which dare not meet the light, I profess before God & Man, is among the leading Motives of all my Actions." Wilkinson alleged that Wayne's untimely death deprived him of an investigation that would clear his name.[13]

Wilkinson's plea struck a nerve with Adams, who was just completing his first year in office and felt aggrieved by numerous attacks on his own character and competence. In his February 1798 reply to Wilkinson, Adams stated that he had "been tortured for a greater part of the year past with written, anonymous insinuations against several persons in conspicuous public Stations; that they had formed improper connections with Spain, and among others against yourself—It has frequently been asserted, that you held a Commission and received pay as a Colonel in the Spanish Service." Adams concluded his letter by stating, "I shall give not countenance to any imputations unless accusations should come, and then you will have room to justify yourself; But I assure you I do not Expect that any Charge will be seriously made."[14]

Adams's broad dismissal of any allegation against Wilkinson would shield Wilkinson from any inquiry for the remainder of his administration. It is unclear why Adams would provide this assurance to a man he hardly knew. Adams did not participate as vice president in the battle between Wayne and Wilkinson following the Battle of Fallen Timbers, and if Washington felt any lingering concerns about Wilkinson, he apparently did not share them with Adams before leaving office. Adams may also have decided that with growing problems with the Jeffersonians on the domestic front and with France on the international front, he did not need an additional headache to confront. He also may have viewed Wilkinson as a temporary caretaker of the army. Five months later, when relations with France continued to deteriorate and the possibility of war began to rise, Adams ignored Wilkinson entirely and reappointed Washington as the expanded army's new commander, in a position superior to Wilkinson. Wilkinson once again was Washington's problem.

With his Philadelphia flank secure from attack from his enemies, Wilkinson devoted most of his time to administrative matters in running the army. Following his September 1796 meeting with Power in Detroit, Wilkinson decided to move the army's headquarters to Pittsburgh. As a growing western city, Pittsburgh provided a central location between the seat of government in Philadelphia and the western forts located in the Ohio and Mississippi River valleys. Because his wife and family would be accompanying him, Wilkinson wanted to obtain as much comfort as appropriate for the army commander's wife. But because Wilkinson had severed his relationship with Spain, thereby ending the annual $4,000 supplement to his income, he required an alternative source of enrichment. Having demonstrated that he was a poor businessman with no talent for honest commerce, he turned to the next readily available source of income for the army's senior commander: extortion of government contractors. The series of peace treaties entered into by the United States with the major Indian tribes required the annual disbursement of food and supplies and the operation of trading posts located in Indian territories. Since the War Department was the only federal agency actually located near the tribes, disbursement was made through contracts it awarded. Wilkinson saw an opportunity to use his influence, for a price, in the awarding of contracts to favored companies. In at least one instance he approached a contractor seeking to obtain a trading contract and offered "to apprise you of my ready disposition *to enter into your service & of my determination to do it well for you*" (emphasis in original).[15]

In the spring of 1798 Wilkinson chose to again move his headquarters to the newly established Mississippi Territory. Traveling with 400 troops in a grand style in a convoy of twenty-seven boats, Wilkinson visited the fort at Chickasaw Bluffs near Memphis before arriving at Natchez in May 1798. Wilkinson's presence in Natchez would provide an opportunity to communicate discretely with newly appointed Spanish governor Gayoso in New Orleans as well as monitor and meddle in the affairs of Andrew Ellicott, who was in Natchez with the survey expedition. Prior to his departure from Pittsburgh, Wilkinson sent a letter to Gayoso stating, "I dare not communicate with you, nor should you try to do so with me; Marshall has attacked my honor and fidelity. You should not trust the western people, because some are traitors. Fortify your frontiers well. While I remain as at present all is safe. Have buried my cipher, but I will recover it. You have many spies in your country. Do not mention me nor write my name, I implore you in the name of God and our friendship."[16] Wilkinson's close proximity to Gayoso in Natchez and later New Orleans significantly simplified Wilkinson's correspondence with his former handler.

Ellicott continued to plot the newly established border between the United States and Spain as required by the 1795 treaty, and Ellicott and his small staff continued to work to overcome continuing Spanish intransigence. Ellicott's staff included his nineteen-year-old son, Andy; Thomas Freeman, chief surveyor; and Lieutenant John McClary, military escort. By the fall of 1798 tensions ran high among the small survey party. Ellicott disliked McClary for being lazy and the Ellicotts had come to despise Freeman because of his lack of professionalism and inattention to detail.[17] (Ellicott reported to his wife that Andy once had almost challenged Freeman to a duel.[18]) Freeman's side of the argument was somewhat more sordid: he believed that Ellicott was dilatory in his work because of Ellicott's preoccupation with a prostitute that had accompanied them on the expedition.[19]

Wilkinson's appearance in Natchez provided Ellicott with an opportunity to commiserate with Wilkinson about his personnel troubles. Wilkinson, acting in his typical style, saw an opportunity for mischief. He first stated that Ellicott was correct in his mistrust of McClary and that he would remove McClary from Ellicott's staff. Wilkinson then added that Freeman had been in communication with Wilkinson's staff in a manner that violated the new anti-sedition laws. The Alien and Sedition Acts, passed by Congress earlier in the year at the request of the Adams administration, were widely seen as an attempt by Adams to stifle dissent. Wilkinson assured Ellicott that he had more than sufficient grounds to remove Freeman from his staff.[20] Ellicott then fired Freeman and departed Natchez with his new staff to continue his surveying work. No sooner had Ellicott departed than Wilkinson hired Freeman to work as a surveyor on his staff. By purchasing Freeman's loyalty, Wilkinson had obtained a source that he would later use to impeach Ellicott's credibility.

Ellicott did a fine job impeaching his own credibility by reporting Wilkinson's suspicious behavior to Pickering while simultaneously assuring Wilkinson of his belief in Wilkinson's honesty and loyalty. While in Loftus Heights, Wilkinson met with Daniel Clark, who, with Ellicott's support, had been named US consul in New Orleans and was now seeking to become a citizen of the United States. To demonstrate his loyalty to his new country, Clark approached Wilkinson with a plan to seize New Orleans from the Spanish and make it part of the United States. Clark's efforts were in part motivated by a fear that if the United States did not move to seize New Orleans, the French would avail themselves of the opportunity to reestablish their empire in the Western Hemisphere. When Wilkinson declined to support the effort, Clark suspected that Wilkinson was motivated by his continuing loyalty to Spain. Shortly after the rebuff, Power approached Clark with a copy of a letter from Gayoso to Power. In the letter Gayoso informed Power that at a recent meeting between Gayoso and Wilkinson, Wilkinson expressed a concern about his Spanish correspondence. Gayoso stated that the papers were safe and would never be used against Wilkinson if Wilkinson "conducts himself with propriety."[21] Clark immediately passed this information to Ellicott.

In a November 1798 report to Pickering, Ellicott provided the contents of the Gayoso letter, directly avowing that the commanding general of the US Army was being blackmailed into silence regarding his relationship with Spain.[22] Unfortunately, in December 1798, Ellicott proceeded to inform Wilkinson of his letter to Pickering and of the fact that Power was the source of the information.[23] Ellicott asked Wilkinson to hide the fact that Power had been exposed and assured Wilkinson that, if the design of the letter "has been to injure you in my opinion, it has failed in its effect, for in the most material point I am confident it is false."[24] Wilkinson now knew that Power and Clark were behind the current rumors and that he had nothing to fear from Ellicott. Furthermore, considering Adams's February 1798 assurance that he would ignore allegations against Wilkinson unless adequate facts were produced, it is not surprising that Pickering once again chose to ignore Ellicott's warning, particularly since Ellicott himself did not believe it.

Adams's carte blanche exoneration of Wilkinson did not stop Ellicott from gathering additional incriminating facts regarding Wilkinson's paid relationship with Spain, but it did stop Ellicott from forwarding this intelligence to Pickering. In October 1799, Ellicott encountered Spanish captain Tomas Portell, another courier, who informed Ellicott that the 1796 payment to Wilkinson of $9,640 was for Wilkinson's Spanish pension, not a payment for a commercial transaction.

This statement by a credible Spanish official, which would have rebutted Wilkinson's cover story, was never reported by Ellicott until his 1801 letter to Jefferson and his statement at the 1808 court of inquiry.[25]

Wilkinson's decision to move his headquarters down the Mississippi during the summer of 1798 removed him from the discussions that were taking place in Philadelphia about the expansion of the army to address a perceived threat from revolutionary France. Since the 1794 Jay Treaty had solved many of the outstanding areas of disagreement with Great Britain, relations between the two former antagonists continued to improve. Conversely, with the violent overthrow of King Louis XVI of France and the rise of the revolutionary government, relations between the two former allies continued to deteriorate. Though remaining neutral in the growing hostilities between Great Britain and France, the United States insisted on continued commercial relations with both parties. France responded by authorizing privateers to raid the growing American commerce with Great Britain. In December 1796 the French government refused to recognize Charles Cotesworth Pinckney as the new American minister, effectively severing diplomatic relations with the United States. In April 1798 Adams informed Congress about the XYZ Affair, when French foreign minister Talleyrand insisted on the payment of a £50,000 personal bribe and a substantial loan to the French government in order to resume diplomatic relations.[26]

Adams recognized that the United States was poorly equipped to take on the French militarily, either on land or sea. The American army was mostly stationed on the western border and its mission was intended to monitor Indian relations; the American navy had been abolished after the Revolution and no longer had any "blue water" capability. Adams proposed a significant expansion of the army and the creation of the Navy Department to address the threat from France. His proposal was placed before Congress during the growing fight between two emerging political parties: Federalists under Hamilton and Democratic-Republicans under Jefferson. Hamilton and the Federalists were viewed as pro–Great Britain and in favor of a strong central government. The Democratic-Republicans, viewed as pro-France and opposed to a strong central government, including a standing army and navy, generally opposed the expansion of the military to confront the French. Adams, with the support of a Federalist congress, was successful in establishing the Navy Department, which expedited a crash program, commenced in 1794, to build six frigates to protect American commerce at sea. The subsequent "Quasi-War" with France was fought mostly at sea and resulted in a series of resounding American naval victories.[27]

The expansion of the army presented a different set of challenges. Unlike the French naval threat, which was active and ongoing, there was no immediate threat to the United States by French land forces. As Adams noted, "At present there is no more prospect of seeing a French army here, than there is in Heaven."[28] France maintained a significant military presence in the Caribbean, but those forces did not pose an immediate threat to the territorial integrity of the United States. Though coastal fortifications could be improved and expanded, Hamilton and the Federalists also envisioned a significant growth in the size of the army. Ultimately, in the summer of 1798 Congress approved a limited expansion of twelve regiments with 12,000 men; Adams was required to choose new leadership for this expanded force.[29]

Wisely, Wilkinson was never considered for this position and, uncharacteristically, he never appears to have sought it. Instead, Adams concentrated on recruiting sixty-six-year-old George Washington to emerge from under his "vine and fig tree" to head up the "New Army." Washington's selection as the new lieutenant general in command of the army was, to Adams, the clearest and most logical choice. It would also keep command out of the hands of Hamilton, who was viewed by Adams as a political rival within the Federalist ranks. While Adams was pleased when Washington accepted the new position, his hopes were soon crushed when it became apparent that Washington was accepting the position in name only and intended to have the army run by his chosen second in command, Hamilton. Weeks of political infighting followed, with Secretaries McHenry and Pickering actively supporting Hamilton behind Adams's back. Finally, by September 1798 the new command structure was in place with Lieutenant General Washington commanding on paper. Hamilton, as major general, served as the commander of the Northern Department but actually commanded the whole army as Washington's second in command. Charles Pinckney was the major general commanding the Southern Department. Wilkinson remained a brigadier general and reported to Hamilton.

Hamilton's first task was to organize the New Army by recruiting officers, launching a professional training program, and restructuring the military establishment. Many Democratic-Republicans viewed Hamilton's recruitment efforts as a blatant attempt to populate the army's officer ranks with loyal Federalists. In addition to recruiting new officers, Hamilton sought to identify and eliminate Democratic-Republican-leaning officers within the existing force and determined that Wilkinson had the best knowledge of the political leanings of the existing officer corps. In February 1799 Hamilton directed Wilkinson to return "with all practical expedition" to Philadelphia to assist him with the army's reorganization.[30]

Wilkinson was notoriously slow in responding to these directions to return east. In May he was still in Natchez, getting his family settled into Concord, an estate he rented from Gayoso. Hamilton sent a second letter on May 23, urging him to comply with the February directive.[31] Wilkinson finally left Natchez, then visited Gayoso in New Orleans and did not arrive in New York until August 1799.[32] Gayoso died shortly after Wilkinson's departure, and the cause of his death was reported as being either yellow fever or entertaining too heartily with Wilkinson.[33]

Acting completely out of character, Wilkinson did not bristle at Hamilton's promotion over him. Unlike his violent reaction to Wayne's promotion, Wilkinson sought to charm Hamilton rather than undercut him. The two had virtually no prior history of working together. During the Revolution, Hamilton had served on Washington's staff and had been thrust into the Conway Cabal when Gates, aided by Wilkinson, falsely accused Hamilton of stealing the incriminating correspondence that had alerted Washington to the existence of the cabal. While the true source of the correspondence had been Wilkinson's drunken exposure of the plot to Washington's allies, Hamilton seemingly bore no ill will toward Wilkinson for his role in falsely implicating him in the affair. At their first meeting in August 1798, Wilkinson reminded Hamilton of the slanders he had suffered when Hamilton was secretary of the treasury.[34] Such an approach may have struck a nerve with Hamilton and formed a common bond. In the summer of 1797 muckraker James Callender had exposed Hamilton's sordid affair with Maria Reynolds and the illicit payments made by Hamilton to Reynolds's cuckholded spouse. (Callender may have obtained the information from James Monroe, who was upset by Hamilton's role in having Monroe recalled as minister to France. Callender's publication was underwritten by Thomas Jefferson.[35]) The public firestorm unleashed by Callender's screed was further enflamed by Hamilton's own published explanation of the affair in July 1797. Two years later Hamilton still bristled at the controversy and may have been overly sympathetic to Wilkinson's false tale of woe regarding public slanders.

At this first meeting on September 6, Wilkinson also demonstrated his amazing ability to maintain relations with all sides of a political fray. Since returning to New York, Wilkinson had wanted to renew his prior relationship with Aaron Burr. Recognizing that there was a political rivalry between Hamilton and Burr, Wilkinson sought Hamilton's permission before he met with Burr. Hamilton remarked that his disagreements with Burr were limited to politics and that he had no issue with Wilkinson meeting with Burr.[36]

Wilkinson's views on the officer corps and the status and location of the army in the West so impressed Hamilton that the following day in a letter to Adams he endorsed Wilkinson's promotion to major general. Hamilton's missive to Adams demonstrated that he had thoroughly become enthralled by Wilkinson. In the letter Hamilton stated that Wilkinson had served with distinction in the Revolution and had served with distinction under Wayne. Regarding the negative rumors surrounding Wilkinson, Hamilton concluded, "I as well as others have heard hard things said of the General but I have never seen the Shadows of proof, and I have been myself too much the victim of Obloquy to listen to detraction unsupported by Facts."[37]

Hamilton's letter shows how thoroughly he was fooled by Wilkinson's demonstration of loyalty and how desperate he was to obtain Wilkinson's support in instituting change in the current army structure. In addition to blindly repeating Wilkinson's characterizations about himself, Hamilton also represented to Adams that the promotion had the endorsement of Washington and Secretary McHenry. His assurances were a gross overstatement. In June Hamilton had floated to McHenry the idea of promoting Wilkinson and McHenry's response was anything but a glowing endorsement. McHenry begrudgingly informed Hamilton that he would not oppose Wilkinson's promotion but urged Hamilton to first obtain Washington's approval. McHenry's endorsement also contained another significant qualification: "Of this however be assured that until the commercial pursuits of this gentlemen with, and expectations from Spain are annihilated, he will not deserve the confidence of government. Further I recommend it to you most earnestly to avoid saying anything to him which would induce him to imagine government had in view any hostile project, however remote or dependent on events against any of the possessions of Spain."[38]

Simultaneous with his solicitation to McHenry, Hamilton also sought the endorsement of Washington. Hamilton's rationale for Wilkinson's promotion was exceedingly specious:

> I am aware that some doubts have been entertained of him and that his character on certain sides gives room for doubts. Yet he is at present in the service—is a man of more than ordinary talent—of courage and enterprise—has discovered upon various occasions a good zeal—has embraced military pursuits as a profession and will naturally find his interest as an ambitious man deserving the favour of his Government; while he will be apt to become disgusted, if neglected through disgust may be rendered really what he is only now suspected to be. Under the circumstances, it seems to me good policy to avoid all just ground of discontent and to make it in the interest of the individual to pursue his duty.[39]

Regrettably, Washington concurred with Hamilton's shallow rationale regarding Wilkinson's promotion, observing that a promotion "would feed his ambition, sooth his vanity, and by arresting discontent, produce the good effect you contemplate. But in the appointment of this Gentleman, regard must be had to time, circumstances and dates; otherwise by endeavoring to avoid Charybdis we might run upon Scylla."[40]

Hamilton's and Washington's cynical decision to support Wilkinson's promotion is inexplicable. Both men served as able combat commanders during the Revolution and both were aware of Wilkinson's meager record. They knew that Wilkinson had never held a combat command and that his promotion by Gates to brevet brigadier general had prompted a virtual mutiny among other Continental officers. Wilkinson's only other contributions in that war were his dubious and unintentional role in exposing Gates as a participant in the Conway Cabal, his brief service as secretary to the Board of War, and a failed term as civilian clothier-general, from which he was fired. His subsequent military service was equally scant in accomplishments, and his only federal combat role involved open and disloyal warfare with General Wayne, Washington's handpicked commander. Since his reentry into federal military service in 1791, Wilkinson had been constantly suspected of maintaining an improper relationship with Spain. Yet, despite repeated warnings, neither Washington nor Hamilton ever conducted a serious inquiry of it. McHenry's tepid endorsement of Wilkinson's promotion was tempered with yet another warning to conduct a full inquiry into Wilkinson's relationship with Spain and to avoid sharing any intelligence with Wilkinson regarding US plans involving Spain. Instead of heeding this warning, Washington and Hamilton performed no due diligence and chose to endorse the promotion of the minimally qualified general in the hopes that the promotion would purchase his loyalty and prevent future treasonous actions.

None of the doubts or qualifications expressed by Washington, Hamilton, or McHenry were shared by Hamilton in his glowing endorsement letter to Adams. Wilkinson was to carry the letter with him and conduct a personal meeting with Adams in Braintree to seal the deal. Though Adams did receive the letter, there is no record that Adams and Wilkinson ever met in the fall of 1799 to discuss the promotion. If a meeting did take place, it was unsuccessful, because Adams never approved the promotion.

In the fall of 1799, two major developments transpired which obviated the need for three major generals and even for the New Army. First, Adams began receiving reports from numerous sources that France, now under the leadership of Napoleon Bonaparte, was willing to settle its differences with the United States. In October 1799, over the objections of Hamilton, McHenry, and Pickering, Adams sent a peace delegation to France that eventually resulted in the cessation of undeclared hostilities and the reopening of diplomatic relations. A formal peace agreement between the two countries, the Convention of Mortefontaine, was signed in

October 1800. Second, on December 14, 1799, George Washington died, leaving Hamilton as the senior general in the army.

The peace with France combined with Washington's passing made the New Army unnecessary. By the summer of 1800, Congress had reduced the army to an end strength of 3,429 regulars.[41] Neither Adams nor the rising Jeffersonians had any interest in a large military force under Hamilton's command. Although Hamilton was the ranking officer, Adams refused to promote Hamilton to Washington's three-star rank. Tensions between Hamilton and Adams continued to rise in the early part of 1800. In May, fearing their alliance with Hamilton, Adams demanded the resignations of McHenry and Pickering. (Pickering eventually was replaced by John Marshall, who served in the position until he was selected by Adams to be chief justice of the US Supreme Court.) In June Hamilton resigned his commission and commenced open opposition to Adams, and Pinckney resigned his commission and agreed to serve as the Federalist candidate for vice president. Wilkinson was, once again, the last man standing in command of the army.

Following the failure of his promotion efforts in the fall of 1799, Wilkinson once again chose to leave the capital. In November 1799 he returned via New Orleans to his wife and family in Natchez. While en route aboard the USS *Patapsco*, he learned of Washington's death and commiserated his passing in a letter to Hamilton. In addition to expressing his sorrow, Wilkinson once again raised his disappointment at not being promoted: "I cannot anticipate the probable Effect of this misfortune on our profession, but it must be a consolation to those who know you, & particularly the military, to find the chief command in Hands so able to administer the functions of the Station—for myself I cannot more safely consign my own Interests, than to the delicacies & the sensibilities of your own Bosom—20 years a Brigadier, a *patient* one too, I pant for promotion, yet I shall be content with my present Commission, so long as I hold my relative rank" (emphasis in original).[42] Wilkinson was clearly overstating his service when he claimed he had served twenty years as a brigadier general. His actual time as a federal brigadier general was less than eight years.

In January 1800 Wilkinson reunited with his wife in Havana, where she had traveled to meet him.[43] In February the Wilkinsons arrived in New Orleans, where the general met the newly appointed governor of Spanish Louisiana, Sebastian Casa Calvo, and in March Wilkinson and Nancy were reunited with their sons in Natchez.

Wilkinson's stay in Natchez was relatively short. Nancy was apparently tired of living on frontier posts, and arrangements had been made, through the good graces of Aaron Burr, to have the Wilkinson sons enrolled at Princeton University. Wilkinson requested and received a formal naval escort to return east. In

May 1800 the Wilkinsons departed New Orleans on the USS *General Green* and, following a brief stop in Havana, the *General Green* arrived in Norfolk and the Wilkinsons traveled on to Georgetown, part of the new capital city of Washington, DC, on July 21. There Wilkinson met Samuel Dexter, whom Adams had selected to replace McHenry as secretary of war.

Dexter was a career politician from Massachusetts, the first secretary of war to have no prior military experience. He had been appointed to the US Senate and resigned after less than a year to serve as Adams's replacement for McHenry. He served in the position for barely seven months, being moved by Adams to be secretary of the treasury during the last weeks of the Adams administration. Because he had no background in military affairs and did not know Wilkinson, he was in no position to exercise any meaningful oversight over Wilkinson during his brief stint in the War Department.

Wilkinson arrived in the nation's new capital at a tumultuous time. Washington, DC, had become the official new capital in June 1800, and Congress and the executive offices were preoccupied with physically establishing the government in the partially constructed new city. Adams was struggling with the disintegrating Federalist party and the rising Democratic-Republican party under Jefferson. With the first truly contested presidential election rapidly approaching, the Adams-Pinckney ticket faced a ticket comprising Vice President Thomas Jefferson and Aaron Burr. Domestic tensions caused by the Quasi-War with France and the enforcement of the unpopular Alien and Sedition Acts continued to vex Adams's administration. In June, muckraker James Callender was convicted of violating the Sedition Act in a trial before Supreme Court Justice Samuel Chase. Callender had been secretly employed by Jefferson in Richmond as a Democratic-Republican propagandist, and in published screeds he praised Jefferson while decrying Adams as a "repulsive pedant," a "gross hypocrite," and a "hideous hermaphroditical character which has neither the force and firmness of a man, nor the gentleness and sensibility of a woman."[44] Callender was arrested, tried, convicted, and sentenced by Chase to a $200 fine and nine months, imprisonment. He was released on the last day of the Adams administration in March 1801.

Wilkinson's arrival into the chaos of the declining months of the Adams administration provided ample opportunities for exploitation. Wilkinson noted to Hamilton that the written records of the War Department were "greatly deranged and disordered."[45] The cause of the confusion may have been the result of McHenry's swift (and forced) departure, his poor record-keeping, and the transfer of the records from Philadelphia to Washington for the establishment of the new capital. Wilkinson graciously offered to help in tidying up the mess. Since Secretary Dexter was engaged in other matters, the opening gave Wilkinson the opportunity to identify and remove records in the War Department that were critical of him or that may have documented his illicit relationship with Spain. Wilkinson's housecleaning became a purely academic exercise because on November 8, 1800, a mysterious fire swept the War Department, destroying most of its records.[46] Wilkinson's possible role in causing the fire was never established, but he clearly was the beneficiary of the disappearance from the department's files any paper trail linking him to Spain. Shortly after the fire, Wilkinson and his wife decided to leave Washington and travel to army headquarters in Pittsburgh.[47]

Wilkinson also used his time in Washington to renew and improve on relations with Jefferson and Burr. Believing that his role as a Federalist general in the Adams administration was secure, Wilkinson sought to hedge his bets by establishing good relations with the opposing party. Prior to this time Wilkinson had relatively little contact with Jefferson. In 1792, when Washington was consulting his cabinet regarding the selection of an army commander, Jefferson noted that Wilkinson had "many unapprovable points in his character." However, eight succeeding years presented few opportunities for the two to meet. In January 1798 Wilkinson was elected to the American Philosophical Society, where he served with Jefferson on a committee to seek natural history information about North America. In May 1800 Wilkinson dispatched his good friend Philip Nolan to present to Jefferson two supposed Italian busts. Wilkinson introduced Nolan as a person who could provide Jefferson with details about the climate and population in the southwest.[48] (Despite the glowing introduction, Nolan and Jefferson did not meet at this time. Nolan soon left Washington to engage in a filibustering expedition to Texas. He was caught and executed by Spanish authorities, who also cut off his ears and sent them as a gift to the Spanish governor of Texas.[49]) Other than these few contacts, Wilkinson had little interaction with Jefferson before Jefferson's election to the presidency.

By contrast, Aaron Burr and Wilkinson had a long and friendly relationship, having first met during service with the Continental Army in Canada in 1776. Burr was instrumental in getting Wilkinson's sons admitted into Princeton University, Burr's alma mater. In October 1800 Burr suggested to Wilkinson that their future letters should be in cypher.[50] Correspondents in this period frequently used cyphers in their letter communications because the nascent postal service was often unreliable and letters were often intercepted and read by postal officials. By and of itself the use of cyphered communications between the soon-to-be vice president and the army's commanding general would not be viewed as remarkable. But this encrypted correspondence takes on new meaning when viewed in the light of the Burr Conspiracy.

The Wilkinsons spent the holiday season in Pittsburgh in high style. As army commander Wilkinson was easily the most prominent celebrity in the city, and he appears to have enjoyed entertaining with his stylish and fashionable wife. He attended parties and official functions dressed in a pompous uniform of his own design that matched his pompous style of communication. Wilkinson's portrait by Charles Willson Peale from the time shows a heavyset officer dressed in a uniform resplendent with gold braid and facings, gold buttons, and epaulettes. When he traveled by horse, Wilkinson's saddle was placed on a leopard's skin.

Wilkinson was soon making plans to return to Washington to attend the inauguration of the new president, whoever that might be. The internecine battle taking place inside the Federalist party, which set Hamilton High Federalists against Adams's New England Federalists, guaranteed a win for the Democratic-Republicans in the popular vote. Burr's efforts in New York were instrumental in shifting the state behind the Democratic-Republican Party, and that state's vote ensured victory for the Jefferson-Burr ticket. However, due to a deficiency in the Constitution at the time, the Electoral College vote gave an equal number of votes to the two Democratic-Republican candidates, Jefferson and Burr. Democratic-Republicans always intended that Vice President Jefferson would lead the party's ticket and would become president after the election victory. Unfortunately, the tie vote of the Electoral College, giving Jefferson and Burr seventy-three votes each, required the winner to be determined by a vote of the House of Representatives. It is not clear whether Burr sought to exploit the confusion and seize the presidency in a contest before the House or if he merely failed to adequately communicate to Jefferson and others that he would support Jefferson for president. Burr's failure to clearly support Jefferson resulted in Burr's subsequent banishment from any meaningful role in the Jefferson administration. When the final House vote was taken, Jefferson was selected as president on February 17, 1801.

The final two months of the Adams administration were a busy time for both lame duck president Adams and president-elect Jefferson. Adams used the remaining time to fill several outstanding vacancies in the judiciary and in his cabinet. His most notable selection was the nomination and confirmation of Secretary of State John Marshall as the chief justice of the Supreme Court. In January, Samuel Dexter was dual-hatted as secretary of both the War and Treasury Departments, and in February 1801 Adams nominated Wilkinson's son James to be a second lieutenant in the army.[51]

Jefferson lost no time in having his cabinet in place by the start of his administration in March 1801. He selected James Madison, his closest confidant, as secretary of state; Albert Gallatin as secretary of the treasury; and Revolutionary War veteran Henry Dearborn as secretary of war. Dearborn had joined Benedict Arnold on his up-country march to Quebec in 1775, was captured by the British in the failed New Year's Eve assault on Quebec, and was exchanged in a prisoner swap in March 1777. He served admirably as a commander of light troops at the Battles of Saratoga under Arnold and went on to serve under Washington through the British surrender at Yorktown. Following the war he was appointed the first US marshal for the District of Maine and served two terms as a Democratic-Republican congressman. Dearborn's first task as secretary was to implement the new legislation to reduce the army's authorized strength from 5,438 to 3,300 men.

In addition to seeking to frustrate the last-minute appointments made by the Adams administration, Jefferson also sought to remove Federalist officers from the army and replace them with Democratic-Republican loyalists.[52] The new army organization approved by Congress in March 1801 required the elimination of many officers, providing an adequate pretext for the political cleansing. Less than a week after his selection by the House and before his inauguration, Jefferson commenced the process by contacting Wilkinson and asking for the detail of Lieutenant Meriwether Lewis, to serve on the president's staff with Lewis as his personal secretary. Jefferson couched his request as a personal favor; he knew Lewis from their time together in Charlottesville and wanted Lewis to advise him regarding issues related to the western territories and the army.[53]

Wilkinson was undoubtedly alarmed by this request. As the army's commanding general who had spent significant time in the West, Wilkinson believed that he, rather than Lewis, was in the best position to advise the president on western matters and the army. The fact that Jefferson sought out a junior officer and not Wilkinson clearly conveyed to Wilkinson the belief that he had been identified by Jefferson as a Federalist officer destined for elimination. To retain his job Wilkinson would have to demonstrate that he had been a closeted Democratic-Republican all along and was worthy of the new president's trust.

Wilkinson started his chameleon-like charm campaign by seeking to pay attention directly to Jefferson. Wilkinson departed Pittsburgh and arrived in Washington in time to attend Jefferson's inauguration and then sought out social opportunities where he could meet the president, Dearborn, and other prominent officials of the new administration. Less than a week after the inauguration Wilkinson attended a dinner held on Jefferson's behalf at Gadsby's Tavern in Alexandria. In April 1801 Wilkinson issued an order directing the soldiers of the army to cut their hair and eliminate the queue, which had been popular since before the Revolution. Wilkinson's justification was twofold: short hair was healthier and easier for troops to maintain in the field and the queue was thought to symbolize British military style. Wilkinson wanted to demonstrate to Jefferson, a known Francophile, that he planned to model the army on republican France. Wilkinson also tested his status by lobbying to be appointed governor of Mississippi Territory. Winthrop Sargent, the presiding governor of the territory, was in ill health and Wilkinson sought the position through the office of his ally, Senator Samuel Smith of Maryland. (Wilkinson had informed his Spanish handlers that if he obtained the position, he would consider resuming his work for Spain.) His lobbying efforts were unsuccessful and in May 1801 Jefferson chose William C. C. Claiborne as governor.

Wilkinson's charm campaign may also have been stymied by Secretary Dearborn. Dearborn had been a supporter of Benedict Arnold prior to Arnold's treasonous departure. As an Arnold supporter and subordinate at Saratoga, Dearborn was familiar with Wilkinson's betrayal of Arnold in favor of Gates and of Wilkinson's efforts to deny Arnold of any credit for winning the battle. As a combat commander of note, Dearborn also recognized that Wilkinson brought little military prowess to the position of commanding general. While the political culling of officers would take place through the efforts of Meriwether Lewis, Dearborn wanted to get Wilkinson out of Washington and away from command responsibilities. In May Wilkinson was dispatched to supervise roadbuilding in Pennsylvania and construction of the Natchez Trace in Tennessee and Mississippi. When not supervising roadbuilding, Wilkinson was sent on a series of trips to negotiate settlements with various Indian tribes, keeping him away from Washington and the army for the rest of 1801 and much of 1802.

Prior to his departure in May, Wilkinson sought to prevent Andrew Ellicott from reviving his concerns with the Jefferson administration about Wilkinson's Spanish pension. Following Ellicott's last report to Pickering in 1798 of his suspicions, Ellicott had carried on his onerous responsibilities of mapping the border between the United States and Spanish Florida. By the start of the Jefferson administration Ellicott had completed the task and was back in Philadelphia, seeking more than $8,000 in back pay. Knowing that Ellicott was in difficult financial straits and wishing to keep him quiet about Spain, Wilkinson suggested to Ellicott that he would support him for the position of surveyor-general of the Northwest Territory. The position would pay Ellicott $2,000 per year, with an additional $500 per year for a clerical position for his Ellicott's son, Andy.[54] When the offer was finalized in June by President Jefferson, the position had been expanded to that of surveyor-general of the United States. Ellicott ultimately turned down the position, undoubtedly upset by the fact that he still had not been paid for his previous federal job as surveyor of the Florida border. He ultimately accepted a surveying job offered by the government of Pennsylvania, which allowed him to remain closer to his home in Philadelphia.[55]

Ellicott later maintained that in June 1801 he had sent a letter to President Jefferson outlining the details of Wilkinson's illicit relationship with Spain. In the letter he set forth Washington's oral directive to Ellicott to beware of Wilkinson as well as the information he had received from Power, Clark, and Thomas Portell rebutting Wilkinson's cover story, establishing that the $9,640 sent to Wilkinson in 1796 was a Spanish pension and not the delayed return on a commercial investment. The letter has never been found and Jefferson subsequently denied that he had received the letter or any other negative information about Wilkinson until sometime in 1808.[56]

The probable receipt of the letter in 1801, and its subsequent communication to Dearborn, may account for Wilkinson's banishment from Washington and the army for much of 1801 and 1802. However, other than banishment, it appears that neither Dearborn nor Jefferson took any meaningful steps to investigate any allegations against Wilkinson. Their failure to act is as inexplicable as the previous failures of Washington, Knox, Adams, Hamilton, McHenry, and Pickering. Wilkinson was anything but irreplaceable to Jefferson. They had no meaningful prior relationship, and Wilkinson had no embarrassing information about Jefferson or his administration that could be used to coerce Jefferson into keeping Wilkinson. Furthermore, Jefferson's purge of the officer corps provided the perfect opportunity to eliminate Wilkinson and replace him with any other faintly qualified officer who had demonstrated Democratic-Republican loyalty. The only close relationship Wilkinson had with a member of the Jefferson administration was with Aaron Burr, but given Burr's persona non grata status from the outset of the administration, that relationship would have been more of a hindrance than a help and his close relationship with Hamilton and Adams clearly established his Federalist bona fides and should have placed him at the top of the officers to be removed.

In addition to suspicion regarding his loyalty to the Democratic-Republican cause, Wilkinson's loyalty to Spain was known to Dearborn at this time, and presumably to Jefferson as well, despite Jefferson's later denial of harboring any suspicions. In 1802, while banished, he wrote Jefferson, seeking to be made governor of the Mississippi Territory. Jefferson denied the request, stating that it would be improper to hold the position of general and territorial governor simultaneously.[57] Wilkinson then wrote to Dearborn and offered to resign his commission if he could be appointed to the position of surveyor-general. Dearborn denied the request, stating that "such a situation would enable him to associate with Spanish agents without suspicion."[58] It is astounding that Jefferson and Dearborn could believe that his Spanish connection would make him unworthy of a surveyor position but not bar him from command of the army.

A possible explanation for Wilkinson's retention is that Jefferson cared so little for military affairs that he believed that the political effort that would be required to remove Wilkinson would not be worth the expenditure of the administration's time and trouble. By March 1802 the army had been further diminished to an authorized strength of 172 officers and 3,042 enlisted men. The cavalry was eliminated entirely, the artillery was reduced to a single regiment lacking the horses needed to pull the guns, and the infantry was cut to only two regiments. The engineer corps had a mere seven officers and ten cadets. The command staff included only Wilkinson as brigadier general, plus an adjutant, an inspector, three military agents for purchasing, two surgeons, and twenty-five surgeon's mates.[59] The entire force was scattered throughout frontier forts and coastal fortifications, making it incapable of any meaningful large-scale operations. Little was expected from this force, and little was expected from its commander.

In many respects Wilkinson did not even command the army for much of 1801 and 1802. His direction from Dearborn to supervise roadbuilding in Pennsylvania and the building of the Natchez Trace in Mississippi and Tennessee and to conduct Indian relations with the Choctaws, Chickasaws, Creeks, and Cherokees. Together these kept him away from army headquarters and Washington and prevented him from participating in the "chaste reformation" of the army that Jefferson pursued during the first two years of his presidency.[60] As part of this chastening, Meriwether Lewis would be Jefferson's instrument to cull the Federalist officer corps. Lewis had grown up in a wealthy family in Albemarle County, not far from Jefferson's residence at Monticello. Following a brief militia service during the Whiskey Rebellion, Lewis had obtained a commission in the federal army in 1795. Shortly after enlisting Lewis was assigned to a company of riflemen under the command of Captain William Clark; eight years later the two would co-command the famous Corps of Discovery. Following his subsequent assignment to the First Infantry Regiment, Lewis took a leave of absence to attend to family affairs, and upon his return in 1798 was first assigned to recruiting duties in Charlottesville and then promoted to lieutenant and assigned to Detroit as regimental paymaster. In December 1800 he was promoted again to captain and shortly thereafter was selected by Jefferson to serve as his personal secretary. At the time the president's personal staff was exceedingly small and the twenty-six-year-old Lewis would be called on to serve the president in numerous capacities.

One of Lewis's first tasks was to assist Jefferson in the identification of Federalist officers for removal. Jefferson did not entrust this task to Wilkinson, the army commander, for at least two reasons. First, Jefferson did not know Wilkinson well. Prior to his election, Jefferson had little contact with Wilkinson and did not realize how elastic Wilkinson's loyalty could be. Wilkinson's survival under Washington, Adams, and Hamilton suggested that he was a staunch Federalist who would not greatly assist in the removal of Federalist officers. Second, while Lewis's military experience was limited, he was a known commodity to Jefferson. Although

Lewis had barely five years of military experience in minor western posts, he had a genteel background and was a neighbor of Jefferson in Charlottesville. These social contacts likely led Jefferson to believe that he would be personally loyal to him.

Lewis completed his assessment of each of the 269 men serving in the officer corps by July 1801, considering several factors including military acumen, demonstrated performance, and demonstrated loyalty to the Democratic-Republican or Federalist parties. In the list he also noted the worst of the group, those "most violently opposed to the Administration and still active in its vilification."[61] List in hand, Jefferson and Dearborn could commence the removal of officers who were unfit, either militarily or politically. Curiously, while Wilkinson was on the list, Lewis did not set forth an assessment of Wilkinson's military worth or political leanings.

Dearborn recommended significant military cuts that were enacted in March 1802. The same legislation established the US Military Academy at West Point. As this legislation moved through the House, there was a simultaneous attempt to eliminate the position of brigadier general, which would have demoted Wilkinson to the rank of senior colonel. However, through the efforts of Burr, Wilkinson's general officer rank was retained in the final legislation.[62] Wilkinson played no role in the force reduction and was constantly on the move, inspecting roads and conducting talks with Indian tribes. He once again began to suffer significant financial difficulties. He received a brigadier general's salary of $255 per month with an additional allowance of $8 per day when working on Indian relations.[63] The additional per diem allowance was subject to abuse and brought Wilkinson to the attention of War Department accountant William Simmons, who later charged Wilkinson with improperly receiving over $7,000 in compensation.[64] Wilkinson's absence from the seat of power, as well as his economic distress, caused him to approach Jefferson and Dearborn to seek the position of governor of the Mississippi Territory or surveyor-general. His efforts were unsuccessful.

Ironically, a decline in US-Spanish relations literally brought Wilkinson back from the wilderness and into direct contact with Spain and President Jefferson. As the Napoleonic Wars continued in Europe, Napoleon eyed the expansion of French power in the Western Hemisphere. In addition to his disastrous campaign to reclaim the French colony of Sainte Domingue in the Caribbean, Napoleon set his sights on reestablishing a French colony in Louisiana. On October 1, 1800, Spain and France signed a secret treaty that transferred Louisiana to French control. Spanish officials would continue to administer the colony while France made plans to assume control.[65] In an attempt to improve trade for France at the expense of the United States, Juan Morales, the acting Spanish *intendant* in New Orleans, canceled the right of deposit for American goods in New Orleans, thereby once again shutting the port to American trade. Once Sainte Domingue was pacified, French troops under Napoleon's brother-in-law, General Charles Leclerc, would be dispatched to New Orleans to occupy the newly reacquired French territory. However, French hopes for a new Western Hemisphere empire soon turned to dust. Despite the wholesale slaughter of former enslaved persons in Sainte Domingue, Leclerc's troops were decimated by climate, disease, and combat. By the end of 1802 thousands of French troops had died, including General Leclerc.

When the United States learned of the proposed transfer of Louisiana to France, Jefferson sent a delegation to Paris to explore the purchase of New Orleans. In early 1803 the delegation, headed by James Monroe, joined US minister Robert Livingston in Paris to negotiate the sale of New Orleans for $10 million. By the time the delegation arrived in Paris, Napoleon had abandoned his goal of reestablishment of a French empire in America and offered to sell the entire province of Louisiana to the United States for $15 million. Despite the administration's qualms about improperly expanding the power of the executive branch, the negotiators knew a good deal when they saw one and agreed to buy the Louisiana Territory on April 30, 1803. The purchase doubled the size of the United States at a cost of less than three cents per acre. Under the terms of the treaty, announced by Jefferson in July 1803, Spain would formally transfer the territory to France on November 30, 1803, and France would in turn formally transfer the territory to the United States on December 20, 1803.

As negotiations for the transfer progressed, Wilkinson and 500 troops were dispatched to Fort Adams, the US post closest to New Orleans. If the negotiations with France proved unsuccessful, Wilkinson was under orders to seize New Orleans to keep it from falling into French hands.[66] Fortunately, the completion of the purchase agreement made military action unnecessary. However, Wilkinson's close proximity to New Orleans combined with his knowledge of the city made him a logical choice by Jefferson as one of the two US commissioners authorized to accept the transfer on December 20. That day, Wilkinson stood with Mississippi governor William Claiborne at the Place d'Armes in front of the New Orleans city hall and formally accepted the new territory into the United States.

Claiborne and Wilkinson made a poor impression on the departing French officials. Pierre de Laussat, the French commissioner, later communicated his impression:

> It was hardly possible that the Government of the United States should have a worse beginning, and that it should have sent two men more deficient in the proper requisites to consolidate the hearts of the Louisianians. The first, [Claiborne] with estimable qualities as a private man, has little intellect, a good deal of awkwardness,

and is extremely [inadequate to] the position in which he has been placed. The second, [Wilkinson] who has been long known here in the most unfavorable manner, is a rattle-headed fellow, full of odd fantasies. He is frequently drunk, and has committed a hundred inconsistent and intemperate acts. Neither the one nor the other understands one word of French or Spanish. They have, on all occasions, and without the slightest circumspection, shocked the habits, the prejudices and the natural dispositions of the inhabitants of this country.[67]

It is unclear whether Jefferson's selection of Wilkinson was a sign of renewed trust in the banished general or merely the result of the happenstance that Wilkinson, a senior federal official, was already in the area. Whatever the reason, being chosen for this important but largely ceremonial post was an opportunity for Wilkinson to both demonstrate his utility to the Jefferson administration and simultaneously capitalize on his apparent newfound status by reopening his paid relationship with Spain.

The sale resulted in a significant loss of Spanish territory to the United States, but the two countries still maintained significant borders. In addition to the border with Spanish Florida, the Louisiana Purchase created a largely undefined border between the United States and Spanish Mexico. It was clearly in Spain's interest to deter American border explorations that would encroach on the remaining Spanish territory and useful to have an American official who could provide them with insight into American intentions and explorations and minimize American efforts to broadly define the boundary.

While he was awaiting orders at Fort Adams to travel to New Orleans for the ceremonial transfer, Wilkinson made a trip to Pensacola to meet with Vincente Folch, the governor of Spanish Florida. Following the transfer, Folch traveled to New Orleans in February 1804 and had a series of clandestine meetings with Wilkinson. At the first meeting, Wilkinson shocked Folch by demanding a payment of $20,000, which represented an alleged ten-year arrearage in his back pay as a Spanish pensioner. In return for this payment and his reinstatement on the Spanish payroll, Wilkinson offered to provide Folch with a "reflection" that would set forth Wilkinson's recommendations on how to thwart US efforts to explore and defend the new territory. Wilkinson also knew that he was soon to return to Washington to meet with Jefferson and his cabinet, and he offered to use these meetings to obtain further intelligence on Jefferson's plans. (Wilkinson's reflection and Folch's report were discovered in the early twentieth century in Spanish archives in Havana, which became available to American scholars after the Spanish American War.[68])

Wilkinson's agreement with Folch represents one of the greatest intelligence coups in American history. The commanding general of the US Army was offering to use his position to gather intelligence from the president of the United States and provide it to a foreign power. Wilkinson also offered to learn intelligence requirements from his Spanish handlers and gather sensitive information from the highest levels of government, then report back to Spain on an ongoing basis. Recognizing the secrecy that would be needed to maintain his relationship with Spain, Wilkinson urged limited distribution of the written reports that Folch required him to produce and urged reinstatement of his old cover identity as Agent 13.

Wilkinson's reflections and memorials of the 1780s were of a completely different nature. While those observations provided the Spanish with insight into the political issues that affected citizens of the western states and territories and gave guidance for separating the western states, they were the observations of a private citizen. However much they were designed to help the Spanish at the expense of American interests, Wilkinson was still acting as a private citizen and only provided commercial and geopolitical information and gossip to which he had access. By contrast, the 1804 reflection was based on Wilkinson's actual knowledge of US plans and capabilities, obtained in the course of his employment as commanding general of the army. His offer to proactively collect additional intelligence also relied on his unique access as commanding general to the highest levels of government. Unlike his earlier civilian pronouncements, this intelligence was a clear violation of Wilkinson's oath and duty as an American officer.

Wilkinson's action, while heinous, was not technically treason. Treason is one of the few offenses defined in the Constitution. Article III, Section 3, defines it as levying war against the United States or giving aid and comfort to their enemies. While the meaning of the clause was not fully explained until the Supreme Court's decision in *Ex Parte Bollman* during the Burr trials of 1807, the United States was not at war with Spain in 1804 and therefore Spain was not technically an enemy. As a military officer Wilkinson was subject to the Articles of War, and his conduct could be seen as violating several articles, such as engaging in conduct unbecoming as an officer (Section XIV, Article 21) or violating the "general article" (Section XVIII, Article 5). In his 1811 court-martial Wilkinson faced two charges related to his Spanish connections: corruptly receiving money from a foreign power and carrying on correspondence with Spanish officials regarding the dismemberment of the United States. Prosecuting authorities in 1811 were not aware of the 1804 reflection nor of Wilkinson's offer to gather intelligence from Jefferson and his cabinet on behalf of the Spanish.

While Folch was obviously interested in the intelligence that Wilkinson could produce, he informed Wilkinson that he did not have access to $20,000 in available funds. Folch suggested, however, that Spanish boundary commissioner Sebastian Casa Calvo might have funds available for immediate payment. Wilkinson met with Casa Calvo, who agreed to an immediate payment of $12,000. Wilkinson then prepared his reflection in writing and renewed his demand for the full $20,000 in back pay and an increase in his annual pension to $4,000. He also sought a commercial license from Spain that would allow him to personally export sixteen thousand barrels of flour per year to Havana. Upon receipt of the report, Casa Calvo paid Wilkinson the $12,000, which Wilkinson immediately invested in a quantity of sugar that he proposed to take with him when he returned east. Wilkinson's sudden wealth caused rumors to spread regarding new improper payments from Spain, and Wilkinson again defended himself with his well-worn cover for action story about delayed payments from old commercial transactions.[69]

When added to the income Wilkinson received from his earlier Spanish pension payments, Wilkinson's total income from Spanish bribes was over $38,000, which amounts to over $1 million in today's value. This sum makes Wilkinson one of the highest-paid spies in American history.[70]

Wilkinson used his knowledge of the current state of affairs in the Jefferson administration to fashion a course of conduct for Spain that would allow them to best understand the goals and concerns of the Jefferson administration and adjust their approach to relations accordingly. This kind of intelligence would have significant value for Spain in the upcoming negotiations about the border and was made all the more valuable coming from a highly placed American source, the commanding general of the army. (In June 1804, Jefferson dispatched Monroe and future War Department secretary John Armstrong to Madrid to negotiate an agreement over the border.[71])

Wilkinson also played on Spanish fears of threats to its remaining empire in Mexico and South America. He urged the Spanish to preserve control of the Mississippi River to protect Mexico and Peru from "hardened armies and adventurous desperadoes who, like the ancient Goths and Vandals, would precipitate themselves upon the weak defenses of Mexico, and overturn everything in their path, and would propagate in their course the pestilential doctrines that have desolated the most valuable parts of Europe, and which have deprived whole kingdoms of their foundations."[72] While the relevant document was originally thought to have been written by Folch, historian I. J. Cox has established that the document was actually written by Wilkinson.[73]

Wilkinson urged the Spanish to appear firm militarily, because the United States did not want to call up an army to oppose them: "There exists no idea so frightful and odious to the common mass of the people of the United States, as that of seeing a powerful standing army, not only for the expense caused them but more particularly for the danger in which they see their democratic institutions as the result of such measures."[74] He also observed that Americans, besides fearing a standing army, were most concerned about the current state of the public debt. Wilkinson revealed that the acquisition of the Floridas was a major diplomatic goal of the Jefferson administration and Wilkinson urged that Spain could play on the Americans' fears by proposing a deal to undo the Louisiana Purchase. Under his proposal Spain would offer to swap the Floridas and pay a large sum of money in return for the United States' relinquishment of the Louisiana Territory west of the Mississippi.[75]

Wilkinson urged Spain to exploit regional differences within the United States. He observed that if western states and territories grew, it would be at the expense of the established eastern states along the Atlantic seaboard. In a naked demonstration of self-promotion, he also urged that in order to win over Jefferson's cabinet, Spain should "make use of men who enjoy the confidence, intelligence, character, and influence in the government of the United States, in order that the ministry of Spain may make use of the most favorable time and methods to direct the said arrangements or purposes as best conduces to the interests of his Majesty's crown."[76] In order to obtain the services of such men, Wilkinson urged that an annual secret fund be established for bribes, placed under the control of the Florida border commissioner, Casa Calvo. In his reflection Wilkinson hinted that, in the absence of a more permanent vehicle for the funding of future bribes, Spain was in danger of losing his services.[77]

In addition to providing an insight into the current situation in the Jefferson administration, Wilkinson proceeded to reveal a series of strategic and tactical insights that would allow Spain to resist American westward advancement. He urged Spain to strengthen its established posts in Florida, build new forts along the Texas border of the Louisiana Territory, and build a fort in western Florida to control the mouth of the Mississippi, thereby choking off New Orleans. He recommended that Spain covertly support American efforts to resettle the Choctaws, Chickasaws, Creeks, and Cherokees west of the Mississippi because such resettlement efforts were likely to backfire and increase the tribes' hostility toward the United States. Wilkinson urged the Spanish to support the Indian tribes in "destroying every settlement west of the Mississippi."[78]

On a more tactical level, Wilkinson recommended that Spain take immediate action to thwart American explorations and settlements in the Louisiana Territory. While Spain was aware of Jefferson's prior interest in finding a route to the Pacific, they were unaware of the state of Jefferson's ongoing efforts to mount an exploratory expedition. Wilkinson not only confirmed the existence of the expedition but also named Meriwether Lewis as its commander and urged that a warning be sent to Spanish officials in Santa Fe and Chihuahua to dispatch cavalry units to force Lewis to retire or to capture the expedition. He also urged the Spanish to send a force to drive off a settlement that had been established by Daniel Boone on the Missouri River.[79]

Wilkinson's warnings about Lewis were specifically designed to compromise a valued project of Jefferson: an exploration of the western territory to the Pacific Ocean. Since early in his administration Jefferson had promoted exploratory expeditions west of the Mississippi, before it became US territory. As some point after joining Jefferson's "family," Meriwether Lewis was designated by Jefferson to commence planning for one such expedition. Recognizing that much of the expedition would travel through Spanish territory, in 1802 Jefferson reached out to Spain's minister to the United States, Marques Carlos Martínez de Yrujo, to learn whether Spain would permit the passage of an American expedition. Yrujo informed Jefferson, in no uncertain terms, that "an expedition of this nature could not fail to give great umbrage to our Government."[80] Despite this rebuff, Jefferson sought and obtained funds from Congress to conduct such an expedition, even before the Louisiana Purchase had been completed. By the time of Wilkinson's February 1804 meeting with Folch in New Orleans, Lewis's plans were well under way to launching the expedition in May 1804. In addition to gathering supplies and maps and recruiting a staff for the Corps of Discovery, Jefferson arranged for Lewis to meet with noted scientists who could provide valuable information about the western territory and provide technical and scientific skills that would be needed on such a journey. Among those asked by Jefferson to meet with Lewis was Andrew Ellicott, whose expertise in mapmaking and surveying would prove to be of great value to the expedition.

Since many of the staff and all of the supplies of the expedition would be drawn from the army, Wilkinson was aware of the plans that were being developed to launch the expedition and had information on parts of its probable route. He was also aware of the importance of this expedition to Jefferson and the threat it posed to Spanish interests west of the Mississippi. Wilkinson's reflection was designed to appeal to Spanish fears by emphasizing that the expedition would jeopardize Spanish interests in Texas and New Mexico, and he urged the Spanish to "detach a sufficient body of Chasseurs to intercept Captain Lewis and his party . . . and force them to retire or take them prisoners."[81] Wilkinson was urging the Spanish to use armed force in a way that would both compromise United States interests and put American lives at risk.

This was neither the first nor the last time that Wilkinson would urge the Spanish to use force to resist American land expeditions. In 1790, Wilkinson learned that an exploratory party under Major John Dougherty was to be dispatched to reconnoiter a route from Kentucky to New Orleans. Wilkinson contacted Spanish governor Miro and urged him to incite local tribes to attack the expedition.

Dougherty's party was subsequently attacked by Indians and 5 soldiers were killed and another five wounded.[82] While Wilkinson later expressed regret to Miro at the casualties that had been suffered, in the same series of correspondence he also solicited a $10,000 "loan" from Miro.[83]

Wilkinson's February 1804 warning to Folch about the Corps of Discovery had an immediate impact on the Spanish. The following month, Casa Calvo, citing the warning of Agent 13, issued directions to Spanish troops in Santa Fe and Chihuahua to intercept the expedition.[84] Eventually four Spanish search parties, involving 200 troops, scoured the western territories in a fruitless search for the Corps of Discovery.

Other Wilkinson warnings to Spain about American exploratory expeditions met with greater Spanish success. In July 1806 Wilkinson directed his loyal subordinate Captain Zebulon Pike to conduct an exploration of the area that would later become the state of Colorado. The true purpose of the Pike expedition remains clouded in mystery. Some historians have suggested it was a spying expedition for Wilkinson to map out a route to Spanish Santa Fe and that Wilkinson intended for Pike to be captured and taken by the Spanish to Santa Fe, thereby identifying the route.[85] Others have contended it was a covert reconnaissance mission by Wilkinson for the Burr Conspiracy.[86] Wilkinson's son Lieutenant James Wilkinson initially accompanied Pike. However, the younger Wilkinson soon quarreled with Captain Pike and was eventually directed to take a separate party to explore the Arkansas River basin, allowing him to avoid capture with Pike. While on detached service, many of young Wilkinson's troops deserted and he returned east.

Whatever the true purpose of Pike's expedition, based on another alert from Wilkinson the party was captured without violence by the Spanish in February 1807. After bringing the party to Santa Fe, Pike and his soldiers were released and traveled back to report to Wilkinson. Once again Wilkinson demonstrated that he was willing to compromise Jefferson's plans, his oath as an American officer, and the safety of his friends and subordinates in order to obtain favor with his Spanish handlers.

Further treachery was apparent in Wilkinson's betrayal of the Freeman expedition. While the Lewis and Clark expedition was designed to explore the Missouri River to the Pacific, the southern border of the Louisiana Territory remained largely undefined by the terms of the agreement. Jefferson aspired to establish the border on the Rio Grande River, while Spain wanted the border drawn miles to the north and east. The Red River flowed through much of the disputed borderland, and Jefferson understood that an American exploration of this river would greatly assist the United States in perfecting a claim to the disputed land. Jefferson believed that the river and all its tributaries were within the territory purchased by the United States from France. However, not until a year after the departure of the Lewis and Clark expedition did Jefferson finally identify a leader for the Red River exploration. In November 1805 Jefferson summoned Thomas Freeman to Washington and offered him the leadership of the expedition.

When Freeman was fired by Andrew Ellicott from the Florida border mapping expedition in 1798, he was hired by Wilkinson to be a surveyor on his army staff. From 1799 to 1800 Freeman worked for Wilkinson in establishing Fort Adams near Natchez and several surveying jobs in the West, eventually coming to Jefferson's attention. At his dinner meeting with Jefferson, Freeman learned that Jefferson wanted him to lead a new expedition to follow the Red River from Louisiana to its source. Recognizing that the expedition would be opposed by the Spanish, Freeman was directed to return if confronted by a superior force.[87] Similar to the Corps of Discovery, the expedition was rounded out by the addition of other scientists and a military escort. Freeman's expedition was not the first Jefferson-sponsored exploration of the Red River: in 1805 he had encouraged an exploration by William Dunbar, but it, too, was turned back by Spanish authorities based on a warning from Wilkinson.[88]

To avoid diplomatic incidents, most American exploratory parties obtained passports from nations that might be encountered on their journeys. The Lewis and Clark expedition had passports from France and Great Britain, and, unaware of Wilkinson's treachery, Jefferson had sought to obtain a similar passport from Spain but was only able to obtain what he thought was a "quiet understanding" with the Spanish minister. In reality the Spanish did not share this "understanding."[89] Spanish authorities rejected the request, based in part on intelligence provided by a source whose identity needed to be protected but who was "implicitly" reliable.[90] That source could only have been Wilkinson. While Wilkinson was encouraging Jefferson in the exploration of the Red River valley, he was keeping his Spanish handlers informed of Jefferson's goal to explore the border with Spanish Mexico. Furthermore, because a significant portion of the staff of the Freeman expedition was to be drawn from troops under his command, Wilkinson had firsthand knowledge of the makeup of the expedition as well as the timing of its departure and ultimate goal.

In April 1806 the expedition departed Natchez and proceeded up the Red River. On July 28, after having traveled more than six hundred miles, the expedition was confronted by a large Spanish army detachment that had been dispatched to intercept them. Obedient to his orders from Jefferson and heavily outnumbered, Freeman reversed course and returned to Natchez.[91]

This pattern of treachery shows that from 1804 to 1806 Wilkinson sought to serve his Spanish handlers by compromising each of the three major explorations sponsored by Jefferson. The attempted compromise of the Lewis and Clark expedition was unsuccessful, but the other two explorations were halted well short of their goals. While the true goal of the Pike expedition remains unclear, the Freeman expedition was a practical failure in failing to add any meaningful insights into the southwestern border of the Louisiana Territory. Jefferson rightly and proudly promoted the results of the Lewis and Clark expedition but made little mention of the Freeman expedition because of its premature end.[92]

This pattern of treachery demonstrates Wilkinson's willingness to compromise his friends and loyal subordinates, including Lewis, Clark, Pike, and Freeman, in order to satisfy his greed. In return for Spanish gold Wilkinson was also willing to compromise the wishes of President Jefferson to gain a greater understanding of the Louisiana Territory and establish US sovereignty in the region. Though Wilkinson would continue to seek Jefferson's confidence and approval, he was more than willing to betray his prospective benefactor and American interests.

Wilkinson also demonstrated his willingness to use and compromise pawns like Thomas Freeman. Freeman was unaware that Wilkinson had urged Ellicott to fire him, and, once he was fired, Wilkinson turned around to "save" Freeman from the ignominy of Ellicott's dismissal by hiring him as a surveyor on his staff. Wilkinson was then willing to sacrifice Freeman by surreptitiously compromising the expedition Freeman was leading and putting Freeman's life in danger through an armed confrontation with Spanish forces. Freeman remained oblivious to Wilkinson's role in his firing and betrayal to the Spanish, and Freeman went on to support Wilkinson in his vicious attacks on Ellicott during Wilkinson's 1811 court-martial.

Following the official cession of the Louisiana Territory, Wilkinson's role as commissioner ended. Dearborn sent a series of communications to Wilkinson seeking information about the ceremonies and directing Wilkinson to return to Washington. Wilkinson ignored these directions as he negotiated his bribe with Folch and Casa Calvo, wrote his reflection, collected his bribe, and purchased his sugar. Jefferson became concerned about Wilkinson's continued presence in New Orleans and feared that by remaining there he was "turning on us the batteries of our friends in aid of his own."[93] He directed Dearborn to remind Wilkinson that his duties in New Orleans as commissioner had ended upon the completion of the turnover and that he should return to Washington immediately. With his usual lack of alacrity, Wilkinson stayed in New Orleans until April, when the last of the French and Spanish forces departed, and did not arrive back in Washington until June.

When his ship first docked in New York in May 1804, Wilkinson immediately sought to stay overnight at the residence of Aaron Burr. In arranging for the meeting, Wilkinson urged that their meeting be "without observation."[94] In seeking this clandestine meeting before reporting to Jefferson, Wilkinson recognized that he was creating a significant political risk. By this time in his career Burr knew that he had no reasonable political future with Jefferson. On the national level, his break with Jefferson was complete, and Jefferson was moving to have him replaced by George Clinton as vice president in the next election. Burr's future on the local level was also equally dismal because of his recent loss in the New York gubernatorial election. While no record of their discussion exists, it is likely that this secret meeting was the start of Wilkinson's role in conspiring with Burr in what became known as the Burr Conspiracy.

Following his secret meeting with Burr, Wilkinson and his wife left New York, visited their son Joseph at Princeton, and arrived back in Washington in early June. Recognizing that he owed a comprehensive report on his journey, Wilkinson proceeded to repackage his Spanish reflection in a report to Dearborn, presenting a mirror image of the strategic issues that he had described for the Spanish five months earlier.[95] Wilkinson clearly understood that by surreptitiously urging opposing courses of conduct to both Spain and the United States he was creating a significant likelihood of armed or diplomatic conflict between the two countries. Given Wilkinson's position within each of these countries, any such conflict would increase his value both as a source and as a military commander.

Following the delivery of his report to Dearborn, Wilkinson departed to Frederick Town, Maryland, having made it the summer home of the army's headquarters. After suffering long periods in frontier forts and separation from her husband, Nancy Wilkinson was in declining health from tuberculosis. While Frederick Town normally offered a relief from pestilential Washington summers, Wilkinson considered moving army headquarters to Sulphur Springs, Virginia, to allow her to take advantage of the healing waters located there.

Once in Washington in the fall, Wilkinson commenced his next campaign: to obtain an appointment as governor of one of the two new territories that had been created by the Louisiana Purchase. In March 1804 Congress passed a law dividing the newly purchased land into two territories. Orleans Territory, comprising the southern portion of the Louisiana Territory in the area that would later become the state of Louisiana, had its headquarters in New Orleans. Wilkinson saw Claiborne as a rival for this position and commenced an unsuccessful campaign to discredit him. Despite Wilkinson's efforts, Claiborne was nominated governor of Orleans Territory and was confirmed by the Senate.

The second territory was originally known as the District of Louisiana and was made a subdivision of the Indiana Territory under Governor William Henry Harrison, Wilkinson's former subordinate. Louisiana Territory encompassed the remainder of the land gained through the Louisiana Purchase and included all the remaining land surrounding the Missouri and Mississippi Rivers. The size of the new territory proved to be too large for effective governance from Indiana, and in March 1805 Congress voted to split it into the Louisiana Territory and the Indiana Territory, with the new territory having its headquarters in St. Louis. The new territory would become official on July 4, 1805, and would require its own territorial governor.

Wilkinson set his sights on obtaining this position and its $2,000 annual salary, but he wanted it only if he could also maintain his position as commander of the army. Two years earlier, Jefferson and Dearborn had rejected Wilkinson from assuming the governorship of the Mississippi Territory, citing both his ties to the Spanish and the impropriety of holding civil and military commissions simultaneously. Wilkinson had done nothing in the intervening years to lessen suspicions regarding his illicit ties to the Spanish, though objections were not raised by either Jefferson or Dearborn when Wilkinson's nomination for governor was put forward by Jefferson in early 1805.

One possible reason for Jefferson's sudden endorsement of Wilkinson may have involved a bargain Jefferson struck with his departing vice president. Burr, still under indictment for murder in New York and New Jersey following his July 1804 duel with Hamilton, returned to Washington in the fall of 1804 to assume his duties as vice president and rule as presiding officer of the impeachment trial of Supreme Court Justice Samuel Chase. Chase had overseen the sedition trial of James Callender and had also outraged Jefferson through a series of seemingly pro-Federalist judicial rulings. Jefferson wanted to intimidate Federalist jurists by removing Chase through the impeachment process. Obedient to those wishes, the Democratic-Republican controlled House impeached Chase in March 1804 by a vote of 73–32; Chase was then brought to trial before the Democratic-Republican controlled Senate in February 1805, with Burr presiding. Jefferson expected the same unquestioning support from the Senate in convicting and removing Chase. To ensure the conviction, Jefferson repeatedly dined with Burr in the weeks leading up to the trial. He bestowed on the lame duck vice president several patronage appointments in the governments of the newly established territories, including naming Burr's brother-in-law, Joseph Browne, territorial secretary in the Louisiana Territory and Burr's stepson, Bartow Prevost, a judge in the Orleans Territory. (Wilkinson was also seen making repeated surreptitious trips to Burr's boarding-house during Burr's last weeks in Congress.[96])

As a final inducement, Jefferson agreed to appoint Burr's friend Wilkinson to the position of governor of the Louisiana Territory.[97] If Wilkinson's appointment was indeed a subtle bribe for Chase's conviction, Burr failed to deliver on his end of the deal. On March 1, 1805, Chase was acquitted on all counts, and two days later Burr was gone from the vice presidency as Jefferson and Clinton were sworn into office.[98]

Jefferson's decision to nominate Wilkinson to the position of territorial governor in 1805 remains a mystery. While he was certainly familiar with the territory, the conditions that had made Wilkinson unfit for the Mississippi territorial governor two years earlier remained in full effect. Neither Jefferson nor Dearborn had taken any actions to investigate the continuing allegations of Wilkinson's illicit relations with the Spaniards. If Dearborn's fears that Wilkinson's relations with the Spanish made him unfit to be a surveyor, surely such relations would have disqualified him from being governor of a new territory that shared hundreds of miles of unexplored border with Spanish Mexico. Jefferson had previously objected to Wilkinson being dual-hatted as army commander and territorial governor of Mississippi. Inexplicably he now ignored those same objections when naming Wilkinson army commander and governor. Jefferson justified his disingenuous opinion by stating that the Louisiana governor position was primarily a military assignment and therefore did not contradict his previous objection to joint civil and military assignments.[99] Wilkinson had capably performed the ceremonial duties regarding the transfer of the Louisiana Purchase and brought back to Washington important information on the geography of the territory, yet these relatively minor accomplishments could not offset Wilkinson's shallow credentials as army commander and late conversion to Democratic-Republican principles.

Whatever minimal skills Wilkinson brought to the job, he succeeded in sufficiently charming Jefferson and his cabinet into believing that he was qualified for this important position of trust. In a letter to Jefferson, Treasury Secretary Albert Gallatin demonstrated the ambivalent support behind Wilkinson:

> Of the General I have no very exalted opinion; he is extravagant and needy and would not, I think, feel much delicacy in speculating on public money or private lands. In both these respects he must be closely watched; and he has now united himself with every man in Louisiana who has received or claims large grants under the Spanish government. But tho' not very scrupulous in that respect and although I fear that he may sacrifice to a certain degree the interests of the United States to his desire of being popular in his government he is honorable in his private dealings and to betraying it to a foreign country I believe him to be altogether incapable.[100]

Jefferson's decision to select Wilkinson as governor would change the essential nature of their relationship even if he could be considered a holdover from a prior administration. Jefferson might face criticism for not addressing Wilkinson's previous inadequacies, but he could still point to the fact that he inherited Wilkinson from Washington, Adams, and Hamilton. However, once he was selected by Jefferson as territorial governor, Wilkinson would now be identified as "Jefferson's general." Once again, a failure of due diligence by a president regarding Wilkinson's capabilities, let alone his loyalty to the United States, gave Wilkinson even greater opportunities for plunder and treachery. All of Wilkinson's failings as a commander and loyal officer would be exposed, and Jefferson would be drawn into a growing series of questionable actions to ignore, cover up, or publicly support his underling's treacheries.

Following his nomination by Jefferson and his confirmation by the Senate, in April 1805 Wilkinson departed down the Ohio River for his new headquarters in St. Louis and his full-scale entry into the Burr Conspiracy.

7

WILKINSON AND THE BURR CONSPIRACY

1805–1808

> The greatest traitor on the face of the earth.
> —Aaron Burr

> Wilkinson is the only man I ever saw who was from the bark to the very core a villain.
> —Rep. John Randolph

> A scoundrel. . . . Pity the sword at the traitor's belt, for it's doubtless of honest steel!
> —Andrew Jackson

Determining the exact nature and extent of the Burr Conspiracy has proved to be a difficult challenge, both for contemporary observers and many subsequent historians. Because of the varying motivations of the many participants, determining the true nature of the conspiracy resembles the quandary presented in the parable of the blind men viewing an elephant: each observer sees a different creature.

At its core, the Burr Conspiracy was an effort by former vice president Aaron Burr to recapture some lost form of personal glory. Having been rejected by Jefferson from any role in his administration and having lost any opportunity to reestablish himself in New York politics, Burr recognized that upon his departure from the vice presidency he would have to find a new role for his unquenchable ambition. After briefly and unsuccessfully exploring a potential congressional seat in one of the new western territories, Burr decided to craft a plan that could capitalize on the national and international chaos percolating along the United States' western border with Spain. To accomplish his plan, Burr needed the political and economic support of dissatisfied and ambitious western political leaders, financial and military support from foreign countries, and the benign endorsement of the United States. To appeal to the varied interests of these different parties, Burr crafted a multifaceted plan tailored to meet the individual and often conflicting desires of different participants. Burr's plan would succeed only if he could somehow forge an alliance among different forces without letting many of these same participants know that he was proposing different courses of action that were diametrically opposed to other portions of his plot. Ultimately the bold plan failed because he relied on schemers such as James Wilkinson to carry it out.

One part of Burr's plan was to promote a filibustering expedition into the Spanish Floridas and Mexico. Burr would appeal to western political and economic supporters by proposing an expedition that would seize some or all of the remaining Spanish holdings in North America. Under this plan, Burr proposed establishing a new pro-American country that would eliminate Spanish influence and provide a new opportunity for American investment. To avoid any domestic concerns, Burr would represent to certain western politicians, such as Andrew Jackson, that his expedition would be mounted alongside an American declaration of war against Spain. Rising tensions between the United States and Spain over the border between American Louisiana and Spanish Mexico, combined with an American army under the command of James Wilkinson sent to the disputed area, would create the clear impression that Burr's filibustering proposal had the tacit support of the Jefferson administration. Wilkinson's role would be to provoke an incident with Spain that would lead to war, the signal for Burr to launch his filibustering exploit.

To other dissatisfied western politicians Burr proposed leading a newly revitalized version of the Spanish Conspiracy. Burr would seize New Orleans and lead western states along the Mississippi in seceding from the United States, forming a new republic (under himself). Burr approached British minister Anthony Merry to obtain funds and the support of a Royal Navy squadron that would assist in capturing New Orleans and seizing control of the Mississippi. Since diplomatic and economic tensions were rising between the United States and Great Britain, Burr had to carefully avoid discussing with many western politicians his efforts to gain British support. Burr did have numerous meetings with British minister Anthony Merry in 1805 and 1806 regarding this plan, but no British endorsement was ever achieved.[1]

A third variation of the plan was an amalgamation of the first two: Burr would lead a filibustering expedition that would separate the western states and seize the Spanish provinces, creating a new country under his control. This version of the plan had to be hidden from western politicians such as Jackson, who would strongly oppose the separation of western states.

Meanwhile, Burr also proposed a contrary plan to Spain. In a series of meetings with former New Jersey senator Jonathan Dayton and Spanish minister Carlos Yrujo in Washington, Burr and Dayton proposed not only a separation of the western states but also a coup d'état against Jefferson. Burr's proposal to Spain may have merely been intended to provide a cover story to mislead Spanish officials regarding his true actions against them, but it did succeed in having the Spanish pay him $2,500 for his efforts against the United States.[2] Burr's treasonous proposal to the Spanish had to be hidden from the American participants opposed to Spain and who would certainly oppose the violent overthrow of the American government.

During his two-month journey from Washington to New Orleans in 1805, Burr met with numerous western figures and politicians who would be central or peripheral players in the conspiracy. Burr met with Dayton and current Ohio senator John Smith in Cincinnati, then traveled to Frankfort, Kentucky, to meet with Senator John Brown, a longtime member of Wilkinson's Spanish Conspiracy. (Wilkinson also sought to arrange a meeting between Burr and newly elected Kentucky senator John Adair, but their schedules did not coincide.) Following his meeting with Brown, Burr traveled to Nashville and spent several days meeting with Andrew Jackson before returning down the Cumberland River to meet with Wilkinson at Fort Massac on June 8.

Wilkinson commenced his journey from Washington to St. Louis, his territorial headquarters, in April 1805. According to cyphered communications between Wilkinson and Burr, they planned to meet in Pittsburgh and travel together down the Ohio. But Wilkinson was delayed and Burr began the journey without him.[3] (Most of Wilkinson's record of communications between himself and Burr are copies of Burr's letters to Wilkinson. Wilkinson admitted at his 1811 court-martial that he did not maintain any of his letters to Burr.[4]) Wilkinson caught up with Burr on June 8 at Fort Massac at the confluence of the Cumberland and Ohio Rivers. They then spent four days together and Wilkinson prepared letters of introduction for Burr to present to Daniel Clark and Spanish representative Casa Calvo in New Orleans. Burr departed for New Orleans on an army barge provided by Wilkinson and arrived there on June 25.

While in New Orleans, Burr met with Clark and Edward Livingston. Clark, a longtime resident of New Orleans and Wilkinson's business partner, had intimate knowledge of the laundering of Spain's payments to Wilkinson. Livingston was a member of the wealthy New York Livingston clan who had moved to New Orleans after his brother Robert helped to negotiate the Louisiana Purchase. Clark and Livingston introduced Burr to other members of the Mexican Association, a loose-knit group of New Orleans businessmen who favored seizing Spanish Baton Rouge and "liberating" Spanish Mexico. Clark, one of the wealthiest men in New Orleans, pledged financial support to Burr and departed on a reconnaissance mission to Vera Cruz to scout Mexican attitudes and defenses. Burr then retraced his steps north to meet again with Jackson in Nashville before journeying by river to rejoin Wilkinson in St. Louis on September 12.

Upon his reunion with Wilkinson in St. Louis, Burr found that Wilkinson's brief tenure as territorial governor had gotten off to a difficult start. In his haste to leave Washington to assume his new role, Wilkinson had neglected to take the oath of office. In an apologetic letter to Jefferson, Wilkinson admitted this error and explained that his delay in arriving at St. Louis was caused by the need to track down an appropriate official to administer the correct oath.[5] This detour, in addition to Wilkinson's usual lethargic pace, delayed Wilkinson's arrival in St. Louis until July 3. By comparison, Burr's journey from Fort Massac to New Orleans took eight days fewer than Wilkinson's journey to St. Louis, even though it was more than twice the distance.

Upon his arrival, Wilkinson confronted numerous difficulties in adjusting to his dual role as commanding general and civilian territorial governor. He got off to a fractious start with Major James Bruff, the commander of the military garrison at St. Louis. Bruff, a veteran of the Revolutionary War who had served in several posts in the West, knew Kentucky newspapers were speculating about Wilkinson's endorsement of yet another plot to separate the western states and that Wilkinson had met at length with Burr at Fort Massac before his arrival. Wilkinson snubbed Bruff by refusing to attend an arrival-day luncheon prepared in his honor and instead visited with a group of French Creoles. A few days later, following a series of political discussions, Wilkinson referred to a "grand scheme" he was contemplating that would make a fortune for himself and Bruff. When Bruff refused to participate, Wilkinson called him a "damned cunning fellow." Later, when Wilkinson had authorized a military cantonment on swampy and unmilitary ground owned by Wilkinson, Bruff objected to the arrangement. After being severely reprimanded by Wilkinson, Bruff observed, "I replied it was my duty and inclination to obey his military arrangement; but should I discover any *plans or measures* which might put to hazard the peace and safety of the United States, I would not keep silence, be the consequences what they might. He understood me; and from that moment I believe my ruin was determined on" (emphasis in original).[6]

Bruff further aggravated Wilkinson by informing him that it was inappropriate to serve as both civilian territorial governor and commanding general of the army.

Such simultaneous appointment to civil governorships and military commands, however, was not unusual and was at times directed by statute. For example, Arthur St. Clair was appointed by Washington to be both commanding general of the army and governor of the Northwest Territory. Later, William Henry Harrison served as both governor of Indiana and commander of the troops that fought at the Battle of Tippecanoe. William Hull was appointed to be both governor of the Michigan Territory and commander of the troops on the northwest frontier. Bruff recalled that at the time of Burr's return to St. Louis, he met repeatedly with Wilkinson and Judge Rufus Easton. Following these meetings, Easton approached Bruff on Burr's behalf to inquire whether Bruff would be willing to lead an expedition to Santa Fe in Spanish Mexico.[7] Following Burr's departure, Wilkinson informed Bruff that war with Spain was likely and directed Bruff to travel to Fort Adams in Natchez and prepare for an attack on Baton Rouge.

When Bruff and other officers raised questions regarding the propriety of Wilkinson serving in the dual roles, Wilkinson demanded that all of the officers under his command send an obsequious letter to Jefferson, praising Wilkinson as "Generous, benevolent and humane; his heart, his hand, and his purse are ever open, and ready to succor distress and relieve misfortune; hardy, enterprising, daring and brave."[8] Ten of the eleven members of Bruff's subsequent court-martial panel signed the document. The treacly language of the missive is typical of Wilkinson's writing style and suggests that the actual verbiage was written by Wilkinson himself.

Wilkinson again turned to the military justice system to discipline the officers who refused to sign. Court-martial charges were preferred against Bruff, charging him with acting contemptuously toward Wilkinson, which Bruff did not deny. Bruff was convicted by a court chosen by Wilkinson and sentenced to a year's forfeiture of pay. (Bruff appealed the sentence to Jefferson, who subsequently repealed the punishment.) Wilkinson initiated similar military justice proceedings against officers who did not sign the petition. In September he raised allegations made by Major Seth Hunt against Captain Amos Stoddard, commander of the garrison at St. Genevieve, regarding improper land grants. Stoddard requested a court of inquiry, which did clear Stoddard of misdeeds, but the dispute undoubtedly raised tensions among the officers under Wilkinson's command.[9]

Those tensions were on full display in a separate case regarding Major Hunt, who had also raised concerns regarding the constitutionality of Wilkinson's simultaneous appointment as commanding general and territorial governor. Refusing to serve under Wilkinson, Hunt had requested a medical transfer. Wilkinson responded by gathering statements showing Hunt's disrespect, placed him under arrest, and brought a request for Hunt's removal from the army to the attention of

Secretary Dearborn.[10] While awaiting Dearborn's decision, Hunt was challenged to a duel by two other officers, including Wilkinson's son James, who demanded satisfaction for Hunt's alleged insults to his father. When Hunt refused young Wilkinson's challenge, stating that his father was more than capable of defending himself in a duel, a group of officers repeatedly assaulted Hunt in his quarters. Among the assailants was Wilkinson's nephew Benjamin Wilkinson. Following the assaults, young James Wilkinson and another officer intimidated a group of civilians in St. Louis into signing statements in support of Wilkinson. When Hunt challenged the assaulting officers to a duel, Wilkinson intervened and prohibited further fighting. Eventually Dearborn dismissed Hunt from the army, but Hunt's criticisms of Wilkinson were introduced into evidence at Wilkinson's 1811 court-martial. The public quarrel involving multiple members of Wilkinson's family caused certain civil officials to call for Wilkinson's removal as governor.[11]

As Wilkinson quickly provoked conflicts between his supporters and opponents in the officer corps, he also provoked similar conflicts between rival civilian factions. Prior to his arrival, the Louisiana Territory was awash in fights between the traditional French and Spanish Creoles and the newly arrived settlers regarding land grants and trade. Wilkinson was seen as siding with the Creole faction, prompting a series of attacks and growing demands by various civil officials, who contacted James Madison and President Jefferson, alleging misconduct by Wilkinson and demanding his removal.[12] Much like he demanded from his officers, Wilkinson solicited letters of support to Jefferson by civilians.[13] One of the civil leaders opposed to Wilkinson, Judge John B. Lucas, alleged that some of the signatures were collected through intimidation by armed army officers and Wilkinson's relatives.[14]

Wilkinson's second meeting with Burr in St. Louis took place during this rising military and civil tension and may have resulted in a certain coolness between the conspirators. Burr likely learned from Clark about Wilkinson's side deal with the Spanish, leading to concern as to the true nature of Wilkinson's loyalties. Wilkinson also likely learned of the different versions of Burr's proposed insurrection and became concerned with some versions of Burr's plans. The two parted as friends, but there is no evidence of any further direct communications between the two for several months.

Wilkinson's public take on the September meeting with Burr was of course more benign. According to his statement in *Burr's Conspiracy Exposed*, Burr discussed the possibility of a Spanish war and a vague "splendid enterprise," but he provided no details and certainly did not propose anything traitorous.[15] However, in an October 1805 communication that would figure prominently in his 1811 court-martial, Wilkinson sent a vaguely worded warning about Burr to Secretary of the Navy Robert Smith. Later, in a September 1806 letter to Dearborn, Wilkinson appeared to be distancing himself from Burr but also urged that consideration should be given to mounting an American assault on west Florida and Santa Fe, an essential part of Burr's filibustering plan.[16]

Recreating the full context of the conspiracy between Burr and Wilkinson over the next few months is problematic. Wilkinson destroyed or did not maintain copies of his correspondence to Burr, and Wilkinson subsequently produced correspondence from Burr that was either forged or altered to diminish Wilkinson's participation in Burr's schemes. Much of the communication that has been identified was in cypher and contains vague references to "a certain speculation" involving Burr, Wilkinson, Adair, and Dayton.[17] However, certain movements of the conspirators eventually brought the scheme to Jefferson's attention.

In December 1805, Dayton and Burr met in Philadelphia, and at Burr's behest Dayton met with Spanish minister Yrujo. In the hope of obtaining Spanish support, Dayton informed Yrujo that Burr's plot involved the seizure of the president, the vice president, and the president of the Senate, plus the seizure of the funds of the Bank of the United States and the seizure of arms and vessels from military installations in the Washington area. Burr would then take the captured loot and move to seize New Orleans, where he would proclaim the independence of Louisiana and the western states.[18] Burr reinforced the message that the expedition was targeted at the separation of the western states in a final meeting with the Spanish minister in May. Yrujo eventually paid $2,500, primarily to stay in contact with Burr and Dayton as a source of information regarding filibustering expeditions that might be targeted at Spanish possessions in North and South America.

At the same time, Dayton introduced Burr to "General" William Eaton, a colorful former captain in the Legion of the United States who had been appointed as consul to Tunis by President Adams. Following the commencement of hostilities between the United States and Tripoli in 1804, Eaton met with a rival to the pasha of Tripoli. Eaton signed a contract with the rival, was appointed general of the opponent's forces, and led a mixed force of local nationals, eight US Marines, and two navy midshipmen in a six-hundred-mile march across the North African desert, where they seized the city of Derne. (The marines' exploits under Eaton are celebrated in the first verse of the "Marine Corps Hymn.")

Despite Eaton's victory, an armistice between the United States and Tripoli was reached without his involvement, and he returned to Washington, embittered by the fact that his exploits had been ignored in the diplomatic settlement. Eaton also sought reimbursement for expenses that he had incurred as part of his expedition. Feeling abandoned by the Jefferson administration, he soon became the Federalist's cause célèbre. During his meetings with Eaton, Burr described his plan to seize Spanish Mexico and offered Eaton a prominent role in the armed force to be raised. According to Eaton, Burr then expanded on this scheme by proposing Jefferson's assassination and seizing control of the federal government. Eaton was so appalled by this suggestion that he met with Jefferson in early 1806 and suggested that Burr could be dissuaded from his course of action by the appointment of Burr to a diplomatic post in Europe.[19] Jefferson ignored the warning.

This was not the only warning regarding Burr and Wilkinson that Jefferson ignored at this time. In January, Joseph Hamilton Daviess, the Federalist US attorney for Kentucky, commenced a series of written warnings to Jefferson regarding Wilkinson's nefarious relationship with the Spanish government. (Daviess, related by marriage to the Kentucky Marshall clan who were longtime enemies of Wilkinson, was the brother-in-law of Chief Justice John Marshall and was later killed in 1811 serving with the Kentucky militia at the Battle of Tippecanoe.) In early January 1806, Daviess contacted Jefferson, stating that in light of the rising tensions with Spain, Jefferson's appointment of Wilkinson as governor of the Louisiana Territory was ill-considered because Wilkinson was a known Spanish pensioner. Daviess reminded Jefferson that he had previously been warned about Wilkinson by Andrew Ellicott and concluded his letter by saying, "Depend on it; you have traitors around you to give the alarm in time to their friends."[20] Subsequent warnings from Daviess implicated Wilkinson, Burr, and a host of other politicians who were also in the longtime pay of Spain (e.g., Judge Harry Innes and Judge Benjamin Sebastian) or were currently conspiring with Burr and Wilkinson (e.g., Senator Smith from Ohio and Senator Adair from Kentucky). Despite passing on Daviess's communications to Madison and Albert Gallatin, because Daviess identified a number of prominent Democratic-Republicans as possible participants, Jefferson and his cabinet chose to ignore him. In increasingly frantic communications to Jefferson and Madison, Daviess accurately recounted Wilkinson's historic receipt of pay from Spain as well as his current efforts with Burr, and he offered to investigate the ongoing plot were Jefferson to approve his expenses. Jefferson ignored every warning.

Jefferson also chose to ignore the furor caused by a series of sensational stories in a new Kentucky newspaper, the *Western World*. The publication, founded by Federalist journalists John Wood and Joseph M. Sweet and closely tied to Kentucky Federalists, released a series of articles recounting the historical ties of many Kentucky Democratic-Republicans to payments made by the Spanish during the Spanish Conspiracy. The paper linked these historical connections to Daviess's ongoing efforts to warn the Jefferson administration about the ongoing efforts of Burr.[21] The stories, which continued throughout the summer and fall of 1806, sent shockwaves through the Kentucky political establishment and eventually renewed concerns in Washington about Wilkinson's historical ties to the Spanish.

Many of the conspirators endorsed Burr's plans to seize Spanish Mexico only as part of an official US military action against Spain. A steady deterioration in Spanish-American relations in early 1806 caused Dearborn to direct troop movements that unintentionally gave cover to the Burr and Wilkinson story that an official American military movement against Spain, under Wilkinson's command, was imminent.

A lack of precision in the border of the Louisiana Purchase with Spanish Texas created ripe conditions for conflict. While it was informally agreed that the Sabine River would be part of the border, in 1806 Spanish troops moved east of the river in violation of this informal agreement. To address the threat, in March Secretary Dearborn directed Wilkinson to send troops under Colonel Thomas Cushing to Natchitoches and to send most of the troops in the Louisiana Territory to Fort Adams near Natchez, where they would be more readily available to address the Spanish incursion.[22] On May 6, Dearborn directed Wilkinson to leave St. Louis and assume command of all the regular and militia troops in Orleans Territory. Wilkinson was also directed to repel by force all Spanish incursions from west Florida or the Sabine River.[23]

While willing to comply with Dearborn's directives, Wilkinson worried that his reassignment to the Orleans Territory might be the end of his governorship in the Louisiana Territory.[24] On April 28 his ally, Senator Samuel Smith from Maryland, contacted Jefferson and expressed his concern regarding any contemplated replacement of Wilkinson.[25] In his response Jefferson assured Smith that no such move was contemplated at that time and that "not a single fact has appeared which occasions me to doubt that I could have made a fitter appointment than Genl. Wilkinson."[26] By this remarkable endorsement Jefferson indicated his rejection of the warnings about Wilkinson's treachery provided to him by Ellicott in 1801 as well as the more recent warnings of Eaton, Judge Lucas in St. Louis, and US Attorney Daviess in Kentucky. (Smith continued to defend Wilkinson to Jefferson throughout the summer, even when Jefferson finally began to question Wilkinson's role in the Burr Conspiracy.[27]) As the summer progressed into fall, Jefferson found it increasingly difficult to defend his governor and general in light of growing concerns that he was in league with whatever mischief Burr was planning.

Despite the assurance provided by Jefferson to Smith, over the summer of 1806 Wilkinson continued to receive hints that his replacement was imminent. In July former senator Dayton sent Wilkinson an encrypted letter, relaying that Jefferson intended to replace him when the next session of Congress was convened.[28] At the same time, Burr in Philadelphia queried Treasury Secretary Gallatin about rumors regarding Wilkinson's removal.[29] The provision of these rumors to Wilkinson by the conspirators was clearly designed to promote fears in Wilkinson that he would shortly be removed and that he should be prepared to abandon any lingering feelings of loyalty toward Jefferson. Jefferson formally replaced Wilkinson as territorial governor with Meriwether Lewis in March 1807.

On June 11, Wilkinson received Dearborn's May 6 directive to take command of forces in the Orleans Territory, but Wilkinson's usual dilatoriness in complying with directions was further exacerbated by the illness of his wife. Nancy's tuberculosis was worsening and Wilkinson was hesitant to expose her to the swampy climate of the Lower Mississippi in summer. He finally decided to move her to Concord, the mansion they had previously rented from the late governor Gayoso in Natchez, and informed Dearborn of their belated departure from St. Louis on August 2, finally arriving at Natchez on September 8. In his letter to Dearborn, Wilkinson set forth the actions he was taking to repel possible Spanish incursions as well as his own planned strike to seize Mobile and Pensacola were hostilities to break out.[30] He then left Natchez and arrived at Natchitoches on September 24.

While Wilkinson slowly made his way to the Spanish border, perhaps planning to create an incident with Spain that would provide the needed spark for Burr's filibuster or insurrection, Burr gathered men, supplies, and support and commenced his journey to New Orleans and Spanish Mexico. In August his "force" arrived at Blennerhassett Island on the Ohio River, which was to serve as a staging area for boats, men, and supplies. Burr then left the island to journey to Nashville, where he intended to meet again with Andrew Jackson. On his way to Nashville, Burr stopped in Cincinnati to meet with Senator John Smith, where he confirmed that his target was Mexico, unless he was resisted by federal troops at Fort Adams. If Burr encountered resistance there, he proposed to seize the fort before heading on to Mexico.[31] Burr departed Cincinnati and traveled on to Frankfort, where he met with Kentucky senator John Brown, finally arriving in Nashville on September 24. During a series of meetings with Jackson, Burr emphasized that his plan was to counter Spanish aggression. Jackson agreed to gather the Tennessee militia under his command to assist in repelling the Spanish and to build boats to transport troops and supplies under Burr's command.[32] Burr then returned to Lexington, Kentucky, where he met with his daughter Theodosia; her husband, Joseph Alston; and Harman Blennerhassett to plan further movements.

Following his arrival in Natchitoches, Wilkinson initially maintained a belligerent posture with the neighboring Spanish forces. Although he later claimed that the Spanish outnumbered them by a three-to-one margin, in reality Wilkinson's force was significantly greater than the Spanish forces present. In addition to communications with the secretary of war, Wilkinson maintained an active correspondence with many of the prominent conspirators besides Burr. On September 26 he sent a letter to Ohio senator Smith, stating that if negotiations failed, he would need Smith to send a massive force that would enable Wilkinson to march toward the Rio Grande, Mexico, California, and Panama.[33] At the same time, Wilkinson reached out to Kentucky senator Adair, indicating that the time was ripe to subvert the Spanish government. "Unless you fear to join a Spanish intriguer come immediately—without your aid I can do nothing."[34] Wilkinson's call to two senators who were prominent members of the Burr Conspiracy, asking for troops outside of his chain of command to mount a military expedition far in excess of his orders or in any proposal he ever made to Dearborn, is the clearest evidence that as of this date, Wilkinson was fully prepared to support Burr's plan to seize Spanish Mexico.

Events over the following three weeks changed everything. In violation of his orders from his Spanish superiors, the local Spanish commander unilaterally withdrew his troops to the west bank of the Sabine River. Wilkinson continued to send bellicose warnings to the Spanish of his intention to march his troops from Natchitoches to the Sabine. However, on October 29, before reaching the Sabine, Wilkinson proposed to the Spanish a "neutral ground agreement" whereby American forces would be restricted to Natchitoches and Spanish forces would be limited to Nacogdoches, leaving an unoccupied gap in the Sabine River basin. The agreement's sudden acceptance by the Spanish ended the tense confrontation between the two countries and removed the war with Spain as the trigger for the Burr filibustering expedition. Acceptance of the agreement by the Spanish may have been expedited by bribe money provided by Wilkinson. War Department accountant William Simmons alleged in 1810 that Wilkinson failed to account for $16,883 in "secret service" funds provided to him at this time. At the Burr trials Wilkinson denied that any monies were paid to the Spanish.[35] (One source has alleged that it was Wilkinson who was bribed by the Spanish.[36])

Wilkinson's abrupt reversal was driven by the unexpected appearance of Samuel Swartwout in Natchitoches on October 8, carrying encrypted letters to Wilkinson from Dayton and Burr.[37] Dayton's letter was the July 24 letter to Wilkinson, warning him about his imminent replacement by Jefferson. Burr's letter, dated July 29, remains one of the most contested items of correspondence in American history. (Another copy of this letter was delivered to Wilkinson shortly thereafter by Erick Bollman, another Burr associate and Hanoverian national who had previously gained fame in the United States for his attempted rescue of Marquis de la Fayette from an Austrian prison.)

The letter's authorship remains in dispute, with competing theories variously claiming that the letter was written by Burr or by Dayton or it was forged in whole or in part by Wilkinson himself. In the decrypted version of the letter ultimately produced by Wilkinson, Burr announced that he had commenced the "enterprise" and that naval support would be provided by Great Britain and elements of the US Navy. Burr's armed force would rendezvous on the Ohio River and proceed westward with 500 to 1,000 men in boats, where they would meet Wilkinson and consider the seizure of Spanish Baton Rouge. In the most direct linkage to Wilkinson, Burr wrote, "Wilkinson will be second to Burr only. Wilkinson shall dictate the rank and promotion of his officers."[38]

This letter is an unequivocal statement that Burr intended Wilkinson, the commanding general of the US Army, to act as his deputy and not under the orders and directions of Dearborn and Jefferson. It also placed Wilkinson on the horns of a dilemma. Given the multiple schemes proposed by Burr and some of his supporters, Wilkinson was confronted by the fact that, if he agreed to shed Jefferson and sign on as second in command to Burr in a filibustering expedition into Spanish Mexico, he might be signing on to an enterprise that was also seeking to sever the western states and possibly lead to the violent overthrow of the American government. If he stayed true to his oath as an American officer, he would be turning against Burr and a variety of other western politicians whom he had encouraged in their wild scheme to create a new country under Burr's leadership. Recognizing that such duplicity would force him to betray either Jefferson or Burr, Wilkinson ultimately concluded that his best course of action was to stick with Jefferson.

Wilkinson also correctly calculated that his allegiance to Jefferson would provide the necessary support to remain in command of the army and weather the growing concerns regarding his competence as a military commander and his loyalty toward the United States. Wilkinson expected that Jefferson would reciprocate by continuing to ignore attacks on Wilkinson's character out of fear that they would diminish Wilkinson's usefulness in Jefferson's campaign against Burr. Wilkinson correctly guessed that Jefferson would go to extraordinary lengths to protect him from all criticism. Meanwhile, armed with a better picture of Wilkinson's divided loyalties, Spanish minister Yrujo assumed that Wilkinson was primarily driven by greed. Yrujo wrote in January 1807 to his superiors in Madrid that Burr's plans jeopardized Wilkinson's "honorable employment [as US Army commander] . . . and the generous pension he enjoys from the King. These considerations, secret in their nature, he could not explain to Burr; and when the latter persisted in an idea so fatal to Wilkinson's interests, nothing remained but the course adopted."[39]

Wilkinson struggled with his decision over a period of two weeks. Colonel Thomas Cushing, a close friend of Wilkinson, later stated that Wilkinson exposed the contents of Burr's communications and plot to him on October 9, the day after Swartwout's arrival, but Cushing was probably lying.[40] If Wilkinson had been an active participant in the scheme, intending to incite war with Spain as a pretext for launching Burr's filibustering expedition, it is inconceivable that Wilkinson had not previously included Cushing, his loyal subordinate and highest-ranking deputy in Natchitoches, in the plans. Cushing would loyally support Wilkinson through numerous military justice proceedings, and his ardent support was likely driven by the fact that he actively supported Wilkinson in his machinations with Burr. When Wilkinson decided to betray Burr, the loyal Cushing would be willing to fashion a corroborating story that Wilkinson only discovered the true nature of the plot following Swartwout's arrival.

If the commanding general of the army suddenly discovered a massive plot by the former vice president to launch an illegal private expedition against Spain and the western states with the direct involvement of the British government and a potentially mutinous portion of the American navy, why did he decide to do nothing and to say nothing to his chain of command for two weeks after receipt of this explosive disclosure? Knowing that an illegal expedition was being launched in the timetable set forth in Burr's letter, Wilkinson should have immediately arrested Burr's messengers, Swartwout and Bollman, and immediately sent a message to Dearborn and Jefferson that the former vice president was acting illegally in raising an armed force to promote an armed insurrection against Spain, if not the United States. Instead, Swartwout remained unmolested in Wilkinson's camp for ten days and then was allowed to leave. Wilkinson waited two weeks after his receipt of Burr's message before deciding to alert Jefferson to Burr's enterprise.

On October 20, Wilkinson prepared a written message to Jefferson, stating that he had recently discovered that a "powerful association" had been formed to raise 8,000 to 10,000 men in an operation against Mexico. The force would descend the Mississippi, where it would be joined by auxiliaries from Tennessee before reaching New Orleans.[41] The following day, Wilkinson penned another letter to Jefferson in which he promised to reach a compromise with the Spanish and "throw myself with my little band into New Orleans, to be ready to defend that capital against usurpation and violence."[42]

Strangely, a copy of the decrypted version of the Burr letter was not included in his warnings to Jefferson, and neither of Wilkinson's letters revealed the most important fact known to Wilkinson at the time: the direct involvement of the former vice president of the United States. Instead, Wilkinson chose to convey this essential fact through high and unnecessary melodrama. Wilkinson directed his aide, Lieutenant Thomas Smith, to carry Wilkinson's two letters to Jefferson in Washington and orally inform Jefferson that Burr was at the center of the "unlawful or treasonous" plot. To disguise his mission, Smith would need to resign his commission then speedily deliver the message to Jefferson, with the understanding that his resignation would eventually be rejected. Smith performed his mission without incident, with the letters to Jefferson hidden in his slipper.[43] Smith arrived in Washington on November 25, removed his slipper before Jefferson, presented Wilkinson's letters, and informed the president that Burr was the party behind the expedition. Smith later was hand-selected by Wilkinson to serve on the panel of his 1811 court-martial and also testified as a witness at the trial corroborating Wilkinson's defense and voted for his acquittal.

Smith's arrival in Washington could not have come at a more propitious time for Wilkinson. Despite Jefferson's early May assurances to Senator Smith that he had full confidence in Wilkinson, a litany of Wilkinson's misdeeds overwhelmed Jefferson during the following months. In addition to continued complaints from St. Louis officials, Jefferson faced the series of articles in the *Western World* about Wilkinson's ongoing role with Burr as well as renewed concerns regarding Wilkinson's Spanish pension and loyalty to the United States. Dearborn expressed concern that he had not heard from Wilkinson since July and rumors from numerous sources regarding Burr's various movements began to arrive in Washington and with greater frequency.

Finally, on October 16, Postmaster General Gideon Granger wrote Jefferson a letter setting forth statements made to him by "General" Eaton regarding Burr and Wilkinson fomenting unrest in the West. Jefferson had ignored or rejected similar statements from Eaton in the past, but Granger's letter and rumors of Burr's movements forced Jefferson to reconsider the validity of Eaton's claims.[44] Jefferson convened a cabinet meeting on October 22 and, with Madison, Gallatin, Dearborn, and Granger in attendance, tried to determine an appropriate course of action. Their first reaction was nothing short of panic. After recounting the series of warnings they had received from Eaton, Daviess, and others, they were convinced that Burr's goal was the formation of the western states into an independent confederacy. With the cabinet's approval, Jefferson directed western governors to watch for any overt moves by Burr. If any such moves were detected, the officials would be authorized to arrest Burr and any of his conspirators for treason.

Jefferson and the cabinet also expressed a concern that, given the "suspicions of infidelity in Wilkinson being now become very general," combined with Wilkinson's apparent delay in complying with orders to move from St. Louis to confront the Spanish, Wilkinson's loyalty to the United States was in doubt.[45] Following a second cabinet meeting on October 24, Jefferson directed two naval officers, Captains Stephen Decatur and Edward Preble, to repair to New Orleans and assume command of all ships stationed there. Orleans territorial secretary John Graham, who happened to be in Washington at the time, was directed to depart immediately to consult with western governors and to pursue and arrest Burr.

Burr's brother-in-law, Joseph Browne, who had been appointed to be Louisiana territorial secretary under Wilkinson, was to be removed from office. Again, no final decision was reached on Wilkinson.[46] A third cabinet meeting was held the following day but in the absence of any new information that Burr was actively conducting illegal acts, the movement of the naval officers was canceled and Graham's mission was amended: he would follow Burr west and make inquiries regarding Burr's movements, arresting Burr if necessary; place the western governors on guard; and replace Wilkinson as governor of Louisiana.[47]

While awaiting a reply from Jefferson regarding his October 20 promise of loyalty, Wilkinson took several steps to reposition himself as the implacable enemy of Burr's treason. He quickly moved from Natchitoches to Natchez, claiming to prepare defenses against Burr and directing his "little band" of troops to move from Natchitoches to New Orleans to be prepared to repel Burr's suspected thousands of troops that were allegedly soon to descend on the city. Wilkinson wrote another letter to Jefferson on November 12, stating his intention to place New Orleans under martial law.[48] Finally, he dispatched another aide, Captain Walter Burling, to carry a message to Viceroy José de Iturrigaray in Mexico City. To Burling, and ultimately to Jefferson, the trip was described as a reconnaissance mission but, unbeknownst to Burling, the mission's real purpose was set forth in a sealed document that Burling delivered to the viceroy. In the document Wilkinson described his efforts to thwart Burr's filibuster against Mexico: "In order to ward off these calamities, from which sight and mind recoil in horror, I will hurl myself like a Leonidas into the breach, defending it or perishing in the attempt." For this sacrifice on Spain's behalf, Wilkinson asked for reimbursement of $121,000 in out-of-pocket expenses.[49] Wilkinson was unsuccessful in obtaining any money from the Spanish to thwart Burr's invasion. Four months later Wilkinson wrote Jefferson and deliberately misrepresented the true purpose of Burling's trip by stating that Burling was instead gathering intelligence on fostering Mexican independence from Spain. Wilkinson also had the temerity to request that Jefferson reimburse him for the cost of the Burling trip. Eventually Jefferson agreed to pay $1,500.

Jefferson's receipt of Wilkinson's October warnings on November 25 provided the certainty Jefferson needed regarding the loyalty of his army commander and gave him an opening to commence a course of action for addressing Burr's actions.[50] Within forty-eight hours of receiving Wilkinson's messages, Jefferson issued a proclamation to the country, warning about the formation of an illegal filibustering expedition against Spain, urging all western civil and military officials to be vigilant against any such expeditions and to arrest any such participants and seize their goods and supplies.[51] The proclamation made no mention of Burr and contained significantly less information about the plot than John Graham was providing as Jefferson's personal messenger to the western governors. On the same day, Secretary Dearborn authorized Wilkinson to arrest any participants in the plot. However, Dearborn's directive to Wilkinson also indicated the lingering uncertainty in Washington regarding Wilkinson's role with Burr: "There can be no doubt but colonel Burr is generally at the head; but his real object has been so covered, as to prevent any conclusive evidence of his ultimate views. Your name has very frequently been associated with Burr, Dayton, and others; and the new addition of the Old Stories, lately published in Kentucky, served to increase the suspicions now in circulation."[52]

Prior to the receipt of an endorsement by either Dearborn or Jefferson regarding the "defense" of New Orleans, Wilkinson commenced his martial law reign of terror against participants in Burr's plot and any citizen of New Orleans who stood in the way of Wilkinson demonstrating his newfound unquestioning loyalty to the United States. With Orleans governor Claiborne's begrudging assistance, Wilkinson began efforts to uncover Burr's open and covert supporters in New Orleans society. Swartwout and Bollman were arrested without a warrant, denied counsel, and placed on a military transport to face imprisonment and trial in Washington. A surprised Senator Adair, arriving in New Orleans in response to Wilkinson's September summons to assist him in opposing the Spanish, was similarly arrested without a warrant (by 120 troops sent by Wilkinson) and summarily dispatched east for trial, as was Peter Ogden, Dayton's nephew, and James Alexander, an attorney seeking Bollman's release. When Orleans judge James Workman had the temerity to consider habeas corpus relief for some of the conspirators, he, too, was arrested without a warrant.[53]

On November 12 Wilkinson composed another missive to Jefferson explaining the need for martial law in New Orleans and providing further details of the July letter he had received from Burr.[54] Wilkinson's decrypted and altered version deliberately overstated the treasonous aspects of Burr's plot and significantly understated Wilkinson's role in the affair. Another special messenger was selected to deliver the message, which Jefferson received on January 18.

In addition to his military duties, Wilkinson was concerned with the deteriorating health of his wife. In December he moved Nancy from Natchez to New Orleans, where he had established his new headquarters. She was housed in the home of Creole millionaire Bernard de Marigny but died in February 1807 with Wilkinson and their son James at her side.[55] While her passing was noted in some of Wilkinson's private correspondence, it received no mention in his memoirs.

Unaware of his betrayal by Wilkinson and the proclamation issued by Jefferson, Burr and his "armada" of less than 100 men gradually made their way down the

Ohio and Mississippi Rivers. At the same time, Jefferson envoy John Graham was slowly pursuing Burr but was delayed by the need to meet with western governors to spread the alarm. While he obtained the support of each governor he briefed, their subsequent efforts to halt Burr were of no use because Burr had already passed their locations. Equally unaware of either Wilkinson's betrayal or Jefferson's proclamation, in early December federal district attorney Joseph Hamilton Daviess arrested Burr as he passed through Kentucky. Lacking any useful evidence, Daviess was unable to obtain an indictment and Burr was released. (Burr's release was also aided by the efforts of his counsel, Henry Clay, and the opposition of federal judge Harry Innes, a longtime member of the Spanish Conspiracy. Federalist Daviess would be fired shortly thereafter by Jefferson.) By January 10 Burr and his few actual supporters had made their way to Bayou Pierre, thirty miles above Natchez on the Mississippi River. Once there, Burr learned of Wilkinson's betrayal and Jefferson's proclamation. A further attempt was made by Mississippi territorial authorities to charge Burr, but the attempt again failed for lack of evidence. Burr abandoned his descent down the river and proceeded overland for Spanish Pensacola. He was intercepted near Fort Stoddert by troops under the command of Lieutenant Edmund Gaines on February 18 and was sent under military guard to stand trial in Richmond.

As Wilkinson's reign of terror in New Orleans continued and the hunt for Burr and his supporters proceeded to its conclusion, Jefferson felt increasing pressure to provide Congress and the nation with a more complete picture of the possible domestic insurrection. In response to a House resolution, Jefferson issued a message to Congress on January 22 that set forth details of the plot and publicly named Burr for the first time. Unlike his cautious statement made in November, Jefferson now announced that the plot was not only an illegal filibuster against Spain but was also a treasonous conspiracy to separate the western states. Proclaiming Burr's guilt and fugitive status, the message also praised Wilkinson as acting "with the honor of a soldier, and fidelity of a good citizen." Jefferson's statement disclosed Wilkinson's role in unmasking the plot and clearly signaled that Jefferson would be relying heavily on Wilkinson to prove his charge of treason against Burr.[56]

Jefferson's reliance on Wilkinson's credibility appears to have increased over the spring of 1807, but the disclosure of Wilkinson's role in exposing the plot caused numerous persons to inform Jefferson that his reliance on Wilkinson was misplaced.[57] In February, Major James Bruff appeared in Washington to appeal the sentence imposed on him by Wilkinson's 1806 court-martial. In a March 1807 meeting with Dearborn, Bruff again recounted his knowledge regarding Wilkinson's true role with Burr and the Spanish. Dearborn responded that "there had been a time when General Wilkinson did not stand well with the Executive;

but his energetic measures at New Orleans had regained his confidence and he [Jefferson] would support him."[58] Bruff inquired whether an examination of Wilkinson's role in the affair would ever be conducted, and Dearborn replied that any such inquiry would be conducted "after the present bustle was over." Bruff went on to meet with Dearborn a second time as well as with Attorney General Caesar Rodney, insistent about the existence of an illicit connection between Burr and Wilkinson. At a final meeting with Dearborn and Rodney, Bruff recounted all his knowledge regarding Wilkinson's connection to Spain and Burr. While Bruff's information did not diminish their reliance on Wilkinson, Dearborn and Jefferson dismissed the penalty that had been imposed on Bruff by Wilkinson's court-martial and Bruff resigned from the army. If the remission of the sentence was an attempt to purchase Bruff's silence, it was unsuccessful. Bruff testified prominently against Wilkinson's credibility in one of the Burr trials.

In July, Senator John Smith of Ohio contacted Jefferson and informed him that although he was a friend of Wilkinson, he had recently learned of information possessed by Federalists that Wilkinson had been on the Spanish payroll for years and that the Federalists were hoping to ambush Jefferson with the information.[59] By this time Smith was under indictment as a Burr conspirator, so Jefferson might be excused for ignoring Smith's warning. Taken in context, however, it was yet another in a series of warnings received by Jefferson from multiple parties that it was foolish to rely on Wilkinson's credibility. (Smith, one of Ohio's first senators, was indicted in Richmond with Burr. Although the charges against him were dismissed following Burr's acquittal, the Senate commenced proceedings to have him expelled from the Senate. The resolution failed to pass by a one-vote margin, and Smith resigned from the Senate in disgrace in April 1808.)

Wilkinson recognized that in being cast as Jefferson's champion in the campaign to discredit and convict Burr, he would be subjected to relentless attacks by the conspirators he had betrayed and that his paid relationship with Spain needed to remain completely hidden. Since Daniel Clark was unwilling to have his own relationship with Burr exposed, Wilkinson believed that Clark would not expose the true nature of his Spanish payments. Nevertheless, Wilkinson reached out to Spanish governor Vincente Folch and obtained a declaration falsely stating that Folch was not aware of any document in Spanish archives that would show that Wilkinson was a Spanish pensioner.[60] This was the first in a series of times that Folch would be called on by Wilkinson to lie to American officials in order to protect the identity and activities of his most valuable American agent. Wilkinson eventually reached out to Thomas Power and obtained yet another statement denying Wilkinson's paid relationship with Spain.[61] (Power provided the statement to Wilkinson with the understanding that it would only be shown to Jefferson and never published. Wilkinson subsequently reneged on this promise, turning Power into an enemy.) Having repelled Burr's faux invasion, Wilkinson left New Orleans on April 20 and commenced his three-month journey to appear as Jefferson's star witness in the Richmond trials of Aaron Burr.

The Burr Conspiracy trials presented the ultimate clash between Jefferson and Burr in the greatest criminal trial of the early republic. Both sides were represented by the finest American legal minds of the early nineteenth century. The trial explored a host of legal issues—the definition of treason, the concept of executive privilege, and the role of the courts in subjecting the executive branch to judicial process—that continue to affect American jurisprudence today. The conflict also cast Jefferson in the personal role as the primary accuser against Burr. In this capacity Jefferson publicly proclaimed Burr's guilt before trial, personally interrogated witnesses, offered grants of immunity, and directed trial strategy, all in an unremitting campaign to convict Burr of some crime, somewhere, in retaliation for Burr's betrayal. The ultimate outcome of the case demonstrated both Jefferson's willingness to abuse the power of the presidency to convict his enemy and the strength of the new constitution's ability to protect the country from the overreach of executive authority.

Much of the legal drama had already played out before the arrival of Burr and Wilkinson in Richmond. As a result of Wilkinson's illegal actions to seize the conspirators without a warrant and ship them east for trial, many of Burr's codefendants, including Swartwout, Bollman, Ogden, Alexander, and Adair, had their initial court appearances prior to the start of the Burr trials in Richmond. Using the process of the "Great Writ" of habeas corpus, each challenged the authority of Wilkinson to arrest them without a warrant and the authority of Jefferson to hold them incommunicado on felony charges of treason, for seeking to separate the western states, and on misdemeanor charges of violating the Neutrality Act of 1794 for mounting a filibustering expedition against Spanish Mexico.

On January 23, the day after his statement to Congress, Jefferson agreed to meet with Erick Bollman, who was imprisoned in a cell in the marine barracks in Washington. Jefferson was accompanied by Secretary of State Madison, to serve as a witness to the meeting. The meeting was unique in the history of American criminal law: an imprisoned defendant, facing federal criminal charges, was interrogated by the president of the United States, while the secretary of state took notes. Jefferson clearly wanted and expected Bollman to produce firsthand evidence of Burr's treasonous plot. According to Madison's notes of the meeting, in order to induce Bollman's cooperation, Jefferson personally promised Bollman that nothing he said to the president would be used in evidence against him.[62] Having received this promise of immunity, Bollman proceeded to provide a version of the story that Jefferson did not want to hear.

According to Madison, Bollman related that the sole purpose of the Burr expedition was as a filibustering campaign. Troops, money, and supplies were raised solely to support Burr's effort to seize Spanish Mexico and install Burr as the new king of Mexico, "the people not being fit for a republican government." At no time did the expedition have as its target the separation of the western states from the union. Bollman admitted that he was aware of the fact that Burr had represented to Spanish minister Yrujo that the purpose was to overthrow the federal government, but this was meant to dupe the minister from divining the real purpose of the plot. Bollman also explicitly informed Jefferson about Wilkinson's role in the plot. Burr had informed Bollman that, once the filibuster had commenced, Wilkinson would resign his commission and assume command of Burr's troops. The following day, Jefferson again repeated his pledge of immunity for Bollman, on "his word of honor that they shall never be used against himself [Bollman]," and asked Bollman to provide a full written statement.[63] Bollman submitted to Jefferson a detailed written statement which again only established that Burr's plot was a filibuster and not an insurrection against the US government.[64]

At a minimum Bollman's statement significantly undercut Jefferson's case that Burr was engaged in felonious treason, an idea primarily built on Wilkinson's statements to Jefferson. It also provided yet another reason for Jefferson to question Wilkinson's loyalty and credibility. Rather than engaging in a careful examination of the evidence at hand, Jefferson doubled down on Wilkinson's version of the facts. On January 30, he personally delivered Wilkinson's December 26 affidavit to federal district attorney Walter Jones and ordered him to file felony treason and misdemeanor Neutrality Act charges against Bollman and Swartwout.[65] Jones did as instructed, demonstrating a willingness to comply with questionable presidential direction on how to try a case.

Jones and Attorney General Caesar Rodney argued that Wilkinson's statement, coupled with Jefferson's presidential pronunciation of Burr's guilt in his January 22 message to Congress, presented sufficient grounds for establishing and arresting Bollman and Swartwout for the crime of treason, that is, levying war against the United States. Their argument sought to substitute presidential direction for the constitutional requirement that an arrest must be based on a finding of probable cause and supported by facts under oath or affirmation as determined by a neutral and detached magistrate. When the lower court refused to issue a writ directing their release, Swartwout and Bollman, represented by Charles Lee, Robert Goodloe Harper, Luther Martin, and Francis Scott Key, appealed the decision to the Supreme Court. In a landmark decision regarding the law of treason, Chief Justice John Marshall ruled that "there certainly is not in the letter delivered to Gen. Wilkinson, so far as that letter is laid before the Court, one syllable which has a necessary or a natural reference to an enterprise against any territory of the United States."[66] Given the absence of any evidence of treason, the court granted the writ of habeas corpus and ordered the pair's release.

Jefferson was outraged at Marshall's ruling and spent three days with Attorney General Rodney planning the next legal move.[67] Relying on Wilkinson to provide the necessary evidence of treason, Jefferson directed Virginia US attorney George Hay to pursue felony treason charges against the conspirators in Virginia. Virginia was chosen as the appropriate venue for the trial because the charged overt act of treason was the gathering of troops and supplies on Blennerhassett Island, then in Virginia. Hay, the future son-in-law of James Monroe and longtime Jefferson ally, had defended James Callender for violating the Sedition Act and later clubbed Callender on the streets of Richmond for threatening Jefferson. Hay later served Jefferson as one of the prosecuting counsels at the impeachment trial of Justice Chase and took directions from Jefferson on charging decisions and trial strategy throughout the Burr trials. (Hay's performance may have been impacted by the fact that his first wife died the week before the commencement of the Burr trial. He later married the daughter of James Monroe in 1808.) Burr was arraigned in Richmond on March 30 before Chief Justice Marshall, who would serve as trial court judge throughout the proceedings. The immediate charge was the high misdemeanor of violating the Neutrality Act against Spain. Hay then sought to impanel a grand jury in Richmond that would consider the felony charge of treason against the United States.

While the grand jury proceedings themselves were conducted in secrecy, the appearances of witnesses in Richmond as well as in court proceedings ancillary to the grand jury hearing quickly captivated the public's attention. The court proceedings were moved to the Virginia House of Delegates to accommodate the expected crowds. Eager spectators flocked to see the finest American legal minds practice their craft. Burr actively participated in his own defense and was also represented by Luther "Old Brandy Bottle" Martin, who, despite a rampant addiction to alcohol, was considered to be the premier trial lawyer in Maryland, if not the United States. The sixteen grand jurors were a collection of Virginia political and social notables; Representative John Randolph of Roanoke was selected by Justice Marshall as foreman.[68]

A host of colorful witnesses, including "General" Eaton, who appeared in Arab garb, and Andrew Jackson, recovering from a dueling wound, made their appearance before a courtroom audience that included Meriwether Lewis, an observer for Jefferson; future general Winfield Scott, an aspiring young attorney; and Washington Irving, a journalist. However, the most colorful witness to make an appearance was Wilkinson, the government's star witness, who was sarcastically described by the defense as "the *Alpha* and *Omega* of the present prosecution" (emphasis in original).[69] Grand jury sessions had been repeatedly continued, awaiting the slow arrival of Wilkinson from New Orleans. Randolph even speculated to Andrew Jackson that, because Wilkinson was a Spanish pensioner, he would never appear before the grand jury.[70] When he finally appeared, Wilkinson was resplendent in a uniform of his own design, awash with gold buttons and braid, astride a horse festooned with a leopard skin saddle blanket. When he appeared before the grand jury, Wilkinson was also wearing his sword, which Randolph demanded he remove out of a concern for jury intimidation.[71] Irving compared him to a strutting turkey-cock and described a tense look exchanged between Wilkinson and Burr as Wilkinson walked through the courtroom to enter the grand jury's secret chamber.[72] Wilkinson described a different visage to Jefferson: "My Eyes darted a flash of indignation at the little Traitor."[73]

Wilkinson and Jefferson exchanged a series of letters during the lengthy Burr trials. In his letters Wilkinson decried the attacks of his enemies, which he suffered with amazing fortitude while doing Jefferson's bidding in condemning Burr before the grand jury. Jefferson sought to commiserate with his general by raising his spirits to withstand the onslaught: "Your enemies have filled the public ear with slanders & your mind with trouble on that account. . . . No one is more sensible than myself of the injustice which has been aimed at you."[74] Jefferson later found that it would take more than offers of moral support to be able to save his general from exposure and accountability for his repeated acts of treachery.

Even before his grand jury appearance, Wilkinson had ensnared Jefferson in a constitutional dispute that still reverberates in the courts today: Can a sitting president be required to participate in an ongoing criminal trial? Recognizing that Jefferson's January 22 public condemnation of Burr was based on multiple letters he received from Wilkinson, Burr and his defense team requested that Marshall issue a subpoena duces tecum to the president, requiring him to appear before the grand jury and produce the Wilkinson correspondence. Citing Wilkinson's record of perfidy in New Orleans, Luther Martin demanded that the actual correspondence of Wilkinson to Jefferson be produced for Burr's perusal.[75] After four days of hearings Marshall granted the request for a subpoena. Jefferson did not react well to being subjected to judicial process. In one of his many letters to George Hay on trial strategy, Jefferson called Martin an "unprincipled and impudent federal bull dog" and recommended that Hay consider charging Martin with misprision of treason for his alleged foreknowledge of Burr's plot.[76] Hay ignored the suggestion.

Wilkinson's appearance before the grand jury was an unmitigated disaster. Under harsh questioning from the grand jurors it soon became apparent that Wilkinson had manipulated the July 1806 letter from Burr to implicate Burr and lessen his own role in the plot. At the completion of the grand jury's work, Wilkinson himself narrowly avoided an indictment for misprision of treason. Foreman Randolph was so incensed by Wilkinson's testimony and by Jefferson's unquestioning support of Wilkinson that he later commenced a three-year campaign in Congress to hold Wilkinson accountable for his role with Burr and the Spanish. Hay and the other prosecutors recognized that, despite Jefferson's support, Wilkinson's presence on the stand as a government witness would become a lightning rod for cross-examination and probably lead to a verdict of acquittal. They chose instead to build their case without the trial testimony of their "alpha and omega."

Contrary to the promise of immunity he had received from the president, Bollman was brought before the grand jury and confronted with his January statement to Jefferson and Madison. To compel his testimony, Jefferson directed Hay to offer Bollman a grant of immunity if he would implicate Burr in the treason plot and not just the filibustering expedition against Mexico. Jefferson also directed Hay to charge Bollman with treason if he did not implicate Burr. Bollman refused the offer and limited his testimony to the filibuster. Jefferson also provided Hay with several blank pardons and instructed him to use them liberally, in a vain attempt to get some witnesses to offer testimony that Burr was engaged in treason.[77] (Jefferson sent more than thirty letters to Hay during the Burr trials about trial strategy and commiserating with Hay on the perceived bias shown by Chief Justice Marshall.)

Finally, on June 24 the grand jury returned a treason indictment against Burr, former senator Dayton, current senator Smith, and several other minor players, but refused to indict Bollman, Swartwout, or Adair. The trial commenced in August, and Hay and the prosecution team proceeded without Wilkinson as a witness. After the testimony of fourteen witnesses it became apparent that the government could not establish that the mere act of gathering armed men and supplies on Blennerhassett Island amounted to an act of levying war against the United States, the sine qua non of the charge of treason as required by Treason Clause of the Constitution. Marshall's ruling on the definition of treason and his instruction to the jury guaranteed Burr's acquittal, which the jury quickly returned on September 1.

Having lost the felony charge of treason, Jefferson immediately directed Hay and the prosecution team to commence a second trial on the high misdemeanor violation of the Neutrality Act of 1794 in the mounting of a filibustering expedition into Spanish Mexico. "I am happy in having the benefit of Mr. Madison's counsel on this occasion, he happening to be with me, we are both strongly of the opinion that the prosecution of Burr for misdemeanor should proceed at Richmond."[78] Again, Wilkinson played no role in the government's case because of his dismal credibility as a witness, and Marshall's legal rulings once again hamstrung the prosecution. Since the indictment charged that Burr had commenced a filibustering expedition on Blennerhassett Island but did not charge him with the act of conspiring to commence a filibuster, Marshall restricted the government to producing evidence that a filibuster was indeed commenced on the island. All evidence relating to conduct that took place off the island and to the conduct of co-conspirators off the island was ruled inadmissible.[79] Following Marshall's ruling, Hay moved to dismiss the case, but Burr insisted that the matter be sent to the jury. Marshall denied Hay's motion, charged the jury, and sent them to deliberate. They returned a not guilty verdict in twenty minutes.

The vindictive Jefferson believed the government was not done. He directed Hay to recharge Burr with treason at a different time and location, the second time regarding the plotters' actions in Kentucky and Ohio instead of in Virginia. Hay filed a motion in Richmond seeking Marshall's approval to try Burr and Blennerhassett in another district. Marshall agreed to a hearing to determine whether there was sufficient evidence, and this time Hay unfortunately tried to buttress his case by putting Wilkinson on the stand. On direct examination Wilkinson admitted that he had not accurately decrypted the July 29 Burr letter and intentionally left out portions of the letter that inculpated him. Wilkinson was evasive in his answers to direct questions, with many repetitions of "I do not recollect." He committed perjury by denying that he had had communications with Spanish officials regarding the Burr expedition, and he falsely stated that he did not recall communicating with Spanish officials in cypher. On cross-examination he could not recall the content of any of his communications with Burr in 1806 and he refused to answer certain questions put to him by the defense on the grounds of self-incrimination. He admitted that he could not find the original encrypted Burr letter of July 29 and that he had destroyed copies of his correspondence with Burr.[80]

The defense practically leapt at the chance to present evidence attacking Wilkinson's credibility, stating, "We do intend to shake the credibility of General Wilkinson, and to make him produce the shake himself."[81] Former major Bruff was called to portray his dealings with Wilkinson and his warnings to Jefferson, Dearborn, and Rodney regarding Wilkinson's relationship with Burr and Spain as well as their statements that no action should be taken to address these concerns until Wilkinson's appearance as a witness for the government against Burr was over.[82] Wilkinson was allowed to testify in response to Bruff: "But I can state before you sir, (addressing the judge,) and before God (turning his eyes to Heaven

and placing his hands on his heart,) that his whole narrative is either a vile fabrication, or a distortion of facts."[83] Three grand jurors were called to highlight
inconsistencies in Wilkinson's testimony. The defense team then sought to prove
that as a Spanish pensioner Wilkinson had a motive to falsely concoct a Burr
treason plot to serve two masters, the United States and Spain. Marshall allowed
testimony regarding Wilkinson's Spanish pension for the sole purpose of exploring
Wilkinson's ulterior motives in disclosing Burr's plot.

Wilkinson's Spanish cash courier, Thomas Power, was then called to testify
regarding his knowledge of cyphered communications between Wilkinson and
Spanish officials. Prior to his appearance in court Power had met with Wilkinson
and assured him that he would not implicate him in any role with Spain.[84] Burr
also subpoenaed Daniel Clark to testify regarding his knowledge of Wilkinson's
relationship with Spain but did not call him as a witness. On the stand, Power at
first refused to answer, citing the fact that as a Spanish official he could not provide
testimony contrary to the interests of Spain. However, when Marshall overruled
his refusal, Power admitted that Wilkinson and Carondolet had communicated
by cypher using a dictionary code.[85] At the conclusion of almost one month of
testimony, Marshall ruled that sufficient evidence existed to commit Burr for trial
in Ohio.

Despite Marshall's final favorable ruling for the government, Jefferson shifted
his mode of assault on Burr. Charges against all the conspirators were eventually
dropped, and Jefferson proposed that Congress examine the issue, and for good
measure he strongly suggested that additional controls on the judiciary and the
possible impeachment of Marshall would be in order. Most of the legislative efforts failed, and Burr drifted into relative obscurity from the national scene. Burr's
remaining life was awash in tragedy. Following the dismissal of all charges, he fled
overseas to avoid his creditors, then subsequently traveled to France and Britain
in search of foreign support for various schemes relating to the conquest of Mexico. Burr then returned and opened a practice of law in New York. His daughter,
Theodosia, lost her ten-year-old son to illness and shortly thereafter she was lost at
sea to either a storm or coastal pirates. Burr's second marriage failed, and he died
following a stroke in 1834.

At the conclusion of the trial, Jefferson received yet another warning about
Wilkinson, this time from George Hay, the chief prosecutor. In a gloomy assessment of the final stages of the trial, Hay expressed his regret at ever relying on
Wilkinson and stated that while he had vouched for Wilkinson's credibility in
court, he now regretted doing so. "My confidence in him is shaken, if not destroyed. I am Sorry for it, on his own account, on the public account and because
you have expressed opinions in his favor. But you did not know then what you will

soon know, and what, I did not learn until after, long after my declaration mentioned above."[86] Hay's remarks may have resulted from a meeting he had at this time with Wilkinson. According to John Randolph, Burr had subpoenaed Daniel Clark to testify about Wilkinson's Spanish pension, and Wilkinson informed Hay that Clark's testimony would ruin him. Clark did not testify at the hearing.[87] If Hay hoped that this warning would succeed in halting Jefferson's support for Wilkinson, when so many other such warnings had failed, he was sadly mistaken.

Throughout the trials Wilkinson and Jefferson shared several communications wherein Wilkinson kept Jefferson informed of the trial's progress and Jefferson urged Wilkinson to keep up his spirits. Following Burr's acquittals, Wilkinson urged Jefferson to seek another trial away from Kentucky and Tennessee, "an unpolished coarse People are apt to be governed by Events, & are easily duped by artifice and cunning."[88] Wilkinson condemned Marshall and suggested that he was a party to the Burr Conspiracy,[89] leading Jefferson to express his hope that the verdicts would spur an amendment to the Constitution subsuming the judiciary to the will of the people.[90]

However, in communications to both Hay and Jefferson, Wilkinson raised his desire to have a military court of inquiry or congressional investigation that would result in the endorsement of his conduct in the Burr matter. While Jefferson was wise enough to ignore these requests, Wilkinson's subsequent foolishness would soon compel Jefferson to take extraordinary steps to protect his general.

The trial and its aftermath resulted in a rash of affairs of honor among the many southern gentlemen participants. Wilkinson's inflated sense of honor arising from his father's deathbed command to never let an insult go unanswered led to many disputes. Toward the end of the trial, Samuel Swartwout pushed Wilkinson on the street in Richmond and subsequently challenged Wilkinson to a duel. Wilkinson declined, stating that he held no correspondence with traitors.[91] Under the informal code duello governing affairs of honor, any aggrieved party denied the honor of a duel was entitled to "post" the offending party who had rejected the challenge, publishing in a newspaper a notice of the offending party's misconduct and cowardice in avoiding an affair of honor. Swartwout posted Wilkinson, calling him "a COWARD and a POLTROON."[92] While deflecting those challenges from Swartwout, Wilkinson sought to challenge Burr defense attorney John Wickham for his attacks on Wilkinson's credibility during the Burr commitment hearing, believing that Wickham's cross-examination had accused him of perjury and forgery. In his reply Wickham denied accusing Wilkinson of forgery and asserted that his charge of perjury was appropriate courtroom behavior and not an appropriate subject for an extrajudicial affair of honor.[93] No duel between them took place.

While Wilkinson wisely allowed his affair with Wickham to quietly disappear, he foolishly pursued an affair of honor against grand jury foreman John Randolph, which had the unintended consequence of turning two of his closest confidants into open and avowed enemies. It also made Wilkinson the prominent target of a sustained attack by one of the most feared members of Congress. Randolph, a scion of the extended Randolph dynasty of Virginia, was first elected to Congress in 1799 as a member of the Democratic-Republican party. Originally a supporter of his cousin, Thomas Jefferson, he was the floor manager for Jefferson in the House impeachment of Justice Chase in 1801. However, by 1807 Randolph believed that Jefferson had abandoned the original agrarian principles of the Democratic-Republican party, leading him to become the head of a splinter group, the Quids, that was opposed to Jefferson's big government initiatives.

Randolph publicly questioned Wilkinson's role with Burr even before the trial commenced. Prior to his departure from New Orleans, Wilkinson had informed his close friend Senator Samuel Smith of Maryland that a duel with Randolph was likely, saying, "The World is too small for us both."[94] Randolph had harshly questioned Wilkinson before the grand jury and had unsuccessfully argued for Wilkinson's indictment with Burr. In a letter to a friend, Randolph reflected on the failure to indict Wilkinson: "But the mammoth of iniquity escaped; not that any man pretended to think him innocent, but upon certain wire-drawn distinctions that I will not pester you with. W[ilkinson] is the only man I ever saw who was from the bark to the core a villain."[95]

Having failed to indict Wilkinson, following the trial Randolph looked for evidence that could be brought before Congress to establish Wilkinson's role with Burr and demonstrate that Wilkinson had been a Spanish pensioner for years. Ironically, Wilkinson was directly responsible for providing the needed evidence to Randolph. At the Richmond commitment hearing Thomas Power had provided little useful testimony for Burr in establishing Wilkinson's relationship with Spain. However, despite Power's successful effort to avoid testifying about Wilkinson's pension, after the trial Wilkinson felt a need to dispel any lingering concerns that may have resulted from intimations made at the trial regarding his Spanish payments. Prior to trial Wilkinson had obtained a deposition from Power, denying any payments from Spain, which was intended by Power to aid Spain by protecting the identity of Agent 13.[96] Power provided the perjurious statement to Wilkinson with the understanding that it would only be shown to Jefferson, in order to quell the president's concerns regarding Wilkinson's loyalty. Despite this assurance, Wilkinson published the deposition on October 21, calling Power's limited testimony into question. Wilkinson's duplicity turned Power from a trusted ally into a deadly enemy willing to cooperate with others seeking to destroy Wilkinson.[97]

At the same time, Wilkinson needlessly created a fatal rift with Daniel Clark, another person who had intimate knowledge of Wilkinson's true relationship with Spain and who was in a unique position to unmask Wilkinson's cover story about payments from Spain. Though the Burr trial did not delve into Clark's relationship with either Burr or Wilkinson, Clark had been subpoenaed to testify at the commitment hearing in order to introduce evidence regarding Wilkinson's Spanish pension. Justice Marshall allowed a limited exploration of this issue to impeach Wilkinson, but Clark was never called to testify. However, his appearance on the witness list led Wilkinson to have a panicked meeting with prosecutor Hay on the harm that Clark's testimony could cause.

Having avoided a potentially difficult exchange with Clark in Richmond, Wilkinson needlessly provoked a fatal rift between them shortly after the trial. At a party in Annapolis, Maryland, in November, Wilkinson indiscreetly suggested that Clark was in financial distress, a statement that eventually came to the attention of Richard Caton, a wealthy Baltimore merchant whose daughter was being courted by Clark. Caton banned his daughter from seeing Clark and shipped her off to England, where she married into British royalty.[98] According to Wilkinson, as a result of this missed romantic and financial opportunity, Clark, "who had always been professed my friend and obsequious servant, as his correspondence will testify, was suddenly converted into a remorseless enemy."[99] Now serving as the Orleans territorial delegate to Congress, Clark was aware that Randolph was looking for evidence against Wilkinson. He approached Power and between them they provided Randolph with a packet of information that could be used against Wilkinson. Recognizing that Randolph was preparing a condemnation, Wilkinson chose to strike first, and on December 24 publicly challenged Randolph to a duel.[100] Randolph declined the challenge, stating that there was a stain on Wilkinson's character that precluded him from the rights of a gentleman. Wilkinson responded by posting handbills in the District of Columbia, calling Randolph a calumniator and poltroon. (Wilkinson's challenge to Randolph and subsequent posting of Randolph were both criminal offenses under the Articles of War, but Jefferson obviously had no interest in prosecuting Wilkinson for harassing Randolph and no charges were ever preferred against him.)

Wilkinson renewed his challenge in a December 28 letter to Randolph, which Randolph again rejected, stating that he refused to descend to Wilkinson's level. Wilkinson's letter in response called Randolph "an insolent, slanderous, prevaricating poltroon."[101] Randolph, like Wilkinson, had no moral qualms about settling disagreements through violence, but he chose a more deliberate way to respond to Wilkinson.[102] On December 31 he appeared in the House and published a series of documents, mostly obtained from Clark, that set forth Wilkinson's illicit relationship with the Spanish.[103] Included were communications from Spanish officials describing payments to Wilkinson and Wilkinson's plea that they refrain from mentioning his name. A declaration from Power was also included, which set forth his role as a Spanish cash courier for Wilkinson and contained the following rationale for his previous denial of a relationship between Wilkinson and Spain:

> Let us now for a while suppose that I was a secret agent of the Spanish Government, and that General Wilkinson was a pensioner of said Government, or had received certain sums for co-operation with and promoting its views, and that those views and projects were inimical to that of the United States, should I be worthy of the trust reposed in me by my Government, were I to refuse to give General Wilkinson any document that might contribute to raise him in the good opinion of the Administration of his country, blazon his integrity and patriotism, and fortify him in their confidence, and by their means enlarge his power of injuring them and serving us? Surely not; or if I did, I should deserve to be hooted as an idiot.[104]

Power's statement of the lengths that he had gone to, to protect the sources and methods of the Spanish intelligence apparatus is a classic example of the duplicity that is needed to effectively conduct double agent operations. Randolph completed his bombshell by introducing a resolution calling on Jefferson to investigate Wilkinson's relationship with Spain.

Few times in American history has more compelling evidence been introduced into Congress that clearly demonstrates that a senior American official was working for a foreign power. Randolph produced Spanish documents with exact sums paid to Wilkinson and statements of Wilkinson's incriminating desire to avoid detection, corroborated by the testimony of a Spanish official who had carried taskings and cash to Wilkinson. However, Randolph underestimated the steps that Jefferson would take to ignore and cover up the crimes of his general. To stifle any mischief that would arise from a congressional investigation beyond his control, on January 2, 1808, Jefferson directed that a court of inquiry be convened under the Articles of War, to examine the Spanish pension allegations made against Wilkinson. In order to avoid the appearance of responding to congressional intimidation, Jefferson couched the court as having been convened at Wilkinson's request.[105]

Jefferson's directive effectively neutralized Clark's efforts to have the House conduct a thorough investigation. In a letter to Power dated January 2, Clark set forth the efforts that the House would have to take to examine Wilkinson's forged commercial transaction documents and the false statement provided by Folch denying any knowledge of Wilkinson's employment by the Spanish.[106] Clark would insist on the production of various corroborating business documents by Wilkinson, which he knew did not exist, and use the absence of these documents to undercut Wilkinson's defense. No such demand or scrutiny was ever done by Jefferson's military court of inquiry.

Randolph's resolution set off a lengthy debate in the House, much of which centered on Congress's authority to investigate misconduct by military officials or compel the executive branch to conduct such an investigation. (Randolph suggested that if Jefferson did not conduct an inquiry, the House should move to impeach him.) Daniel Clark, who was sitting in the House when Randolph made his motion, stated that he had repeatedly sought to warn the administration about Wilkinson, both verbally and in writing, "to which a deaf ear had been turned."[107] Questions arose regarding the authority of the House to compel a member of the House (i.e., Clark) to provide additional information.

While the House debated, Clark was busy amassing additional information against Wilkinson. In response to a House resolution, he provided a sworn statement to the House on January 11 that made several allegations against Wilkinson based on his own personal knowledge. He stated that he knew that in 1788 Wilkinson had prepared a list of individuals who, upon the receipt of a Spanish pension, would support the separation of the western states; he was not aware of Spanish payments to Wilkinson before 1794 or 1795, but became aware of them at that time and described attempted Spanish payments made to Wilkinson, including one incident when the cash courier was murdered; and he described a statement made to him by Power setting forth a Spanish payment made in 1796 and Power's travel to Detroit to deliver Spanish plans to Wilkinson to sever the western states. He also described a meeting he had had with Wilkinson in 1798 at Loftus Heights, where Wilkinson discussed monies owed to him by the Spanish government and Wilkinson had suggested that Clark negotiate the transfer to Wilkinson of Governor Gayoso's plantation in Natchez as settlement for this debt. Clark also stated that he was aware that in 1804 he had heard stories in New Orleans of Wilkinson's receipt of $10,000 from Spain. Clark was able to determine that no tobacco transactions had taken place at the time, which might have accounted for such a sum being provided to Wilkinson.[108]

Following Clark's statement, the House passed a two-part resolution requesting that Jefferson investigate to determine whether Wilkinson had ever corruptly received money from the government or agents of Spain while in the service of the United States and provide the House with all information ever received by the executive branch regarding discussions between citizens of the United States and any foreign government about the dismemberment of the union or showing that any officer of the United States had "corruptly received money from any foreign government."[109] The first part of the resolution was already being addressed by the court of inquiry ordered by Jefferson on January 2, but the second part would cause Jefferson additional trouble.

Jefferson subsequently conducted an "exhaustive" search of all federal records, taking only a week to accomplish the task. His response to the House, one of the most mendacious documents ever issued by an American president, was designed to defend the repeated efforts over a period of fifteen years by all presidential administrations to ignore any evidence showing Wilkinson's improper relationship with Spain. Without implicating Wilkinson, Jefferson admitted that certain information had been provided to former president Washington regarding efforts with a foreign government to dismember the union, but no record of any such information during Washington's administration existed in federal records. Jefferson admitted that Andrew Ellicott had provided the secretary of state with certain reports during the Adams administration and that those reports would be provided to the House. Jefferson admitted that Ellicott might have another report which he wished to keep secret but that Ellicott was being directed to appear as a witness before the court of inquiry. (Ellicott was a civilian at this time and Jefferson had no authority to direct his appearance.) Jefferson also claimed to have found a 1798 letter from Daniel Clark to the State Department and agreed to provide it to the House. Jefferson asserted that the 1800 fire in the War Department may have destroyed other records, and he declared that a diligent search was continuing but that the noted records were the only documents in the executive's possession relating to dismembering the union or receiving corrupt foreign payments.[110] Regarding his own administration, Jefferson stated that one year after he took office he recalled that Daniel Clark had provided some verbal information regarding the dismemberment of the union. Those written records were delivered to the secretary of state at the time but now could not be found.

On February 4, 1808, Jefferson sent another letter to the House stating that the missing Clark letters addressed to the secretary of state had been found. Jefferson assured the House that none of the newly found papers were related to the dismemberment of the union or corrupt payments by any foreign agent.[111] Jefferson stated that Clark's information only related to dismemberment actions under previous administrations and that those officials had considered the information and found it unworthy of action. Since Clark's information did not relate to any corrupt payments, the information provided by him was considered by Jefferson to be a "dead letter." Jefferson admitted that during the Burr Conspiracy some "suspicions and insinuations" had been received against Wilkinson. Since much of this information was provided by anonymous persons, they too had resulted in no action. Finally, Jefferson assured the House that

no other information within the purview of the request of the house, is known to
have been received by any department of the government, from the establishment of
the present federal government, that which has recently been communicated to the
House of Representatives & by them to me, is the first direct testimony ever made
known to me, charging General Wilkinson with a corrupt receipt of money: and
the House of Representatives may be assured that the duties which this information
devolves on me shall be exercised with rigorous impartiality. Should any want of
power in the court to compel the rendering of testimony obstruct that full & im-
partial enquiry which alone can establish guilt or innocence and satisfy justice, the
legislative authority only will be competent to the remedy.[112]

Jefferson was undoubtedly attempting to justify his ignorance and denial of repeated concerns and inquiries that had been raised throughout Wilkinson's career.
The letter vaguely referred to allegations raised by Washington and the flawed reports of collaboration discovered by Ellicott. It made no reference to the warnings
provided to and information developed by Anthony Wayne, nor the fact that all
inquiries under the Adams administration were halted, not because there was a
lack of information but because of Wayne's untimely death. Jefferson's letter also
ignored the written warning provided to Jefferson by Andrew Ellicott in the first
year of his administration or the fact that, prior to his appointment as governor
of Louisiana, Dearborn and Jefferson were hesitant to appoint Wilkinson to various positions out of concern over Wilkinson's ties to the Spanish. It ignored the
multiple written warnings provided to Jefferson and Madison by Joseph Hamilton
Daviess, William Eaton, and Gideon Granger. It deliberately ignored the statements of James Bruff regarding direct allegations of Wilkinson's paid relationship
with Spain, which had been made the previous year to three cabinet members
and repeated in sworn testimony during the Burr trials. It ignored information
provided to Jefferson by Senator John Smith regarding Wilkinson's relationship
to Spain. (Jefferson had good reason not to mention the Smith letter. At the time
of Jefferson's letter to the House, the Senate was conducting hearings on expelling
Smith from the Senate because of Smith's role in the Burr Conspiracy.) Finally, the
letter made no reference to the October 1807 written warning to Jefferson from
prosecutor Hay regarding his own loss of faith in Wilkinson. All these documents
and warnings were known to Jefferson. Jefferson's assurance to the House that
Clark's recent warnings were the first evidence he had received regarding Wilkinson's corrupt receipt of money was a plain and deliberate misrepresentation.

The Jefferson-directed court of inquiry commenced at Morin's Tavern in Philadelphia on January 14. Under the provisions of Article 91 of the Articles of
War, the president was authorized to convene a court of inquiry to conduct a

fact-finding proceeding. The inquiry would include a board of three officers and a judge advocate (who would serve as recorder); the court could take evidence regarding "any transaction, accusation or imputation against any officer." The court would have the ability to compel the production of evidence in the same manner as a court-martial, meaning that it could compel only military witnesses and only military documents. A court of inquiry was usually limited to a fact-finding role and was prohibited from opining on the merits of a case, unless specially required to do so by a convening order. Under Article 91 the accused was allowed to cross-examine witnesses and present relevant evidence in his defense. The convening authority, in this case President Jefferson, could also use the court's factual conclusions to determine the need to convene a subsequent court-martial over the same issue.[113]

Following the controversy surrounding Arthur St. Clair's debacle on the Wabash in 1791, presidents had been conflicted on the appropriate way to conduct inquiries into misconduct by the commanding general of the army. Since all the officers of the army are subordinate to the commanding general, there was clearly a concern that officers on a court of inquiry could not be expected to conduct a meaningful inquiry into the possible misdeeds of their commander. In 1792, while Washington struggled with finding the appropriate manner for conducting an inquiry regarding St. Clair, Congress took the lead and conducted fact-finding hearings that ultimately produced an incomplete record at best. Washington later confronted the issue in the internecine squabbles between Wilkinson and Wayne and obtained a legal opinion from the attorney general that even the commanding general of the army could be subjected to a court of inquiry. Washington's quandary ended when Wayne died before any such court could be convened.

As early as the fall of 1807, Wilkinson had lobbied for a court of inquiry regarding allegations that had arisen against him regarding his relationship with the Spanish. When Jefferson directed Dearborn to convene a court on January 2, he was motivated by two factors.[114] First, a court of inquiry would remove the need for fact-gathering to be conducted by the House. While various House members debated the propriety and constitutionality of a House inquiry, Jefferson cut short the debate by providing his own inquiry, relieving the House from further consideration of the issue. Second, Jefferson and Dearborn knew that they and Wilkinson could control the conduct and outcome of the military court in a way that would exonerate Wilkinson from any Spanish connection and support Jefferson's decision to ignore any incriminating evidence against the primary accuser in the Burr trials.

The first step of control exerted by Wilkinson was the selection of the court's members. Traditionally, selection was supposed to be made by Secretary Dearborn

and President Jefferson, the convening authority, but Wilkinson undoubtedly influenced the selection of officers who were to reach the preordained conclusion.
Since the time of the Wilkinson-Wayne controversy in 1794, the army officer
corps had been divided into pro- and anti-Wilkinson camps.[115] As the courts-
martial of Colonels Butler and Bruff demonstrated, Wilkinson was not hesitant
to use the military justice process to attack his opponents in the officer corps, and
by 1808 most officers were outspoken in their support of or at least cautious in
their discussions of their commanding general.

   The first officer chosen by Dearborn and Jefferson was Colonel Henry Burbeck, a Revolutionary War veteran, who was appointed president of the court.[116]
Burbeck was the only officer on the panel who was not an outspoken friend of
and advocate for Wilkinson and was probably selected to give the appearance of
fairness. No such appearance was expected from the other two officers. Colonel
Thomas Cushing, long considered a strong supporter of Wilkinson, had been one
of the signatories in the tribute letter to Jefferson that Wilkinson had demanded
that his loyal officers sign. The other officer was Lieutenant Colonel Jonathan
Williams, a person related to Wilkinson by marriage and who was widely believed
to be a close friend of Wilkinson.

   To complete the court, Walter Jones, the civilian US attorney for the District
of Columbia, was selected as the judge advocate for the court. Under the Articles
of War the judge advocate directs the presentation of evidence before the panel
and prepares the record of proceedings for the review and approval of the convening authority, the president. Jones, a political appointee with no background
in military justice, had already demonstrated his pliability in serving Jefferson by
attempting to justify before the Supreme Court Wilkinson's illegal arrest of Swartwout and Bollman. Once again he was being called on by Jefferson to produce
a flawed legal product that suited the president's needs. As Jefferson stated to a
correspondent at the outset of the proceedings, he expected the court of inquiry
to "crush" Clark.[117]

   As set forth in the convening order, the purpose of the inquiry was to determine whether Wilkinson had been a pensioner of the Spanish government while
holding a commission from the United States. From the outset of the proceedings
it was clear to all that the true purpose of the inquiry was not to investigate the
charge but rather to provide Wilkinson with a forum to rebut the charge. Jones
surrendered the role of recorder and judge advocate and allowed Wilkinson to
control the proceedings before a pliant audience.

   At the first session on January 14, Jones was asked by Burbeck if he was ready
to proceed. Jones stated that he was not and that he instead expected Wilkinson
to present the witnesses he wanted to summon.[118] From that point forward most

witnesses during the hearings, which stretched from January to June, were produced by Wilkinson, with Wilkinson calling over a dozen witnesses and Jones calling only two. Jones subsequently stated that because of his other responsibilities, he "contrived" to be present whenever Wilkinson presented witnesses and evidence. But from the meager record of the proceedings, it appears Wilkinson presented testimony without any attempt at cross-examination by Jones.[119] To ensure that whatever record was produced by the court was carefully controlled by Wilkinson, Jones requested that the court issue an order at the outset of the proceedings that prohibited notes from being taken by anyone other than Jones and Wilkinson. The subsequent gag order prohibited reporters in attendance from producing verbatim records of the testimony given.[120] The only contemporaneous records of testimony and other evidence considered were copies of Wilkinson's lengthy addresses to the court (which Wilkinson gave to the press) and carefully edited summations of certain witnesses' testimony. The reporting newspapers described the person who provided the information as a reliable source, but this person was undoubtedly Wilkinson.[121] In addition to regularly leaking to the press, Wilkinson had several exhortations published in important newspapers, urging the public to await the final judgment of the court.[122]

At the outset of the proceedings Jones sought to invite three prominent congressional critics, Randolph, Clark, and John Rowan, to voluntarily appear before the court. Each refused to attend. Rowan and Randolph responded that they had no personal knowledge regarding the matter. Clark stated that he had already provided a statement under oath to the House but would be willing to appear before a court of competent jurisdiction, and not a military tribunal, to provide further information. Clark noted that the military court of inquiry did not have the ability to compel nonmilitary witnesses who could corroborate testimony and therefore he would not attend. Jefferson noted in his letter to the House that if Congress was not satisfied with the investigatory powers of the court of inquiry, they were free to pass legislation expanding the power of the military court.[123] A bill was introduced at this time to allow military courts to call civilian witnesses, but because of concerns about subjecting civil officials to military process, the legislation never passed.

Wilkinson's defense rested on four pillars. Power and Clark had previously stated that Wilkinson was not the recipient of a Spanish pension, and Wilkinson sought to impeach them both with their prior inconsistent statements. Jones did nothing to buttress their credibility. Wilkinson also sought to show that Clark had become biased against Wilkinson and therefore had a motive to forge documents showing Spanish payments. Wilkinson also sought to show that Clark was a Burr co-conspirator and that Clark had contrived the documents to deflect attention from those actions. Finally, Wilkinson provided false testimony and manufactured documents supporting his cover story that any Spanish money was merely a delayed payment for old commercial tobacco transactions.

Wilkinson's theatrics were on full display before the court. "I repel the infamous charge, of having received base bribes from the Spanish government for corrupt purposes. By the holiest affections of the soul, and the most noble feelings of the heart, I protest it is the fabrications of ferocious revenge, and being false my only avenue to justice is to shew, that those who prefer it are governed by impure motives, and are unworthy of credit."[124] In addition to lengthy perorations against Clark, Wilkinson presented testimony from numerous witnesses who attacked the credibility of Clark and Power, including Representative Walter Jones Sr., Walter Jones's father. During the conduct of the court of inquiry, Clark introduced additional documents before the House that showed further communications between Wilkinson and the Spanish. It is not clear whether these additional Clark documents, set forth in the records of the House, were ever brought before the court of inquiry.

Realizing that Jefferson had placed Andrew Ellicott's prior reports, which mentioned Wilkinson's Spanish pension, before the House, Wilkinson reached out to Ellicott to see what Ellicott planned to say about the matter. Ellicott responded with an accurate representation of the contents of his reports to the secretary of state but concluded by saying that despite the clear evidence of illegal Spanish payments, Ellicott still felt that Wilkinson behaved correctly in all of the conduct he witnessed.[125] Ellicott's naive refusal to condemn Wilkinson may have been among the reasons why previous administrations had ignored his warnings and greatly diminished the strength of his evidence against Wilkinson at future proceedings. While he was assuring Wilkinson that he had seen no improper conduct, Ellicott was also providing information to Clark that directly conflicted with his letter to Wilkinson. On January 14, Ellicott wrote Clark and stated that the Gayoso letter mentioned in his previous report "places the improper conduct of General Wilkinson . . . in a point of view not to be mistaken. If corruption is criminal, this letter establishes criminality." Ellicott went on to say, "To my knowledge, the present administration has been minutely informed of the conduct of general Wilkinson, and why he has been supported, and patronized, after this information, is to me an inexplicable paradox."[126]

Because of Jones's supine posture during the proceedings, very little evidence was actually presented to prove the allegations and Jones admitted that his attempts to bring forward evidence to support the charges against Wilkinson were fruitless. On February 16, Wilkinson, not Jones, moved for the introduction of Clark's January statement before the House, in order to enable Wilkinson to open

General James Wilkinson, the highest-ranking federal official ever to be tried as a spy. *Artist unknown. National Portrait Gallery.*

General Benedict Arnold. Prior to his acts of treason, Arnold was probably the finest combat commander in the Continental Army. He was the first victim of Wilkinson's betrayals. *Artist: John Trumbull. Library of Congress.*

General Horatio Gates, Wilkinson's first mentor. As a result of Gates's lying to George Washington, his relationship with Wilkinson descended into a series of duels. *Artist: Charles Willson Peale. National Portrait Gallery.*

The Surrender of General Burgoyne. The American victory at Saratoga led to France's entrance into the war. The central figure is General Horatio Gates. Wilkinson can be seen behind Gates's right elbow. *Artist: John Trumbull. Yale University Art Gallery.*

(MAJOR GENERAL ANTHONY WAYNE)

General Anthony Wayne. During the Northwest Indian War, Wayne accused Wilkinson of trying to murder him in order to take command of the Legion of the United States. *Artist: George Graham. National Portrait Gallery.*

General Alexander Hamilton. As commander of the US Army in 1798, Hamilton unsuccessfully sought to promote Wilkinson to the rank of major general. *Artist: John Trumbull. National Portrait Gallery.*

Andrew Ellicott. Although he was a famed cartographer, Ellicott proved to be a poor spy hunter for President Washington. At his 1811 court-martial Wilkinson attacked Ellicott for Ellicott's dalliance with a prostitute. *Artist: Jacob Eichholtz. New York Historical Society.*

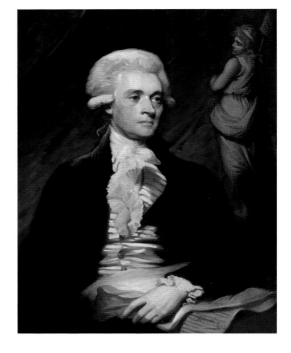

President Thomas Jefferson. In return for Wilkinson's betrayal of Aaron Burr, Jefferson shielded Wilkinson from congressional attacks by arranging for a sham court of inquiry. *Artist: Mather Brown. National Portrait Gallery.*

Vice President Aaron Burr. Burr foolishly trusted Wilkinson to be a co-conspirator in Burr's plot to establish a western empire. Wilkinson betrayed Burr to Jefferson in order to remain in command of the US Army. *Artist: Charles Balthazar Julien Févret de Saint-Mémin. National Portrait Gallery.*

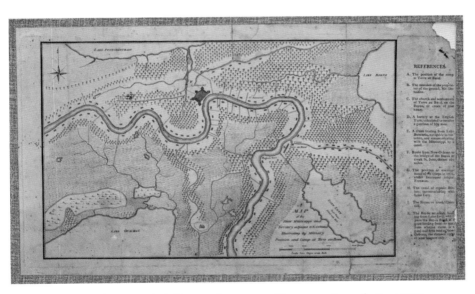

Map of New Orleans and Wilkinson's camp at Terre aux Boeufs. In 1809 Wilkinson led the army to its greatest peacetime disaster, in the swamps near the Mississippi River. *Digital Commonwealth.*

General Winfield Scott. As a young officer Scott was court-martialed for stating that he would carry a pistol to use on Wilkinson, his commanding general. *Artist unknown. National Portrait Gallery.*

Representative John Randolph of Roanoke. Randolph called Wilkinson a villain from the "bark to the very core" and led the congressional effort to remove Wilkinson. *Artist: John Wesley Jarvis. National Portrait Gallery.*

Roger Brooke Taney. As a young attorney Taney agreed to represent Wilkinson for free at his 1811 court-martial. Taney went on to become the Chief Justice of the Supreme Court and authored the infamous proslavery *Dred Scott* decision. *Artist unknown. Dickinson College.*

President James Madison. In order to cover up Wilkinson's treachery and incompetence, Madison arranged for a sham court-martial of Wilkinson that was guaranteed to clear Wilkinson from twenty years of misconduct. *Artist: Chester Harding. National Portrait Gallery.*

Secretary of War William Eustis. Dr. Eustis, Madison's first secretary of war, stated that Wilkinson was "the most profligate unprincipled servant the public ever had." *Artist: Gilbert Stuart. Metropolitan Museum of Art.*

Secretary of War John Armstrong Jr. President Madison's second secretary of war, Armstrong was responsible for placing Wilkinson in command of a disastrous invasion of Canada during the War of 1812. Armstrong was fired by Madison shortly after British troops burned Washington, DC, in 1814. *Artist: John Wesley Jarvis. National Portrait Gallery.*

an attack on Clark's credibility.[127] Jones also succeeded in getting Ellicott to voluntarily consent to answering written questions posed by Wilkinson. Since the questions were only posed by Wilkinson, Ellicott's statement provided yet another example of Ellicott's naivete and confusion regarding the effect of Wilkinson's Spanish pension.[128] Jones also obtained a statement from Maryland attorney Robert Goodloe Harper, who stated that while attending a Supreme Court hearing in early 1807, he had heard it mentioned that Wilkinson had accepted a $10,000 bribe from the Spanish in 1804. Harper discussed the bribe allegation with Clark, who denied any knowledge of a bribe at that time. However, Clark later informed him that he had changed his opinion regarding Wilkinson and the bribe, based on the receipt of additional information. Harper further related that after the Burr trials he had met Thomas Power, who felt that Wilkinson had made him appear to be a liar during the trials. Power said that he had documents to support his recent condemnation of Wilkinson. Harper learned that Power had provided the documents to Clark, and Harper urged Clark to provide the documents to Randolph.[129]

While presenting his cover story defense before the court, Wilkinson took additional steps to ensure that his Spanish handlers would support that story. Wilkinson introduced the false statement from Governor Folch to Governor Claiborne, stating that Folch was unaware of any documents showing that Wilkinson was a Spanish pensioner.[130] Folch went on to provide an assurance that any correspondence between Wilkinson and Gayoso alleging such a relationship was a forgery.

To ensure that any documents relating to Wilkinson's true relationship with Spain were beyond the reach of anyone hostile to Wilkinson's interest, Folch later informed Wilkinson that such documents had been shipped to Havana:

> My dear friend: I believe that you are already well convinced that I have acted befitting a faithful servant of the noble Spanish Monarchy, and that I have sincerely fulfilled the obligations which friendship imposes on me. I have done even more, for I have sent to the archives in Havana all that pertains to the ancient History, persuaded that before the United States are in a situation to conquer that capital, you and I, Jefferson, Madison, with all the Secretaries of the different departments, and even the prophet Daniel himself, will have made many day's journey into the other world.[131]

With his Spanish flank secure, a friendly court selected, and a complicit judge advocate in place, Wilkinson proceeded to dominate the inquiry. The proceeding was completed with Wilkinson's two-day summation to the court on June 24–25. During his summation Wilkinson repeatedly referred to documents and affidavits that had never been submitted into evidence. (Jones later estimated that fifty-five new exhibits were produced by Wilkinson during his two-day summation. None of them had been introduced during the proceedings and none were ever examined by Jones.[132]) Jones and Wilkinson were then excused from attendance while the panel members deliberated their conclusion. On June 28 Jones was brought before the panel and witnessed the signing of its final decision of exoneration. Based on Wilkinson's demand that the results be approved and published by July 4, the record was quickly referred to Dearborn and Jefferson, who approved the finding on July 2. The approved finding was then published, in according with Wilkinson's demand, on July 4.[133]

In its public statement the court accepted Wilkinson's cover story in its entirety. Ignoring all evidence to the contrary, if any had even been presented, the court concluded,

> It is therefore the opinion of this court, that there is no evidence of Brigadier-general James Wilkinson, having, at any time, received a pension from the Spanish government, or of his having received money from the government of Spain, or any of its officers or agents, for corrupt purposes; and the court has no hesitation in saying, that, as far as his conduct has been developed by this enquiry, he appears to have discharged the duties of his station, with honour to himself, and fidelity to his country.[134]

The court's exoneration far exceeded the narrow confines of its convening order. Under Article 91, courts of inquiry are limited to findings of fact and prohibited from opining on the merits of a case unless specially required. No such special requirement was in the January 2 convening order.

To Wilkinson's and Jefferson's supporters, the court's finding was an endorsement of Wilkinson's conduct and Jefferson's unwavering support of his general. To their opponents, the verdict was nothing short of an appalling whitewash that did nothing to dispel the taint of corruption that surrounded all of Wilkinson's actions and Jefferson's blind refusal to address them. However, with this exoneration Wilkinson was now able to return to his duty as commanding general without facing the threat of immediate removal. He would now lead the army into its worst peacetime loss of life in the nation's history.

DEATH OF AN ARMY ON THE MISSISSIPPI
1808–1809

A liar, traitor and scoundrel . . . , an unprincipled imbecile.
—Winfield Scott

The court of inquiry whitewash freed Wilkinson to continue to serve Jefferson during the final months of the Jefferson administration. Because Jefferson's likely successor in the election of 1808 was expected to be James Madison, Wilkinson felt a good deal of comfort that he would continue to thrive under the new administration. In the past Wilkinson had carefully groomed his relationship with each new president as he arrived in office, and though Wilkinson had not worked closely with Madison under the Jefferson administration, he was confident that Jefferson's good graces toward him would carry over into the new administration.

Unfortunately for Wilkinson, a final set of orders from Jefferson deprived him of the opportunity to charm Madison as the president-elect or establish a personal working relationship with whomever Madison would select to replace Henry Dearborn as the secretary of war. On December 2, 1808, Dearborn, operating on instructions from Jefferson, directed Wilkinson to assume the responsibility for the defense of New Orleans from an anticipated attack by Great Britain.[1] Relations between the United States and Great Britain had continued to deteriorate during the endless series of struggles arising from the Napoleonic Wars. Jefferson's attempt to avoid getting embroiled in the affair resulted in the passage in 1807 of the first in a series of Embargo Acts designed to deny the European belligerents from gaining access to American goods. While the embargoes had virtually no adverse effect on the belligerents, they did deprive American farmers and manufacturers of a European market for their crops and wares and caused a significant amount of economic distress throughout the United States. The 1807 embargo specifically did not deter Britain from its campaign of impressment of sailors taken from US vessels, including American warships.

Relations with Britain remained tense, and the American public's reaction to Napoleon's forays in Europe was unsettling. The Embargo Acts also prohibited trade with France, and applied to all French allies, including Spain. Because Spain still controlled Florida, the acts prohibited trading through Spanish ports in St. Augustine, Pensacola, and Mobile. Since many American settlements in Alabama, Georgia, and Mississippi relied on these ports, the embargo had an adverse impact on the southern and western American settlements as well. Relations with Spain were further confused when Napoleon forced the abdication of the Bourbon Spanish king, installing Napoleon's brother, Joseph, in his place. On May 2, 1808, the Spanish population of Madrid rose in armed opposition to Napoleon's actions.

With Spain in open rebellion against Napoleon, Jefferson saw an opportunity to capitalize on the confusion regarding the status of Spanish colonies in the Americas. Jefferson's first priority was to determine whether either Napoleon or Spain would be willing to sell the Floridas to the United States. Jefferson had long wished to acquire Spanish Florida but was hesitant to formally commence negotiations during the diplomatic chaos of the Napoleonic wars. Furthermore, Jefferson's House of Representatives enemy, John Randolph, chairman of the House Ways and Means Committee, was adamantly opposed to funding any Jeffersonian purchase of the Floridas.[2] Jefferson's secondary priority was to encourage independence of the Spanish colonies from Spain rather than becoming part of a French American empire.[3]

Wilkinson was, of course, adept at playing to the desires and fears of both sides regarding the future of the Spanish colonies. In November 1806, he sent Captain Walter Burling to Mexico City to remind the Spanish governors of Wilkinson's previous efforts to protect Spain from the supposed depravations of Aaron Burr. Wilkinson had been unsuccessful in getting the Spanish to reimburse him for his efforts, so he sought to have Jefferson pay for the trip by misleading him into believing that the real purpose of the trip was to assess the viability of Mexican independence.[4]

In October 1808 Wilkinson urged Jefferson to send a message to the Spanish colonies in an effort to deter their alliance with Great Britain. To ensure that the message was delivered by someone trusted by the Spanish, Wilkinson volunteered to be the messenger. Oblivious to the lingering suspicions around his dealings with the Spanish, Wilkinson told Jefferson, "I Know More of Spanish America, and am better Known there by name and Military Character (which is impressive in despotic Governments) than any other American."[5] Wilkinson couched his request as a way of demonstrating his loyalty to the United States: "The unexampled persecutions and Vindictive Spirit by which I am pursued, have produced an ardent desire for some interesting appointment, which may evince the public confidence, and put in my power to justify it, by a display of zeal, discretion, integrity, perseverance and successful evidence, to Strike dumb my Slanderers and revilers."

Within two months of Wilkinson's offer to deliver Jefferson's message, Jefferson found the opportunity to have Wilkinson perform a multipart mission. Recent rumored British troop movements in the Caribbean had increased American fears that the British might have designs on fomenting unrest in the Spanish colonies. Furthermore, were relations between the United States and Great Britain to continue to deteriorate, those British troops might be used to seize New Orleans. Wilkinson was chosen to accomplish two simultaneous missions: command the defense of New Orleans (the American army was being significantly expanded and these newly recruited troops would be dispatched from numerous locations throughout the United States and sent to Wilkinson in New Orleans) and deliver a message to Spanish governors to avoid British entanglements and assure them of American support for their independence from Spain.

Wilkinson also sought to use the trip as an opportunity for personal enrichment. With Jefferson's knowledge and permission, as part of the mission Wilkinson was allowed to ship fifty barrels of flour and apples he owned in order to sell them to Spanish officials in Havana and Pensacola, in contravention of the Jefferson embargo.[6] While the terms of the embargo allowed the president to waive its restrictions on a case-by-case basis, granting permission to Wilkinson for his personal enrichment was yet another way Jefferson sought to reward Wilkinson for his betrayal of Burr.

On January 24, 1809, six weeks after he received the order to proceed to New Orleans, Wilkinson finally departed Baltimore aboard the schooner *Wolf*. At a stop in Norfolk, Virginia, Wilkinson attended a public dinner, where he offered a toast: "The New World, governed by itself and independent of the old."[7] The Spanish minister formally protested Wilkinson's remarks, which were disavowed by Treasury Secretary Gallatin, who attributed them to "the vanity, the indiscretion and the ordinary inconsistencies of that General."[8] After stopping in Charleston, Wilkinson transferred to the brig USS *Hornet* and arrived in Havana on March 23. He sold his flour and apples, then briefly met with Captain-General Marquis de Someruelos, assuring him that the American troops that were amassing in New Orleans were for the defense of that city and not for an invasion of Spanish Florida. Wilkinson departed Havana on April 2, aiming to sell more flour in

Pensacola and meet with his old Spanish paymaster, Vincente Folch. Unfortunately for Wilkinson, Foch had departed for Baton Rouge and a meeting with him would be delayed until Wilkinson arrived in New Orleans in late April.[9]

The citizens of New Orleans did not greet Wilkinson's arrival with open arms. Many residents were still chafing from Wilkinson's heavy-handed declaration of martial law in 1806, when Wilkinson was preparing the city for the alleged arrival of Aaron Burr's army. Furthermore, the recent court of inquiry whitewash had failed to quell the continuing rumors of Wilkinson's Spanish pension. One local publication, *The Pensioners Mirror*, greeted Wilkinson's arrival with the following ditty: "When his serene highness entered the city, the bells they rung, *The pensioner is come, um, um, um*" (emphasis in original).[10] The social opprobrium did not stop Wilkinson from seeking to renew his ties with the city's elite, and at some point he either met or renewed his acquaintance with Charles Laveau Trudeau, the former surveyor-general of Spanish Louisiana. Trudeau, designer of what was later to be named Jackson Square in New Orleans, had remained in New Orleans when it was sold to the United States and possessed an intimate knowledge of the lands surrounding the city. Even more enticing to Wilkinson was Trudeau's daughter, Celestine, a woman thirty years his junior with whom he commenced an immediate courtship. Wilkinson's preoccupation with this courtship had a serious impact on his later decision to continue to station his sickly troops in and around New Orleans during the deathly summer of 1809.

The military establishment that Wilkinson had been chosen to lead in early 1809 was in a sad state of repair. Jeffersonian neglect of all things military had scattered troops across numerous frontier posts to monitor Indian relations or operate as customs inspectors to enforce Embargo Act restrictions.[11] A clash with Great Britain during the Burr trials, however, forced Jefferson to reconsider the limited role of the army. On June 22, 1807, the American frigate USS *Chesapeake* departed Norfolk and soon encountered the British frigate HMS *Leopard*, which had been stationed off the Norfolk coast to intercept and inspect American vessels for the presence of British citizens as passengers or crew.

In order to man the Royal Navy for its ongoing war with Napoleon, Britain enforced an impressment policy that asserted its right to force British citizens to serve in the navy. Many British sailors had rebelled against harsh Royal Navy conditions, deserting and then serving as crew on American vessels, where they would find better accommodations and pay. Britain maintained that British sailors could not renounce their citizenship and that the Royal Navy could forcibly stop American vessels on the high seas to search for British deserters. The policy resulted in the kidnapping of thousands of sailors from American vessels, which become a primary cause of war with Great Britain in 1812.

Prior to the encounter with the *Chesapeake*, the Royal Navy's actions had been limited to the search of American commercial vessels only. The *Chesapeake* was unprepared for a confrontation with the Royal Navy, and most of its guns were not prepared for action. In a major escalation of hostilities, the *Leopard* demanded the *Chesapeake*'s submission to an inspection for British deserters among its crew. The captain of the *Chesapeake* refused, leading the *Leopard* to open fire, killing three American sailors and wounding eighteen. After token resistance, the American vessel surrendered and allowed the British to board and seize four British sailors from among its crew.[12]

Jefferson's reaction to this assault on American sovereignty was twofold: he commenced a series of embargoes against trade with Great Britain and he proposed a significant expansion of the army. At Jefferson's request, Congress passed a law in early 1808 that authorized the massing of eight temporary regiments. By the time of their deployment to New Orleans in 1809, however, these units consisted of mostly raw recruits led by an officer corps largely selected for adherence to Democratic-Republican politics rather than military skill. Winfield Scott, one of the officers recruited at the time, later observed, "The appointments [from the Democratic-Republicans] consisted, generally, of swaggerers, dependents, decayed gentlemen, and others—'fit for nothing else,' which always turned out *utterly unfit for any military purpose whatever*" (emphasis in original).[13] Scott was equally as dismissive of the old officers, describing them as "sunk into either sloth, ignorance, or habits of intemperate drinking." Jefferson's parsimony continued to be reflected in the staffing of the new regiments. For example, the 1808 legislation called for the recruitment of a regiment of light artillery but provided no funds for acquiring horses to pull the guns or the caissons.[14]

The expanded military envisioned by the 1808 legislation was completed by Jefferson and Dearborn without any meaningful input from Wilkinson, who was primarily engaged in defending himself at the Burr trials and the 1808 court of inquiry. In recognition of the perception that the officer corps had long been divided into pro- and anti-Wilkinson camps, the act also called for the creation of two new brigadier general positions, reducing Wilkinson's overall influence on the army's officers. To provide for a geographic balance, New Yorker Peter Gansevoort and South Carolinian Wade Hampton were selected for the new general officer positions, and each would figure prominently in Wilkinson's future travails. Gansevoort served as the presiding officer at Wilkinson's 1811 court-martial, and Hampton, an avowed enemy of Wilkinson, eventually became the head of the anti-Wilkinson faction of the army's officer corps. Disputes between Hampton and Wilkinson had a significant detrimental impact on the fortunes of the army during the War of 1812.[15]

The neglect shown by Jefferson toward the military, as clearly demonstrated by his choice of Wilkinson to remain in command, was continued if not compounded by the neglect shown by Jefferson's successor, James Madison. Madison followed Jefferson's example of ignoring the weaknesses within the military establishment, even though the growing strain with both Great Britain and France demonstrated a greater need for a competent military force. Madison was a great constitutional scholar and adept politician, but he had no military background and he failed to attract any recognized military talent to his cabinet. (James Monroe, who had significant military experience in the Revolution, was initially not in favor with the new Madison administration. Monroe did not enter the Madison administration until 1811, when he replaced Robert Smith as secretary of state.) Madison replaced Secretary of War Henry Dearborn with William Eustis, a veteran of the Revolutionary War who had served as a military surgeon, not as a combat commander. Following the war Eustis had entered Massachusetts politics as a Democratic-Republican in a Federalist-dominated state, and his selection as secretary of war was designed to provide a geographic balance to Madison's cabinet but was in no way based on Eustis's military background or skill. In many ways Eustis was the least qualified man to hold that office to date.

Eustis's lack of a military background was compounded by a host of other issues. At the time, the staff of the War Department consisted of fewer than ten civilian clerks.[16] The authorized strength of the army before the 1808 expansion was set at 3,350 men, although the actual strength was considerably lower.[17] The troops were organized into eight new and three old regiments, many of which were scattered to locations that were unknown to Eustis. Finally, Eustis had to work with Wilkinson, a man whom he did not know and who had over ten years of experience in circumventing secretarial control. Making the transition even more difficult, when Eustis took over the office, Wilkinson was deployed with the bulk of the army fifteen hundred miles away at New Orleans.

Dearborn's order to Wilkinson of December 2, 1808, to proceed to the defense of New Orleans caused the greatest concentration of US Army forces after the campaign at the Battle of Fallen Timbers in 1794. The order was based on faulty intelligence that British troop movements in the Caribbean were a precursor to an invasion of the Mississippi valley and capture of New Orleans. A British fleet and 10,000 troops did descend on the Caribbean in January and February of 1809, but the target was the French island of Martinique, not New Orleans. The invasion force was under the command of Rear Admiral Sir Alexander Cochrane, and the British succeeded in capturing Martinique on February 19, 1809.

Dearborn's December 1808 order directed four regiments of infantry and an assortment of dragoons, light artillery, and riflemen from scattered posts throughout the United States to move to New Orleans and be deployed as Wilkinson saw fit in defense of the city. The troops were ordered to proceed via ocean packet from Atlantic ports or by river boat down the Ohio and Mississippi Rivers.[18] The order led to more than 2,000 troops descending on New Orleans in the winter, spring, and summer of 1809 and demonstrated the failure of the Jefferson and Madison administrations to provide the necessary logistical infrastructure for action.

Many of the troops came from the new regiments raised in response to the April 1808 expansion of the army. They were unfamiliar with large troop movements over long distances and were commanded by inexperienced officers unfamiliar with the health hazards inherent to living in the Lower Mississippi Delta during the summer months. To the extent that these troops were deployed for the first time away from their usual posts of duty, they would soon be exposed to the inadequacy of the army's ability to sustain them.

The 1808 legislation provided for the establishment of the first light artillery unit in the army. However, recruitment of field grade officers to command the unit was still lacking eighteen months later. A seasoned artillery captain, George Peter, was transferred into the unit in May 1808 to acquire the necessary guns, wagons, and horses needed to form the unit. When the December 1808 order was received to proceed to New Orleans, the unit proceeded overland in winter from Baltimore to Pittsburgh, where it was loaded onto boats and floated down to New Orleans.[19] As the unit prepared to deploy under Wilkinson in the summer of 1809, the newly appointed secretary of war Eustis concluded that the cost of maintaining horses to pull the unit's guns and wagons was too expensive and the unit was directed to sell its horses.[20] How an artillery unit was expected to function without horses was left unsaid.[21]

Of all the senior officials in the Madison administration, Wilkinson was the most familiar with the challenges related to climate and disease that would confront a military force in the Lower Mississippi. Since 1787 he had engaged in commercial operations in New Orleans. In 1798 he supervised the construction of Fort Adams at Loftus Heights, the southernmost outpost of the United States on the Mississippi. In 1801–2 he supervised the construction of the Natchez Trace. In 1803–4 he commanded US troops in Natchez and New Orleans as part of the acquisition of the Louisiana Territory from France. In 1806 he had commanded troops in Natchitoches during the "neutral ground" incident with Spain and in New Orleans in the "defense" of the city from the anticipated depravations of Aaron Burr. In addition to his knowledge of the challenges of the climate, Wilkinson was the most experienced officer in the army who would be familiar with the command of and logistics for a large body of troops. Were he at all competent, he would have used this knowledge to take effective command of the forces at New

Orleans and acted to ameliorate the adverse effects of climate and disease. Furthermore, having intimate knowledge of the inadequacies of the army's logistical system, he could have urged reforms on Dearborn, Jefferson, Eustis, and Madison before and during the deployment.

Instead, Wilkinson did virtually nothing to prepare the army. While the troops slowly trickled into New Orleans, he delayed his own departure for New Orleans and did little to prepare the necessary quarters and supplies that would be needed to house the troops. To the extent that prior to his arrival in New Orleans he sought to address the logistical difficulties that he would face, it was based on reestablishing the corrupt relationship with the contractor he had used to frustrate Anthony Wayne in 1794. In one of his first communications to Secretary Eustis, Wilkinson urged the hiring of Eli Williams to serve as quartermaster.[22] Williams, a partner in the firm of Elliott and Williams, was the provisioning contractor for the Legion in its advance into Ohio in 1794, and Wilkinson, behind Wayne's back, had urged the contractor not to perform in order to cause the campaign to fail and lead to Wayne being replaced by Wilkinson.

Williams was not selected as quartermaster, but Wilkinson did enter into a corrupt relationship with the army's current provisioning contractor, James Morrison. Wilkinson and Morrison had served together at Saratoga and then met again when they were both businessmen in Kentucky.[23] By 1809 Morrison had been selected by the War Department to provide provisions to the troops under Wilkinson's command in New Orleans. Recognizing that his economic success was contingent on Wilkinson's satisfaction with his substandard work, Morrison gifted Wilkinson with eleven Kentucky horses for his personal use. The expense incurred by the government in transporting and feeding these personal animals of Wilkinson from Kentucky to New Orleans was one of the charges brought against him at his 1811 court-martial. Based on the price the army subsequently paid to Wilkinson for some of these horses, the fair market value of this "gift" of eleven horses was worth $2,200.[24]

Having gained Wilkinson's attention with this valuable bribe, Morrison reached out to him in July to establish his expectations in return:

> You know whether the contract is profitable depends on the commander-in-chief. . . . Should I visit New Orleans in winding up my contract I will make arrangements on this head as will no doubt be satisfactory to you. On this head don't have a moment's uneasiness. Be as serviceable to me as you can, where you are, keeping the public in view, and it may be in my power to be of some way serviceable to you. . . . Should a part [of the flour] become unfit for use, I have directed them [his agents] to purchase and mix with sweet flour as to make it palatable. Don't I pray you order an examination unless the last resort.[25]

Some of the flour provided was so badly damaged that "when the barrel was sep-
arated from its contents, the cemented mass retained the shape given to it by the
cask, and stood firmly erect like a block of wood." Axes were needed to break up
the block before the flour could be used.[26] Hundreds of troops were suffering from
diseases caused by malnutrition from the tainted food provisioned by Morrison.
Yet he solicited Wilkinson's aid to ensure that his fraudulent performance would
not be held against him in the renewal of the contract and allow him to bid for
maximum profit: "Will you oblige me, by giving me your opinion on the price
which you conceive the Ration will be furnished at each post, calculating on a
moderate profit—write briefly and without reserve marking the letter *Private*"
(emphasis in original).[27]

Fraud within the military contracting system ran rampant, typically perpetrated
by contractors passing off substandard goods by tricking overworked contracting
officials. When trickery did not suffice, corruption of low-level government contracting officials would often ensure that substandard goods were accepted without complaint. The Morrison-Wilkinson correspondence demonstrated a much
higher level of corruption. Rather than tricking or corrupting low-level contracting officials, Morrison recognized that in bribing the senior officer, he could ensure that substandard performance would be accepted and that complaints by
contracting officials or sickly and malnourished troops would be ignored.

Under the provisioning contract awarded to Morrison, if the commanding general determined that the provisions provided were "unsound, unfit for use, or of an
unmerchantable quality," a survey would be conducted to determine if the provisions should be condemned.[28] The contract also had a provision that in the case of
deficient or failed performance by the contractor, the commanding officer could
procure supplies directly from the public economy and charge the cost against
the contractor. Morrison's bribe to Wilkinson ensured that he never conducted a
survey and only once procured goods directly against the contractor's account.[29]

In the late winter and early spring of 1809, the units from diverse locations began to arrive in New Orleans and were housed in the city in a haphazard manner,
with no one being in overall charge.[30] No military housing had been constructed
in advance, forcing the units to find their own accommodations in the city and
charging the costs to the military agent. When Wilkinson arrived in late April, he
described the conditions as he found them:

> Picture to yourselves, gentlemen, a body of two thousand, undisciplined recruits,
> men and officers (with a few exceptions) sunk in indolence and dissipation; without
> subordination, discipline or police, and nearly one-third of them sick; extend your
> prospects, gentlemen, to an army without land, or water transport, for a single
> company; medical assistance for two thousand men, dependent on two Surgeons,

and two Mates, one of the former confined to his bed; the majority of the corps, without paymasters; the men deserting by squads; the military agent, representing the Quarter-master's department, without a cent in his chest, his bills protested, and he on the eve of shutting his office; a great deficiency of camp equipage; not a haversack in store; the medicines and hospital stores scarcely sufficient for a private practitioner; and you may, then, form a correct ideal of the conditions in which I found the detachment of recruits, at New Orleans.[31]

Though Wilkinson did indeed seek to exploit the relationship with the provisioning contractor, many of the other supplies needed were out of his control. Under "reforms" passed in 1798 and refined in 1802, the position of quartermaster general and commissary general had been abolished and were replaced by civilian military agents who reported directly to the secretary of war, not the local commander.[32] All food, clothing, and medical supplies had to be procured through military agents in accordance with congressional appropriations and War Department directives. Agents were paid on a commission basis on the cost of goods purchased and therefore had little reason to control costs. The agent for New Orleans was directed to commence purchases of needed supplies by Secretary Dearborn on December 12, ten days after the troops were ordered to head to New Orleans. However, the agent submitted his resignation shortly after receiving this direction and left in mid-July. On May 4, Eustis appointed a replacement agent, but that agent died shortly after arriving in New Orleans in July. Just prior to his departure from Terre aux Boeufs in September, Major Zebulon Pike was detailed to the position for his remaining time at Terre aux Boeufs, but only after two other candidates had refused the appointment and a third had died while considering it.[33]

The confusing presence and authority of the military agent had a direct impact on the provision of goods and supplies in New Orleans. Medical supplies and hospital stores were ordered in December 1808 but did not start to arrive in New Orleans until four months later, long after many of the troops had arrived and become ill. Similarly, fresh clothing for troops was not even ordered until July 1809 and did not arrive until the end of August. Many of the troops had not received new clothing in over a year.

Eustis assumed the position of secretary in March 1809 with no background in the procurement process of the War Department, which was directly under the control of the secretary of war. Furthermore, he arrived in the middle of the largest deployment of American forces in fifteen years and was immediately confronted with information that the deployed troops were becoming ill at an alarming rate and that the deployment was too expensive. As a physician and not a military professional, Eustis understood the reports of the poor health of the troops but was at a loss on how to improve the conditions, other than sending increasingly distressed directives to Wilkinson to move the troops out of the unhealthy environment of the city.

Never having run a large organization or military force, Eustis had no background in the congressional appropriations process or the costs inherent in deploying a large body of troops. He was particularly ill-equipped to understand the frantic messages he was receiving from William Simmons, the Treasury Department accountant assigned to the War Department, which stated that the New Orleans deployment was out of fiscal control. Simmons had been installed fourteen years before, by Treasury Secretary Alexander Hamilton, to provide internal controls over War Department expenditures. Hamilton had a legitimate reason to create an independent review of military expenses: military officers would otherwise go unchecked in their personal approval of military expenses. Simmons, reporting to the secretary of the treasury, was to provide a level of independent review and approval prior to payment by the War Department. Unfortunately, Simmons believed in accounting with a vengeance, and he delayed approval of many legitimate expenses by insisting on the production of massive volumes of invoices and expense records prior to approval. As a result, military officers were often personally liable for expenses incurred by their commands and many fought for years with Simmons over the adequacy of their expense documentation.[34] (Just prior to the end of the Jefferson administration, Dearborn had grown tired of Simmons's accounting practices and recommended his removal.[35] Jefferson did not act, and Dearborn apparently did not pass on an adequate warning to Eustis. Simmons remained the accountant to the War Department until he was finally fired during the War of 1812.)

Given his questionable history of financial transactions, Wilkinson was a consistent target of Simmons's fiscal ire and scrutiny. Wilkinson's alleged expenses to travel to the Burr treason trials in Richmond were the latest skirmish between the two. Simmons questioned expenses claimed and Wilkinson appealed Simmons's denial to Dearborn. The matter was eventually escalated through the attorney general and Secretary of State Madison, making its way to Jefferson, who approved payment shortly before leaving office. Simmons did not take kindly to losing the fight and published one of the first whistleblower documents in American history, "Public Plunder." In the report the anonymous Simmons denounced Wilkinson for taking bribes from a foreign power and for improperly claiming $56,116 in expenses for items that included the cost of 18 bottles of wine *per day*, 339 bottles of porter and ale, 74 gallons of brandy, rum, and whiskey, 1 case of gin, 3 barrels of cider, and 350 cigars. The author castigated Dearborn, the attorney general, the treasury comptroller, and Jefferson for approving Wilkinson's excessive claim.[36]

The massive deployment of troops and supplies to New Orleans, all under Wilkinson's command, attracted the immediate attention of Simmons, who began communicating with the newly appointed Eustis regarding the exorbitant cost of the expedition. The ever-alert Simmons focused on the cost affiliated with transportation of the eleven horses for Wilkinson (the bribe from contractor Morrison). Simmons uncovered the fact that housing and forage for these personal horses were being charged by Wilkinson to the government at an exorbitant rate. Apparently not understanding the context of Simmons's concerns, Eustis immediately directed Wilkinson to cut costs across the board. For example, on June 22, he informed Wilkinson that, based on information provided by Simmons, the costs for housing and feeding the horses of the artillery would soon "devour our appropriations." Eustis directed that the horses either be moved to a cheaper location or be sold.[37] Later, when Wilkinson attempted to procure enhanced provisions for the sick, Simmons flagged the purchase, and Eustis directed the military surgeon not to purchase additional supplies for the sick.[38]

Even before his arrival Wilkinson realized that the army needed to be removed from the temptations of women and alcohol available to the troops in New Orleans. As he stated, the attractions in New Orleans "divert our green officers, from due attention to their profession, and will expose them, as well as the men, to the arts, intrigues, dissipation and corruption, of my personal enemies, and the enemies of the administration and the government; who are as busy, under the management of [Daniel] Clark and his cabal, as fiends of hell to corrupt and seduce men and officers from their duty, and to excite discontent and sedition."[39] Since under the December 2 directive from Dearborn, Wilkinson had unlimited discretion on the deployment of the forces guarding New Orleans, and since his primary charge was to defend New Orleans from an assault from the Gulf of Mexico, he sought to move the troops to an appropriate location south of New Orleans.

Unfortunately, because his troops were sick and dying, it took six weeks to find an alternate location. By May 29, Wilkinson, without consulting any other senior officer,[40] had selected an encampment at Terre aux Boeufs (Land of oxen), at a spot on the Mississippi known as the English Turn, twelve miles downstream from New Orleans; by June 4 the movement of the troops to the new location had commenced.[41]

From a tactical perspective regarding the defense of New Orleans, this location twelve miles distant had significant merit, but the selection was compromised by two factors. One was the common belief that the campground had been chosen not for its tactical worth but because it would result in an economic benefit to Charles Laveau Trudeau, the father of Celestine Trudeau, the woman that Wilkinson was actively courting. Trudeau had been the surveyor-general for the Spanish government prior to the transfer of Louisiana to the United States. Given Trudeau's active involvement in surveying land for the Spanish government, it is possible that Trudeau maintained a hidden interest in the property to be rented for the encampment. In addition to paying $640.34 in rent for the property during its three months of occupancy, the army would improve the value of the property by clearing underbrush and constructing roadways and drainage systems that would benefit the owner when the army left. Although records from the subsequent congressional investigation and court-martial hinted at an improper relationship, no direct evidence indicates that Trudeau had an interest in the land. At his 1811 court-martial, Wilkinson denied any fraud with Trudeau:

> It has boldly been asserted, by one class of my enemies, and industriously circulated by another, that I had sacrificed the lives of my associates in arms, and exposed my own hazard; for the improvement of a plantation, belonging to the honourable, and virtuous Lavau Trudeau, my respected father-in-law, who did not own a foot of land, within three leagues of the spot! And, as if nothing could be too gross for credulity, wherein my destruction was concerned, this monstrous tale was circulated by my enemies, with as much confidence, as if it had been a solemn truth. The court will pardon me, for anticipating the regular order of my defense, by the introduction of this foul calumny, which has been too successfully propagated: the infamous falsehood, has filled my mind with indignation and horror; for surely, I am among the last of the human race, who might rightfully be charged with sordid speculations.[42]

The second compromising factor was the land itself: a swampy and flood-prone area three feet below the level of the Mississippi. That year the river had been particularly subject to overflowing its levees, resulting in flooding of the camp and bringing an accompanying plague of disease, insects, and vermin. A 1976 study by the director of the Walter Reed Army Institute of Research concluded that the troops were suffering from "a combination of vitamin deficiency, starvation, and malaria as the common substrate upon which diarrhea, dysentery, hepatitis, typhoid, and pneumonia were laid, all being helped along by poor housing, poor clothing, and demands for hard physical labor, with a shortage of moderately effective medicine and the overuse of a useless or dangerous therapy. Any one man didn't have to have everything—just a few would kill him."[43] Moving an army that was already suffering from sickness and malnutrition into this area eventually led to a debacle that has been described as "one of the army's worst peacetime disasters of any era."[44]

Upon his arrival in New Orleans at the end of April, Wilkinson commenced corresponding with Eustis regarding the challenges that he faced. On April 13, from aboard the USS *Hornet* docked at the mouth of the Mississippi, he sent his first letter to Eustis, relaying his intention to move the army out of New Orleans.[45] On April 19 his first letter to Eustis from within the city described the sickness confronting his command; Wilkinson reported that 598 troops were already sick (one-third of the entire command) and stated that the army needed to be moved quickly out of New Orleans. Over the following weeks a series of letters to Eustis complained about the limited ability of the military agent in supporting his command;[46] the lack of tents to house the troops in the tropical climate;[47] the effects of floods and the rising sick toll;[48] and the lack of bunks, mosquito nets, and horses.[49]

Eustis first responded to Wilkinson on April 27, seven weeks after being sworn into office. In the letter he bemoaned the fact that upon assuming office he hoped to find knowledgeable people who could assist him in successfully assuming the role of secretary but that these persons were dispersed throughout the country and were unavailable to assist him. One person who had contacted him was Simmons, the accountant, who had already raised concerns about improper expenditures in New Orleans. Eustis also hinted to Wilkinson that Simmons continued to mention Wilkinson's "past animadversion" (i.e., his relationship with Spain).[50] Barely three days later Eustis was much more strident and direct, and on April 30, after expressing concern regarding the dismal health of the troops in New Orleans, he directed the immediate removal of most of the troops from New Orleans to Fort Adams and Natchez.[51] Those two locations were clearly in a higher and healthier location on the Mississippi, but they were also three hundred miles upriver from New Orleans. Recognizing that the original deployment of troops in the vicinity of New Orleans may have been driven by Dearborn's December 2 directive, Eustis specifically removed that restriction.

At the time of the April 30 letter, Eustis had not yet received any of Wilkinson's letters regarding the New Orleans deployment. Only one mail courier per week traveled between Washington and New Orleans, and the average transit time was nineteen days.[52] However, Eustis's April 30 order to move to Natchez should have reached Wilkinson before he decided to move the army to Terre aux Boeufs on May 29. At his 1811 court-martial, where he was charged with disobeying Eustis's April 30 order to move the troops, Wilkinson claimed a two-part defense: that he did not receive the April 30 letter until June 5, five weeks after it was sent and the day of the commencement of the movement to Terre aux Boeufs,[53] and that, given the language used by Eustis, the April 30 letter regarding movement to Fort

Adams in Natchez was merely a "suggestion" on where to move the troops, not a "directive."

Both defenses ring hollow. Wilkinson offered no further explanation for the unusual delay of the mail, nor did the prosecutor seek to rebut his assertion at trial. Most likely Wilkinson received the directive in time but chose to ignore it. Furthermore, while Wilkinson and Eustis did not have an established history of communication, and even leaving room for the possibility of an honest misinterpretation, Wilkinson's history of resentment toward and circumvention of secretarial control was well established. Had Wilkinson indeed received the order to move to the healthier climate of Natchez before the commencement of the movement to the pestilential Terre aux Boeufs, why would he continue to insist on the move to the unhealthy location? Furthermore, why did he insist on remaining there when casualty figures continued to rise and his own subordinates were increasingly raising objections? Some historians believe that Wilkinson directed the movement to Terre aux Boeufs out of a spiteful resentment of Eustis's micromanagement.[54] Others believe that he was driven by the need to consummate a corrupt bargain that had been struck with his prospective father-in-law. In June 1809 Wilkinson was actively pursuing his courtship with Celestine Laveau Trudeau, and a move to Natchez instead of Terre aux Boeufs may possibly have been viewed as reneging on an illicit financial commitment Wilkinson made to her father. Trudeau's social connections allowed Wilkinson to overcome the stigma that attached to his reputation in New Orleans and were key to revitalizing his personal finances. Personal greed was also a motivation for ignoring Eustis's April 30 directive and for maintaining the army for three months in the swampy and disease-ridden environs of Terre aux Boeufs at the height of summer.

From the day he arrived in New Orleans, Wilkinson understood that the health of his troops required moving them out of the city and he assumed sole responsibility for seeking an alternate location. He searched for six weeks for a new location, all while his army endured mounting casualties by remaining there. The ultimate selection of Terre aux Boeufs, twelve miles downstream from New Orleans, was Wilkinson's alone, and considering his movement of troops there in direct defiance of the secretary's instruction, his decision was the immediate cause of the suffering that was to follow.

On June 3 Wilkinson dispatched Zebulon Pike, his loyal subordinate, and nine companies of soldiers to commence clearing the land and installing drainage ditches to alleviate flooding. Before the work was completed the remaining troops began departing New Orleans, and by June 9 the entire compliment was located at Terre aux Boeufs. Many were without tents, and many of the tents that had been erected did not have floors, making them particularly prone to flooding, which commenced in earnest shortly after the troops arrived. Until floors were installed, most troops slept on straw or blankets on the damp and flooded ground. (Later the barges that had been used to bring the troops down from New Orleans were broken up, and many of the tents finally received flooring.)

In addition to the discomfort caused by the Mississippi overflowing its levees, the flooding caused the camp's rudimentary sanitation system to overflow, spreading human waste throughout the camp. Mosquitos and flies swarmed the encampment at night, and few mosquito nets were available to provide some moderate form of protection. Medical professionals at the time were not aware of the fact that malaria was spread by mosquitos, so to the troops the presence of mosquitos was an annoyance and not a health hazard. Soldiers were allowed to use their own funds to purchase mosquito nets in New Orleans, but since most troops had not been paid in months, few personal purchases were made.[55] As early as May, Wilkinson sought special authority to purchase more nets, but Eustis never authorized the purchase.[56] In lieu of mosquito nets, some soldiers installed curtains over tent openings, but since rampant dysentery forced most soldiers to make multiple trips to the primitive toilets during the night, the curtains provided little relief from the insect swarms.

None of the troops had clothing that was appropriate to the climate, which was consistently hot, humid, and rainy. At the time the army issued one standard woolen uniform once a year, no matter where a soldier was stationed. Heavy fatigue duties, to create and maintain the camp, resulted in many of the soldiers being half naked before they were eventually evacuated. To the extent that the men had clothes, they were filthy, and the army lacked laundry facilities to provide even a minor level of sanitation. Soldiers were expected to do their own laundry in the water that was also used for drinking, cooking, and bathing. Under Morrison's provisioning contract, four pounds of soap were issued with every one hundred rations, and little effort was made to procure additional soap. During the army's time in the New Orleans vicinity, 28,436 additional rations of whiskey were provided but only two additional pounds of soap.[57] After a time, many soldiers were too sick to do laundry and stayed in clothes that had been repeatedly soiled by bouts of diarrhea.

Few medical facilities, surgeons, or supplies were available to support the sick. In addition to insect-borne illnesses, troops began to suffer from dysentery, caused by poor field sanitation, and scurvy, caused by poor nutrition. The increasing number of dead were buried in shallow graves that soon became exposed through repeated flooding. Makeshift hospitals were full, leading many of the sick troops to stay with their units, thus increasing sanitation woes and the further spread of infectious diseases. The men's shrieks and groans reverberated throughout the camp at night.[58] According to one army surgeon, "a number, in a state of delirium, wandered from their lodgings into the fields and swamps and there expired."[59]

The consistently poor quality of food delivered by Morrison also began to exact its toll on the soldiers' health. "Fresh" beef and pork were often rancid, and the flour was either spoiled or damp. On numerous occasions troops threw away spoiled food rather than eat it.[60] The poor quality of rations was observed by many officers, and Wilkinson did little to hold the contractor accountable for poor performance. Even when Wilkinson attempted to procure additional fresh foodstuffs for the sick, he was reprimanded by Eustis for exceeding the budgetary allotment.

By early July the poor condition of the camp caused many soldiers to be in a near state of mutiny.[61] Enlisted soldiers continued to desert, and a sizable number of officers resigned their commissions rather than remain at Terre aux Boeufs. A group of remaining officers collected a petition begging Wilkinson to move the camp to a safer location. Wilkinson dismissed them as "crazy" and stated that he could not move the camp without a specific authorization from Eustis.[62] In his summary dismissal of their concerns, Wilkinson was again being mendacious. The April 30 letter from Eustis clearly provided adequate authority to move away from Terre aux Boeufs. Wilkinson, who by his own admission received the letter on June 5, hid Eustis's letter from his staff throughout the months of June and July. However, on July 22, he received Eustis's latest orders and could no longer plead ignorance or lack of clarity regarding the secretary's direction. On receiving Wilkinson's letter of May 29, where he stated his intention to move the army to Terre aux Boeufs, Eustis was nothing short of apoplectic and on June 22 he sent a blistering directive to Wilkinson, which removed all doubt about the secretary's direct order to immediately move the army to safer ground at Fort Adams.[63]

Eustis's June 22 letter also mentioned information provided to him by Simmons, documenting the exorbitant expenses incurred by the army since its arrival in New Orleans. Wilkinson's response to the directive was a perfect example of passive resistance; he immediately responded by stating that the directive had "relieved me from an oppressive load of responsibility" and that he would proceed to commence the withdrawal to Natchez. Despite this promise of immediate action, however, Wilkinson and his army would spend another six weeks in the pestilential swampland before the withdrawal commenced.

Some of the delay arose from Wilkinson's petulance at being forced by Eustis to abandon Terre aux Boeufs. Wilkinson later expressed his regret at obeying Eustis's direction to move from Terre aux Boeufs, blaming the move, and not the encampment, for the heavy casualties his troops endured. Wilkinson justified his obedience to secretarial direction on impaired judgment caused by "the deluge of calumnies which poured in on him from all quarters."[64] In subsequent communications to Eustis, Wilkinson raised a variety of health concerns about the wisdom of traveling on the Mississippi in late summer. Because Spanish authorities refused permission for Wilkinson's army to march through Florida, any trip to Natchez had to be made by boat. Eustis's June 22 letter included a directive that had been issued by navy secretary Paul Hamilton, which directed Captain David Porter, the naval commander at New Orleans, to provide Wilkinson with boats that would be responsible for the movement of the troops. However, because of the illnesses that were affecting his crews, Porter reported on September 6 that only three vessels were available and that it was unlikely that these vessels would be able to ascend the river.[65]

Given the failure of the navy to provide sufficient vessels, Wilkinson and his staff hired private barges to move the troops. Most were not equipped with cabins or sleeping accommodations, which meant that the troops would mostly ascend the river on open decks, subject to the sun and insects of the Lower Mississippi in summer. Most evacuations took place between September 3 and 8, with the final troops departing on September 13, almost two months after the order for withdrawal had been received. Wilkinson himself made it no further than New Orleans, where he became violently ill and remained behind in the city until November. Some days later the virtually leaderless armada reached Point Coupee, north of Baton Rouge. Several sick were taken off and placed in a makeshift hospital. Because no funds were available, the officers took up a private collection to build a hospital to support the sick left behind. Boats stopped nightly to bury the dead and cook the evening meal. In the morning, burial parties were again dispatched to bury troops who had died overnight.

When the barges finally reached Natchez and nearby Fort Washington at the end of October, they met yet another disappointment. Colonel Thomas Cushing, another Wilkinson loyalist, was in command at Fort Washington, and even though Wilkinson had received orders to move the army to Fort Washington, sixty days before, Cushing did little to prepare the site for the arrival of a thousand sick and weary troops. Though the climate in Natchez at that time of year provided some relief, the sick and wounded continued to die at an alarming rate. According to official returns, by the end of October, 56 percent of the surviving troops at the fort were listed as sick.[66] Total casualty figures for the period February 1809 to January 1810 were the highest percentage of peacetime casualties in American military history. Of the 2,036 enlisted troops deployed, over 900 deaths had occurred. To this number must be added 166 desertions and approximately 40 officers who either died or resigned their commissions.[67] Wilkinson's losses at

Terre aux Boeufs by death and desertion (1,066) far exceeded St. Clair's combat losses on the Wabash (630).

Wilkinson was never to return to his disastrous command. As a result of either his aversion to serving with a sick army, his own illness, or his courtship of Mademoiselle Trudeau, Wilkinson left his troops and remained in New Orleans until November. While in New Orleans he received a September 10 letter from Eustis relieving him of his command and directing him to report to Washington. To add to his miseries, in September his former business partner, Daniel Clark, published a book intriguingly titled *Proofs of the Corruption of Gen. James Wilkinson, and His Connection with Aaron Burr*. In the book Clark presented a compelling record of Wilkinson's twenty-year history of improper dealings with the Spanish, involvement in the Burr Conspiracy, and mockery of the 1808 court of inquiry. Wilkinson would later return to Washington to face an unfamiliar president, a hostile secretary of war, and a series of congressional investigations primed to investigate his entire military career.

9

THE RISING STORM

1810–1811

Sooner be shot than take a command under Wilkinson.
—James Monroe

A man is as much disgraced by serving under General Wilkinson as by
marrying a prostitute.
—Winfield Scott

Wilkinson's return to Washington was marked with a great deal of uncertainty. His prior relationship with Jefferson had been sealed by his betrayal of Burr, but he was uncertain that this positive relationship would persist under the new administration. Jefferson continued to serve as Madison's mentor, and Madison viewed his own administration as a continuation of Jefferson's, but Wilkinson was concerned that, considering the Terre aux Boeuf scandal, Madison might not be willing to turn the same blind eye to his failings. Jefferson had rebuffed previous congressional concerns about Wilkinson's misconduct through the use of a whitewash military court of inquiry, but Madison displayed no immediate support of another military whitewash or presenting a defense of Wilkinson before Congress.

During his first year in office Madison had few direct dealings with Wilkinson, delegating most of his contact with Wilkinson to take place through Secretary of War Eustis, who had grown increasingly frustrated with Wilkinson's actions at Terre aux Boeufs and the steady flow of fiscal concerns raised by War Department accountant Simmons. Now with renewed congressional hearings being threatened, Madison was forced to take his first in-depth look at the senior general of the army. The first warning came through an unlikely source: former president

Jefferson. Jefferson had supported Wilkinson through the end of his administration, but that support was more circumspect following the debacle at Terre aux Boeufs and the continuing calls for a reexamination of Wilkinson's role with the Spanish and with Burr.

Madison continued to rely on Jefferson's advice in numerous matters, and in November 1809 he asked Jefferson to speak with James Monroe regarding a place for Monroe in the Madison administration. Monroe had served with distinction in the Continental Army and, following the end of the war, formed a close bond with Jefferson and, through Jefferson, with Madison as well. During the Washington administration Monroe had served as US minister to France and later was elected governor of Virginia, all the while a staunch Jefferson supporter. During Jefferson's administration he again served as minister to France and assisted in the negotiation of the Louisiana Purchase. Following the purchase Jefferson selected him to be the US minister to Great Britain. In that capacity he negotiated the Monroe-Pinkney Treaty in 1806, which would have extended many of the terms of the expired Jay Treaty of 1794. However, because Great Britain refused to renounce the impressment of American sailors, Jefferson refused to submit the Monroe-Pinkney Treaty to the Senate for ratification.

Monroe blamed Secretary of State Madison for the treaty's failure and returned to Virginia in 1807, displaying a significant chill in his relationship with Jefferson and Madison. However, at Jefferson's urging, by late 1809 Madison considered a possible role for Monroe in his administration. In November 1809 Jefferson agreed to meet with Monroe to discuss a variety of roles for Monroe. Monroe rejected Jefferson's offer of the governorship of the Orleans Territory, stating that he was only willing to serve in a position where he would report directly to the president. Given Monroe's Revolutionary War career, Jefferson asked whether a military position would be acceptable, but Monroe responded that he would sooner be shot than take a command under James Wilkinson. In a letter dated November 30 Jefferson relayed this bleak assessment and concluded by stating that Monroe would only consider a cabinet position, or a military position, were he to report directly to the president.[1]

Monroe's abrupt condemnation of Wilkinson did not have an immediate effect: Jefferson's letter did not offer an independent evaluation by Jefferson of Wilkinson, nor did it provide a concurrence of or rebuttal to Monroe's condemnation. However, while Madison did not offer any employment to Monroe at this time, Monroe's break with Jefferson's unquestioning support of Wilkinson must have given Madison a new reason to examine the role and worth of his army chief. (In April 1811, Madison picked Monroe to replace Robert Smith as secretary of state.)

At the same time, another Jefferson ally provided Madison with a similar warning about the political liability that Wilkinson had become. On January 18, 1810, Madison sent a letter to Representative John Wayles Eppes, a congressman from Virginia and Jefferson's nephew and son-in-law, having married Jefferson's daughter Mary. Eppes's letter set forth details of the tragedy at Terre aux Boeufs, and stated,

> I have no hesitation in stating that he [Wilkinson] has completely lost the confidence of nine tenths of all persons with whom I am acquainted either here or elsewhere. He hangs like a dead weight upon the administration and so completely has suspicion pervaded the great mass of the community that men of the purest patriotism and best dispositions towards the administration, would if difficulty or danger should occur withhold from the public their services if he was to be their commander.[2]

Eppes may have been dismissive of Wilkinson's worth as a general, but he apparently recognized Wilkinson's skill as a duelist. In January 1811, Eppes challenged Representative John Randolph of Roanoke to a duel. In preparing for the duel, which never happened, Eppes engaged Wilkinson as a dueling instructor.[3]

These warnings were not the only negative information about Wilkinson brought to Madison's attention. In December 1809, satirist, reporter, and author Washington Irving published his novel *Diedrich Knickerbocker's History of New York*.[4] The book, a satirical take on Dutch New Yorkers, was an immediate hit. One of its characters, a bloated and pompous fool named General Jacobus Von Poffenburgh, seemed to be modeled on the persona and history of James Wilkinson. Irving had been a reporter at Burr's 1807 treason trials in Richmond and had taken an immediate dislike to Wilkinson and his demeanor. Irving's thinly veiled description of Von Poffenburgh clearly was meant to mock the pretentious Wilkinson and further eroded any of his popular support.

Though these developments jeopardized Wilkinson's standing in Washington, he displayed his usual lack of alacrity in complying with Eustis's September 1809 directive to return to Washington. Wilkinson did not commence his return journey until April 1810, using his protracted residency in New Orleans and Natchez to punish enemies and complete his courtship of Celestine Trudeau.

One of the unfortunate by-products of Wilkinson's campaign against General Anthony Wayne was the division of the army's officer corps into separate camps, one supporting Wilkinson and one supporting Wayne. Wayne had been gone from the army for over a decade, but the officer corps was still divided into pro- and anti-Wilkinson camps, with the anti-Wilkinson officers favoring General

Wade Hampton. Wilkinson had a long history of actively using the military justice process to promote allies and intimidate and punish enemies, and the most
recent victim of his military justice ire was Captain Winfield Scott. Scott had
originally pursued a career as an attorney, and in the summer of 1807 he attended
the Burr treason trials and observed some of the finest legal practitioners of the
day arguing before Chief Justice John Marshall. Scott was also able to observe the
poor performance of the chief government witness, James Wilkinson. Scott came
away with the belief that Wilkinson was as treasonous as Burr and that Wilkinson
had escaped justice only because of the intercession of President Jefferson.[5]

In light of the growing tensions with Great Britain, Scott decided to abandon
the practice of law in favor of a military career and he entered the army in 1808.
Although he later decried the political loyalty test used by Jefferson to expand the
officer corps, Scott used political connections and took advantage of the process
to obtain a captain's commission in the light artillery. He and his unit, ordered
to report to New Orleans, arrived there on April 1, 1809. Shortly after arriving
he came under Wilkinson's command and was directed to assist in clearing the
ground at Terre aux Boeufs. Scott, disillusioned with his posting to a swamp and
being led by Wilkinson, quickly submitted his resignation and returned to Virginia to await its acceptance by Eustis. Unfortunately, prior to his departure Scott
could not resist imparting to his military colleagues his opinions about Wilkinson's sordid role at the Burr Conspiracy trial.

Upon his return to Virginia and before his resignation was accepted, Scott
learned that allegations of misconduct had been made against him by a Wilkinson
loyalist, William Upshaw, a surgeon in the Fifth Infantry Regiment, who alleged
that Scott had stolen money intended for his troops and had made disparaging
comments against Wilkinson before his departure from Terre aux Boeufs. (Upshaw was among Wilkinson loyalists who had signed a fawning letter in support of
Wilkinson's actions at Terre aux Boeufs.[6]) Scott chose to confront these aspersions
by withdrawing his resignation and returning to the army. He arrived in Natchez
in November 1809 and demanded a court of inquiry, which found grounds to
bring two court-martial charges against him, as alleged by Upshaw on Wilkinson's
behalf. (According to Scott's memoirs, both Upshaw and Wilkinson denied that
Wilkinson had any role in bringing the court-martial charges against Scott, which
is likely a false claim.[7] The charges may have indeed been referred to court-martial
by General Hampton as the convening authority, but Wilkinson's probable role
in urging Upshaw to press the charges is consistent with Wilkinson's history of
using officers loyal to him to attack his enemies.) One charge alleged that Scott
had improperly withheld two months of pay from his men; the second alleged that
Scott had used seditious and insubordinate language about Wilkinson when he

stated that "if he should go into the field with him, he would carry one pistol for his enemy and one for his general."[8]

The first charge probably resulted from the chaos in paymaster records during the Terre aux Boeuf deployment and from Scott's lack of familiarity with military fiscal matters. The court-martial acquitted Scott on this count. However, the second charge had significant merit. During his first deployment at New Orleans and Terre aux Boeuf during the summer of 1809, Scott was probably liberal in his imprudent condemnation of Wilkinson, his commanding officer. When he returned to Natchez in the fall he also expanded on his condemnation of Wilkinson. Among the statements attributed to him: Wilkinson was "a liar and a scoundrel"; he "never saw but two traitors, General Wilkinson and Burr"; and "A man is as much disgraced by serving under General Wilkinson as by marrying a prostitute."[9] Scott's defense at trial rang hollow. He contended that the charge of insubordination toward his commander was improper because, at the time of his November outburst, Wilkinson had been relieved and was no longer his commander.[10]

No military organization could countenance such statements by a junior officer against the commanding general of the army, and Scott's conviction on the disrespect charge was assured. However, while the military jury could have expelled Scott from the army, it instead imposed a punishment of a year's suspension from duty. The jury also recommended that nine months of the suspension be lifted, but General Wade Hampton, the convening authority, rejected the jury's recommendation and insisted that the full time be served. Wilkinson was in turn outraged by the light sentence and harbored a continuing resentment of Scott.

In many ways Scott and Wilkinson shared similar personality traits. Both were imperious, with an affinity for military dress and pomp. Both served over forty years and rose to the highest position in the US Army. Both wrote memoirs at the end of their careers that were filled with attacks on perceived slights by presidents, politicians, and military rivals, with a portion expressing a mutual dislike of the other, and both used their memoirs as a recitation of their defenses to court-martial charges. However, there is one critical difference between the two: Scott, despite his many faults, was probably the finest military officer produced by the American army in the first half of the nineteenth century. From his brilliant leadership on the Canadian frontier in the War of 1812 to his astonishing conquest of Mexico City in the Mexican-American War, to his development of the Anaconda Plan to strangle the Confederacy at the outset of the Civil War, Scott is widely recognized as an outstanding military commander, despite his ego and pomposity. By contrast, Wilkinson never demonstrated any noteworthy skill as a military commander and his memoir's attacks on Scott are filled with his jealous recognition that, in 1816, Scott's career was on the ascendant while his had been destroyed.

Some historians have alleged an even darker instance of vengeance at this time by Wilkinson against a perceived foe: the murder of Meriwether Lewis. Following Wilkinson's tumultuous tenure as governor of the Louisiana Territory, Jefferson nominated Meriwether Lewis to succeed him in February 1807. Lewis did not arrive in St. Louis until March 1808. In the interim he commenced a protracted series of negotiations with War Department accountant William Simmons, seeking reimbursement for the expenses paid for the journey to the Pacific. Lewis submitted a claim for $38,772 and immediately ran into the typical bureaucratic dispute with Simmons. Like Wilkinson, Lewis had attracted Simmons's adverse attention both by failing to document his claims promptly and fully to Simmons's satisfaction and by missing several meetings with Simmons during the early summer of 1807. When he finally met with Simmons that August, Simmons informed Lewis that, instead of being reimbursed for the claimed amount, Lewis had been overpaid by $9,685.77 and was expected to promptly repay the overage.[11]

Lewis's fiscal problems were also exacerbated by the economic mess he had inherited from the poor governance of Wilkinson in St. Louis. In addition to addressing Wilkinson's mismanagement and clearing "Burrites" from posts of authority in the territory, Lewis continued to confront Simmons's refusal to reimburse him for legitimate territorial expenses, resulting in many delayed payments, when payments were made at all. By September 1809 Lewis was deeply in debt from advances he had made from his personal finances for territorial expenses and from the unpaid claims to the Corps of Discovery. Lewis felt he had no choice but to return to Washington to confront Simmons directly.

On September 4, Lewis, accompanied by his free mixed-race servant John Pernier, departed St. Louis by riverboat for New Orleans, with the intention of booking passage there on an oceangoing vessel headed for the East Coast. By September 15 Lewis was incapacitated with malaria and commanded the riverboat to stop at Fort Pickering at Chickasaw Bluffs (Memphis, Tennessee). While recovering at Fort Pickering, Lewis made the decision to proceed overland to the Natchez Trace (thereby avoiding pestilential New Orleans and the possibility that his ship could be intercepted by a British warship and his as-yet-unpublished journals of his trip to the Pacific would fall into British hands).[12] Lewis chose to leave with Pernier and Major James Neely, a local Indian agent who needed to get to Nashville on business. Lewis, Pernier, Neely, and Neely's servant departed Fort Pickering on September 29 and by October 10 had arrived at Grinder's Stand, an overnight inn for travelers on the Natchez Trace. On the evening of their arrival shots were heard from Lewis's room and the following day Lewis died.

The manner of Lewis's death remains swirled in controversy. The traditional viewpoint, as set forth in President Madison's letter to Jefferson at the time, is that Lewis committed suicide.[13] The controversy arises from attaching the label of "suicide" to the death of a famous historical figure. On its face, accepting the conclusion of suicide would require acknowledging that Lewis was in a damaged mental state and in a fit of depression had taken his own life or that he was suffering from the pain and delirium from a severe bout of malaria or the onset of syphilis.[14]

Some recent scholarship has sought to cast doubt on the traditional story. Questions have arisen regarding the authenticity of some of the original reports of his death and the plausibility of the account, considering the existence of two pistol shots and subsequent self-mutilation by stabbing. Given the opprobrium that attaches to suicide, however, some have suggested that Lewis could not have committed suicide, so his death must have been the result of homicide. Since none of the immediate witnesses—Mrs. Grinder, Lewis's servant Pernier, or Neely's unnamed servant—mentioned anything but suicide, each has been suggested as the murder culprit or as a co-conspirator of others wanting Lewis dead.

Given his propensity for intrigue, some have suggested Wilkinson was the prime suspect for Lewis's murder.[15] This theory says Wilkinson wanted to prevent Lewis from bringing evidence to Washington that could demonstrate Wilkinson had benefited from land fraud schemes during his tenure as Louisiana territorial governor or evidence that Wilkinson was plotting yet another filibustering expedition to seize Spanish Mexico and, when he learned of the purpose of Lewis's journey, he set out to intercept Lewis, assassinate him, and seize the incriminating documents. This theory is based on little more than coincidence and speculation. Using the means, motive, opportunity analysis that is typically used to identify a suspected killer, little evidence supports the theory that if Lewis had been murdered, the act was carried out at Wilkinson's direction. Historical speculation that Wilkinson was responsible for Lewis's murder seems to be based on little more than the knowledge that Wilkinson was a scoundrel and that any untoward thing that happened in his vicinity or inured to his benefit must have been his doing.

After recovering from his latest bout of malaria, Wilkinson spent the next few months assisting Hampton assume command at Fort Washington near Natchez and finalizing his courtship of Celestine Trudeau. On March 5, 1810, Wilkinson and Trudeau were married in a Catholic service in New Orleans and Wilkinson finally departed New Orleans for his return to Washington, arriving on April 17.[16] Upon arrival Wilkinson was confronted by the fact that two different congressional committees were commencing investigations into charges old and new against him. While the 1808 congressional inquiry of him had been spurred by House members Randolph and Clark, the 1810 inquiries involved a broader base of congressional support.

Given the debacle at Terre aux Boeufs, on March 13 the House adopted a resolution with little debate to create a committee, chaired by Representative Thomas Newton Jr. (Virginia), to investigate the cause of the high mortality numbers during the army's devastating deployment there. On March 21 Representative Joseph Pearson (North Carolina) introduced an additional resolution calling for the House to create a separate committee to examine Wilkinson's relationship with Spain and with Burr.[17] On April 3–4 this matter was brought to the House floor and resulted in a heated debate. Some members again questioned Congress's authority to even conduct an inquiry, believing that Congress's authority to act was limited to impeachment. Furthermore, since the constitution allowed impeachment of civil officers only, some members suggested that Wilkinson's misconduct as commander in chief was beyond its purview. These opponents believed that only the president had the authority to make such an inquiry into allegations of Wilkinson's misconduct. As stated by Rep. John Taylor, "If there was a Constitutional power in this House of getting rid of this officer, I for one would be most willing to get rid of him. He is a mill-stone around our necks; but I will not take upon myself the responsibility for his conduct. . . . I hold the President responsible for continuing this man in office, and will not take upon myself his responsibility."[18] Others repeated Jefferson's comments from 1808 by stating that Clark's charges were merely a repeat of well-worn allegations of misconduct under previous administrations, and since neither Washington nor Adams had found grounds to act and Jefferson had conducted a court of inquiry that exonerated Wilkinson, there was no need for Congress to act now.

A different group of members dismissed this constitutional pettifogging and mounted a strong case for congressional action. Rep. Timothy Pitkin (Connecticut) observed,

> When we have evidence staring us in the face, (which, if true, makes Wilkinson a Spanish pensioner,) they will say we have no right to make the inquiry? Sir, it is due to the character of the Commander-in-Chief of our Army, as well as to ourselves, that the inquiry should be made. If Daniel Clark is perjured and has told an untruth, let it be known to the world that what he says is untrue. . . . If the facts stated by Mr. Clark are true, General Wilkinson should not hold his commission an instant. And if the President was satisfied of the facts, and did not remove him, I would impeach him. If he was satisfied that an officer in the Army was a Spanish pensioner, and did not remove him, he ought to be impeached.[19]

Pitkin went on to observe that even in the army Wilkinson's standing was diminished by the allegations of misconduct. He noted that in the court-martial of Captain Winfield Scott, the jury refused to expel an officer who was convicted of accusing Wilkinson of being a traitor. "What can be the situation of an army in which such allegations against the Commander-in-Chief are so slightly punished? The officer ought to have been cashiered if he had said that which was not true. If the Commander-in-Chief be suffered to remain in office when treated thus, your Army will not be worth a straw."[20]

Debate also circulated around the adequacy of the 1808 congressional attempt at oversight and the adequacy of the 1808 court of inquiry at addressing the allegations against Wilkinson regarding Spain and Burr. Some defended the court's exoneration of Wilkinson by noting that under the Articles of War, Clark's 1808 declaration to the House was inadmissible before the court and Clark had refused to testify at the proceeding. (The claim by some representatives that the court of inquiry did not consider Clark's January 1808 deposition is incorrect. Article 74 of the Articles of War allowed testimony to be taken by deposition and admitted into evidence if both prosecution and defense are present when the deposition is made. Since Clark's deposition was not taken in the presence of these parties it would have been inadmissible. However, in his deposition before the Butler committee, board recorder Walter Jones testified that Wilkinson waived any objection to the Clark deposition and that it was admitted into evidence, subject to Wilkinson's right to impeach Clark's credibility.[21])

Others had no trouble calling the court of inquiry a "petty military tribunal" and "whitewash"; they urged a meaningful examination of the allegations by the House. Some argued that the Constitution gave the House the authority to pass appropriations for military affairs, and as part of that authority the Constitution also empowered the House to conduct inquiries into how those funds were spent. Many members drew a parallel to Congress's actions in 1792: the examination of General Arthur St. Clair's defeat created a precedent for congressional oversight into Wilkinson's misconduct. On April 4, the House voted 80–29 to appoint a committee to conduct an inquiry into Wilkinson's relationship with Spain and with Burr and selected Representative William Butler (South Carolina) as chairman.

Much of the Butler committee's work was spent in publicly replowing ground covered by the 1808 whitewash. Since little of the testimony and other evidence produced by that inquiry had ever been made public, the committee sought to obtain records from the Madison administration and depositions and records provided by Daniel Clark that were published in 1809 in his *Proofs of Corruption* screed against Wilkinson. Clark had amassed a volume of documents and witness statements that portrayed a thorough and accurate picture of Wilkinson's treasonous relationship with Spain and improper relationship with Burr. His book was prepared in the hopes that the Madison administration would hold Wilkinson accountable in a way that Jefferson didn't.[22] Clark accurately set forth that Wilkinson had received $34,563 from Spain and that these monies were a Spanish bribe/pension and not a delayed return on commercial transactions. He produced copies of Spanish documents, such as Wilkinson's September 1796 letter to Governor Gayoso in which Wilkinson urged the governor not to mention his name in any correspondence, because President "Washington is wide awake." Clark also produced a deposition from former Spanish official Thomas Power, now a Wilkinson enemy, setting forth Wilkinson's paid relationships with Spain and documenting specific trips Power had taken to carry cash and instructions from Spanish New Orleans to Wilkinson when he was located at various military posts throughout the West. Power detailed his multiple trips, taken in coordination with Wilkinson, to bribe various western officials into severing the western states into an alliance with Spain. Power also described Wilkinson's treasonous advice to the Spanish in the 1790s, when he urged them to erect forts at critical points on western rivers to frustrate American efforts to explore the border with Spain.

Clark accurately described how Wilkinson created a false defense of obfuscation to sway the 1808 Jefferson court of inquiry: "Having established the receipt of the money, let us now inquire to what account it is placed by the general and his friends. Here every one who has at all attended to the nature of his defence, must have remarked a studied obscurity, a confusion of dates, sums and circumstances, that evidently show a design to avoid inquiry."[23] Clark alleged that Wilkinson had obtained statements from Power and Spanish governor Vincente Folch denying an improper Spanish relationship with Wilkinson, perjured evidence introduced at the court of inquiry. Clark also produced a January 1808 letter from Andrew Ellicott to Wilkinson that described Washington's suspicions regarding Wilkinson's relationship with Spain. Ellicott declared that Washington asked him to conduct a "thorough, though private investigation" of the matter, and as part of that inquiry Ellicott subsequently uncovered rumors of Wilkinson's illicit relationship with Spain and Power's 1797 trip to bribe western officials as part of the Spanish Conspiracy. Ellicott also described his October 1799 conversation with Spanish captain Thomas Portell when Portell informed him that the recent Spanish shipment of $9,640 to Wilkinson was a direct payment from the Spanish government and not a reimbursement for a commercial transaction.[24] Clark alleged that while Ellicott's letter was available to the court of inquiry, it was never introduced into evidence. (Ellicott did respond to a series of questions that Wilkinson proposed at the hearing.[25])

Clark then launched into a full-scale assault on the conduct of the court of inquiry. He alleged that the three court members were under Wilkinson's control and decried the fairness of the proceeding, since the court could not compel the testimony of nonmilitary witnesses. Thus, though Clark did not testify, Wilkinson was able to present evidence attacking his credibility. Clark noted that while Jefferson published the court's conclusion of exoneration,[26] Jefferson never produced the evidence on which that conclusion was reached.[27] Clark surmised that the lack of evidence that Wilkinson was a Spanish pensioner could only have been reached if no evidence of the pension had been introduced.

Clark also mounted an assault on Jefferson's deceitful letter of January 20, 1808, to the House of Representatives, wherein Jefferson had set forth an inaccurate picture of his knowledge of the allegations against Wilkinson involving Spain and made a hollow promise of a full investigation by a military court of inquiry.[28] Clark rebutted many of the points in Jefferson's letter, including Jefferson's claim that the 1808 allegations by Randolph and Clark were the first that he had heard regarding Wilkinson's Spanish pension. Clark pointed to Jefferson's acknowledged receipt of written communications from Joseph Hamilton Daviess, US district attorney for Kentucky, wherein Daviess expressed concern that Wilkinson was a Spanish pensioner. Clark also produced evidence of a letter from Ellicott to Jefferson in June 1801, setting forth multiple allegations involving Wilkinson's paid relationship with Spain, as well as a January 14, 1808, letter he had received from Ellicott in which Ellicott alleged that "the present administration has been minutely informed of the conduct of General Wilkinson, and why he has been supported, and patronized, after this information, is to me an inexplicable paradox."[29]

Clark's diatribe also inspired another line of attack. Andrew Jackson, a rising Tennessee political star and militia general, had also witnessed Wilkinson's shameful performance during the Burr trials. Nursing a conspicuous hatred of Wilkinson, Jackson was solicitous of any information that might further implicate Wilkinson in Burr's conspiracy or in an inappropriate relationship with Spain. Clark's book and January 1808 declarations described a business relationship between Wilkinson and Michael Lacassange that was improperly tainted with Spanish pension money. (Lacassange had served as a cash courier for Wilkinson.) In January 1810, Jackson's neighbor, William Oliver Allen, contacted Jackson and provided him with records he had obtained from Lacassange's estate. According to Allen, the records corroborated certain aspects of Clark's allegation of an improper relationship among Wilkinson, Lacassange, and the Spanish.[30] Upon review, Jackson concluded that the Lacassange papers were appropriate to bring to the attention of Tennessee senator Jenkin Whiteside. In his February letter to Whiteside, Jackson alleged that the papers corroborated Clark's accusation regarding Wilkinson's receipt of a Spanish pension and urged Whiteside to share the Allen letter with President Madison so that "he may see the effects of over grown treason treachery and corruption when cloathed with power and supported by the smiles of government." Jackson hoped that his attack on Jefferson's court of inquiry whitewash would lead Madison to conduct a real investigation "that can enforce the production of those letters which are in the handwriting of the General it will with other proofs before the publick *completely unmask* him—What my Dear Sir Just on the eve of war, and a Treator at the head of the army—a commander in chief in whom the citizens that is to fight your Battles have no confidence" (emphasis in original).[31]

From the outset both committees faced a daunting challenge in being able to complete their work before Congress adjourned on May 1, 1810. Both committees sought to gather relevant documents from the War Department and obtain testimony from critical witnesses in the Washington area who could provide depositions. Newton's committee commenced taking depositions on March 16 and completed ten depositions by April 24. Most depositions were taken from army officers who had been stationed at Terre aux Boeufs, recounting their first-hand knowledge regarding Wilkinson's selection of the site, the fetid conditions of the camp, the lack of food and medicine, and the ultimate movement of the troops to Natchez. Wilkinson's actions in providing provisions and medical care for the troops were described and copies of the correspondence between Eustis and Wilkinson were also examined and placed in the record.

Wilkinson finally arrived in Washington on April 14, after the investigations had commenced, and immediately sought to inject himself into the hearings process. On April 19 he wrote a letter to House Speaker Joseph B. Varnum, claiming that his delay was caused by the need to review the mass of documents that were necessary for his defense and demanding the right to confront his accusers as part of the congressional investigations.[32] All such requests were denied. Wilkinson provided a deposition to the Newton committee on April 24, blaming the loss of life at Terre aux Boeufs on an act of providence and the inexperience of the troops deployed to New Orleans, stating that his selection of Terre aux Boeufs had been endorsed by Colonel Alexander Smyth and that Eustis's April 30 directive to move to Natchez was merely a "conditional order" that did not require compliance. Wilkinson concluded by saying that "the tales of ignorant, discontented, seditious, and worthless subalterns, and the fictions and falsehoods of my personal and political enemies, have been industriously circulated to wound my character; but being conscious that, in this, as in every other instance of public service, I have done, and more than done my duty, I court inquiry, and defy investigation."[33]

The Newton committee produced a final report by April 27, 1810.[34] The report concluded that the loss of life in New Orleans and Terre aux Boeufs was caused by a variety of factors relating to logistical failures, but other than setting

forth its conclusions for cause of the mortality rate, the report did not seek to assign blame nor did it recommend any action to either Congress or the president.[35]

The Butler committee took a different approach. Relying on its enabling resolution, the committee described its task in four pieces: examine the circumstances
surrounding Wilkinson's receipt of money from Spanish agents, examine Wilkinson's role in the conspiracy to separate the western states, examine Wilkinson's
role with Arron Burr, and examine questionable expenses claimed by Wilkinson as commanding general. The committee identified and gathered numerous
documents previously produced by Clark and Randolph, including the original
records obtained by Randolph in 1808, Clark's January 1808 sworn statement
to the House, and other documents and depositions described in Clark's book.
The committee also took from Wilkinson numerous documents, including forged
accounting records, in support of his cover story that the monies received from
Spain were delayed payments from commercial transactions and not bribes or
pension payments.[36]

Overall the Butler committee took relatively few new depositions. War Department accountant William Simmons was examined at length regarding Wilkinson's
1809 questionable expenses in transporting, at government expense, personal
horses to New Orleans and personal goods to sell in Cuba and Florida.[37] George
Peter testified regarding the improper shipment of Wilkinson's horses to New
Orleans.[38] Kentucky resident Elisha Winters testified regarding his knowledge of
Wilkinson's receipt of payments from Spain.[39]

Since many of the allegations involving Spain were allegedly examined as part
of the 1808 whitewash, the committee asked the War Department to produce
the records of that proceeding and were surprised to learn that whatever record
had existed of that proceeding had "mysteriously" been turned over to Wilkinson
and never returned. In one of the few depositions taken by the committee, Walter
Jones, the recorder of the court of inquiry, was called to explain the disappearance
of the official records. Jones had been appointed by Jefferson as a special judge
advocate even though he was not a soldier and had no military background. Jones
supervised the gathering of evidence by the court, including which documents
would be examined and which witnesses would be called to testify. Given the
court's published conclusion that there was no evidence seen by the court that
established a connection between Wilkinson and Spain, it can be assumed that
Jones presented no such evidence and that the court ignored all contradictory
documents and evidence from Randolph and Clark.

Rather than second-guessing Jones's trial strategy before the court of inquiry,
the committee instead focused on obtaining the official War Department files
relating to the court of inquiry. When the Articles of War were revised in 1806,

Congress recognized that courts of inquiry could be "considered as engines of destruction to military merit, in the hands of weak and envious commandants, they are hereby prohibited unless directed by the President of the United States or demanded by the accused."[40] To ensure accuracy in the results of any proceeding, Article 92 required the record of the proceeding to be signed by the recorder (Jones) and the president of the court (Colonel Henry Burbeck) and to be delivered to the convening authority (Jefferson). Produced in this manner, the record of the court was then admissible in any subsequent court-martial. When the official record of the 1808 proceeding could not be found by anyone in the War Department, Jones was deposed by the committee on the last day it met and provided a disturbing tale of professional malpractice on his part and active subterfuge by Wilkinson and Jefferson in the conduct of the proceedings.

According to Jones, the court had met at various times from January to June 1808. The court finished its inquiry with defense testimony presented by Wilkinson on June 24 and June 25. Jones stated that at the time he was busy with other court appearances but that he "contrived" to attend the court of inquiry on the days of Wilkinson's defense. Upon Wilkinson's conclusion of testimony, Jones gathered up the records of the proceeding, including the fifty-five exhibits Wilkinson produced for the first time during his summation, and left them for the perusal of the three court members. On June 28 he was called back by the members and found that they had reached a written decision exonerating Wilkinson. Jones acknowledged that, as judge advocate for the court, it was his responsibility under the Articles of War to prepare the record of the proceedings for transmission to the convening authority (Jefferson). Because of the pressures of his other responsibilities as US attorney, Jones estimated that it would have taken him ten days to a fortnight to complete this task, but he had been informed by Secretary Dearborn that Wilkinson wanted the president's endorsement of the report's conclusion to be issued by July 4, less than a week after the court had issued its decision. Dearborn had directed Jones to gather up all available court records and send them to Jefferson, with the understanding that the records would be returned to Jones after Jefferson issued his final ruling. Jones had arranged the papers in bundles and transmitted them to Dearborn for transmission to Jefferson. Jones became aware of Jefferson's final July 2 decision when he read about it in the press on July 4, even though a final report still needed to be prepared and signed by him as recorder and Colonel Burbeck as board president. Since Jefferson had already issued a final decision, however, he assumed the final preparation of the record could wait until Burbeck returned to Washington. Jones thought nothing more of the matter until fifteen months later (September or October 1809), when he learned that Burbeck had returned. He requested the records from the War Department only to discover that the records were missing. An inquiry that took place through the winter of 1810 subsequently concluded that the records had at some point been given to Wilkinson and never returned.[41] In his deposition Jones attempted to recall the numerous witnesses who had testified before the court of inquiry three years before. He also tried to recall the substance and theme of Wilkinson's defense and stated his opinion that the documents Wilkinson had provided to the committee from the missing records were actual records examined by the court.[42]

Jones's account of Wilkinson's removal of the records was corroborated by the testimony of John Smith, chief clerk of the War Department. In his deposition Smith stated that a few weeks after the president's July 4 decision, Wilkinson came to the War Department and noticed the records of the proceedings lying on the absent secretary's desk. Wilkinson informed Smith that the records belonged to him or had been promised to him and that he was taking them. Smith voiced no objection and allowed Wilkinson to take the records and had not seen them since then. Smith also recalled informing the secretary of war of Wilkinson's action.[43]

With Jones's admissions to the committee on the last day of the congressional session, the Butler committee recognized that a complete accounting of Wilkinson's conduct would not be possible. The committee's report, issued the same day as Jones's deposition, concluded that due to time constraints and the complicated nature of the facts, the committee was unable to make "a thorough and conclusive investigation of the objects of their inquiry." The committee noted that, because War Department records were missing and Wilkinson was unable to produce certain accounting records considered by the court, they were not able to reconstruct the information that had been considered by the court of inquiry when it exonerated Wilkinson.[44] Wilkinson maintained that he did not provide critical documents to the Butler committee out of fear that they would have been lost or destroyed.[45] Since many of these documents were forgeries supporting his cover story, it is understandable why Wilkinson did not want a close examination of the documents.

Wilkinson's pattern of forgery and interference frustrated the Butler inquiry on multiple levels. By forging documents and providing perjured corroboration from his Spanish handlers, Wilkinson had been able to convince a compliant court of inquiry in 1808 that there was no evidence of a Spanish pension. By improperly removing the records from War Department custody after the conclusion of the inquiry, Wilkinson ensured that no subsequent examination of the forged documents or the perjured testimony could ever be conducted. In light of the strength of information produced by the Butler committee regarding Wilkinson's misconduct, Jones's malpractice, and the disappearance of evidence directly related to

Wilkinson's misconduct, the committee's report indicated that more congressional oversight was needed.

In June 1810 Wilkinson requested Eustis to convene a court of inquiry to opine on certain matters covered by the Butler and Newton reports.[46] Wilkinson wanted the court to review allegations raised by Simmons regarding the improper transportation of horses to New Orleans and the transportation of flour and apples to Cuba and Florida in violation of the Embargo Act. He also wanted the court to review the deployment of troops to Terre aux Boeufs. Wilkinson included a list of witnesses he wanted to be called before the court. Wilkinson's request was designed to serve two purposes. First, Wilkinson hoped that such a court of inquiry would once again forestall a further congressional investigation. Such a trick had worked with Jefferson in 1808, and Wilkinson hoped that Madison would support a similar diversion of congressional interest. Second, Wilkinson recognized that, unlike in a military inquiry, in a congressional investigation he could not control the production of evidence. A military court would allow him to influence the selection of court members, gather evidence from friendly witnesses, and attack the credibility of his accusers, all techniques that had succeeded for him during the 1808 court of inquiry.

Four days after Wilkinson's request for a court of inquiry, Eustis informed him that Madison had denied his request.[47] Not satisfied with this denial, Wilkinson then made an unusual request to have Eustis to confirm that, as the commanding general of the army, Wilkinson had the right to direct certain military officers to be recalled to Washington (at the government's expense) to allow Wilkinson to depose them. This request for production of witnesses, outside of any ongoing military justice proceeding, was highly unusual and caused Eustis to express his displeasure to Madison. Eustis stated that the cost of travel would be prohibitive and that the duties of the witnesses would be disturbed for the sole purpose of being interviewed by Wilkinson. Eustis also asserted that it was his understanding that, with Wilkinson's December 1809 recall to Washington, Wilkinson had no current command in the army and was without any authority to direct any officers.[48] On July 20 Madison concurred with Eustis's conclusion not to allow Wilkinson to order the appearance of officers.[49]

Recognizing he lacked the authority to direct the appearance of officers outside a military justice proceeding, Wilkinson commenced a yearlong personal project of gathering the witnesses and evidence that would be needed in any subsequent congressional investigation or court-martial. When he returned from New Orleans he hired John B. Colvin, former editor of the Frederick Town *Republican Advocate*, to assist him in gathering information for the publication of his memoirs and to use in any future proceedings. In May 1811 Wilkinson published much of the information that he would later use in his defense in a book titled *Burr's Conspiracy Exposed, and General Wilkinson Vindicated against the Slanders of His Enemies on That Important Occasion.*[50]

When Congress reconvened in December 1810, it again took up the question of completing the investigations left unfinished by the previous session. Once more objections were raised regarding the House's constitutional authority to examine Wilkinson's acts and once more it was agreed that further inquiries would be conducted. Newton was again appointed to continue his committee's work and Representative Ezekiel Bacon (Massachusetts) was chosen to replace Butler as chairman of the second committee. Unlike the previous committees, the new committees were charged with including input from Wilkinson, and within days of its re-creation, Bacon's committee invited Wilkinson to present evidence on his own behalf. The committee also agreed to issue subpoenas on Wilkinson's behalf for documents and testimony from others.[51] Wilkinson promptly accepted the committee's invitation but repeated his criticism that Congress had no right to question his conduct as a military officer.[52] Wilkinson was more confrontational with Newton's committee, and in a series of letters to the committee he repeatedly demanded the right to cross-examine witnesses called by the committee. All such requests were ignored.[53]

Both committees were confronted by the fact that they had to complete their work by March 4, 1811, the closing date of the 11th Congress. Ultimately the remaining inquiries did little to complete the record. On February 23 Bacon proposed to send to Madison "an immense mass of documents collected on the subject, without any opinion expressed thereon by the committee."[54] Bacon's report also noted that in November 1810, Wilkinson had returned several documents to the War Department that allegedly comprised the records of the 1808 court of inquiry that Wilkinson had previously removed. These documents, which the committee noted were generally exculpatory of Wilkinson, were obtained from the War Department and admitted into evidence.[55]

The House approved an amendment to include the transmission to Madison of the report, issued during the last session by Representative Butler.[56] Newton's 1811 report, which reaffirmed the findings of the 1810 report, was apparently never even sent to Madison. Based on objections raised by Wilkinson ally Representative William Crawford (Pennsylvania), the work of the Newton committee was shelved.[57] Though the House vote suppressed the Newton committee's report from being finalized and sent to Madison at this time, Wilkinson sought to ensure that Madison was aware of Crawford's opposition to the report. On April 20 he wrote to Madison for the first time in two years and provided him with Crawford's opposition to the report.[58]

In the end, other than creating a record of misconduct that was difficult for Madison to ignore, the 1810–11 congressional attempts at accountability and oversight were a complete failure.[59] Twenty years had passed since adoption of the Constitution, yet Congress still was uncertain of its authority to conduct oversight hearings, particularly as they related to possible criminal misconduct by a senior military official. Furthermore, due to time constraints and a lack of investigative experience, Congress had demonstrated an inability to investigate a complex subject when no clear answers were readily apparent. Their efforts were further frustrated by Wilkinson's successive obfuscations via forged documents, confusing and perjured testimony, and the loss and destruction of official records. Congress was also confronted with clear evidence that three prior presidents had been given evidence of Wilkinson's misconduct yet chose to do nothing. Had Wilkinson been a traitor and a thief, the thinking went, surely that fact would have been realized and acted on by Washington, Adams, and Jefferson. Their lack of action must have been the result of a considered choice, that there was insufficient evidence to take any such action. The committees chose to attribute a degree of wisdom to these presidential decisions that they did not deserve.

As the congressional inquiries concluded, Wilkinson commenced a multifaceted effort to curry favor with Jefferson and Madison. On January 21 he sent a long letter to Jefferson, with whom he had lost touch. Repeating the familiar complaint of persecution by numerous sources, he provided Jefferson with a review copy of the portion of his memoirs dealing with his role in the Burr Conspiracy trials.[60] Jefferson, no doubt pleased that Wilkinson's memoirs favorably interpreted both of their roles in the trials, responded by urging Wilkinson to ignore his detractors.[61] Wilkinson proceeded to display Jefferson's friendly letter before multiple people, and eventually Madison informed Jefferson of Wilkinson's liberal use of the letter.[62] Jefferson responded to Madison by stating that his letter was only meant to be a friendly acknowledgment of the receipt of Wilkinson's memoirs. Regarding Wilkinson and Burr, Jefferson observed that "I never believed that Wilkinson would give up a dependence on the government under whom he was first, to become a secondary & dependant on Burr."[63] However, Jefferson must have realized from Madison's letter that Wilkinson might abuse any communication from him and that having a close association with Wilkinson would be problematic and might result in further scrutiny by Congress. Jefferson ceased all further communications with Wilkinson, a silence that lasted seven years.

Wilkinson had little direct contact with Madison following his April 1810 return to Washington. According to Wilkinson's memoirs, Eustis assured Wilkinson, prior to his departure from New Orleans, that he could *rest assured of a disposition in the executive, to shield me from persecution, and to afford me every aid*

in my exertions to assert and maintain the uprightness of my character and conduct"
(emphasis in original).[64] Wilkinson also stated that he had been assured by three of
Madison's ministers that Madison was "satisfied of my innocence in relationship
to Burr's conspiracy and the Spanish pension."[65] However, Wilkinson was trou-
bled by the fact that, following the adjournment of Congress, Eustis had advised
Wilkinson to return to New Orleans to await further developments. Recognizing that such a move would remove him from influencing decision-makers in
Washington and place him in close proximity to his army rival, Wade Hampton,
Wilkinson informed Eustis "*that sooner than consent to such degradation, I would
bare my bosom to the fire of a platoon*" (emphasis in original).[66] Wanting to obtain
a more direct reassurance that Madison would stand up to pressure, Wilkinson
wrote to Madison and complained about the injustice of the congressional investigations and the successful efforts of Crawford and others to prevent the House
from reporting out the results of the Newton committee's investigation of Terre
aux Boeufs.[67]

Wilkinson's instinct that something was apparently amiss in his relationship
with Eustis and Madison was well founded. In addition to the concerns raised
by the congressional document dump, Madison was conducting his own inquiry
into Wilkinson's relationship with Spain. The existence of the records of Wilkinson's late business partner Michel Lacassange, which established that Wilkinson's
payments from Spain were not in return for a business transaction, had come to
Madison's attention; he directed Eustis to ask William O. Allen, who possessed
the records, to provide them to territorial governor Benjamin Howard for transmission to Washington. Allen did as requested, and Madison directed Eustis to
confront Wilkinson with their contents. On May 13 Eustis requested a meeting
with Wilkinson the following day but provided no hint about the subject of the
meeting.[68]

According to Wilkinson, at the May 14 meeting, which was his first meeting
with Eustis in six months, Eustis assured him that Madison was convinced that
Wilkinson was without fault relating to the "Spanish business" and the "Burr business." However, Madison felt that the Terre aux Boeuf matter should be referred
to a general court-martial. Wilkinson agreed that a military trial was needed to
clear his honor but objected to the trial being held in New Orleans because of
the presence of General Hampton.[69] Eustis ended the meeting with a promise to
discuss the matter further with Madison.

On May 15 Wilkinson wrote to Eustis and expressed his reluctant support of a
court-martial: "In a case where I waive the privileges of my rank, and the immunities secured to me by law and by custom immemorial, to accommodate the views
of the executive, I trust I may, with propriety, offer to your consideration, such

precautions as appear to me essential to a fair and unbiased trial." Wilkinson urged
that the trial be held at Fort McHenry in Baltimore and that the court members
be selected from officers in Pittsburgh and posts east of the Alleghenies. Wilkinson said that he would agree to a trial in New Orleans but only if Hampton was
transferred out of that post and provided a list of officers whom he felt could serve
as jurors. Wilkinson also explained that he wanted a trial away from Washington
to spare Madison from allegations of fixing the trial. "As I am to be prosecuted by
his order, should a tribunal, composed of his dependents, hold their deliberations
immediately under his eye, the invidious, who do not understand the principles
and motives of his conduct in this case, may misinterpret them, and cast censures
where none are due." Wilkinson also asked whether he could retain his sword until
the time of trial.[70] (Under Article 77 of the Articles of War, whenever an officer is
charged with a crime, the convening authority is to confine the defendant to his
quarters and "deprive him of his sword.")

Under the guise of protecting Madison, Wilkinson was attempting to manipulate the military justice process in his usual way. By allowing Wilkinson to control
the location of the trial and be tried by a jury of subordinate officers he selected,
Madison would be visibly compromising the process from the start. Once again
Wilkinson was attempting to ensure that a jury pool would be selected from officers who were loyal to him. (Wilkinson's memoirs do not list most of the officers
that he recommended to serve on the jury, so it is unclear how many were actually
selected. Of the two names that he does mention, Lieutenant Colonel Thomas
Smith was indeed chosen by Madison and Eustis, and Smith testified as a witness
for Wilkinson.) It is not clear what "privileges" and "immunities" Wilkinson was
waiving by submitting to court-martial. Ironically, it was Wilkinson's attacks on
Anthony Wayne fifteen years before that had established the legal principle that
the president could direct the court-martial of any subordinate military officer,
including the commanding general.

A second meeting with Eustis took place on May 18. According to Wilkinson,
Eustis "expressed his abhorrence of his situation, which obliged him to become
my accuser, and thought the charges could be reduced to a narrow compass; I
wished them to be extended as far as possible."[71] If Wilkinson is to be believed,
the sweeping nature of the final charges, which encompassed allegations that
took place before Wilkinson was even a soldier and which were well beyond
the statute of limitations, was Wilkinson's own idea. From this statement it is
clear that Wilkinson intended that his court-martial, and anticipated acquittal,
would completely exonerate him for twenty years of treason, theft, and incompetence. To provide a record to support charges of such a broad nature, Wilkinson
helpfully provided Eustis and Madison with a copy of the record of the various

congressional proceedings that they allegedly had not yet seen or reviewed, even though the House had directed the transmission of the Bacon committee documents more than two months before. Eustis and Madison were apparently fast readers, because on June 1 Wilkinson was informed that the broad charges he requested had been referred to a general court-martial.[72] Eustis even offered to place a government vessel at Wilkinson's disposal to expedite his return to New Orleans, pending the commencement of trial. When Wilkinson rejected the offer, Eustis informed him on June 14 that the court-martial would be convened in early September in Frederick Town, Maryland. On July 7, Walter Jones, again chosen by Madison to serve as judge advocate, provided Wilkinson with the sweeping charging document requested.

10

SPY TRIAL IN FREDERICK TOWN

1811–1812

An officer renowned for never having won a battle or lost a court-martial.
—Robert Leckie, *From Sea to Shining Sea*

The stain which our government has sustained by having such a
character in command of the army must be washed out by a just
and public punishment.
—Andrew Jackson

Frederick, Maryland, had a long relationship with the army, predating the early years of the Republic. Founded as Frederick Town in 1745 by German immigrants, the town (eventually the city of Frederick) was located at an important crossroad of north-south and east-west traffic. In his ill-fated 1755 campaign against French Fort Duquesne at modern-day Pittsburgh, British commander General Edward Braddock took a portion of his army through Frederick and, along with his colonial aide-de-camp, George Washington, met with Benjamin Franklin in an attempt to secure Pennsylvania wagons for Braddock's journey west.[1] During the Revolution the Continental Congress needed interior locations, away from raiding British Army forces, to house captured British and Hessian soldiers. In 1779 the Maryland government responded and constructed the Frederick Town Barracks, which were used to temporarily house the British and Hessian troops of the Convention Army which had surrendered at Saratoga. In 1781, following the American victory at Yorktown, the Frederick Town Barracks was chosen as a site to house the troops that had surrendered at Yorktown and were awaiting repatriation. After the war the garrison continued to house military prisoners, such as French sailors captured during the 1798–1800 Quasi War with France.

Because of the town's barracks and the excellent road connecting it to the new capital at Washington, Frederick was often chosen by military leaders as a place where the army could be headquartered during the pestilential Washington summers. It also was often chosen by army leaders as a place to convene military justice proceedings, such as courts of inquiry and courts-martial, because of its proximity to the seat of government in Washington but also its distance from direct congressional and executive civilian interference in military justice proceedings.

Then, as now, courts-martial were deemed as an important aspect of maintaining discipline in the army. Rather than subjecting army officials to the vagaries of local civilian courts, and to provide a place for adjudicating military as well as civilian offenses committed by soldiers, the American army followed its British forebearers and established a military criminal code, called the Articles of War, and a military criminal justice system to try military members before a military court. The original Articles of War were first issued by the Continental Congress during the Revolution in 1775 and revised by Congress in 1806. With minor revisions, this code remained the primary body of military law until Congress passed the Uniform Code of Military Justice in 1950.

Under the Articles of War, a senior military officer, known as the convening authority, would swear out charges against a military defendant, then convene a court-martial to try the case. General courts-martial were convened to try the most serious offenses and were authorized to impose a full variety of penalties, from reprimands to death sentences. The convening authority would identify thirteen officers to sit on the jury panel. In theory these officers should be of equal or higher rank than the defendant, but, given the small size of the available officer pool during early times, it was not always possible to achieve when the defendant was a senior officer. The government's case was presented by a prosecutor, known as a judge advocate, who may or may not have been an attorney. In addition to prosecuting the case, the judge advocate provided legal advice to the members of the court on issues that arose during trial. (The Articles of War also expected the judge advocate to serve as counsel for the accused. It is not clear how this obviously conflicting role was expected to be carried out in an ethical manner.) However, the judge advocate provided legal advice only; the ultimate legal decisions were made by the president of the court, who was the most senior officer on the panel. The jury's verdict and sentence were not final until they were reviewed and approved by the convening authority, who had the authority to overturn a guilty verdict or mitigate the court-martial-imposed verdict and sentence. In some cases, when dealing with senior officers or an adjudicated sentence of death, the court-martial results had to be reviewed and approved by the secretary of war and the president.[2]

In his role as commanding general, Wilkinson was intimately familiar with Frederick and its citizens. On numerous occasions he directed the relocation of army headquarters to Frederick during the hot summer months.[3] As the army's commanding officer he also directed that courts-martial be convened at Frederick. The most famous, prior to Wilkinson's trial in 1811, was the 1803 trial of Colonel Thomas "Long Hair" Butler. Following Jefferson's election in 1800, Wilkinson decided to make some changes in the dress of the army. Since the time of the Revolution, many officers continued to wear their hair in the British style, which meant long hair gathered in a queue at the back and tied with a ribbon. Wilkinson chose to abolish this style for two reasons: short hair was healthier for troops in the field, and short hair appealed to the Jeffersonians because it was a rejection of British traditions and mirrored the practices of republican France.[4] Colonel Butler, forty-nine, was an obstinate holdover from Revolutionary times and viewed his long hair as a badge of honor. He refused to obey Wilkinson's order, contending that Wilkinson did not have the authority to deprive him of his hair, which he considered to be a "gift of nature." Butler also believed he had incurred Wilkinson's ire because of his stated belief that Wilkinson was a paid Spanish agent.[5] Since Wilkinson could not tolerate defiance by a senior officer, he directed Butler's court-martial in Frederick. As the most senior officer in the army after Wilkinson, Butler was also viewed by Wilkinson as a rival.[6])

Butler spent his trial preparation time wisely. He began by hiring John Hanson Thomas, a well-respected Frederick trial attorney and known Federalist, who was willing to take on cases that would oppose Republican/Jeffersonian principles. Butler also commenced a public relations campaign to obtain political support for his cause, attracting public figures like Andrew Jackson, a rising Tennessee political star, state militia general, and friend of the Butler family. Jackson wrote to President Jefferson on Butler's behalf, protesting the prosecution of a faithful Revolutionary War veteran.

Butler's trial commenced on November 21, 1803, and lasted until December 6. Thirteen senior officers were empaneled to serve on the court, and during the trial the panel members were seen socializing with known Frederick Federalists, including Thomas and Roger Brooke Taney. One of the jurors noted that virtually every officer on the panel was a known Federalist.[7] Owing to the small size of the army's officer corps, many of the panel members and witnesses would have roles to play in Wilkinson's 1811 court-martial. While Butler was convicted of failure to obey Wilkinson's order, the recommended sentence was a simple reprimand. Wilkinson was furious at the court-martial's judgment and appealed to Jefferson to have the entire proceeding thrown out. Jefferson wisely refused to interfere, and Wilkinson begrudgingly approved the verdict in February 1804.[8]

Wilkinson was not done with Butler, however, and following his simple reprimand he ordered Butler to New Orleans and again ordered him to cut his hair. Butler was inclined to disobey these new orders because of the harsh climate and the prevalence of local friends of Wilkinson in New Orleans, and he again sought Jackson's advice on how to proceed. Jackson advised Butler to comply with the transfer order while again lobbying Jefferson on Butler's behalf. Reluctantly, Butler arrived in New Orleans in October 1804 and, as expected, received a new order to cut his hair, and his refusal led to being court-martialed again by Wilkinson. After renewed pleas to Jefferson were rebuffed, Jackson petitioned Congress for relief, citing Wilkinson's order as a "despotic abuse of power."[9] Meanwhile, Wilkinson commenced several lobbying strategies to gather support for his orders to Butler. He contacted former President Adams, asking Adams to confirm that, shortly after Adams's inauguration in 1797, Adams and Wilkinson discussed Wilkinson's authority to issue regulations governing army dress.[10] Adams responded that he could not recall the exact conversation but he believed that only the legislature had that authority.[11] As usual, Wilkinson portrayed himself as the victim of smear tactics by his many enemies. Because he felt that courts-martial were given to "caprice, prejudice and ignorance," he also sought to have Secretary Dearborn administratively discharge Butler.[12] Dearborn chose not to intervene, and the court-martial went forward in New Orleans in July 1805 to its inevitable conclusion: Butler was convicted. This time the court-martial administered more than a wrist slap—Butler was found guilty of failing to obey orders and of engaging in mutinous conduct, then sentenced Butler to be suspended from service for a year. The court-martial finding was then sent to Wilkinson for his review and approval as the convening authority. Following the verdict, but before Wilkinson's approval of it, Butler died in New Orleans of yellow fever.[13] Butler's untimely death did not prevent Wilkinson from approving the sentence, postmortem, in September 1805, but Butler did have the last laugh. He had directed special handling of his remains at burial: "Bore a hole through the bottom of my coffin right under my head and let my queue hang through it, that the damned old rascal may see that, even when dead, I refuse to obey his orders."[14]

Following Wilkinson's confrontation with Secretary of War Eustis in early 1811 and the apparent agreement between Wilkinson and Madison that a trial on all outstanding allegations was needed to clear the record, Wilkinson began preparations for a court-martial to complete his exoneration. Since his relief from command in late 1809, Wilkinson worked full time on the preparation and polishing of his defense.

Remarkably, the location of the trial was negotiated with Wilkinson. Because many of the witnesses to be called at the court-martial were stationed in the Lower Mississippi, the trial was originally set to be held in New Orleans. However, Wilkinson was afraid to be tried there since it was still under the command of Wade Hampton, who was clearly hostile to Wilkinson. Wilkinson then indicated he wanted the trial to be held in Baltimore, at Fort McHenry. But Eustis came to believe that Wilkinson had too many friends in Baltimore and he directed the trial to be conducted at Frederick. Wilkinson strenuously opposed the location. Based on his experience with the citizens of Frederick during the Butler court-martial in 1803, Wilkinson felt that the citizens of Frederick were openly hostile to him and posed a physical threat. However, Wilkinson's concerns regarding Frederick were apparently ameliorated by the fact that two Federalist leaders of the Frederick bar, John Hanson Thomas (Butler's counsel) and Roger Brooke Taney, agreed to represent him. On June 1, 1811, the site of Frederick was agreed on and the trial was set to begin that September.

Under the Articles of War, the thirteen officers selected as jurors would be officers equal to, or senior in rank to, the defendant, but in this case such a selection was impossible.[15] For more than ten years Wilkinson had been the senior general in the army and virtually every officer then on active duty had served under Wilkinson's command. There were no officers senior to Wilkinson and, because of the required size of the court-martial panel, the nature of the offenses charged, and the small size of the army's officer corps, it was virtually impossible to find officers who had not in some way been involved with Wilkinson or the actions leading to his court-martial.

Of even greater concern was the fact that Wilkinson attempted to influence Eustis in his selection of appropriate jurors. In his May 15 and 17 letters to Eustis, Wilkinson identified several officers that Wilkinson recommended should be selected to sit in judgment on his case.[16] While his memoirs do not identify all the officers he recommended, one identified officer, Lieutenant Colonel Thomas Smith, was subsequently chosen by Madison and was called by Wilkinson as a witness to corroborate a major portion of his defense. It is hard to imagine how Madison could have expected any outcome other than complete acquittal when the defendant was allowed to influence the selection of the jury.

After receiving Wilkinson's recommendations, Madison and Eustis, probably working with Walter Jones, the civilian judge advocate, picked several officers who were a cross-section of the existing officer corps. Some were elderly Revolutionary War holdovers with a mixed military record. For example, senior officer and president of the panel was Brigadier General Peter Gansevoort, sixty-two, who had a service record that dated back to the Revolution and who had served under Wilkinson at the Battle of Fallen Timbers.[17] Next in seniority was Colonel Jonathan Williams, sixty, the first superintendent of West Point; Williams was related to Wilkinson by marriage and was widely known to be a friend of Wilkinson.[18] Williams had served on the 1808 court of inquiry that had whitewashed Wilkinson on many of the same charges that were now under review by the court-martial. Colonel Jacob Kingsbury, fifty-five, was another Revolutionary War holdover who also had served under Wilkinson at Fallen Timbers and had previously signed a petition to Jefferson protesting unfair attacks on Wilkinson.[19] In 1801 Kingsbury had named his firstborn son after Wilkinson and eventually testified as a witness for Wilkinson at the trial.[20]

Other senior officers on the panel included Colonel William Russell, another Revolutionary War veteran who had served under Wilkinson for years and would be called by Wilkinson as a witness to vouch for his conduct at Terre aux Boeufs. Colonel William D. Beall was also called by Wilkinson as a witness to his exemplary conduct at Terre aux Boeuf.[21] The aforementioned Thomas A. Smith, thirty, was a former aide to Wilkinson and was called by Wilkinson as a witness to directly corroborate Wilkinson's defense to the charges related to the Burr Conspiracy.

Other officers included Major Moses Porter, fifty-five, a Revolutionary War veteran and noted artillerist and Wilkinson loyalist,[22] and Major A. Y. Nicoll, forty-five.[23] Major Joseph G. Swift, twenty-seven, the first graduate of West Point, replaced a different officer challenged by Wilkinson. Swift went on to have a long and distinguished career as an engineer officer and future superintendent of West Point and eventually served as a witness for Wilkinson.[24] Lieutenant Colonel Alexander Macomb, twenty-nine, another seated panel member, had an exemplary record as a combat commander during the War of 1812 and rose to Wilkinson's position as commander of the army after the war. Just prior to the court-martial, Macomb published an extensive treatise on military justice.[25] Unfortunately, Macomb was also heavily biased in favor of Wilkinson. In his memoirs published years after the trial he described Wilkinson as his friend and as "a man of genius and courage, of military experience, learning, and resources, and yet the victim of misfortune."[26] The overall poor quality and bias of the panel quickly became apparent to the prosecution and gave rise to the belief that the panel had been handpicked to acquit Wilkinson.

Other senior officers who might have been chosen to sit on the panel were unavailable because they themselves were pending court-martial charges in matters not directly related to Wilkinson's case. These included Wilkinson ally Colonel

Thomas Cushing, who had been placed under arrest by General Wade Hampton pending court-martial in New Orleans. At the start of the trial Wilkinson fought to have Cushing released from custody to enable him to testify; Cushing's testimony was eventually provided by deposition. Still other senior officers were unavailable because they were engaged in combat operations taking place under the direction of General William Henry Harrison, leading to the Battle of Tippecanoe in November 1811.

Though Madison, Eustis, and Jones had the advantage of handpicking the court members, military practice gave Wilkinson the right to challenge members for cause.[27] At the start of the trial he moved to have three officers removed. His first challenge was of Colonel Henry Burbeck, fifty-seven, a Revolutionary War veteran who had presided at Wilkinson's 1808 court of inquiry.[28] Based on Wilkinson's objection that Burbeck had publicly commented on Wilkinson's guilt, Burbeck was removed but later called as a witness for the government. Next Wilkinson challenged Colonel Constant Freeman, who had served as president of the court-martial in "Long Hair" Butler's 1805 trial in New Orleans; he was removed on the same grounds as Burbeck and was also called as a witness for the prosecution. Wilkinson also successfully challenged Lieutenant Colonel Electus Backus, who appeared as a witness for the prosecution.[29] In anticipation of successful challenges for cause, Jones and Madison had identified five additional officers as alternate jurors. As a result of Wilkinson's successful challenges, Major Amos Stoddard, forty-nine, another Revolutionary War veteran, and Major Walker K. Armistead, thirty-eight, were chosen as alternates to sit on the panel, along with Swift.[30]

The panel represented a small group of officers who knew Wilkinson well and who were already familiar with, or directly involved in, many aspects of the case. Of the thirteen officers ultimately seated on the panel, five were called as defense witnesses by Wilkinson. While the Articles of War did not prohibit a panel member from also serving as a witness, the direct involvement of almost half the panel in some aspect of Wilkinson's defense to the charged misconduct clearly presented the possibility of bias in the panel's proceedings.[31] It is hard to believe that Madison was not aware of this conflict when he selected these officers.

The clubby atmosphere of the military panel continued throughout the three-month trial in Frederick. Panel members often attended social events in Frederick sponsored by known Federalists and even attended by Wilkinson.[32] The members witnessed the Great Comet of 1811 from Frederick on September 16, and during frequent breaks in the trial many of the panel members took advantage of their close proximity to Washington to pay their respects to Secretary of War Eustis and President Madison. This socializing with the convening authority of the court-martial may have been common during military justice proceedings of the time but nevertheless created the appearance of impropriety.

Madison, as the convening authority, also played a direct role in addressing legal issues that arose during the trial. However, unlike Jefferson's direct involvement in prosecutorial decisions in the Burr trial of 1807, Madison took a much more circumspect approach to his involvement with Wilkinson's prosecution. Under the Articles of War the court-martial convening authority, in consultation with the judge advocate, determined what charges were to be brought. In this case, dealing with the senior military officer of the United States, the convening authority was Madison, and in all likelihood, he made specific charging decisions after consultations with Eustis and Walter Jones Jr., who served as judge advocate.

Jones was an experienced civilian trial attorney and should have known that a prosecutor may harm his or her case by overcharging the defendant. Overcharging, or "throwing in the kitchen sink" on every possible offense, may have some benefit in that multiple charges in a big case can lead to conviction on at least some portion of the charges. But overcharging can often confuse or exhaust the jury. If a prosecutor appears to be unfairly or unnecessarily charging numerous offenses, particularly petty ones, it can have the negative effect of causing the jury to become sympathetic to the defendant. The overcharging of Wilkinson proved to be a serious mistake.

However, if the selection of broad charges had been done as an accommodation to Wilkinson's desire to be cleared by the panel of all outstanding allegations that had arisen over his twenty-year career, Madison's and Jones's overcharging can be viewed as a deliberate decision and not a tactical error. While Wilkinson might have desired an exoneration by a military panel on the host of charges that continued to vex him, Madison, Eustis, and Jones were under no obligation to furnish him with a proceeding that would provide the necessary coat of whitewash. According to Wilkinson, while Eustis had first proposed limiting the charges to allegations relating to Terre aux Boeufs, it was Wilkinson himself who demanded the trial include the broad set of charges dealing with twenty years of misdeeds.[33] Madison's decision on the charges and the way the trial was subsequently handled by Jones certainly create the appearance that an acquittal was preordained.

Under military and civilian procedures of the day, there existed no criminal investigative organization to interview witnesses and gather documents in preparation for trial. Jones and Madison were required to fashion a set of charges based on existing factual records. However, a remarkable record of testimony that exposed Wilkinson's misconduct existed. Numerous congressional hearings had produced volumes of testimony and correspondence regarding Wilkinson's involvement with the Spanish and with Burr as well as his failures at Terre aux Boeufs. Additionally, the 1808 court of inquiry, at which Jones also served as judge advocate, produced a great deal of evidence, even though much of the record was subsequently lost by Jones and the War Department or stolen by Wilkinson. Wilkinson's chicanery appeared in the transcripts of the Burr 1807 trials in Richmond, where Wilkinson testified so poorly regarding his role in the Burr Conspiracy. Daniel Clark's book provided a host of documentation condemning Wilkinson's involvement with the Spanish. Wilkinson's anticipated defense to these issues was also well documented: at the 1808 court of inquiry he was allowed to call witnesses and present evidence in his own defense and he took full advantage of the opportunity to produce volumes of conflicting documents and forgeries supporting his cover story. Furthermore, just prior to the convening of the 1811 court-martial, he published his rebuttal to Clark's book.[34] At each stage Wilkinson expanded on and enhanced his proposed defense. A wise prosecutor would have understood the thrust of Wilkinson's defense and charged accordingly, using available documents and witnesses to rebut Wilkinson's defense. Unfortunately, Jones either failed or refused to benefit from the tactical advantage these earlier proceedings provided.

Under military justice, a "charge" is a general statement of the offense and a "specification" is a specific factual act evidencing a violation of the charge. Seven general charges and twenty-five specifications of misconduct were leveled against Wilkinson, and they can be broken into four separate categories. The first category of charges related to charge 1, corruptly receiving a pension from Spain, and charge 2, treasonably conspiring and corresponding with Spanish agents to dismember the United States. The government claimed Wilkinson had taken payments from Spain and corresponded with various Spanish officials with a goal of severing the western states from the United States and align those states with Spanish Mexico and Florida The charges alleged that Wilkinson's acts started in 1789 and continued in various forms until 1804. Article 57 of the Articles of War identifies correspondence with the enemy as a capital offense.[35]

Three problems with this first category of charges were immediately apparent. First, the charges alleged acts of misconduct by Wilkinson during the period 1789–91, but Wilkinson was not a soldier at this time, so his acts were not covered by the Articles of War. Indeed, it was widely believed at that time that Wilkinson had commenced his improper role with Spain before rejoining the army in 1791, but charging these acts as misconduct by a person then not subject to the Articles of War was clearly wrong. Second, the Articles of War clearly established a two-year statute of limitations.[36] All the alleged acts in this category of charges were well beyond the statute of limitations. Third, treason per se was not an offense covered by the Articles of War.[37] The Articles did prohibit corresponding with or giving intelligence to the enemy, but those articles did not cover peacetime interactions with a foreign power. Wilkinson's peacetime treachery with Spain was technically espionage, which was not a crime in the United States before the passage of the Espionage Act of 1917.

The second category (related to charge 3, confederation with known traitors; charge 4, failure to discover and frustrate treasons and conspiracies against the United States; and charge 5, unlawfully conspiring to commence a military expedition against Spain) alleged that Wilkinson had engaged in a conspiracy with "known traitors," that is, Aaron Burr and his associates. But four years earlier Burr and his associates had been acquitted of treason and mounting an illegal campaign into Spanish Mexico—of course, based in part on the government's reliance on Wilkinson's poor evidence, making it unclear how Jones expected to obtain a conviction on Wilkinson's conduct.

The third category (on charge 6, disobedience of orders, and charge 7, neglect of duty) covered Wilkinson's disastrous leadership during the Terre aux Boeufs debacle. The specifications cited Wilkinson's delay in complying with orders to evacuate the camp and failing to provide adequate housing, food, medicine, and medical care to the troops, which resulted in the death of a significant portion of his command. Wilkinson was also charged with failure to hold the supply contractor accountable for failed performance.

The final category (on charge 8, misapplication and waste of public money and supplies) identified a variety of allegations involving Wilkinson cheating on numerous travel vouchers as well as authorizing improper payments to the supply contractor at Terre aux Boeufs.

One charge that was not brought was bribery, although the circumstances surrounding bribery were hinted at within some of the charges that were brought. In 1809 Wilkinson had accepted the "gift" of eleven horses from James Morrison, the provisioning contractor for the Terre aux Boeuf deployment. Wilkinson had this personal property shipped at government expense from Louisville to New Orleans, though he subsequently sold some of the horses to the army for use by officers and the artillery. Wilkinson also failed to hold Morrison accountable for failing to provide adequate and healthy provisions. Under these known facts a case could be made that the "gift" to Wilkinson was bestowed in exchange for ignoring Morrison's failure to perform. This corrupt quid pro quo is the essential element of the offense of bribery.

Under federal law at the time, bribery was one of the few crimes explicitly mentioned in the Constitution as grounds for impeachment of certain civil officers.[38] However, neither the existing federal criminal code nor the Articles of War specifically addressed corruption by a federal officer.[39] Given the absence of a clear statutory prohibition, Wilkinson's corrupt relationship with Morrison was apparently addressed in three specifications. Under charge 7, specification 2 (neglect of duty), Wilkinson was charged with failing to hold Morrison accountable for contract nonperformance. Under charge 8 (misapplication of public money and supplies) Wilkinson was accused of assessing the government the cost of transporting of his horses from Morrison (specification 2) and authorizing payment to Morrison when Wilkinson knew that the contractor had not performed (specification 3). Wilkinson was given a copy of the charges in July 1811 and told to report to Frederick for trial on September 2.[40]

Then, as now, major trials proved to be significant public events, with crowds gathered to watch celebrities in court and the legal pyrotechnics of famous attorneys. Here a celebrity trial was taking place, this time of a well-known military officer in a military environment. Walter Jones, a well-respected civilian trial attorney, was selected to be the judge advocate and present the government's case. Since 1804 Jones had served both Jefferson and Madison as the politically appointed US attorney for the District of Columbia. Jones also had a significant career of arguing more than three hundred cases before the Supreme Court, a record that has never been broken. Jones's familiarity with military matters and military law is less certain.

Jones's only other actions in the military justice system was as the judge advocate at Wilkinson's 1808 court of inquiry. However, rather than controlling those proceedings as judge advocate, Jones allowed Wilkinson to dominate the proceedings to their apparently preordained conclusion. The appearance of the whole affair being a whitewash was further enhanced by Jones's actions to obfuscate the meager records of the proceedings. Jones's admission to the House committee that he had failed to complete the record of the court of inquiry, coupled with the loss of the record when it was given to or stolen by Wilkinson, had effectively ended the Butler committee's inquiry.

Was this admission by Jones to Congress in 1810 a simple act of professional incompetence, or was it a recognition by him, a seasoned political appointee of both Jefferson and Madison, that the White House wanted the controversy surrounding Wilkinson to just disappear? Jones was clearly desirous of washing his hands of the whole complicated matter as quickly as possible. In 1808 Wilkinson had been exonerated through the findings of three close subordinates, and that decision had quickly been endorsed by the president without the niceties of a complete report, as required by the Articles of War. Jones likely hoped that he would never have to deal with Wilkinson again. Unfortunately, Jones, a loyal political operative, was brought back into the affair in 1811 as the prosecutor with the best knowledge of the available facts and the defense expected to be mounted by

Wilkinson. Jones's subsequent failure to capitalize on these advantages at the 1811 trial may simply have been another attempt by him to satisfy the White House by once again seeking to make the matter go away through a preordained acquittal.[41]

Jones's poor actions and inactions both before and during the trial, combined with the handpicked selection of friendly jurors, gives the clear impression that the Madison administration was seeking a proceeding that would, once and for all, exonerate "Jefferson's general" from charges of misconduct that reached back over a twenty-year period. Such an exoneration would also have cleared three former presidents, both Federalists and Democratic-Republicans, of failing to address Wilkinson's repeated pattern of treachery, incompetence, and dishonesty.

Wilkinson's defense team represented the top of the Maryland trial bar. Initially Wilkinson had been hesitant about going to trial in Frederick due to the Federalist hostility shown toward him during the Butler trial. He was particularly concerned about the presence of John Hanson Thomas, thirty-two, editor of the *Frederick-town Herald,* who had engaged in attacks on the Democratic-Republican inspired prosecution of Butler. Somehow, Wilkinson overcame his fear of Thomas, who was also an excellent trial attorney and succeeded in having Thomas represent him. At first Thomas believed in Wilkinson's guilt, but he eventually came to believe in his client's innocence and agreed to represent him for free.[42] Described by his colleagues as "the most brilliant and gifted orator of his day in Maryland," Thomas also served in the Maryland House of Delegates.[43]

Completing the defense trial team was another respected Frederick trial attorney, Roger Brooke Taney, thirty-four. Following Wilkinson's trial, Taney went on to the highest levels of the American legal community. After marrying the sister of Francis Scott Key, Taney served in the Maryland House of Delegates and became an ardent supporter of Andrew Jackson. He was elected the attorney general of Maryland in 1827 and was selected by President Jackson to replace the deceased John Marshall as chief justice of the US Supreme Court. As chief justice he is primarily remembered for the infamous 1857 Supreme Court decision *Dred Scott v. Sanford*. Taney, the author of the opinion, was an avowed supporter of slavery who sought to "heal the nation" by ruling that Congress had no authority to restrict the practice of slavery. Rather than healing the nation, the decision is widely regarded as a leading cause of the Civil War.

Thomas and Taney had a difficult task in devising an effective defense strategy and were hampered by a significant procedural impediment. Under military justice practice at the time, defense counsel were prohibited from speaking to members of the court.[44] Despite the constitutional guarantee under the Sixth Amendment of a right to counsel, the Articles of War improperly limited that right to consultation and not representation at trial.[45] Ironically, Wilkinson, in his previous role as a court-martial convening authority, had been particularly outspoken in his opposition to defense counsel taking an active role at trial. In one case he rejected the findings of a court-martial because defense counsel was allowed to address the court. "No one will deny to a prisoner, the aid of Counsel who may suggest Questions or objections, to prepare his defence in writing—but he is not to open his mouth in Court."[46] The defense team's legal wisdom and trial strategy thus had to be communicated through Wilkinson, who was incapable of being anything but bombastic and imperious. The fact that they devised a strategy that suited their client's personality is a tribute to their skill.

As a result of the numerous congressional and military justice reviews of Wilkinson's conduct, the defense had a full picture of the government's case. Furthermore, Wilkinson was a notorious pack rat, and he had prepared a voluminous record of correspondence and depositions that would serve the defense. Whether the defense attorneys discerned that a significant portion of Wilkinson's defense would be based on lies and forged documents is unknown. Whether Wilkinson shared with his defense team the true nature of his dealings with Spanish authorities and with Burr is equally unclear but probably unlikely. Wilkinson's carefully crafted cover story, accounting for his Spanish pension, was a secret that could be disproved only through documents and testimony from Spanish authorities complicit in Wilkinson's actions, and obviously they were not available for trial. No doubt Wilkinson realized that the knowledge of the truth might impede his defense team. It would be neither the first nor last time that a defendant lied to his own counsel.

When the court-martial convened on September 2, 1811, the judge advocate began by reading the convening order, reading the charges before the court, and having the defendant make his initial appearance and plea.[47] Under the Articles of War, a prisoner facing court-martial was required to surrender his sword.[48] However, as a result of his agreement with Eustis, Wilkinson had been allowed to keep his sword until the start of the trial. General Gansevoort, president of the court, noted that Wilkinson still had his sword and demanded that Wilkinson surrender it. Wilkinson did so, using the pompous rhetoric that would be characteristic of his defense at trial: "Mr. President, this sword (unclasping from his side) has been the untarnished companion of my thigh for forty years, with a resolution never to surrender it dishonorably to an enemy. I am now by the order of the government of my country ordered to place it in your hands."[49]

The first few days of court were taken up with the need to find a different location for the conduct of the trial. The first location, probably the Frederick Town barracks, most likely proved unsuitable because the Barracks were undergoing a substantial renovation at the time.[50] An alternative location was found at the Frederick County Courthouse, and the trial recommenced there a few days later. The court then addressed its first issue: Wilkinson's challenges of named court members and demands for their replacement with alternate jurors. Three members were replaced.

The first session of the court, which lasted from September 2 to 11, was also delayed for several days as Jones, the judge advocate, was ill. This was the start of a continuing issue, which clearly upset the court members during the three-month trial. On numerous occasions the trial could not be held because Jones was unavailable. Sometimes he was sick, but he also cited the demands of his duties as US attorney for the District of Columbia, which required him to appear in court in Washington, sometimes to argue cases before the Supreme Court. His absences, and the delays caused by his absences, steadily wore on the patience of the court members. On September 11 Gansevoort contacted Secretary of War Eustis and asked for an assistant judge advocate to be appointed, but Eustis did not appoint an assistant counsel and the trial continued for three months, with many breaks caused by Jones's absence.

From the beginning, and despite the many delays caused by numerous issues, court members were under a great deal of pressure to quickly conclude the proceedings. Barely a week into the trial, President Madison directed Eustis to inform the court members, who represented a significant portion of the army's senior leadership, to hold themselves in readiness to deploy if American-British relations heated up.[51] Madison's missive to Eustis was one of a series of curious back-channel communications during the trial by members of the court, Jones, and Wilkinson with both Eustis and Madison. In addition to legitimately seeking guidance from Madison through Eustis on procedural decisions that were the president's decision to make as convening authority, Jones routinely briefed Eustis on the status and progress of the trial, and much of this information was then forwarded by Eustis to Madison. On October 8 Wilkinson contacted Madison to complain about alleged misconduct by government court-martial witnesses while on the streets of Frederick.[52] Though Wilkinson could and did use this alleged misconduct to impeach the witnesses at trial, his direct communication with Madison was clearly improper. Madison responded four days later to Wilkinson with a short reply, assuring him that he would get a fair trial.[53]

Madison was directly involved in the next vexatious issue raised in the first days of trial. Wilkinson sought the testimony of six army officers who were stationed in the West. Wilkinson and his defense team recognized the impact on a military jury of the favorable testimony of numerous army colleagues regarding his character and actions. Under military justice practices, the defense was required to ask the permission of the judge advocate to issue subpoenas for any defense witnesses. Jones denied all requests, and Wilkinson appealed the denial to the court members. On September 11 Gansevoort granted Wilkinson's motion to compel his colleagues' attendance, and Jones was directed to obtain their appearance. Jones, through Eustis, sought guidance from Madison on September 14. Eustis told Madison that the request was part of a scheme by Wilkinson to inundate the court with the testimony of many of his friends, and he asked Madison if the request should be granted. Undoubtedly based on information from Jones, Eustis also provided a stark assessment to Madison that Wilkinson had "moulded the court to his liking and gained a control over it which as I am well informed has been evident in every instance hitherto."[54] Madison replied on September 21, directing the attendance of all of Wilkinson's witnesses.[55] (General Wade Hampton, the convening authority in the court-martial of Colonel Cushing, had previously threatened to resign if Cushing had been made available for Wilkinson's trial. Hampton did not carry out the threat, and he stayed in the army to serve and quarrel with Wilkinson in their disastrous 1813 invasion of Canada.)

As a result, Jones, Wilkinson, and the court next dealt with a major problem that confronted all trials in the early nineteenth century: delays for witness travel. Eustis informed Madison that it would take at least three months to bring Wilkinson's witnesses to Frederick from their current duty stations in the West.[56] At the time, travel between the military posts in the West and Frederick was long and arduous, and travelers had two choices for journeying east. They could go by keelboat down the Mississippi River to New Orleans, then board an oceangoing vessel or coastal packet to sail to Baltimore, eventually heading west to Frederick via the National Road, which at that time was under construction. This route exposed travelers to diseases associated with the climate of the lower Mississippi and other hazards that were common for coastal and ocean voyages of the time, including interdiction by the Royal Navy.[57] The alternative was to get to Natchez by boat, then take an overland route by foot or on horseback via the Natchez Trace to Nashville, take a boat, coach, or horse to Pittsburgh, then take another coach or horse via the National Road, going east to Frederick. This route involved hazards of hostile Native Americans, robbery by highwaymen, and delays caused by bad weather. In either case, the journey took months to accomplish.

To deal with the delays inherent in the production of witnesses, Wilkinson and Jones agreed on several compromises. First, they agreed that witnesses not immediately available could testify via deposition instead of live testimony before the court, a form of testimony specifically allowed by the Articles of War.[58] Second, rather than insisting on live testimony, they would admit into evidence the entire proceedings of the numerous congressional investigations of Wilkinson's conduct; the record, such as it was, of the 1808 court of inquiry; and portions of the transcripts of the treason trials of Aaron Burr.

Article 92 of the Articles of War specifically prohibited the admission of the records of a court of inquiry unless properly certified by the recorder and the president of the court. Since these steps had never been taken and much of the official record of the court of inquiry was missing due to Jones's negligence and Wilkinson's removal of the records from the War Department, what remained of the "official" records ended up in Wilkinson's personal possession. Jones made no objection and portions of these records were apparently submitted into evidence at the court-martial by Wilkinson, but it proved to be disastrous for Jones and of great benefit to Wilkinson. Records from these earlier proceedings were voluminous in size and contained much evidence that should have been excluded as being either irrelevant or inadmissible. Nevertheless, all these records were put into evidence and were required reading by the court members and President Madison, as the convening authority, all of whom expressed their subsequent displeasure in being put through such torture.

This agreement was probably the worst error of the many that Jones made in trying the case. It eased the burden of in-person testimony and of putting on a case, but it directly harmed his ability to withstand one of the primary defenses mounted by Wilkinson and his defense team: the impeachment of critical government witnesses. It is one of the canons of trial practice that a jury is in the best position to determine the credibility of a witness when able to watch live testimony given under oath and subject to cross-examination.[59] In the presentation of his defenses before Congress and the court of inquiry and in his published rebuttal to Clark, Wilkinson clearly signaled that an assault on the credibility of his attackers would be a primary defense tactic. Jones failed to present his best case through live witness testimony and failed to attack the credibility of Wilkinson's own witnesses, many of whom also testified via deposition and without cross-examination or rebuttal by Jones. Since the burden of proof was on Jones, this flawed strategy consigned the prosecution to failure.

Jones compounded this error at trial. Following Wilkinson's relentless attacks on the credibility of numerous government witnesses, Jones made little effort to rehabilitate the credibility of his own witnesses. Wilkinson mounted an effective assault against the credibility of important government witnesses that included Daniel Clark, Thomas Power, Andrew Ellicott, and William Simmons, accusing them of bias, misrepresentation, and sexual deviancy. These attacks went unrebutted by Jones, leaving the court members with the impression that the government's case was overwhelmingly based on the testimony of scoundrels.

Jones may have recognized that he was doomed to fail, even from the start of trial. The first witnesses had hardly been called when Jones, on September 11, complained to Eustis that the court-martial panel was filled with Wilkinson's friends and that conviction on any count was unlikely. Eustis immediately passed this gloomy assessment on to Madison: "In forming a judgment, it is impossible to exclude from consideration the high presumption (founded on the disposition already manifested by the court) of a complete and I should not be surprized to see attached the word *honorable* acquittal of every charge and specification" (emphasis in original).[60] Rather than seeking to address these weaknesses, Jones's subsequent actions—including frequent absences from court—give the appearance of his acceptance of the fact that the court had been rigged to assure the inevitability of acquittal and he would do the minimum amount of advocacy needed to present the government's case.

Madison was called on to decide yet another issue in the early stages of the trial. Some participant (probably a member of the court-martial panel) raised the issue of the propriety of the court-martial proceeding covering charges that were clearly outside the two-year statute of limitations provided by the Articles of War. Wilkinson, seeking official exoneration from all charges that had plagued him since the early 1790s, had urged Madison and Eustis to bring a broad set of charges and was now willing to waive the statute of limitations to keep all the charged misconduct before the court. Jones contacted Eustis to seek guidance from Madison, the convening authority, on the issue. Jones also raised the possibility that if the bulk of the charges were barred by the statute of limitations, the remaining charges should be dismissed as well. Eustis, in his letter to Madison, raised the possibility of the court not accepting Wilkinson's waiver and dismissing most of the charges, which were clearly outside the statute of limitations.[61] Madison responded a few days later. Recognizing the fact that the House of Representatives had placed the Wilkinson mess firmly in the hands of the executive, Madison felt that he had no choice in letting the matter play out in court: the court would determine if the charges were within its authority, and if the bulk of the charges were dismissed by the court on this ground, the remaining charges would still have to go forward.[62] The court accepted Wilkinson's waiver and the trial on all charged misconduct, just as Wilkinson had desired, began.

Military trial procedures normally followed the practice of their civilian counterparts. The government would present its case through testimony and documents, subject to cross-examination by the defense. The defense would then present its case, subject to government cross-examination and rebuttal by the prosecution. At the conclusion of the evidence both sides would argue their conclusions and the court members would retire to deliberate.[63] Tied to the vagaries of witness availability, the Wilkinson trial did not proceed in an orderly manner, and witness testimony and documents for both the prosecution and defense were randomly presented over three months' time. The voluminous records of the previous congressional and military inquiries into Wilkinson's misconduct were given to the court members with little effort by Jones to bring them together into a compelling story. Significant delays exacerbated the disjointed nature of the proceedings while the court awaited the arrival of distant witnesses or Jones's return from illness or civilian court business. Court members entertained themselves during these gaps by partying in Frederick, inspecting local military installations, watching the Great Comet of 1811, paying their respects to Madison and Eustis in Washington, and contacting the president on the need to establish military seminaries to provide adequate chaplains for the army.[64]

Jones's case regarding Spanish payments relied primarily on the records produced in prior congressional hearings and little actual testimony. For example, one of Wilkinson's main accusers was his former business partner in New Orleans, Daniel Clark, who had loudly and publicly condemned Wilkinson and published his lengthy denunciation of Wilkinson in 1808. Despite his public accusations against Wilkinson and his deposition to Congress, Clark refused to voluntarily appear at the 1808 court of inquiry and, as a civilian, could not be called as a witness at the court-martial. Wilkinson had been preparing his refutation of Clark's charges for years and took full advantage of the fact that Clark was not present to testify. He introduced a significant amount of evidence showing Clark's bias and prior inconsistent statements where he adamantly denied that Wilkinson was a Spanish pensioner.

One critical live witness for the government was Thomas Power, a former official of the Spanish government, who agreed at the last minute to voluntarily appear. In court Power exclaimed to Wilkinson, "It is an unfortunate day for you, Gen., and painful to me, to make these declarations—but it is your own fault. You have placed me in a situation where I must stab or be stabbed."[65] At multiple times Power had served as a courier of messages, orders, and money from Spanish officials to Wilkinson, particularly during the period when Wilkinson was also an army officer. Like Clark, Power's contradictory evidence regarding Wilkinson had been produced in numerous previous proceedings and Wilkinson mounted a full attack on Power's bias and past inconsistent statements regarding Wilkinson's loyalty to Spain. Press reports regarding Power's testimony also alleged that he was intoxicated on the stand.[66]

Wilkinson's boundless determination to attack the credibility of government witnesses is evidenced in the case of Andrew Ellicott. Ellicott did not testify at the court-martial, but his 1808 deposition at Wilkinson's court of inquiry provided considerable evidence against Wilkinson.[67] Ellicott stated that when he was first asked to work on the western boundary in the early 1790s, President Washington had asked him to keep an eye on Wilkinson regarding his relationship with Spanish authorities.[68] In response to this oral direction, Ellicott gathered information regarding Wilkinson's dealing with Spanish authorities and Power as well as information relating to Wilkinson's role in the Spanish Conspiracy. Ellicott stated that in November 1798 he came into possession of a cyphered communication from Spanish governor Gayoso confirming that Wilkinson was in the pay of Spain. Ellicott forwarded this information to Secretary of State Timothy Pickering, who proceeded to ignore it.[69] Ellicott's reports to the State Department, which corroborated his current testimony that he had reported his suspicions about Wilkinson in a timely manner, were never introduced into evidence at the trial.

Wilkinson had had three years to prepare his rebuttal, and his personal attack on Ellicott was relentless. While working in territory under Wilkinson's command, Ellicott had hired Thomas Freeman as an assistant, but Freeman and Ellicott soon had a falling out and, based on Wilkinson's advice, Ellicott had fired Freeman. Never one to pass up an opportunity to be involved with mischief, Wilkinson then reached out to Freeman and hired him for his own staff; Freeman later demonstrated the value of his purchased loyalty by providing impeaching information against Ellicott at the court-martial. In an August 1811 deposition that was admitted into evidence and never challenged by Jones, Freeman represented that during his time with Ellicott, Ellicott was known to employ a woman named Betsy. Freeman stated that while her position was ostensibly that of washerwoman, in fact she was a "prostitute, and of the lowest grade." To make matters worse, Freeman alleged that Ellicott engaged in group sex with the "harlot Betsy" and Ellicott's nineteen-year-old son:

Question 4 [Wilkinson]: Did you observe any particular familiarity and attentions, the intercourse of said prostitute, with Ellicott and his son, and what was the age of the boy? Be particular in times and circumstances.

Answer [Freeman]: I did observe frequent particular familiarities and attentions, in the intercourse of Ellicott and his son, with said prostitute. I cannot now, from recollection, be very particular, in time, place, and circumstance. The boy appeared to be near fully grown, of about nineteen years of age. I recollect that Mr. Ellicott introduce that woman Betsy, to Governor Gayoso, on his first visit to our barge, after we had landed at Natchez; and, that so far as their conduct (Ellicott and son) came within my observations afterwards, they continued to pay mutual friendly and familiar attentions to her. It was said, and generally believed, that that extraordinary trio, father, son and washerwoman, slept in the same bed, at the same time—I did not see but believed it. I even pressed myself by the old sinner, Ellicott, to take part of his bed with his washerwoman and himself, for the night.

Question 5 [Wilkinson]: Was it not your opinion, and that of all other gentlemen of the party, that Ellicott, the father, and son, held criminal intercourse with the said harlot Betsy?

Answer [Freeman]: It was my opinion, and I understood it to be the opinion of every gentleman of both parties, American and Spanish, that the Ellicotts, both father and son, held and continued to have a beastly, criminal, and disgraceful intercourse, with the said harlot Betsy.[70]

Jones's case regarding the Spanish allegations at trial was not only hindered by what he did know and how he presented it but also by what he did not know and could not refute. Wilkinson had indeed been a spy for a foreign power, first as a private citizen, then as an army officer, then as the commanding general of the United States. He was paid for collecting intelligence that would be helpful to a foreign power and damaging to his own country. In intelligence terms, Wilkinson was a "walk-in." He was not directly recruited by the Spanish but instead chose to approach them in 1787 and agreed to work for them in return for money.

Intelligence agencies today study the motivations of the person who chooses to become a spy for a foreign power. It is generally accepted that most people do this based on one or more of the motivations under the acronym MICE: money, ideology, coercion, ego. For example, Aldrich Ames, one of the most notorious spies in CIA history, agreed to spy for the Russians based on his desire for money. Over his ten-year spy career he was paid more than $1 million. Jonathan Pollard, a navy analyst who spied for Israel, was driven by his desire to serve the Israeli government rather than to live up to his oath as an American naval intelligence officer. Clayton Lonetree, a marine guard at the US embassy in Moscow, was blackmailed by Russian intelligence to spy for Russia. Robert Hanssen, the FBI's most damaging spy, was motivated to work for Russia by ego and a belief that his talents were not adequately valued by his employer.

For Wilkinson, ideology was not involved. While he had sworn an oath of allegiance to the Spanish throne in 1787, his oath was initially nothing more than a commercial accommodation to be able to ship goods through the port of New Orleans, which at the time was controlled by the Spanish. Similarly, coercion was not involved: Wilkinson had willingly initiated the dialogue with Spain. What drove Wilkinson was money and ego. During his paid relationship with the Spanish government, Wilkinson received, in today's equivalent, more than $1 million, making him one of the highest-paid spies in US history. Approximately $600,000 of this sum was paid for spying while he was a private citizen, but the remaining $400,000 was paid after he had taken an oath as an officer of the US Army. The mere receipt of a payment from a foreign power by an official of the federal government violates the Emoluments Clause of the US Constitution, but Wilkinson did much more than simply accept a supplement to his salary as an army officer.[71] In return for his payments Wilkinson actively advised the Spanish on how to separate the western states from the United States; he identified other army officers and Kentucky officials who might be susceptible to corruption by Spain; he advised his Spanish masters on where Spanish fortifications should be erected on the Mississippi River, in Florida, and in Texas to prevent encroachment by American forces; he alerted Spanish authorities to filibustering campaigns targeted against Spanish territory mounted by George Rogers Clark, Aaron Burr, and others; and finally, and most treacherously, he routinely alerted the Spanish when US military scouting parties were approaching Spanish territory, to enable Spanish authorities or their Indian allies to capture or kill them.

Unfortunately for Jones and the United States, Wilkinson and the Spanish practiced expert espionage tradecraft. Both parties recognized the need for secrecy and many of their written communications were made in cypher. Wilkinson would then work diligently to create a cover story to explain his receipt of Spanish cash. In September 1796 Wilkinson informed Spanish authorities that, were his payments from Spain ever discovered, he would claim that such payments were merely delayed reimbursements from Spanish authorities that resulted from Wilkinson's pre-army commercial transactions in New Orleans. At trial Wilkinson enhanced this fiction by introducing a forged balance sheet that was created for his cover story.[72] As part of the conspiracy, Spanish officials corroborated Wilkinson's cover story of commercial payments in affidavits provided to Wilkinson and Orleans governor Claiborne. Though the Spanish had kept detailed records of their espionage relationship with Wilkinson, they assured Wilkinson that these records would be removed to Spanish archives in Cuba and Spain, where they would be beyond the reach of Wilkinson's American enemies.[73] As a result, many of the records establishing Wilkinson's treachery were not discovered by American historians until many decades after the court-martial, and most of the Spanish officials with direct knowledge of Wilkinson's actions as Spanish Agent 13 were either dead by the time of the trial or beyond the reach of military justice subpoenas.

Compared to the excellent tradecraft practiced by the Spanish and Wilkinson, the federal government at this time had virtually no capabilities in espionage or counterintelligence and was particularly ill-equipped for spy hunting. During the Revolution, Washington had been an exceptional spymaster, running numerous sources that provided him with tactical intelligence on British capabilities and troop movements.[74] Unfortunately, Washington and the Continental Army had virtually no counterintelligence capability to look for British spies, and Continental efforts were repeatedly penetrated by British agents. Benedict Arnold was the most conspicuous British agent, having fallen for the dual enticement of money and revenge for having been slighted by American officials. Arnold's efforts to betray West Point and deliver Washington to the British were discovered only when his British handler, Major John Andre, was captured by irregular forces, who found incriminating documents in Andre's boot. But Arnold was not the only British espionage success. Benjamin Church, one of the early founders of the army's medical corps, was found to have shared intelligence with senior British military officials. He was expelled from his government positions and allowed to leave the country. The American diplomatic mission to Paris, which was responsible for negotiating the alliance with France, was compromised from the beginning by the presence of Edward Bancroft, a British agent who served as the mission's secretary, which gave him access to all papers and correspondence of Benjamin Franklin and his fellow commissioners. Bancroft kept his British handlers fully informed of the American negotiations.[75]

Despite having mounted successful spy operations during the Revolution, and having been repeatedly penetrated by enemy agents, the United States allowed its espionage and counterintelligence capabilities to wither and die after the Revolutionary War. Neither the War Department nor the State Department developed the capability to conduct routine espionage or counterintelligence operations, even though every administration knew that they were continually being targeted by British, French, and Spanish agents. For example, in 1796 British authorities recruited Tennessee senator William Blount to act as their agent as they sought to mount an expedition to sever Louisiana from Spanish control. The plot was thwarted when, based on a tip from Spain, the State Department hired an agent to conduct an undercover investigation that established Blount's complicity. Following his impeachment by the House of Representatives, Blount faced trial in the Senate but avoided conviction.[76] The lack of understanding of the need for an intelligence organization meant the federal government was particularly unqualified to assess Wilkinson's Spanish relationship with a discerning knowledge of spycraft.

Having hidden the true nature of his relationship with the Spanish from government investigations, at trial Wilkinson, aided by his defense team, did a masterful job of obfuscation. As the defendant he did not have to prove anything and only had to create a reasonable doubt. However, sometimes a defense can successfully present an innocent explanation for the critical facts. Wilkinson's defense to the Spanish pensioner charges was multifaceted. First, he denied any such payments even existed, and to the extent that government witnesses said that such payments did occur, such witnesses were biased liars and sexual deviates. Second, to the extent the government was able to produce any credible evidence of payments, the evidence was merely a record of delayed payments for commercial transactions occurring before he had become a soldier in 1791. Alternatively, Wilkinson suggested that if there were any noncommercial payments from Spain, the government did not prove that he had done anything untoward because of these payments. Finally, Wilkinson suggested that if payments from Spain had been made, they merely represented a generous gratuity to an old soldier who had served as their ally during the Revolution:

> It would therefore seem that, instead of aiding in any plan of dismemberment, or other plans hostile to this union, if I have been bribed by Spain I have only been bribed to preserve my allegiance inviolate to the United States, and that a foreign government has been generous enough to step forward and pension a poor veteran of the Revolution, in order to continue him faithful in his attachment to his country—to that country whose sovereign rights as an independent power, several of you gentlemen as well as myself, some thirty or forty years ago fought and struggled hard to establish and maintain.[77]

Several old soldiers on the jury were also Revolutionary War veterans, but not Spanish pensioners, and it is not clear how far Wilkinson thought this argument would get with the panel.

In addition to denying or explaining away the payments and attacking the character and credibility of anyone who said payments had been made, Wilkinson put on a character defense. He pointed out to the jury that rumors regarding the Spanish payments were known to his commanders, Washington, Adams, Hamilton, and Jefferson, yet these persons kept Wilkinson in command and never found the allegations regarding Spain worthy of investigation.[78] Since both Washington and Hamilton were dead by time of trial, and Jefferson was unlikely to voice any doubts about Wilkinson, only Adams was available to rebut Wilkinson's claim. Protecting that flank, Wilkinson had sent a series of interrogatories to Adams, seeking his assurance that he did not believe the rumors of Spanish payments. Remarkably, Adams responded and assured Wilkinson that, while there were lots of "Rumours, Suspicions, and Insinuations" of his relationship with Spain, no evidence of such misconduct had been produced during his administration or the administration of Washington, and Wilkinson retained his trust.[79] In this response Adams seems to have conveniently ignored the fact that Anthony Wayne had repeatedly demanded an investigation of Wilkinson and that Washington and Adams had repeatedly ignored Wayne's requests. When Wayne died, Adams allowed the requests to die with him. Adams also ignored the warnings provided by Andrew Ellicott to Secretary of State Pickering in 1797 and 1798 regarding Wilkinson's status as a Spanish pensioner.

A defense of obfuscation, character assassination, and alternative facts proved attractive to the jury. The court accepted the commercial transaction defense and rejected the credibility of any evidence that showed that Wilkinson had had an improper relationship with Spain or had actively sought to sever the western states from the United States. Wilkinson was acquitted of all charges and specifications relating to Spain.[80] In its verdict, the court acknowledged that those specifications that alleged misconduct before Wilkinson returned to active duty in 1791 were not properly before the court. While conceding its lack of jurisdiction over these specifications, the court still ruled that no evidence supported them and acquitted Wilkinson of all charges relating to Spain, based on a lack of evidence.

Jones's evidence on Wilkinson's complicity in the Burr Conspiracy charges was almost completely based on the record developed at Burr's trials. Little in the way of new or live evidence was presented on the merits alone. At one point in mid-October 1811, the court considered the dismissal of the Burr charges and specifications. Once again Wilkinson fought to keep the Burr charges in the hope of obtaining a complete exoneration on all the allegations of misconduct that he had been deflecting for twenty years. If the court were to dismiss the Burr allegations, they might continue to haunt him, but an acquittal by a pro-Wilkinson court would hopefully silence his critics on this issue forever. Gansevoort accepted Wilkinson's motion to retain the charges, and the Burr counts remained.[81]

Despite the absence of any meaningful proof of conspiracy with Burr, Wilkinson did not pass up the opportunity to attack the credibility of any available government witness. For example, Jones called Major Seth Hunt to testify about past conversations he had had with Wilkinson regarding some vague plans with Burr. Wilkinson immediately called several witnesses who testified as to Hunt's bias against Wilkinson, including Captain Zachary Taylor, who later went on to the US presidency.[82] Major Amos Stoddard, a court member, also provided testimony regarding Hunt's bias against Wilkinson. In addition to emphasizing the conundrum of whether it was possible to "conspire with known traitors" if those persons were ultimately acquitted of treason, Wilkinson advanced another theory: that he had repeatedly warned Jefferson about Burr. One such warning was delivered to Jefferson in November 1806, when Wilkinson asked his aide, Thomas A. Smith, to hand carry a warning to Jefferson. While Wilkinson's written letter, transported in Smith's slipper, contained no mention of Burr's role in the conspiracy, Smith testified at trial that he was ordered by Wilkinson to provide the information naming

Burr orally to Jefferson.[83] Despite Smith's direct role in establishing Wilkinson's warnings to Jefferson about Burr, Smith was picked by Madison to serve as a juror. During trial, Smith left the jury panel table, took the witness stand when called by Wilkinson, corroborated a critical portion of Wilkinson's defense, and then resumed his seat on the panel to deliberate Wilkinson's guilt.

An earlier alleged warning by Wilkinson to Jefferson's cabinet, cited by the court in its verdict, is more suspicious. In acquitting Wilkinson of any role in the Burr Conspiracy, the court's decision focused on the fact that in October 1805 Wilkinson had communicated warnings about Burr to a cabinet official, Secretary of the Navy Robert Smith. The court, quoting the warning to the cabinet official, stated that Burr "was about something, whether internal, or external, he could not discover, but he ought to keep an eye on him."[84] The proof of this communication, directly cited in the court's verdict, is curious. Wilkinson was a known pack rat, and his defense, set forth in his three-volume *Memoirs* and in the record of multiple congressional investigations, is filled with Wilkinson's records of correspondence and communications with many private and government figures over a forty-year period. But Wilkinson apparently maintained no record of this important 1805 communication with Smith. Wilkinson was not above forgery and perjury to establish his defense, and he proved the existence of this document only through his oral defense statement, when he remembered the contents of the alleged letter and buttressed his recollection through the testimony of Captain Daniel Hughes. In 1805 Hughes was an aide to Wilkinson, and he testified that he remembered the contents of a letter that Wilkinson had written to Smith, warning him about Burr.[85] At trial Hughes repeated verbatim the content of this letter, based on his recollection six years after the event. The recollection of Wilkinson, and Hughes's deposition and testimony, went without challenge by Jones, and the court acquitted Wilkinson of all Burr-related charges.

Several mysteries surround this evidence. First, it is not clear why Wilkinson did not invite former secretary Smith to testify in person or by deposition. Immediately prior to trial Wilkinson had reached out to Smith regarding their correspondence about Burr. Smith responded in a letter to Wilkinson that he did receive the letter and that he remembered its contents, which were consistent with Wilkinson's statements.[86] None of this correspondence was introduced into evidence. Smith, the brother of Wilkinson's constant supporter Senator Samuel Smith, might have proved to be an interesting witness. Following his service as Jefferson's secretary of the navy, Smith was appointed by Madison as secretary of state. At the time of the Wilkinson trial, Madison was in the process of firing Smith from that position and replacing him with James Monroe. Smith's support of Wilkinson may have been an attempt by him to get back at Madison. Second, at the time of the warning, Smith was not in Wilkinson's chain of command. As commanding general of the army, Wilkinson regularly communicated with his superior, the secretary of war, and with President Jefferson, but he had no reason to communicate a warning about Burr to navy secretary Smith.

The third set of charges related to Wilkinson's actions at Terre aux Boeufs. In April 1810 the House issued its report on the deployment, one of the worst peacetime disasters ever suffered by the army.[87] The report did not attach any personal blame to Wilkinson, so the subsequent court-martial charges against Wilkinson reflected either a decision by Madison to hold accountable the most senior military officer in command or a desire by Madison and Wilkinson to be relieved of any responsibility. In addition to introducing into the record the House report, Jones did introduce the testimony of many officers who recounted the suffering of the troops at Terre aux Boeufs. Evidence was presented that when Wilkinson was directed to move the troops to a healthier environment at Natchez, three hundred miles upriver, he was slow to respond. The delay was significant in increasing the sickness of the troops and the number of casualties. However, neither the witnesses nor the House record established any direct personal failing by Wilkinson other than the fact that he was in command, he was slow to recognize that his army was slowly dying on the banks of the Mississippi, and he failed to move the troops to a safer climate.

Wilkinson responded with a vigorous defense. He first contended that Terre aux Boeufs was an appropriate place in which to mount a defense of New Orleans and presented the testimony of numerous military officials familiar with New Orleans—American, French, and Spanish—who all agreed that Terre aux Boeufs was the best defensible ground. (Wilkinson's judgment was later affirmed by Andrew Jackson, who chose the same ground in his successful defense of New Orleans in January 1815.) Wilkinson also demonstrated that the War Department system for purchasing food, tents, and medical supplies was broken on many levels and was inadequate to support his efforts.

Wilkinson introduced testimony, including that of Colonel William Beall, a court member who had served under Wilkinson at Terre aux Boeufs, regarding Wilkinson's efforts to obtain better food, shelter, and medical attention. Beall testified that the delay in evacuating Terre aux Boeufs was in part based on the navy's inability to provide adequate boats to transport the troops. In short, Wilkinson tried the best he could under impossible circumstances.

The excuses presented, while valid, go only so far. Wilkinson was not only an experienced army commander; he had significant experience commanding troops in the West and lower Mississippi. Much of his military career was spent in establishing military posts and commanding troops in Louisiana, Mississippi, Missouri, and Alabama. He was aware of the hazards of geography and the risks that would be faced by an army in the lower river delta, particularly during the summer months. He was also aware of the problems with the inadequacies of the army's fiscal, medical, and logistical systems. And rather than using his experience to avoid or ameliorate the dangers inherent in military operations in the West, Wilkinson sought to use these problems to his advantage, after the fact, to justify his negligent command. However, Wilkinson's argument obviously was appealing to a military jury. As military officers of senior rank and long experience, each of them had probably confronted similar problems with the inadequacies of the army's financial, medical, and logistical systems. Without more evidence of personal culpability by Wilkinson, a not guilty verdict from this panel was assured.

Further evidence of Wilkinson's personal misconduct at Terre aux Boeufs may have been available, but it was never fully explored by the House committee nor by Jones. Numerous contemporary reports circulated that Terre aux Boeufs had been was chosen not because of its military value but because of its value to Wilkinson's future father-in-law, Charles Trudeau, with an appropriate kickback to Wilkinson.[88] While some of the witnesses that provided evidence to the House investigation implied the existence of an improper relationship between Wilkinson and the landowner, Wilkinson vehemently denied the allegation and Jones made no attempt to develop this issue at trial.[89]

Furthermore, it has been speculated by numerous historians that Wilkinson had an inappropriate relationship with James Morrison, the contractor selected to supply poor food to the army.[90] While this would not be the first time that speculation surrounded Wilkinson's corrupt relationship with an army contractor, no meaningful effort was made by Jones or the House to investigate these possible irregularities. Had they been proved, they would have shown that the incredible casualties were directly caused by Wilkinson's greed. Instead, Wilkinson was acquitted of all counts related to Terre aux Boeufs.

The fourth set of charges dealt with a series of allegations regarding Wilkinson's claims for expenses. Charge 8 alleged three separate acts of fiscal malfeasance. The first specification alleged that in 1805 Wilkinson had improperly caused military officials to pay for the transportation of his personal property. The second specification alleged that in 1809 Wilkinson directed a military barge to stop in Louisville and take on the cargo of eleven horses, which were then shipped and fed, at government expense, and delivered to Terre aux Boeufs. The third specification alleged that Wilkinson had authorized payments to Morrison, the provisioning contractor at Terre aux Boeufs, even though Wilkinson knew that the contractor had failed to perform. Much of the evidence surrounding these fiscal irregularities came from War Department accountant Simmons.[91]

Given the irregularities surrounding Terre aux Boeufs, Wilkinson's expenses from the debacle had attracted Simmons's scrutiny. As early as June 1809 Simmons warned Secretary Eustis regarding possible fiscal irregularities in the deployment. In 1810 Simmons commenced a series of appearances before multiple congressional investigations of Wilkinson's misconduct, and as court-martial charges were ordered in 1811, he was readily available to serve as a live witness. Simmons was called on September 10 as one of Jones's first witnesses and was immediately subjected to a multipronged attack by Wilkinson. Several army officers attending the court-martial as witnesses or spectators were staying at a local Frederick inn, the Golden Lamb, owned by a Mrs. Kimball. Multiple persons overheard Simmons making remarks while on the street in front of the inn, demonstrating Simmons's bias against Wilkinson.[92] All of these statements were proper grounds for impeachment of Simmons at trial, but Wilkinson went one step further. On October 9, Wilkinson wrote Madison directly and attacked Simmons, alleging that Simmons was again speaking in the streets of Frederick and was now stating that Madison was in favor of Wilkinson's conviction.[93] Wilkinson stated that this was improper, particularly from someone who was "acting in the Double Capacity as a Witness for the prosecution, and the paymaster to the members of the court." Madison responded by providing Wilkinson with a bland assurance that he would get a fair trial.[94]

While two of the three specifications directly related to Wilkinson's improper relationship with James Morrison, the provisioning contractor, Jones failed to introduce any evidence regarding their corrupt relationship and instead primarily relied on Simmons's testimony regarding arcane accounting issues. Wilkinson responded by attacking Simmons for bias and producing an affidavit from Morrison in which the contractor perjuriously denied any improper relationship with Wilkinson.[95] To buttress Morrison's credibility, Wilkinson asked Colonel William Russell, a court member, to testify about Morrison's bravery at the Battle of Freeman's Farm in 1777 and Morrison's "subsequent conduct in life, [which] has been not only correct, but exemplary."[96] Jones made no effort to buttress Simmons's credibility or rebut Morrison's self-serving affidavit.

Wilkinson's acquittal on this count was guaranteed. Simmons had harassed army officers far and wide and there was probably not a single officer on the panel that had not been the victim of Simmons's fiscal wrath.[97] Regarding the three specifications, the court ruled that as the commanding general Wilkinson was entitled in 1805 to have his goods shipped at government expense. The court also ruled that the transportation of Wilkinson's "gift" horses to Terre aux Boeufs did not result in the public sustaining any injury. The court was strangely silent on explaining its acquittal of Wilkinson for improperly paying Morrison for delivering rancid foodstuffs.

Following the testimony of former Spanish official Thomas Power in mid-November, the court again went into adjournment. Jones left the court and the city in disgust over the conduct of the proceedings, vowing never to return.[98] Gansevoort then visited President Madison and on November 29 wrote to Madison requesting the appointment of a replacement for Jones.[99] Eustis, on behalf of Madison, replied that Jones would be back by the next scheduled court date to complete the trial. When the recalcitrant Jones was back in attendance, Wilkinson was allowed to commence his defense statement to the court on December 6 and proceeded with his address to the court for five straight days. Under military procedure at the time, this was a mixture of testimony and argument, not given under oath and not subject to cross-examination. Wilkinson summarized his story of loyal service and his history of persecution by his enemies, all of whom were liars, traitors, and reprobates.

Following Wilkinson's closing remarks and Jones's response on December 18, the members commenced a review of the records of the other proceedings that had been dumped into evidence. The court members were clearly not happy with the task.[100] They began a series of votes on December 23 and reached a conclusion on December 25. General Gansevoort called the court back into session on that date to announce that a decision had been reached but that the verdict would not be announced until it had been reviewed and approved by President Madison, the convening authority. However, as reported in the contemporary press, the court members gave a clear indication of what their verdict had been. One paper reported that immediately following their adjournment, the members "waited on Wilkinson."[101] This was a clear indication to the public that junior officers, who had once served under Wilkinson, were preparing to do so again.

Following the court's decision, the record was reviewed by Judge Advocate Jones and the secretary of war, then sent to the president for final review and approval. Jones remained silent on the matter and no record exists of his reaction to the verdict. There is also no record of Eustis's formal comments (likely because Eustis at the time was undoubtedly preoccupied with military preparations for the War of 1812, which would be declared by the United States a few months after the trial; the total civilian strength of the War Department at the time consisted of Eustis and eight clerks).[102] Years later Eustis wrote to Madison stating that he believed Wilkinson to be "the most profligate unprincipled servant the public ever had."[103]

Another interesting insight into Eustis's position is provided by a curious item of correspondence to Madison from Senator William Crawford. Crawford had been a member of one of the Wilkinson investigation House committees. By 1812 he had been elected to the Senate and had served as its president pro tempore. (When Vice President George Clinton died in April 1812, Crawford became the acting vice president.) Crawford had apparently heard rumors of the impending court-martial verdict and wanted to ensure that Madison had the full record before him prior to making a final decision. Crawford stated that while he was on a House committee investigating Wilkinson, Eustis was invited to appear. Eustis appeared and stated that he wanted to provide the committee with information and observations about Wilkinson. He then proceeded to read a variety of anti-Wilkinson newspaper articles and stated that his information was not being provided to the committee as an official statement. Crawford wanted to be sure that Madison was aware of this curious appearance by his secretary of war.[104]

Eventually the matter ended up on Madison's desk. As a well-respected attorney, Madison knew the law and knew the stakes if Wilkinson was not acquitted. Much of the charged misconduct took place during the administration of Madison's predecessor and mentor, Thomas Jefferson, and Madison knew that repeated congressional investigations had not established Wilkinson's culpability but also had not adequately cleared the general. Here was an opportunity to provide an end to twenty years of controversy. The 1808 Jefferson court of inquiry had clearly been seen as a whitewash by Wilkinson's many enemies and congressional critics, and this recent handpicked court-martial panel had created an exhaustive record that could be used to justify an acquittal and put an end to further inquiries into Jefferson's failings and Wilkinson's past. Furthermore, Madison was driven by the fact that he needed generals. The war that Madison sought against Great Britain would begin less than six months later and, given the dearth of generals then available to the United States, Madison could not easily afford to lose even one of them, based on charges of twenty-year-old misconduct.

Still, Madison reached his decision only after an appropriate amount of deliberation. While the matter was pending before him, Henry Dearborn was recalled to service and appointed the new commanding general of the army, blocking Wilkinson from that position. Additionally, Madison undoubtedly sought guidance from Jefferson, who was surely also thinking about Wilkinson. While the matter still rested on Madison's desk, Jefferson wrote a private letter to James Monroe, Madison's secretary of state. In the letter he stated that he had a general awareness of the various allegations against Wilkinson and that he would not vouch for Wilkinson, except in the matter of the Burr Conspiracy. Jefferson concluded by stating his hope that Wilkinson would keep his name out of the trial.[105] Madison, too, commiserated directly with Jefferson regarding the Wilkinson trial. On February 7, 1812, in a chatty letter to Jefferson, Madison bemoaned the fact that for the preceding month he had been working through the nearly seven-hundred-page record of the Wilkinson trial.[106] Further correspondence between the two regarding the Wilkinson trial has not been found.

Despite his doubts, Madison knew what needed to be done. On February 14, 1812, he published his final decision: "I have examined and considered the foregoing proceedings of the general court martial held at Fredericktown, for the trial of Brigadier General James Wilkinson—and although I have observed in these proceedings, with regret, that there are instances in the court, as well as the officer on trial which are evidently objectionable, his acquittal of the several charges, exhibited against him, is approved, and his sword is accordingly ordered to be restored."[107]

11

DEATH OF AN ARMY ON THE ST. LAWRENCE

1812–1814

James Wilkinson is, in my opinion, totally and utterly unfit to command.
—General Jacob Brown

He is generally believed to be one of the most abandoned and
profligate of men.
—Senator William Crawford

The War of 1812 remains shrouded in mystery to most Americans today. Although the nation recently celebrated the bicentennial of the conflict, it remains the least studied of all the nation's wars. Aside from eventually providing the country with its national anthem, few Americans recall the events of the war and fewer still understand the cause for or course of this unfortunate conflict. It remains a hidden monument to Madisonian hubris.

One of the causes of the war was the failure of five years of efforts by the Jefferson and Madison administrations to address restrictions by Great Britain on American trade with Europe. Much of the economic well-being of the eastern states was based on seaborne foreign trade with Great Britain, Europe, and the Caribbean Islands controlled by European powers. By 1812 Europe had been at war for almost ten years, as shifting alliances between Great Britain and various European nations sought to address Napoleon's continuing assaults against the established order. To aid their military campaigns, both France and Great Britain established a series of economic and military blockades to prohibit neutral nations, such as the United States, from trading with their enemies and their allies. In retaliation for these economic sanctions, in 1807 the Jefferson administration commenced a series of embargoes that restricted Americans from trading with

Great Britain and France and their allies. When the initial embargo produced no effect on the belligerents, it was extended and expanded by the Madison administration. The Madison administration grew increasingly frustrated with the failure of the new economic sanctions and began to consider a military solution.

A second cause was the Royal Navy's threat to US sovereignty resulting from Great Britain's policy of impressment, which greatly impacted eastern cities that relied on oceangoing commerce. Issues of "free trade and sailors' rights" were of less concern to the southern and western states, a mainstay of Democratic-Republican political support. However, war fever arose among a faction of the party known as the War Hawks; they opposed the continuing support shown by the British government to Indian unrest in the south and west. Under the leadership of Tecumseh (Shawnee), a nascent pan-Indian confederacy of disaffected tribes in the south and west was promoted by British interests in Canada. In November 1811, federal troops under General William Henry Harrison fought the largest battle against the Indian tribes in the Northwest since the Battle of Fallen Timbers.[1] Harrison defeated the Indians at the Battle of Tippecanoe, but his victory only produced greater resentment among the tribes over federal encroachment into Indian lands and over their interests, and an increasing sense among western states that British support of such deprivations could be halted only by an American invasion and seizure of Canada.

Furthermore, Madison and the Democratic-Republicans grossly overestimated the military capability of the United States in 1812. Despite years of politically inspired purges of the army's officer corps, the paucity of capable military leaders in senior positions in the army, and the inadequacy of the army's logistical capability (as amply demonstrated by the Terre aux Boeuf debacle), Madison and party leaders mistakenly thought that the United States could pose a credible military threat to British interests in the Western Hemisphere. Jefferson famously stated that "the acquisition of Canada this year [1812], as far as the neighborhood of Quebec, will be a mere matter of marching; & will give us experience for the attack of Halifax the next, & the final expulsion of England from the American continent."[2]

Madison and the Democratic-Republicans also saw that hostility with Great Britain would provide a way to buttress the declining fortunes of the Democratic-Republican Party. Five years of embargoes had failed to curtail British economic sanctions, and large portions of the nation had suffered severe economic decline as a result of the restrictions on trade. Such decline encouraged a resurgence of the Federalist Party, primarily in the northeast, and jeopardized Madison's reelection and his party's control of Congress. Divisions within the Democratic-Republican party threatened party unity and weakened the hold of the Virginia dynasty over the party's fortunes.[3] Many felt that an easy war with Great Britain would unify the party and the nation. As stated by Elbridge Gerry, Madison's vice presidential running mate in 1812, "By war we should be purified, as by fire."[4]

Madison commenced an eight-month campaign to generate war fever among the public and in Congress. As the new Congress convened in November 1811, Madison inveighed them with an address that set forth the accumulated grievances against British policy toward American trade and the failure of diplomatic efforts to reach a peaceful resolution. In light of continuing economic hostilities, Madison called on Congress to extend army enlistments and create an expanded militia. Henry Clay of Kentucky, a first-term member of the House and noted member of the War Hawks, was elected Speaker of the House and pressed the House to move forward on war preparations. By April 1812 Congress had passed several measures that moved the country to a firmer war footing. Recruiting bonuses were created to enable the army to reach its existing authorized strength of 10,000 and then be expanded to 35,000 regulars.[5]

In March 1812, in the hopes of inflaming pro-war passions and embarrassing anti-war Federalists, Madison informed Congress of a supposed espionage operation by Great Britain against US interests. John Henry, an Irishman by birth, had spent several years in New England. After immigrating to Canada, he returned several times to the United States for commercial purposes, and on at least one such trip he was paid by British authorities to report on political unrest he observed during his trip. When Henry was disappointed with his British compensation, he offered to sell his correspondence to American authorities. In February 1812, Madison approved the expenditure of $50,000, the entire federal secret service budget, to acquire Henry's letters. Secretary of State Monroe negotiated the price with Henry and agreed that the existence of the papers would not be revealed until Henry left for France on the USS *Wasp*.[6] The documents were then sent by Madison to Congress, with the accompanying spin that Henry's real purpose was to recruit New England Federalists to assist Great Britain in destroying the union. However, a closer examination of the documents found no such perfidy and attempts by the House to question Henry were frustrated by the fact that Henry had already been spirited out of the country.[7]

When Britain refused to back down from the economic restrictions set forth in its Orders-in-Council, Madison sent a message to Congress that once again set forth the accumulated grievances against Great Britain regarding economic sanctions, impressment, and the failure of diplomatic efforts to resolve the issues.[8] As one of the authors of the Constitution, Madison recognized that under Article I, Section 8, only Congress had the authority to declare war. His June 1, 1812, message did not specifically ask for Congress to declare war but provided more than sufficient grounds for Congress to do so. On June 4 the House voted in favor of a declaration of war on a 78–45 vote, and the Senate followed on June 17 with a 19–13 vote.[9] None of the thirty-nine Federalist members of Congress had voted in favor. Madison signed the nation's first declaration of war on the following day, but, ironically, the British government had already decided to revoke the offensive Orders-in-Council six days earlier.

As Madison stirred war fever in the winter and spring of 1812, Wilkinson sought to reestablish himself within the post-court-martial army, settling scores with those who opposed him in court and revitalizing his depleted finances. Having been relieved of command in December 1809 and then superseded by Dearborn as the commanding general of the army, Wilkinson realized that his new role in the army would be determined by Madison and Eustis. Shortly after Madison had approved the verdict, Wilkinson commenced his campaign for reinstatement by sycophantically apologizing to Madison for any slights that might have been unintentionally inflicted by his heated court-martial rhetoric: "I can have no hesitation to avow, & I do it with great pleasure, that no language or Sentiment recorded in my defense, was intended either to affect your Mind or derogate from your Character, and I can with equal truth aver, that no instance of my Conduct, before the General Court Martial, was intended to apply to you."[10] He went on to promise Madison that, in the interest of harmony during the impending "Crisis of our public affairs," he had "buried every Sentiment of resentment towards the Secretary of War." Wilkinson used this missive to once again assault War Department accountant Simmons, who would continue to review Wilkinson's claims for compensation.

Even though Wilkinson's defense lawyers represented him for free, his two-year absence from command had severely impacted his finances. He continued to be paid as a brigadier general, but his removal from active service restricted him from his customary practice of using his official position to engage in fiscal misconduct. As a result of other trial expenses and the need to support Celestine in New Orleans in the style that was expected, Wilkinson was forced to sell sixty-five thousand acres of land, including all his remaining holdings in Kentucky.[11] In April, Wilkinson filed a claim for $6,941.89 in outstanding disbursements he had made while in command in New Orleans. In a move that was designed to circumvent Simmons, Madison sought legislative relief to approve Wilkinson's travel expenses related to some of the court-martial charges. Congress quickly approved and Madison signed the special relief bill in July.[12]

Wilkinson's pandering worked. On March 12, Eustis wrote Wilkinson a short letter in which he solicited Wilkinson's views on the defense of west Florida.[13] In September 1810 a local rebellion had seized Baton Rouge and the surrounding parishes from Spanish rule and declared the formation of the Republic of West

Florida. Madison saw an opportunity, and in October 1810 he declared that the 1803 Louisiana Purchase had intended to include West Florida and directed the governors of the Orleans and Mississippi Territories to take possession of the area. Congress endorsed this action on March 3, 1811. (The official Spanish relinquishment of all of Florida would eventually be established in 1821 through the Adams-Onis Treaty.) Wilkinson responded on March 28 with a lengthy treatise on the defense of New Orleans and the Lower Mississippi from British encroachment. He also advocated the seizure of Mobile and Pensacola, to prevent them from falling into British hands.[14] On April 9, Eustis directed Wilkinson to return to New Orleans and assume command of the troops in the territories of Orleans and Mississippi.[15] By April 30, Orleans Territory and the Florida parishes east of the Mississippi were admitted into the union as the state of Louisiana. Louisiana Territory, where Wilkinson had previously served as governor, became the Missouri Territory.

Still smarting from his court-martial for failing to comply with Eustis's orders to leave Terre aux Boeufs, Wilkinson immediately sought clarification from Eustis on the role he was to play in New Orleans, including whether he was authorized to seize Spanish Mobile and Pensacola.[16] In his April 15 reply Eustis informed Wilkinson that he had consulted with Madison and that Wilkinson was authorized to seize the cities if an arrangement was made with local, that is, Spanish authorities and only if there was an attempt to occupy the cities by any foreign power.[17] Wilkinson moved with unusual alacrity in returning to New Orleans. He arrived on July 9 and was greeted with Eustis's letter of June 19, informing him that war had been declared against Great Britain.[18]

Despite the bellicose nature of Wilkinson's request for instructions from Eustis, a combination of factors prevented Wilkinson from taking any immediate action to commence hostilities. In addition to his normal reticence about combat, Wilkinson soon learned about the deplorable state of the troops under his command, which he characterized as "a frightful destitution of means in every branch of service, except the hospital, and that imbecility and disorder prevailed throughout."[19] (Wilkinson's condemnation was likely intended to slight General Hampton, the recently departed commander at New Orleans.) The command lacked small arms, clothing, horses, wagons, powder, and ammunition, and the river and bayou defenses for New Orleans were either weak or nonexistent. Wilkinson convened a council of war among his senior military, naval, and logistical commanders, which voted to remain in a defensive posture until their circumstances improved. However, assistance from the War Department in Washington was not forthcoming because there was none to send. As the war commenced, Madison was quickly confronted by the fact that most of the army's senior leadership, including the secretary of war, were unfit for a wartime role: many were aging Revolutionary War veterans and the remainder consisted of influential politicians with no meaningful military experience.

Most of Madison's war focus in 1812 was directed toward the preservation of American outposts in the Michigan Territory and commencing a multipronged offensive operation against British forces in Canada. Both efforts resulted in resounding failures. The American fort at Michilimackinac in the Michigan Territory surrendered on July 17 when its commander was surprised by the arrival of British troops, who announced the commencement of hostilities to the unsuspecting American garrison. Michigan territorial governor General William Hull was directed to commence hostilities in Canada from a base in Detroit. After a timid entry into Canada in July 1812, by early August Hull's force had been driven back to Detroit, where he was tricked into surrendering the garrison to an inferior British force on August 16. Hull eventually was court-martialed for cowardice and convicted in January 1814, then sentenced to be executed *pour le encourager les autres*, the only American general ever to receive such a sentence. Madison later remitted the sentence to dismissal from the service.[20]

In northern New York, General Henry Dearborn's first reaction to the declaration of war was to enter into a local armistice with General Sir Henry Prevost, his British counterpart.[21] Dearborn expressed shock to Madison to then learn that he was expected to command two initiatives into Canada, one to seize the Niagara frontier and another to seize British forts at Kingston and Montreal.[22] The Niagara initiative was assigned to Brigadier General Alexander Smyth, a notorious braggart, who conducted an unsuccessful campaign that has been characterized as a three-month farce.[23] A brief foray across the Niagara River in October resulted in the capture of a significant portion of American troops, including now-lieutenant colonel Winfield Scott. In what would be a recurring problem at the beginning of the war, local militia troops refused to cross into Canada, believing that such offensive operations were beyond their authority. Relieved of the immediate responsibility for the Niagara frontier, Dearborn dithered for another month before finally moving toward the Canadian border in mid-November.[24] Ignoring the folly of commencing an assault on Canada in late fall, Dearborn was forced to confront the refusal of New York militia to cross into Canada. Without firing a shot, Dearborn retreated to Albany and submitted his resignation, which was not immediately accepted.[25]

By late fall it was obvious to Madison that Eustis could no longer serve as a wartime leader of the War Department. Eustis was a notorious micromanager who unsurprisingly could not manage the country's war machine on a national or strategic level.[26] A loyal political subordinate to the end, Eustis submitted his resignation on December 3, leaving Secretary of State Monroe to be temporarily dual-hatted as acting secretary of war, while Madison and Monroe searched for an acceptable replacement. By early January Madison had chosen John Armstrong Jr., fifty-three, who was confirmed by the Senate on January 18. As part of his continuing infatuation with Wilkinson, former president Adams felt that Wilkinson was a good candidate for secretary but that "his Vanity and the Collisions of Faction have rendered his Appointment improper and impossible."[27]

Armstrong commenced his military career in 1775 as an aide to General Hugh Mercer. Following Mercer's death at the Battle of Princeton, Armstrong shifted to the staff of General Horatio Gates, with whom he served through the Battles of Saratoga. (Armstrong was the aide sent by Gates to recall General Benedict Arnold at the Battle of Bemis Heights. Arnold proved to be the better horseman and outrode Armstrong to lead the American forces to victory.) Following the battles, Armstrong resigned his commission for health reasons, but he was coaxed by Gates to rejoin Gates's staff in 1782. In that capacity Armstrong was with Gates in Newburgh, New York, and was a prominent figure in the quasi-mutiny of American officers in 1783 known as the Newburgh Conspiracy. By the end of the war, many Continental officers had become disgruntled by the failure of the Continental Army to restore years of back pay. In March 1783 an anonymous letter, later identified as being written by Armstrong and circulated among the officers, called for a meeting to discuss grievances and form a plan of action, which might include a direct approach to Congress. Recognizing that such a meeting might be the start of a mutinous revolt, Washington appeared at the meeting. Through his personal appeal, the budding insurrection was diffused.[28]

Following the war Armstrong went into politics and served sporadically as a US senator from New York at the beginning of the Jefferson administration. By that time Armstrong had married into the wealthy New York Livingston family, and in 1804 Jefferson appointed Armstrong to be minister to France. Upon his return in 1810, Armstrong remained active in New York politics and in July 1812 was appointed a federal brigadier general and placed in charge of the defenses of New York City, followed by his selection to War Department secretary six months later. At this stage in his career he was also seen as a northern rival to Monroe to become Madison's successor as president.[29]

Armstrong's first act as secretary that affected Wilkinson served to head off a growing dispute between Wilkinson and another western military rival, Andrew Jackson. In response to Wilkinson's plea for more troops to defend New Orleans, Eustis had issued a call in October 1812 to Tennessee governor Willie Blount to assemble 1,500 militia troops and send them to Wilkinson.[30] Eustis's order allowed Blount to appoint a brigadier general in the federal service to command the troops. The senior Tennessee general selected for the command was state militia Major General Andrew Jackson, but two problems were immediately apparent in complying with Eustis's order. First, Jackson wanted to use this force to seize Mobile and Pensacola from the Spanish, not to reinforce New Orleans. Second, Jackson did not want to be in a subordinate position to Wilkinson. Since Jackson's appearance at the Burr trials in 1807, Jackson had widely and publicly denounced Wilkinson and continued to regard Wilkinson as an incompetent agent of Spain. On November 29 Jackson contacted Tennessee congressman George W. Campbell and urged Campbell to press the administration for Wilkinson's removal from command.[31]

Despite Jackson's machinations, he and his federalized militia departed Nashville for New Orleans on January 10, 1813, proceeding in two columns that would rendezvous at Natchez. While Wilkinson and Jackson maintained a publicly cordial relationship, Wilkinson was greatly concerned about the arrival of a significant body of troops under the command of an avowed critic. Wilkinson would be the senior federal brigadier general, but questions regarding a clear chain of command continued to cause him concern, particularly regarding someone as volatile as Andrew Jackson. Wilkinson first sought to exert control over Jackson and his force by directing that they halt further movement at Natchez, citing the inability of the army's quartermaster to support the force in New Orleans.[32] Simultaneously, Wilkinson reached out to acting War Department secretary Monroe to raise the specter of chaos on the streets of New Orleans if thousands of untrained Tennessee militia were "turned loose on this licentious community, made up of all kinds of countries and colors."[33] Wilkinson requested that Monroe direct the removal of Jackson and provide clear direction that the Tennessee troops would be under Wilkinson's command.

Wilkinson's February 9 request for Jackson's removal was overtaken by events. Armstrong had taken office on February 5, then issued an order directing Jackson to disband his force at Natchez. Armstrong had determined that the Tennessee troops were no longer needed and should return at their own expense to Tennessee. When the order was forwarded to Jackson by Wilkinson, Jackson took great umbrage at the fact that the War Department was abandoning his federalized militia stationed on the banks of the Mississippi. Given the fact that the secretary's orders were arriving through Wilkinson and that the copies contained some inconsistencies, Jackson even suspected that the orders might be forgeries.[34] Contrary to orders, Jackson kept his force intact and led it back to Tennessee, where the troops were discharged and eventually paid. His efforts to protect his men from War Department indifference to their welfare earned him the nickname "Old Hickory."[35]

Jackson's call for Wilkinson's removal was not the only such demand in circulation. Wilkinson's 1812 reappearance in New Orleans was not well received by the local population. Ill will remained from Wilkinson's heavy-handed declaration of martial law in New Orleans during the Burr Conspiracy, and Wilkinson's poor leadership during the Terre aux Boeufs debacle did nothing to improve his standing. In November 1812 Wade Hampton wrote Madison and requested a transfer so that he would not be required to serve under Wilkinson.[36]

Even more ominous was the March 3, 1813, letter directed to Madison from Senator William H. Crawford, requesting Wilkinson's removal from New Orleans:

> I beg leave to suggest the necessity of removing Genl Wilkinson from the New Orleans Station. The importance of that place should induce a selection of a military commander, whose character is above suspicion. That Genl Wilkinson is not an officer of that description, will I believe be universally admitted. Those who adhere to him are constrained to admit, that during the whole time of his public employment, he has been suspected of the want of integrity. In the western and southern states, and especially at New Orleans, he is generally believed to be one of the most abandoned and profligate of men.[37]

Crawford's condemnation carried special weight. A Georgia senator, he had been elected president pro tempore of the Senate, and under the presidential line of succession procedures then in effect he became the acting vice president when George Clinton died in office in April 1812.

The spring of 1813 would result in the high-water mark of Wilkinson's military career and conclude with the only successful military campaign under his command during forty years of service. In February Congress approved the seizure of Mobile, which completed the seizure of Spanish western Florida that had commenced with Madison's annexation of Baton Rouge in 1810. On February 16, newly installed secretary Armstrong directed Wilkinson to seize Mobile and all remaining Spanish territory west of the Perdido River.[38] At the time, Spanish forces consisted of sixty troops located at Fort Charlotte in Mobile and a small detachment at Dauphin Island, located at the mouth of Mobile Bay. On April 7, Wilkinson and 600 troops approached Mobile by boat, while another 400 hundred dred troops departed Fort Stoddert to conduct an investment of Mobile from the north. (On the way, Wilkinson suffered the ignominy of having his boat capsize on Lake Pontchartrain. He was eventually rescued by a passing fishing boat.[39]) On April 12 Wilkinson sent a polite note to Fort Charlotte's commander, Captain Cayento Perez, and requested that he surrender the fort, which was done on the following day.[40] When the Spanish commander at Pensacola politely inquired whether Spain and the United States were at war, Wilkinson replied that he was not aware that the nations were at war and that he was merely complying with his orders from the US president.[41]

The bloodless seizure of Mobile and its environs proved to be the only territorial acquisition by the United States during the War of 1812. Wilkinson had complied with his orders in a timely and efficient manner and completed the seizure of west Florida, a long-sought goal of US foreign policy, without bloodshed. Wilkinson's brief foray into Mobile was, of course, tainted by a whiff of scandal. In 1806, John Forbes & Co., an English trading company, had significant business dealings with Indian tribes in the Gulf and Lower Mississippi. When the tribes did not pay their debts, the company pressured the tribes to sell portions of their land to the United States and reimburse the company with the funds received from the sale. To encourage US participation in the scheme, the firm called on Wilkinson to use his influence with the federal government to help consummate the sale. In return for his assistance, the firm transferred the title of Dauphin Island as a "gift" to Wilkinson.[42] On a personal note, a tragedy for Wilkinson also attended the incursion. During the expedition, Wilkinson was accompanied by his eldest son, Captain James Biddle Wilkinson. When Wilkinson departed the island, he left his son behind as part of the garrison stationed there. In September 1813 young Captain Wilkinson died on the island.[43]

Unknown to Wilkinson at the time of the Mobile campaign, Congress had moved at the beginning of March to promote him and several other generals to the rank of major general. Wilkinson, Hampton, William Henry Harrison, and Morgan Lewis joined Dearborn and Pinckney as senior generals of the army, even though as of the beginning of March not one of them had conducted a successful campaign against the British.[44] And, except for Harrison, none would distinguish himself during the war. However, in apparent response to Crawford's criticism, Armstrong determined that Wilkinson's talents would be best used on the northern campaign into Canada. On March 10 Armstrong directed Wilkinson to move to upstate New York, where he would serve as second in command to the ailing Dearborn for the next offensive against Canada.[45]

Once again, and despite his promise to Armstrong to move swiftly, Wilkinson complied with his orders in the deliberate pace that characterized virtually every movement he made.[46] Notwithstanding the fact that any campaign occurring on the northern frontier had to commence by early June to have any hope of success, Wilkinson did not immediately depart New Orleans for New York. In June he was still in Mobile with Celestine, and in July, while passing through Georgia, he learned of the death of his loyal subordinate, Brigadier General Zebulon Pike, who was killed in the American assault on York, the capital of Upper Canada. Pike's death caused Wilkinson to write to his friend Morgan Lewis about the role of generals in combat. While the letter commenced with Wilkinson's usual florid comments about risking his life in the service of his country, it also contained a passage that was subsequently viewed by many as a hallmark of Wilkinson's innate cowardice. In commenting on Pike's death in combat, Wilkinson remarked, "Farewell my friend, and remember a general officer does not expose his person, but in the last resort. Subordinates execute, while chiefs command: to mingle in the conflict, is to abandon the power of direction."[47] Wilkinson finally arrived in Washington at the end of July and almost another week passed before he met with Armstrong, who informed Wilkinson that he would now replace Dearborn as the commander of the Canadian invasion.

During the summer of 1813, while fighting raged across the Detroit and Niagara frontiers, Armstrong envisioned a third invasion of Canada that would target the St. Lawrence River valley. With Dearborn's removal, Armstrong was left with two major generals in the St. Lawrence–Lake Champlain area of operations: Wilkinson and Hampton, who hated each other. Hampton's 1812 refusal to serve under Wilkinson had resulted in his transfer to the north, and Armstrong was now faced with the challenge of delicately arranging a command structure with them working together. In an August 9 letter to Wilkinson, Armstrong assured Wilkinson that Hampton would be acting under Wilkinson's command.[48] However, despite his assurances, it is not clear that this subordination was ever communicated to Hampton. To ensure full cooperation between the two commanders, Armstrong chose to take the field himself and operate as the de facto commander of the invasion. Despite his political promotion to general officer rank (a rank he held for only six months), while serving as secretary Armstrong insisted on being referred to as "General Armstrong."[49]

Armstrong's decision to assume command was also driven by factors outside of the Wilkinson-Hampton feud. As a rival to Monroe for the 1816 presidential nomination, Armstrong believed that a successful military campaign under his personal direction would greatly benefit his presidential aspirations. Even though prior to the war his only military experience was as a staff aide to Generals Mercer and Gates during the Revolution, Armstrong felt that his personal command would result in a successful invasion of Canada. Wilkinson did not react well to the announcement that "General Armstrong" would be operating and directing in close proximity. On August 24 he sent Armstrong a polite note, urging his civilian superior to keep his distance: "I trust you will not interfere with my arrangements, or give orders within the district of my command, but to myself, because it would impair my authority and distract the public service, two heads on the same shoulders make a monster."[50] Armstrong repeatedly ignored Wilkinson's plea, and Wilkinson's implied chastisement commenced a widening rift between them.

The 1813 Montreal campaign was doomed from the start. The divided command structure among three of the worst American generals was rife with acrimony, poor communications, and conflicting goals and orders. When Wilkinson learned that Hampton was resisting his orders, he insisted on communicating directions to Hampton only through Armstrong.[51] Armstrong encouraged this disjointed coordination but failed to effectively communicate with either Wilkinson or Hampton. When he arrived at Sackett's Harbor, New York, on September 5, Armstrong promptly succumbed to one of the camp diseases that were ravaging the American staging area and, upon his recovery, eventually withdrew to the safer and warmer climes of Albany and out of immediate communications with either wing of the American advance. In addition to his failed communications, Armstrong also directly issued orders to Wilkinson's subordinates without going through Wilkinson, thereby creating chaos and uncertainty in the command and growing hostility from Wilkinson.

Their dysfunctional command structure was immediately apparent when Armstrong and Wilkinson could not agree on the ultimate objective of the campaign. From the outset, two possible objectives were apparent. Montreal was located near the convergence of the St. Lawrence and Richelieu Rivers and was the traditional target of all US campaigns that proceeded from the Lake Champlain valley. Kingston was an important British base located at the juncture of the St. Lawrence and Lake Ontario, approximately 150 miles upriver from Montreal. Since Hampton would be proceeding down Lake Champlain from Plattsburgh, New York, Montreal was always intended as his primary objective. However, because the remaining American forces under Wilkinson were scattered along Lake Ontario, from Fort George on the Niagara frontier to Sackett's Harbor on the lake's eastern shore, their forces would first have to be consolidated then dispatched by boat down the St. Lawrence to either Kingston or Montreal. While the American forces were being consolidated at Sackett's Harbor, Armstrong and Wilkinson repeatedly clashed over the ultimate destination of the American force. If Kingston was the goal for Wilkinson's force, Hampton would be expected to operate independently in the assault on Montreal. If Kingston was to be bypassed by Wilkinson's boats traveling down the St. Lawrence, Hampton would have to eventually link up with Wilkinson at an agreed-on point on the St. Lawrence prior to the joint assault on Montreal. Armstrong and Wilkerson bickered over the final objective for more than a month before Armstrong finally selected Montreal on October 19, far too late in the campaigning season.[52]

Following his departure from Washington, Wilkinson arrived at Sackett's Harbor on August 20 and promptly fell ill. However, rather than remaining at Sackett's Harbor to meet with Armstrong and coordinate the consolidation of the American forces there, on August 30 Wilkinson departed by open boat for Fort George on the Niagara frontier, to oversee the removal of most of the federal troops from that location. This task could clearly have been assigned to a competent subordinate, but Wilkinson nevertheless went himself and did not return to Sackett's Harbor until October 4. Some of the delay may have been driven by Wilkinson's reluctance to be under Armstrong's immediate supervision. During his time away Wilkinson repeatedly wrote to Armstrong complaining about his own illness and the impact it had on his ability to command.[53] When Wilkinson finally arrived back at Sackett's Harbor he was so ill that he required help to leave his boat. The following day, when he was visited at his sickbed by Armstrong, Wilkinson asked to be relieved of command. According to Wilkinson, Armstrong denied his request, stating that there was no one else to take his place.[54] Despite the debilitation from the illness and treatments of laudanum he received, Wilkinson remained in command for the assault on Montreal.

Americans had been fighting in and around the St. Lawrence River valley for more than fifty years and should have been well-versed in the primary factor that affected military campaigns in this region: the Canadian weather. Winter conditions severely impacted all military initiatives that commenced in the fall. Yet the 7,300 troops under Wilkinson's command did not even enter the St. Lawrence until November 1. Plummeting temperatures, hurricane-force winds, and snow squalls had delayed the departure of the three hundred open boats from Sackett's Harbor. Supplies were inefficiently loaded on the boats and some of the boats were lost as they scattered along the lakefront, seeking refuge from the deteriorating weather. Camp diseases (dysentery) and bad provisions added to the misery of the boats as they struggled through the series of rapids that interrupted the river journey toward Montreal.

On November 3 Wilkinson called a halt at French Creek on the south (American) bank of the St. Lawrence River to reorganize the forces under his command. Wilkinson and his second in command, General Morgan Lewis, realigned their forces and examined the dwindling status of their supplies. Nearly half of their supplies had been lost in storms on Lake Ontario before the expedition even entered the St. Lawrence River.[55] Wilkinson's incompetent quartermaster, Brigadier General Robert Swartwout, thirty-five, had little military or logistical experience. A New York merchant and local politician, Swartwout had entered the army with a brigadier general's commission six months earlier. Swartwout did not relish his quartermaster duties and pressed for a field command, which he was foolishly given in addition to his quartermaster role. (Wilkinson was especially concerned about his relationship with Swartwout, the brother of Samuel Swartwout, whom Wilkinson had illegally arrested as part of the Burr Conspiracy. Upon his assumption of command, Wilkinson had General Lewis speak to Swartwout and obtain his assurance of no hard feelings toward Wilkinson.[56]) Supplies that were poorly stored were often looted by hungry troops without regard to logistical assignment. Incompetent quartermasters lost accountability for goods scattered throughout the fleet, and greedy contractors gladly overcharged the army for missing supplies. Shortly after arriving on the St. Lawrence, Wilkinson learned that his expedition had barely two weeks of provisions left for the entire campaign.

Wilkinson's continuing illness (or perhaps his incapacitation from drugs or alcohol) delayed departure from French Creek until November 5. The careful alignment of the fleet did not survive its first encounter with the currents of the St. Lawrence, and the scattered boats landed with "some confusion" along the southern shore at Morrisville that evening. The following day, as the invalided Wilkinson once again attempted to realign his disordered fleet, he was greeted with shattering news delivered by Major William King, adjutant to General Hampton, who had traveled overland to report to Wilkinson: Hampton had been defeated by an inferior Canadian force and was retreating back to New York.

At Armstrong's direction, Hampton and his more than 4,000 troops had departed Plattsburgh for Montreal on September 19. Hampton chose the traditional route of invasion—down Lake Champlain to the source of the Richelieu River, then down that river to the confluence with the St. Lawrence near Montreal. However, barely forty-eight hours into the journey, Hampton convened a council of war, which concluded that Canadian resistance and deteriorating roads precluded the use of the traditional route. Changing course, Hampton and his force traveled seventy miles west to Four Corners, New York, on the Chateauguay River. There, just short of the Canadian border, Hampton built a camp and awaited word from Armstrong and Wilkinson regarding his next move. If his superiors directed him to independently assault Montreal, he could proceed down the river and commence an attack. If they directed him to link up with Wilkinson, he could proceed down the river and join Wilkinson west of Montreal on the St. Lawrence.

In the deteriorating weather of the Canadian fall, Hampton waited more than three weeks for direction. Upon finally receiving Armstrong's directive to link up with Wilkinson, Hampton's force departed Four Corners on October 21 in the middle of a snowstorm. Hampton left the camp at Four Corners in the care of New York militia, who again refused to cross the border into Canada.[57] For four days Hampton struggled north, slowed by the need to widen the cart track that paralleled the Chateauguay River. On October 26, nineteen miles short of the St.

Lawrence, Hampton was confronted by a small Canadian blocking force under the command of Lieutenant Colonel Charles-Michel d'Irumberry de Salaberry, a French *Canadienne* and professional British soldier. De Salaberry commanded a scratch force of 1,700 Canadian militia entrenched on both sides of the Chateauguay River. Hampton's subsequent attack, facing two-to-one odds in the Americans' favor, was soundly repulsed when a significant part of the American troops got lost in the woods.[58] Despite remarkably light casualties, Hampton conducted another council of war on October 27, which voted to abandon the campaign and retreat back across the border to Four Corners. American losses were estimated at 82 killed, wounded, or missing. Canadian losses were 2 killed, 16 wounded, and 4 taken prisoner.[59] After a second council on November 7, Hampton abandoned any hope of linking up with Wilkinson and returned with his force to Plattsburgh.

Whether from the effects of illness, laudanum, liquor, or the shock from the news of Hampton's defeat and retreat, Wilkinson began acting even more erratically. Reports circulated that Wilkinson was drunk, that he had commenced singing songs denigrating the entire campaign, and that he was cursing the army and its officers. Colonel Joseph Swift, a Wilkinson loyalist and member of the 1811 court-martial, was serving on the campaign as Wilkinson's chief engineer. In his memoirs Swift states that under the influence of laudanum, Wilkinson "became very merry, and sung and repeated stories, the only evil of which as that it was not the dignified deportment to be expected from the commander-in-chief."[60] On November 7 the first American troops to enter Canada put ashore on the north bank of the St. Lawrence, under the command of Colonel Alexander Macomb. That force was soon joined by artillery units under the command of Colonel Winfield Scott. On November 8 yet another council of war was called, and the decision was made to continue toward Montreal.[61] The council was informed that Hampton had been defeated but they were not informed that Hampton would not be joining them.

On November 9 a significant portion of the army under the command of Brigadier General Jacob Brown, Wilkinson's ablest general, put ashore and moved forward on the Canadian side of the river to continue the approach to Montreal. Accompanying Brown were capable units under the command of Colonels Macomb and Scott; the rear guard, 3,000 men under the command of Brigadier General John P. Boyd, was deployed near Crysler's Farm to screen the rear of the army from a British force believed to be approaching from the West. On November 10 Wilkinson remained on his boat on the river and, due to illness, relinquished command of the army to General Lewis. Unfortunately, Lewis was equally ill, so Wilkinson continued to issue orders to the troops on shore, prolonging the command confusion that had characterized the entire campaign. By late afternoon

Lewis in turn relinquished command to Boyd, who, being thoroughly confused by the chain of command, attempted to seek clarification from Wilkinson that evening. Upon arrival at Wilkinson's boat, Boyd was informed by Wilkinson's aide that Wilkinson was too ill to see him and that Boyd should defend his position and the fleet from the shore. The following morning Boyd received a series of contradictory orders from both Lewis and Wilkinson. Before clarification could be obtained, the British force at the rear commenced its assault, and Boyd directed the US side of the ensuing battle without any direct involvement from either Wilkinson or Lewis.[62]

In his autobiography Winfield Scott describes Boyd as an able subordinate "but vacillating and imbecile, beyond all endurance, as a chief under high responsibilities."[63] Boyd did demonstrate the accuracy of Scott's observation. The British force, 1,200 men under the command of Lieutenant Colonel Joseph Morrison, attacked the American rear guard. Boyd, with over 2,200 men, responded with a series of uncoordinated piecemeal attacks. Units under General Swartwout were driven back in disarray, and General Leonard Covington, the only capable American general officer on the scene, was fatally wounded in an unsuccessful assault. Eventually Boyd withdrew his force to guard the American boats. Fittingly, Boyd later stated that he had withdrawn under orders from either Lewis or Wilkinson but could not remember which officer had issued the order.[64] Both Lewis and Wilkinson later denied ever issuing such an order. American casualties were over 300 killed and wounded as well as the loss of one piece of artillery.[65] British losses were 179.

The Battle of Crysler's Farm was the first battle in Wilkinson's entire military career when he was in command. In every respect it was an unmitigated disaster. Either through incompetence, illness, medication, inebriation, or a combination of all four, Wilkinson created a command climate that was incapable of functioning effectively and defeating an inferior force. After allegedly relinquishing command to another incapacitated and marginally competent officer, Wilkinson continued to issue orders that only sowed further confusion. While on November 10 a clear threat was presented by the British forces to his rear, Wilkinson divided his command and sent most of his best troops, under the leadership of General Jacob Brown, his best commander, on a fruitless excursion away from the threat. Operational command of the battle was then left to Boyd, who not by choice but through the process of elimination had become the most senior officer on scene. When Boyd sought clarification of his role and responsibilities on the evening of November 10, Wilkinson was unwilling or incapable of providing it. The incompetence of Boyd and Lewis certainly contributed to the outcome, but the ultimate failure in the battle and the entire campaign primarily belongs to Wilkinson.

The defeat at Crysler's Farm did not preclude Wilkinson from carrying on the assault on Montreal, eighty miles further downstream. The inferior British force engaged on November 11 was to the rear of and it did not pose a meaningful threat to Wilkinson's troops as it moved toward Montreal or to the supply lines that could have been reestablished through upstate New York and Lake Champlain. Wilkinson's force also outnumbered the Montreal garrison by a factor of four to one. However, the delays encountered due to the late seasonal start, the poor supply status of the army, and the incapacity and incompetence of the senior leadership, all led to the conclusion that the 1813 campaign was over. On November 12 a council of war unanimously recommended that the campaign be halted and that the army retire to winter quarters at French Mills, a camp to be established less than twenty miles away at a spot across the New York border. The stated reason for the council's decision was of course not the incompetence of the campaign's leadership but the failure of Hampton to rendezvous with Wilkinson's column.[66]

The council's decision was just the first step in the concerted campaign of finger-pointing and obfuscation among Wilkinson, Armstrong, and Hampton, all designed to avoid and deflect responsibility for the campaign's collapse. Despite his illness and alleged incapacitation from command, Wilkinson deftly and immediately commenced his crusade to avoid responsibility for the campaign's demise. His first volley was a November 12 letter to Hampton in which Wilkinson expressed shock and alarm at Hampton's decision not to join forces.[67] Wilkinson then dispatched a November 16 letter to Armstrong, wherein he claimed victory instead of defeat at Crysler's Farm and informed Armstrong that the sole reason for the withdrawal was the failure of Hampton to effect a rendezvous.[68]

Wilkinson dispatched Joseph Swift, his loyal subordinate, on a journey primarily designed to cover Wilkinson's political flanks. Swift was directed to bring another missive to Hampton in Plattsburgh and confidentially report back to Wilkinson on Hampton's reaction. Swift was then directed to report to Armstrong, who was presumed to be in Washington, and deliver the November 16 letter claiming victory and blaming Hampton. After Swift met with Hampton in Plattsburgh, he sent a report to Wilkinson acknowledging that Hampton placed the blame on Armstrong's order to join Wilkinson. Swift then commenced his journey to Washington to deliver Wilkinson's spin to Armstrong. However, as he journeyed through Albany, Swift unexpectedly encountered Armstrong having dinner with the governor of New York and General William Henry Harrison, who had recently defeated the British and killed the Shawnee leader Tecumseh at the Battle of the Thames in Canada.[69] In a telling example of the confusion in the command structure, Wilkinson was unaware of the location of the secretary of war when he sent Swift on his mission. Armstrong had departed Sackett's Harbor in mid-October and arrived in Albany in the beginning of November, and apparently he never informed Wilkinson of his location.

In summing up his conversations with Wilkinson, Hampton, and Armstrong in his memoirs, Swift astutely observed,

> As to the causes of the failure of the campaign on the St. Lawrence, the sojourn of General Armstrong on the frontier in the autumn had excited the jealousy of General Wilkinson. As the event is, both of the generals and the Secretary would gladly attribute the failure to any other cause than their respective errors. The immediate cause of the failure is the delay on the river; overtaking our army by the British on 11th November ended the campaign. My impression is that a junction of Wilkinson and Hampton was not intended, and by consequence an assault on Montreal was not purposed after October, if previously. One of the main causes of delay is bad bread, and its consequent bad health. Our chiefs were old, and from the date of the movement from Sackett's Harbor the two oldest, Wilkinson and Lewis, had not a day of sound health until the winter. If the army had been led by General Brown the end had been better than it is.[70]

Wilkinson's campaign to shift blame had just begun just as the army was confronting the immediate need to create a winter encampment at French Mills. Unfortunately, because of poor planning and inadequate supplies, French Mills became a frozen version of Terre aux Boeufs. In his report the chief hospital surgeon reported that hospital tents were inadequate to protect the sick and injured from the winter cold. The men had inadequate clothing, and the food and hospital supplies were either inadequate or fraudulently produced.[71] Winter quarters required the construction of wooden huts, hospitals, and warehouses to support the winter needs of 6,000 troops, one-third of whom were unfit for duty. No satisfactory facilities existed at French Mills, and the tired and sick had to be housed in tents and shanties until proper buildings could be constructed.

True to form, Wilkinson used the excuse of his own illness to avoid sharing in his men's misery. Wilkinson was carried in a litter by eight men to a comfortable home in Malone, New York, eighteen miles away from his freezing troops.[72] At the same time, senior generals Boyd and Lewis concluded that their presence at French Mills was not needed and departed the area.[73] Less than two weeks later, when the Malone location proved to be inadequate to remove him from the sufferings of his troops, Wilkinson requested Armstrong's permission to move his headquarters to Albany, another two hundred miles away: "Albany, independent of personal consideration, is the proper point for winter quarters of the officer commanding this district, to superintend and press the recruiting service, to imbody the recruits, to have them clothed, armed, organized and instructed in the essential duties of police and personal cleanliness."[74] Armstrong denied the request. Wilkinson then sought to turn the command over to Lewis but concluded that Lewis was too ill to assume command. Wilkinson also tried to assign command to Boyd but found an "insuperable repugnance" by other officers to serve under Boyd. General Jacob Brown, Wilkinson's best subordinate general, threatened to resign if forced to serve under Boyd.[75] To the misfortune of all, Wilkinson remained in command.

When press reports of the failure of the campaign began to circulate, casting Wilkinson as the cause of the failure, Wilkinson sought to deflect responsibility by requesting that Armstrong arrest and press charges against Hampton for disobeying orders to join Wilkinson in Canada: "With respect to the unfortunate issue of the campaign, I disclaim the shadow of blame, because I know I have done my duty, and more than my duty. *To General Hampton's outrage of every principle of subordination and discipline may be ascribed the failure of the expedition*; and that I have not arrested him must be attributed to my respect for you, and my desire that the arrest should proceed from the highest authority" (emphasis in original).[76] When Armstrong failed to respond to his requests for Hampton's arrest, Wilkinson sought to arrest Hampton on his own authority.[77] By the time Wilkinson's court-martial directive was issued, Hampton had left Plattsburgh and Wilkinson's area of control. On December 31, further pressure to assign blame arose when the House of Representatives passed a resolution demanding that Madison produce all correspondence between Armstrong and the responsible generals.

On November 1, following Hampton's defeat at Chateauguay and retreat to Plattsburgh, Hampton again offered his resignation, which was accepted by Armstrong.[78] Shortly thereafter, Hampton departed from Plattsburgh and soon departed the army altogether. Though a court of inquiry would usually be the method through which the War Department would gather facts and assign blame for a failed campaign, Armstrong never recommended that Hampton's failure be subjected to a court of inquiry, and by January 1814 it was apparent that Armstrong would seek to place the failure of the campaign entirely on Wilkinson's shoulders. Following the directive of President Madison, on January 20 Armstrong ordered Wilkinson to abandon French Mills and disburse his troops to Sackett's Harbor and Plattsburgh, which had regular lines of supply.[79] On January 25, in response to the House of Representatives resolution, Armstrong submitted a report to Madison containing carefully edited correspondence between himself, Hampton, and Wilkinson as well as excerpts from a journal he had supposedly maintained during the campaign. Wilkinson later contended that Armstrong's journal had been manufactured after the fact. "Whoever is well acquainted with

General Armstrong's mental organization, will scarcely believe, that he has ever descended to keep, a diary of diminutive incidents; yet, no one can doubt *his capacity*, to form a journal to meet any occasion"[80] (emphasis in original). The report was duly transmitted by Madison to the House on January 31 and published on February 2 under the title "Causes of the Failure of the Army on the Northern Frontier."[81]

Armstrong's report laid the groundwork for a court of inquiry and the ultimate court-martial of Wilkinson, but it was only a part of a concerted campaign by Armstrong to subject numerous bad generals to the extreme sanctions of military justice for failed campaigns. This campaign for accountability also echoed the sentiments of capable junior officers who resented the repeated failures of the army's senior leadership. At Armstrong and Madison's direction, on January 3, 1814, a court-martial was convened in Albany to try General William Hull for his shameful surrender of Detroit in 1812. The charges against him were treason, cowardice, neglect of duty, and "unofficer-like conduct," and the matter was referred to the court-martial as a capital offense. The trial proceeded until March 25, when the court convicted Hull on all counts except treason, then sentenced him to be shot. Madison ultimately approved the verdict but reduced the sentence to dismissal from the army.

The possibility of a court-martial and even an execution was undoubtedly on Wilkinson's mind when he conceived several ill-considered winter expeditions to reclaim some semblance of military success. On January 15 he proposed to New York governor Daniel Thompkins a winter invasion of Canada. While the proposal was farfetched and never carried out, it did succeed in convincing Thompkins to contact Armstrong and assure him that Armstrong had misjudged the general.[82] In late March Wilkinson actually led an assault into Canada, but after a significant portion of his force became lost in the ice and snow, it was repulsed by an inferior Canadian force at Lacolle Mill on March 30.[83] This was the only battle in Wilkinson's career when he actually commanded and led troops on the battlefield, and it was a fitting end to his military accomplishments. Even though he outnumbered his opponents by a four-to-one margin, the troops failed to dislodge the small force of entrenched Canadians and quickly retreated back across the border, thirty miles south to Plattsburgh.

Wilkinson's final campaign was more than too little too late. On February 21 Armstrong recommended to Madison that Wilkinson be relieved from command and that a court of inquiry be convened to examine Wilkinson's role in the failure of the Montreal campaign.[84] Following Madison's approval, Armstrong issued orders on March 24, relieving Wilkinson from command and directing him to a court of inquiry.[85] After the court of inquiry had been scheduled to convene at

Fort Edward in April, Wilkinson commenced his usual approach to such proceedings by quibbling over the composition of the court and the availability of
witnesses.[86] Due to increased British activity on the northern frontier, Armstrong
suspended the court of inquiry on April 28, issued orders for a court-martial
instead, and directed Wilkinson to report to either Philadelphia, Baltimore, or
Annapolis to await further proceedings. Wilkinson once again made technical
objections to the composition of the court and specifically objected to being tried
by only five officers rather than the thirteen usually required by the Articles of
War. Madison sustained the objection, forcing the trial to be delayed until such
time as thirteen serving senior officers would be available to sit as members.[87] On
May 23 Armstrong proposed an initial set of charges, including criminal delay in
prosecuting the Montreal campaign, failing to "take measures, proper and necessary for beating the enemy" at Crysler's Farm, and intoxication.[88]

   As the summer progressed, other affairs impacted the antagonists. In January,
Celestine Wilkinson had given birth to daughter Marie in New Orleans, but the
child died in June. Wilkinson made no mention in his memoirs of either her
birth or her passing. By June Armstrong had become the target of War Department accountant Simmons's fiscal ire when Simmons had the temerity to question
certain food expenses Armstrong had incurred during the Montreal campaign.[89]
Armstrong wrote a scathing letter to Madison in which he set forth his lack of confidence in Simmons, based on Simmons's lack of competence, attachment to the
government, and public and private morals.[90] Madison finally ended Simmons's
twenty-four-year campaign of fiscal terror the following week.[91]

   Of greater concern to Armstrong was his deteriorating relationship with Madison. By mid-summer of 1814, American military fortunes in the war had spiraled
downward. British and American forces continued to clash on the Niagara frontier. While new commanders such as Jacob Brown and Winfield Scott had demonstrated remarkable brilliance in this theater, their overall efforts only resulted in
a standstill of the US military's fortunes in that sector. The British victory over
Napoleon resulted in the release of numerous troops and ships that could be directed at the United States as the only remaining belligerent. Brilliant single-ship
victories by the American navy in the first two years of the war were now only
a memory, as it now was either blockaded in port or defeated at sea by superior
forces. Furthermore, in the summer of 1814 Great Britain prepared three invasions into the United States that were targeted at defeating the United States on
multiple fronts. While the Niagara frontier remained at a stalemate, British forces
prepared for yet another invasion of upstate New York through the traditional
Lake Champlain route. A second invasion was planned with Napoleonic War
veterans at New Orleans and the Mississippi Valley. Finally, for over two years
British troops and ships had raided the Chesapeake Bay with impunity, with little

effective resistance from the few American forces stationed there. The quiescent American response encouraged the planning of another British expedition that was targeted on the destruction of Washington and Baltimore.

Armstrong's failure to effectively confront the British on any of these fronts naturally caused Madison to question the secretary's capability. Furthermore, as Madison's relationship with Monroe grew stronger, Monroe encouraged presidential attacks on his possible rival in the upcoming 1816 election. Armstrong's incessant practice of meddling in small matters of the department provided the catalyst for the ultimate break with Madison. Frustrated by the continuing practice of dueling among army officers, Armstrong issued an order banning the practice and required other officers who were aware of dueling to arrest any participants.[92] Madison took umbrage at the fact that this order, and many other minor decisions affecting army conduct and discipline, had not been approved in advance by the president. In one scathing letter to Armstrong, Madison chastised the secretary for not seeking the president's prior approval on a broad variety of War Department matters. Madison ordered Armstrong to seek presidential approval on various actions large and small and cited a nonexclusive list of ten matters that would require presidential approval, clearly indicating to Armstrong that he was on a particularly short leash.[93]

In response to Madison's chastisement, Armstrong apparently ceased to function as the secretary of war. Unfortunately, the timing of Madison's rebuke and Armstrong's shut down could not have been worse. Less than a week after Madison issued his denunciation, 4,500 British troops came ashore at Benedict, Maryland, a mere forty miles from Washington. Confusion reigned among the American leaders regarding the ultimate destination of the raiding force, but within a few days it became clear that Washington was the intended target. American defenses were entrusted to Brigadier General William Winder, a Maryland attorney and loyal Democratic-Republican who had received a commission at the beginning of the war. (In his memoir of the campaign, Armstrong insists that Winder was Madison's selection as local commander, based on Winder's familiarity with Maryland and relation to Maryland's governor.[94]) Wilkinson, who was already in the Washington area, volunteered to lead the defense if his arrest was lifted, but Madison ignored the offer.[95] Winder drew together various militia units and a small group of regular soldiers, sailors, and marines and sought to halt the British at Bladensburg, Maryland, on August 24.

The Battle of Bladensburg was a disgrace for all the American officials present. Winder's incompetence, Armstrong's reticence, and Madison and his entire cabinet's presence at the battlefield resulted in a surfeit of leaders but a dearth of leadership. The American forces were quickly defeated, and without further resistance the British entered Washington on the evening of August 24 and burned most federal buildings, including the White House and the Capitol Building. Upon the British withdrawal on August 25, Madison and his cabinet slowly straggled back into the charred city, and by the time Madison and Armstrong next met (on August 29), the finger-pointing and assignment of blame had begun. Madison informed Armstrong that "violent prejudices" were being exhibited against his administration and that militia officers threatened to "tear off their epaulets if Genl. Armstrong was to have anything to do with them." Armstrong presented a series of excuses regarding his deficient performance in the defense of Washington and expressed dismay at the personal attacks being made against him. Madison dismissed Armstrong's excuses by stating that Armstrong "had never himself proposed or suggested a single precaution or arrangement for its safety."[96] Five days later Armstrong resigned in disgrace.[97]

Two people directly benefited from Armstrong's demise. James Monroe saw the elimination of his primary rival as Madison's successor and his rising star was further burnished by again being dual-hatted as both secretary of state and secretary of war. The second beneficiary was James Wilkinson. Though the court-martial charges proposed by Armstrong against Wilkinson remained, the primary force pushing the charges was gone and an attractive scapegoat for Wilkinson's failure in the Montreal campaign had appeared.

The commencement of the court-martial had to await the availability of thirteen senior officers to sit in judgment. Fortunately, the fall of 1814 saw a rapid end to most hostilities and the American military experienced a particular upturn in its fortunes. Other than accomplishing the burning of Washington, each of the three British invasions had ended in dismal failure. In early September the British invasion of Lake Champlain was defeated on land and lake and forced to return to Canada, ending all military activity on the northern frontier. In mid-September the Royal Navy was unable to enter Baltimore harbor because of the stout resistance shown by Fort McHenry; a subsequent land advance on the city was then repulsed by entrenched militia, which also killed the British commander.[98] In December, on the southern front, a British force of over 14,000 troops approached New Orleans via the surrounding lakes but on January 8, 1815, General Andrew Jackson soundly defeated the invasion and killed the commander. The last major British force had been driven from American soil.

On the diplomatic front, American and British diplomats began negotiations in Ghent, Belgium, in August 1814. The American delegation was particularly strong, being composed of John Quincy Adams, Henry Clay, and Albert Gallatin. A final agreement was reached on December 24 that returned the two nations to the status quo ante: free trade and sailor's rights had not been resolved but were rendered moot by Napoleon's defeat. By February 1815 the treaty would be ratified by both parties, ending the long and painful affair.

12

COURT-MARTIALED AGAIN, ACQUITTED AGAIN, DISMISSED AT LAST

1815

Shall a coxcomb who merely wants a splendid uniform to gratify his peacock vanity—be allowed unnecessarily to lose his men by hundreds, or by thousands, to surrender them or to cause them to be beaten by inferior numbers;—shall such imbeciles escape ignominious punishment? In every case, Humanity—as loudly as Justice—calls for death.
                                        —Winfield Scott

John Armstrong's removal did not end the administration's effort to subject the losing generals to face accountability through the military justice process. Monroe, as the acting secretary of war and no fan of Wilkinson, was more than willing to continue the process commenced by his predecessor. On November 18, 1814, formal charges were announced, and Wilkinson's court-martial was scheduled to commence in Utica, New York, on January 3 the following year.

Monroe, working with assigned judge advocate Evert A. Bancker, had reworked many of the charges originally proposed by Armstrong the previous spring. Bancker, a New York civilian attorney, was one of five attorneys assigned to the army as judge advocates in 1813. Wilkinson would remark that the "zeal of the judge advocate was always manifest; it was a substitute for capacity."[1] The first charge alleged that Wilkinson engaged in neglect of duty by delaying commencement of the campaign, delaying the conduct of the campaign, failing to hold officers accountable for loss of supplies, improperly sending General Brown to the front of the column on November 11 when the threat was to the rear, and failing to properly engage the enemy at Lacolle Mill. The second charge alleged that Wilkinson was intoxicated on November 6–7. The third charge alleged that Wilkinson engaged in a variety of acts unbecoming an officer, including intoxication; damning the army, the expedition, and himself; singing an obscene and ludicrous song about the expedition; and writing the June 10, 1813, letter to Lewis stating that general officers should avoid danger to themselves. The fourth charge alleged that Wilkinson had countenanced disobedience of orders regarding officers on parole.[2]

The appointing order identified thirteen officers to sit on the panel, with General Henry Dearborn serving as president of the panel. In addition to Bancker, a supplemental order designated rising New York political star Martin Van Buren, a civilian, as a special judge advocate and lead counsel to try the case.[3] Wilkinson was greatly concerned about the appointment of Van Buren, who had led the prosecution team that had won Hull's conviction and death sentence. At the beginning of the trial Wilkinson vehemently objected to Van Buren's appointment as improper since the appointment did not arise out of a presidential direction with Senate approval, as required by law. As one of the first orders of business, the court upheld the objection and Van Buren was removed from the trial team.[4]

The thirteen members of the jury were selected from among the senior officers available on the northern frontier. One member, General Morgan Lewis, was a witness to and participant in some of the charged misconduct and later testified on behalf of the government. (He also testified as a witness for Wilkinson.) Since much of the failure of the Montreal campaign was attached to Lewis as the deputy commander, Lewis's placement on the jury was an obvious conflict of interest. Strangely, Wilkinson never raised an objection to his presence on the panel. Of the remaining twelve members, seven eventually testified at the trial as witnesses for Wilkinson.

Upon receipt of the court-martial order, Wilkinson immediately requested the presence of various other officers to serve as witnesses on his behalf. Wilkinson was informed by the army's adjutant general that Monroe had approved the appearance of all requested army witnesses and that the secretary of the navy had approved the attendance of two requested navy commodores as well.[5] When the court convened in Utica on January 3, it was determined that insufficient quarters existed in Utica to house the members and witnesses, and the trial was reset to commence in Troy, New York, on January 16. When court reconvened, Bancker informed the court that none of the witnesses that had been requested by either the government or Wilkinson were in attendance. The court was repeatedly reconvened through the end of the month, and each time the judge advocate had to report that the requested witnesses were not yet in attendance.

Word of the continuing delay reached acting secretary Monroe, who was concerned that, even though the United States and Great Britain were still at war, a large portion of the senior leadership of the army was involved with Wilkinson's court-martial. Monroe authorized Bancker to depose witnesses off-site, in lieu of their appearance at trial, and allowed him to keep the court in session for extended hours.[6] Bancker subsequently expressed his frustration with proceeding to trial, and in response to Monroe's January 19 letter he stated that he was caught unprepared by Van Buren's unexpected dismissal. Bancker's intention was to interview witnesses as they appeared, but witness unavailability precluded a full development of the government's case prior to trial. Bancker assured Monroe that he would do his best but that Wilkinson had refused to allow the taking of testimony by deposition. Under the Articles of War, any testimony taken by deposition was inadmissible without the assent of the accused.[7]

On January 24, as critical witnesses were still not present, Bancker was required to file a deposition with the court setting forth the status of his efforts to produce witnesses. Bancker dutifully stated that Generals Scott, Boyd, Brown, Macomb, Swartwout, Swift, Edmund P. Gaines, and Eleazer W. Ripley, as well as three colonels, one lieutenant colonel, and one major, had been summoned to testify but that none had responded to the summonses.[8] Under court-martial procedures at the time, a summons by a judge advocate or a court was normally issued through the adjutant general of the army; the direction by these staff officers carried the full authority of the secretary of war. Officers who contumaciously failed to obey were subject to court-martial for disobedience of a lawful order.

The failure of eight generals and five other field-grade officers to obey orders was highly unusual and probably driven by two factors. Some, such as Scott, did not want to be subject to examination by Wilkinson regarding peripheral matters having nothing to do with the charges.[9] Bancker had requested neither Scott nor Macomb to appear as government witnesses. Wilkinson had instead requested their appearances as material witnesses in his defense, and his request had been approved by Monroe and Madison. Wilkinson's hatred of Scott was well known because of Scott's injudicious comments about Wilkinson's morals and capabilities, freely expressed at the Burr trials in 1807 and the Terre aux Boeufs court of inquiry in 1809.[10] Scott had joined the Montreal expedition in November 1813, but as part of the consolidation of forces from Fort George, he reported to Macomb and Brown and mostly avoided any acrimonious contact with Wilkinson during the campaign. (Upon Wilkinson's arrival at Fort George, Scott approached Wilkinson and assured him of his loyalty.[11]) Since the government did not intend to call Scott to prove its case in chief, his presence had been requested by Wilkinson. Were Scott to testify for the government, Wilkinson had every right to cross-examine him regarding his previous statements and subsequent court-martial conviction, in order to show bias. Since Scott was being called by Wilkinson, the only purpose for his testimony would be to allow Wilkinson an opportunity to embarrass Scott, whose career had undergone a meteoric ascent during the war. Scott had started the war as a captain and was now a brevet major general and probably had no desire to revisit the nadir of his career in 1810.

Some officers sought to avoid being dragged into the court-martial for other reasons. Most saw the charges as stemming from an attempt by the now-disgraced and dismissed Armstrong to deflect his failure toward Wilkinson. Armstrong's abrupt departure following the burning of Washington removed any motivation from the subpoenaed officers to loyally support Armstrong's initiative against Wilkinson. Monroe had clearly signaled that he wanted the charges to proceed, but most senior officers sought whatever excuse they could find to avoid being drawn into the case against Wilkinson. Furthermore, most were probably aware of the fact that, as part of the postwar downsizing of the army, Wilkinson's career was finished no matter the outcome of the trial. There was no apparent career gain to be had for participating in the trial.

The reticence of witnesses to appear had a significant impact on Bancker's ability to present the government's case. He first faced the panel's ire by repeatedly requesting adjournments as he sought to compel the attendance of witnesses. Most of the senior officers on the panel wanted to pursue other tasks and resented the almost one month of delay in having the government present its case.[12] Furthermore, as the testimony of the reluctant officers who did appear later showed, the government was not able to present a compelling case against Wilkinson.

Court was again adjourned until January 31, and when it reconvened Bancker again had to report that most witnesses were still not present, including the specific reasons that neither Scott nor Macomb were ever likely to appear. In a letter to Bancker, Scott represented that he was president of a court of inquiry against another general officer being held in Baltimore, and that he would be unavailable for one to two months. (This was the court of inquiry into General Winder's failed defense of Washington. The court exonerated Winder from any responsibility for failure.[13]) Macomb was equally coy in his attempt to avoid testimony, stating that as the commander of the American army on the northern frontier, the possibility of renewed hostilities with Great Britain prohibited him from leaving his command.[14] (Although the peace treaty with Britain had been signed in December 1814, it was scheduled to go into effect only after it was ratified by both governments. The US Senate did not ratify the treaty until February 1815.) Macomb never testified but did provide a series of interrogatories that were later admitted as part of Wilkinson's defense. Bancker also produced a letter from the adjutant general stating that Brown, Ripley, Swartwout, Swift, and Boyd, as well as other subordinate officers, had been issued orders to appear and that Scott, Gaines, and Swift were otherwise occupied and would be excused from attendance. Brown never responded to the summons.[15] With the appearance that day of Swartwout and Boyd, the government commenced the presentation of its case.

On charge 1, neglect of duty and unofficer-like conduct, several officers testified for the government regarding Wilkinson's dilatoriness in commencing and conducting the campaign. Wilkinson cross-examined them regarding the difficulties that weather and broken logistics presented. Wilkinson's defense frequently blamed the absent Armstrong for conflicting and indecisive orders that greatly contributed to the confusion and delay. Other officers testified that Wilkinson did the best he could under difficult circumstances and supported Wilkinson's defense that Hampton's failure to rendezvous, a matter out of Wilkinson's control, resulted in the failure of the campaign.

On charge 2, intoxication, Bancker failed to produce any compelling testimony that Wilkinson was drunk on November 6–7. One of the specifications alleged that Wilkinson was intoxicated at the home of Daniel Thorpe on the night of November 7. Bancker failed to call Thorpe to support this charge, even though Thorpe was apparently available to testify. In his 1840 memoir of the campaign, Armstrong presented sworn statements from Thorpe and two other witnesses to the fact that they were present when Wilkinson was drunk on those dates.[16] None of these witnesses were called by Bancker. While Swift's memoirs stated that Wilkinson was "merry" on the dates in question, Swift never appeared as a witness, even though he had been directed to attend.[17] Wilkinson responded with evidence from numerous witnesses, including the government's own witnesses, attesting to his sobriety in general and specifically on the dates in question. In his unsworn statement to the court Wilkinson admitted that he had been taking laudanum throughout the campaign but that he was never incapacitated by the medication.

Among the acts under charge 3, conduct unbecoming, Wilkinson was charged with singing inappropriate songs and damning himself, the army, and the expedition. Bancker presented testimony from W. M. Ross that at one point Wilkinson stated, "Damn the hospital department."[18] On cross-examination by Wilkinson, Ross admitted that it was a hasty expression and that Wilkinson was ill and under a lot of pressure.[19] Further testimony was presented by Colonel William King, Hampton's adjutant, that upon being informed of Hampton's defeat at Chateauguay, Wilkinson exclaimed, "Damn such an army! A man might as well be in hell as command it!"[20] On cross-examination King admitted that Wilkinson's statement was "more an expression, of the feelings of the moment, than any deliberate sentiment."[21] Wilkinson then called Lewis, a member of the court, to testify that Wilkinson's comments were directed at the poor quality of the recruits assigned to Hampton.[22] On the specification that Wilkinson sang an obscene and ludicrous song on November 7, no evidence was presented.[23]

Regarding the specification that his June 10, 1813, letter to Lewis demonstrated cowardice, Wilkinson's defense was masterful. Wilkinson had written the letter to Lewis while journeying to assume command in the northern department. He expressed regret on the demise of General Zebulon Pike in the assault at York and stated, "Farewell my friend, and remember, a general officer does not expose his person, but in the last resort. Subordinates execute, while chiefs command; to mingle in the conflict, is to abandon the power of direction."[24] When the charges were proposed by Armstrong, this statement was characterized as "striking at the very foundation of military character and service, and calculated to bring shame, and disgrace upon American arms."[25] While Wilkinson's aversion to personal danger was manifested throughout his career, Armstrong's conclusion that this particular statement was encouraging cowardice was unwarranted. Wilkinson demonstrated this by showing how Armstrong initially reacted to the letter. When Wilkinson sent the letter to Lewis in June, it was transmitted in an open envelope through Armstrong as secretary of war. Wilkinson argued that Armstrong read the letter and forwarded it on to Lewis, compellingly contending that if the document had truly been encouraging cowardice, why would Armstrong, knowing its contents, forward it on to Lewis and still retain Wilkinson in command of the expedition?[26]

Wilkinson was on particularly strong ground in his defense against charge 4, countenancing and encouraging disobedience of orders. On January 18, 1814, Wilkinson had issued a general order stating that officers on parole were not allowed to bear arms or perform any professional duties. The parole system, respected by both Great Britain and the United States, allowed captured officers to be returned to their home countries with the understanding that they would not perform any military duties until such time as they were formally exchanged. Parole agreements reduced the burden on belligerents to maintain certain prisoners of war and allow captured officers to be properly cared for in their own countries. Bancker presented testimony from Colonel Simon Learned that Wilkinson had issued a general order in January 1814 that prohibited paroled officers from performing any military duties and that this order was in direct conflict with a different order, issued by Armstrong, that allowed paroled officers to perform garrison duties. Wilkinson was able to show, through the testimony of General Dearborn, the president of the court, that in November 1812 Dearborn had entered into a parole agreement with his British counterpart that paroled officers were prohibited from performing *any* military duties. Dearborn opined that when Armstrong issued his contradictory order, he was not aware of Dearborn's agreement with the British and that when Dearborn informed him of the agreement, Armstrong rescinded the order.[27] Wilkinson also argued that he was never informed of Armstrong's order before he issued the order in question. Wilkinson was able to show that Armstrong's order was clearly improper and that his own order was consistent with military law.

Wilkinson commenced the presentation of his defense on February 20 and continued to present witnesses for seven days. One group of witnesses were officers on the Montreal and Lacolle Mills expeditions. They testified as to the difficult conditions confronted by the American forces and the valiant efforts of Wilkinson to overcome these conditions. They denied ever seeing Wilkinson drunk or incapacitated by drugs, although they often described Wilkinson's illness. Four members of the court, Generals Dearborn, Lewis, Porter, and Bissel provided testimony that supported various aspects of Wilkinson's defense. Five other members of the court, Colonels Simmons, Schuyler, Kingsbury, Brearly, and McFeely, all testified as character witnesses. Each testified as to their long record of service with Wilkinson and provided glowing opinions regarding his soldierly honesty and integrity.

Wilkinson also arranged to have evidence presented from three of the heroes of the American defense against the 1814 British invasions. Maryland senator Samuel Smith, a longtime supporter of Wilkinson, was the militia general in charge of the successful defense of Baltimore in September 1814. While he was unable to make an appearance at court, he submitted an affidavit on Wilkinson's behalf, impeaching the credibility of Colonel King.[28] Commodore Thomas Macdonough, the victor over the British fleet on Lake Champlain in September 1814, provided a tepid testimonial to the fact that fortifications constructed by Wilkinson in early 1814 provided some assistance in the defeat of the British fleet.[29]

The third hero, Major General Alexander Macomb, avoided the government's order to testify but agreed to answer interrogatories promulgated by Wilkinson and Bancker. Macomb had been a member of the 1811 Wilkinson court-martial panel, and since voting for Wilkinson's acquittal he had gone on to a stellar career on the northern frontier, serving under Wilkinson's command on the Montreal expedition and at Lacolle Mills. Following Wilkinson's relief and removal from command, Macomb became the commander of the American army on Lake Champlain and defeated the British Army at the Battle of Plattsburgh in September 1814. For this victory Macomb was breveted to major general, having risen from the rank of major at the start of the war. Macomb was evasive in his answers to many of Wilkinson's questions but ultimately stated that Wilkinson was sober and his conduct proper when he saw him on November 7. He also testified that Wilkinson reacted well under fire at Lacolle Mill. Finally, Macomb recalled his fifteen-year career with Wilkinson and stated, "I have always found him [Wilkinson] desirous of improving the army, a man of honour, a gentleman and a soldier; always willing to do, what he expected from others, as far as it respected personal exposure, personal honour, and individual rights." He stated that Wilkinson was sober throughout the campaign and that Wilkinson always sought to promote discipline and military virtue.[30]

Following the introduction of Macomb's interrogatories, Wilkinson presented his defense statement, which was not given under oath and not subject to cross-examination. In addition to his usual litany of suffering the slings and arrows of outrageous fortune, Wilkinson attacked the charges as a vicious attempt by Armstrong to deflect blame for the campaign's failure. He attacked Armstrong's meddling, inconsistent orders, and contradictory directions given to Wilkinson's subordinates without his knowledge. Wilkinson also argued that Hampton was a significant cause of the campaign's failure and that Armstrong had shielded Hampton from Wilkinson's efforts to bring him to justice.

The court had no problem in reaching a verdict of acquittal on all counts on March 21. On many points the government had simply failed to make a convincing case that Wilkinson was guilty beyond a reasonable doubt. While the 1813 Montreal campaign was an unmitigated disaster, many of the court members had suffered from Armstrong's meddling in their affairs and were hesitant to allow Wilkinson to be assigned the sole blame for the campaign's failure. Since Armstrong, and to a certain extent Hampton, were culpable as well but beyond the reach of accountability from military justice, the panel chose to spare Wilkinson from the indignity of being assigned the role of solitary scapegoat.

The members were also probably affected by the realization that Wilkinson's military career was over. His dismal failures were not out of line with the failures suffered by other Revolutionary War veterans like Dearborn, Lewis, and Hull, and the members understood that a new generation of capable and professional officers—including Scott, Brown, and Macomb—were the army's future and that the failed "relics" would be cast aside in the downsized army desired by Madison. On April 18 Madison approved the verdict of acquittal by the court.[31]

Though the panel's members might have recognized that Wilkinson's career was over, Wilkinson did not. After having risen, phoenix-like, from the ashes of the court of inquiry in 1808 and the court-martial of 1811, Wilkinson thought he could stage another comeback in the new army. In his effort to continue his service, Wilkinson was driven by ego and by finances. The cost of the trial, the burden of his always costly lifestyle, and his inability post-suspension from command to exploit his position for personal financial gain all had a devastating impact on his financial means. Fortunately for everyone else, Madison finally summoned the courage to end Wilkinson's military career.

With the war ending, Congress passed a law on March 3, 1815, reducing the size of the officer corps from 3,495 officers to 674, with only eight general officers.[32] Dismissed officers received no pension and many of the Revolutionary War relics like Wilkinson were without an alternative source of income. To implement the cutbacks in the army required by the March 1815 legislation, acting War Department secretary Alexander James Dallas created a panel of four generals, Scott, Brown, Ripley, and Macomb, to make recommendations on which generals should be retained. Since both Scott and Brown were avowed enemies of Wilkinson, their selection ensured that, without presidential intervention, Wilkinson would be cut. (Dallas, who was also secretary of the treasury, served as acting secretary of war following Monroe's resignation from the post on March 2; he would serve as acting secretary until William Crawford returned in August from his assignment in Europe.)

On April 8 Monroe recounted to Madison a meeting he had had with Wilkinson before the court-martial verdict had even been approved. Wilkinson expressed his willingness to remain in the service and that he needed to "find some employment or perish."[33] Madison responded to Monroe by suggesting that some position, perhaps customs inspector or Indian commissioner, might be found for Wilkinson but that continuing prejudice against Wilkinson in the West might prohibit such a position.[34] Dallas met with Wilkinson and remarked to Madison, "But of all cases Genl. Wilkinson is the most touching, simply on the score of humanity. He has written and spoken the most lamentable accounts of the consequences of his dismission."[35] At one point Dallas explored with Madison the possibility of appointing Wilkinson to a naval position in New York, but he assured Madison that the position had "nothing to do with money."[36] Eventually that position was filled by someone else.

Following the formal approval of the court-martial verdict, Wilkinson's situation took on a more desperate and ominous tone. On April 26, Monroe informed Madison that Wilkinson had stated that he felt dishonored by discussions of his removal, that he had the government in his hands, and that the government must provide for him. "The discontent among the officers, about to be discharged, or expecting to be, natural in such a state, is suspected to be excited by him, and his antipathy to Brown & Scott seems generally to be known, as is their reciprocation of it. I fear he will act so indiscreetly, as to make it more difficult, if not render it impossible, for the admn. to do any thing for him."[37] Wilkinson expressed a desperate interest in any form of employment, and Madison responded by stating that any "insinuations or threats" from Wilkinson would be defied.[38] In addition to pressing the administration for his own retention, Wilkinson also lobbied for the dismissal of other officers, including Colonel King and General Swartwout, both of whom had testified against him at the court-martial. Acting Secretary Dallas found the discussion with Wilkinson "painful and disagreeable."[39]

As the time for deciding on his dismissal versus an alternative form of federal employment drew near, Wilkinson became even more desperate. Dallas reported to Monroe that Wilkinson was "threatening hostilities" by going to the *Philadelphia Aurora*.[40] Monroe responded to Madison by stating, "If he makes the attack he is gone. The admn. will be freed from all anxiety in his account. I am convinced that the appointment of him to any important office, would do it more injury than his attack possibly could."[41] Shortly thereafter Wilkinson was dismissed from service and his government career finally came to an end. Final revenge would have to await his memoirs.

13

WHO TELLS YOUR STORY?

1816–1825

Three ponderous volumes of memoirs, as false as any yet written by man.
—John Bach McMaster, *A History of the People of the United States*

Doubtless the most mendacious book ever published in America.
—Royal Ornan Shreve, *The Finished Scoundrel*

Following his abrupt departure from federal employment, Wilkinson pursued a series of courses that he hoped would fulfill two basic needs: making money and obtaining revenge. Documenting all in his memoirs would allow him to obtain both simultaneously. Following publication of his *Burr's Corruption Exposed* in 1811, Wilkinson was obsessed with amassing a volume of documents that had affected events throughout his career. In addition to keeping copies of correspondence that he had generated or received, Wilkinson engaged in a campaign of seeking out documents from official sources and historical figures that could be woven into a tale portraying himself as both a courageous hero and a victim of systematic vituperation lasting throughout his career.

It is not clear how much documentation Wilkinson himself had personally accumulated. Given the peripatetic lifestyle he maintained for much of his life at a series of frontier posts, it is hard to imagine that he was able to maintain a library of correspondence that withstood military campaigns, transfers to new assignments, floods, hurricanes, lost baggage, and poor storage. A significant portion of Wilkinson's *Memoirs of My Own Times* consists of his correspondence with presidents, military officials, and cabinet secretaries; the rest relates to events surrounding his life but not directly addressed to him. This means that he had to obtain this correspondence from official sources or from the authors or recipients of the correspondence. Given Wilkinson's propensity for forgery and his desire to portray himself in the best possible light while demonizing his enemies, the accuracy and completeness of some of the correspondence remains uncertain.

Significant gaps in his correspondence exist. Wilkinson admitted at his 1811 court-martial that he did not retain any copies of the letters he had sent to Burr.[1] Not surprisingly, none of his incriminating and treasonous correspondence with his Spanish handlers is reproduced in the memoirs. Later historians, such as Gayarre, Shepherd, and Cox, had to find the documents, which either had been destroyed by Wilkinson or hidden by Spanish officials in archives in Spain and Cuba.

Early in the process Wilkinson retained the services of John B. Colvin, a State Department employee and editor of the *Republican Advocate*, a Democratic-Republican paper published in Frederick, Maryland, to help research and ghost-write part of the memoirs. (Colvin had been an early supporter of Wilkinson. During the 1808 court of inquiry Colvin published a series of pro-Wilkinson articles in two of his earlier publications, *Colvin's Weekly Register* and the *Monitor*.[2]) Thomas Jefferson had been an early subscriber to the *Republican Advocate* and Colvin, presuming on this relationship, approached Jefferson in 1810 while writing the portion of Wilkinson's memoirs related to the Burr treason trials. Colvin asked Jefferson to opine on the question: "Are there not periods when in free government, it is necessary for officers in responsible stations to exercise an authority beyond the law—and, was not the time of Burr's treason such a period?"[3] Jefferson's response, ten days later, has often been cited by historians and legal scholars as the first justification of the expansive and extrajudicial power of the presidency, particularly in times of emergency, in potential violation of the Take Care Clause of the Constitution.[4] In his response to Colvin, Jefferson waxed how

> a strict observance of the written laws is doubtless one of the highest duties of a good citizen: but it is not the highest. The laws of necessity, of self-preservation, of saving our country when in danger, are of higher obligation. To lose our country by a scrupulous adherence to written law, would be to lose the law itself, with life, liberty, property & all those who are enjoying them with us; thus absurdly sacrificing the end to the means.[5]

With these words Jefferson defended his actions against Burr as well as Wilkinson's actions in declaring martial law in the defense of New Orleans in 1806.[6] Wilkinson subsequently used Jefferson's justification as part of his defense against court-martial charges involving Burr and sent an advance copy of his memoirs to Jefferson for his review and comment.

As the preparation of the memoirs progressed, Colvin became concerned about the vituperative tone that Wilkinson was injecting into the memoirs and was concerned that its attacks on Madison would adversely impact Colvin's continued federal employment. In his subsequent letter to Jefferson, Colvin admitted that while he had used Jefferson's sentiments on executive power as part of the memoir, he had not cited Jefferson as the source of the comments. Colvin also admitted to Jefferson that the only person with whom he had shared Jefferson's letter was Dolly Madison, to explain to her his limited role in ghostwriting Wilkinson's memoirs about Burr:

> As Gen. Wilkinson is a man of very violent temper, I was apprehensive that he might have introduced into it some abuse of the President, and my enemies would not have failed to ascribe it to me. It is owing to my unceasing representations to him that the language of the volume is as temperate as it is. I fear that of the suc-ceeding volumes will not be so much so. The General is becoming desperate, but his constitution is so peculiar, that it is rather the desperation of Anger than the Despair of fulfilment of Hope deferred.[7]

Jefferson may have been the only president to get an advance review of the memoirs, but he was not the only political figure who was aware of the project. For example, Tennessee governor Willie Blount informed Andrew Jackson in 1811 that Wilkinson was writing memoirs "with the hope of washing away his sins—he will have hard work to effect his purpose."[8]

In 1815 former President Adams engaged in a series of letters with Thomas McKean, a fellow member of the Second Continental Congress. In the letters Adams pondered on who would write the history of the Revolution and McKean informed him that Wilkinson was busy writing the definitive account.[9] McKean stated that while Wilkinson may not be as great a historical talent as Thucydides or Gibbons, he would produce a "history of our Revolution with at least as much regard to the truth as any of them has exhibited." McKean recalled that Wilkinson was charged with bringing the news of Burgoyne's surrender to the Congress and that he had dallied in Reading, romancing Nancy Biddle, his prospective bride. McKean recalled that, in debating what honor should be bestowed on Wilkinson, Samuel Adams had recommended a "pair of spurs."[10] Adams responded by stating that Wilkinson's talents were "by no means inconsiderable. His openness of Soul and a little too much pomp have as usual made him Enemies and given them Advantages." Adams stated that he had never heard the anecdote that Wilkinson's delay in Reading had been caused by his courting of his future wife: "Had I known that he had fallen in Love at Reading with so fine a Woman as his after Wife really was, my rigorous heart would have somewhat relented."[11]

If Adams and McKean had hoped that Wilkinson would produce a nineteenth-century version of *The History of the Peloponnesian War* or *The History of the Rise and Fall of the Roman Empire*, they were sadly mistaken. Wilkinson's three-volume *Memoirs* is many things, but an accurate and stirring account of the Revolution it is not. The memoirs attempt to recount certain famous battles, such as Bunker Hill, where Wilkinson was not a first-person observer or participant, but these portions are inserted at odd locations throughout the memoirs. In over two thousand pages of stilted prose, Wilkinson primarily accomplished three things. First, he repeatedly discussed his role in every meaningful event in a way that overstated his bravery and contributions. The narrative and correspondence are filled with his continuing promise to place his life at risk to defend his country and honor and the great sacrifices he had made on his country's behalf. Second, he continuously recounted the perceived slights and attacks he constantly endured during forty years of public service. Much of the narrative and correspondence with Adams, Hamilton, and Jefferson is filled with a recitation of such slights, presumably in a hope to appeal to their sympathies for having suffered similar attacks during their own careers. Third, he stridently sought to avenge perceived slights by seeking revenge on persons who had the temerity to challenge his schemes or expose his treachery. Arnold, Gates, Wayne, Burr, Eustis, Armstrong, Scott, Jackson, Brown, Hampton, Clark, Ellicott, Randolph, Simmons, and Madison are all prominent targets for Wilkinson's endless denunciations.

Certain historical figures receive strong approbation from Wilkinson, in part for their support for him but also from a recognition of the continuing reverence shown toward these figures in the early 1800s. Even though Washington's support of Wilkinson had been tepid at best, he is treated by Wilkinson as the hallowed icon of the nation's founding. The murdered Hamilton, who championed Wilkinson's promotion, is also treated with respect. Adams, who ignored all evidence against Wilkinson and supported him during his 1811 court-martial, is also portrayed positively. However, the greatest admiration was shown toward Jefferson. Despite the rocky beginning of their relationship, Wilkinson ultimately proved his loyalty toward Jefferson through the betrayal of Burr, and Jefferson had returned the compliment of loyalty in cash payments for dubious secret service expenses and the 1808 court of inquiry whitewash. To Wilkinson, Jefferson was a paragon of presidential virtue in his pursuit of Burr and support of Wilkinson. Despite his public praise of Jefferson, however, in private correspondence Wilkinson described Jefferson as a fool.[12]

How much of the three volumes was penned by Colvin is uncertain. Wilkinson's verbose and bombastic style permeates virtually every paragraph. The first volume speeds through his childhood and education, then quickly shifts to his

Revolutionary War military career. Except for random sections examining battles like Bunker Hill, the book makes no attempt to realistically depict the campaigns of the Revolution nor place in context the recounted events of the war. It is instead a view of the Continental Army through the narrow lens experienced by Wilkinson alone. While he had been a key witness to many of the seminal events in the Revolution up to 1778, everything is viewed from his perspective and no attempt is made to place his view in the context of overall events. Following his resignation from the Board of War, mention of the events of the Revolution disappear and little coverage is provided to his unsuccessful tenure as Washington's clothier-general. The first volume abruptly halts in 1778, resumes with Wilkinson on the Sabine River in 1806, jumps back to his meeting with Hamilton in 1799, then jumps forward to the War of 1812. An entire chapter is devoted to an attack on Winfield Scott. The only attempt at a consistent narrative is his expressions of entitlement to greater glory and rewards and persistent persecution by his numerous enemies.

The second volume is primarily concerned with the charges against him in his 1811 court-martial and the presentation of his defense, which was largely based on his 1809 jeremiad, *Burr's Conspiracy Exposed.* Volume 3 describes his view of the events of the Montreal campaign, includes attacks on Armstrong and Hampton, and is a relatively complete record of his 1815 court-martial and acquittal. The greatest positive contribution is the collection of numerous items of correspondence that appear, which set forth the insights and communications of various important figures of the Revolution and the early republic.[13]

What is missing from the massive volumes is any insight on Wilkinson's view toward his wives, children, and relatives. After a brief description of his childhood, Wilkinson's narrative shifts to the Revolution. While there is a brief mention of his courtship of Ann "Nancy" Biddle, her name is never once mentioned in the memoirs, though she loyally followed him to numerous frontier posts and probably ruined her health in her travels at his side. She remains a mystery. Wilkinson's second wife, Celestine, is also barely mentioned.[14] Wilkinson's correspondence not included in the memoirs refers to her fondly, though a significant part of their fifteen-year marriage was spent apart. And, while there is a brief mention of his first three sons with Nancy, there is no mention of the fact that one of his sons died on Dauphin Island in 1813. Daughters with Celestine are born and die without meaningful notice, and no mention is made of the birth of Wilkinson's fourth son, Theodore. While the wealthy Biddle family probably provided significant economic and employment support to Wilkinson during and after the Revolution, he makes no effort to acknowledge their role. His only mention of his second father-in-law, Charles Trudeau, is a passing reference in Wilkinson's denial of improper dealings with him in the selection of the disastrous camp-site at Terre aux Boeufs. To the extent his family lived, died, added to, or detracted from his personal experience, it appears their existence was not worthy of mention.

The publication of Wilkinson's memoirs in 1816 was neither the financial nor critical success that he envisioned. The three-volume set was offered for $15, a significant sum for the times. Initial sales were strong, and Wilkinson invested the slim profits into a second printing, but those proved difficult to sell. Critical reaction was mixed, and while some reviewers were impressed with Wilkinson's insights, many recounted their exhaustion with his overblown prose and endless bemoaning of the attacks on his character. As one review in the *Raleigh Minerva* noted, "The style of these Memoirs is frequently faulty, the sentences ill constructed, the language sometimes ungrammatical, and more than sometimes laboriously inflated . . . [W]e do not regret the publication of this work. Slander and malice will defeat their own purposes; but what is true, and of importance, and supported by evidence, of which there is much in this work, will be read with considerable interest in the present day and be of use to the American Historians hereafter."[15] Following the book's publication, former secretary Armstrong wrote a series of anonymous articles attacking the work, although he saved his greatest condemnation of Wilkinson and Hampton for his own memoirs, published in 1840 after both of his targets were dead and incapable of response.

When the publication of the memoirs failed to produce a sizable income, Wilkinson commenced a series of campaigns to lobby for a pension for his previous military service. Though he never served in the Maryland Line, Wilkinson successfully lobbied the state of Maryland and in early 1816 the state awarded him a pension equivalent to a colonel's or a dragoon's half-pay for life.[16] He was less successful in two other pension attempts. In January 1819 he petitioned the state of Louisiana for a military pension, which apparently was never granted.[17] Increasingly desperate for funds, in 1819 he unsuccessfully pressed his New York friend Solomon Van Rensselaer to use his influence to have the federal pension of the recently deceased Arthur St. Clair reassigned to Wilkinson.[18]

With his finances still in flux, Wilkinson decided to return to New Orleans in the summer of 1817. Celestine had departed Washington two years before, to return to New Orleans for the birth of their twins, and Wilkinson had not seen her since then, nor his twin daughters, Stephanie and Theofannie, who had been born in January 1816. Wilkinson soon purchased the Magnolia Grove Plantation, a sugar and cotton plantation south of New Orleans and settled into the life of a gentleman planter and slave owner with Celestine and the twins; Theodore was born within a year of Wilkinson's arrival.

Among the commercial enterprises Wilkinson attempted at this time was the odious practice of slave dealing.[19] The purchase and sale of enslaved persons was an inherent part of plantation management, and Wilkinson's views on the evils of slavery are opaque. Having grown up on a tobacco plantation in Maryland, Wilkinson had no historical revulsion for the practice and his memoirs make no mention of any enslaved person accompanying him as a servant during his military career. When he commenced his first commercial journey from Kentucky to New Orleans in 1787, slaves and tobacco were among the "cargo" that Wilkinson sought to trade. However, his active reentry into the slave trade in Louisiana in 1817 did not result in a meaningful improvement to his finances.

Despite his participation, Wilkinson eventually acknowledged the moral and financial pitfalls that slavery entailed. When the new state of Missouri struggled with the legalization of slavery, Wilkinson wrote to Van Rensselaer on the evils inherent in the practice: "You can not find any one of virtue & Intelligence who, viewing negro slavery in the abstract, & to probable results, will not condemn it as a curse. The Missourians will discover too late that the opponents to the introduction of Slavery among them were their best friends."[20] It was one of the few times that Wilkinson assumed a moral stance that was contrary to his economic interests.

The consequences of his previous involvement with Burr continued to plague him with a disastrous impact on his finances. In January 1819, John Adair sued Wilkinson for false arrest, claiming that Wilkinson had no reliable evidence linking him to the Burr Conspiracy in 1806. A court in Natchez found in Adair's favor and fined Wilkinson $2,500. Having no funds to satisfy the judgment, Wilkinson appealed to President Monroe and Congress for financial relief to pay the debt. In May 1820, Monroe signed the relief act passed in Congress, providing Wilkinson with $3,000 to pay the Adair fine.[21]

Because Wilkinson's poor business skills did not provide him with the ability to successfully run a plantation, he again turned to international intrigue as a source of financial gain. In 1819 the Adams-Onis Treaty was signed and sent to the Senate for ratification. In addition to ceding all the Floridas to the United States, the treaty resulted in the United States relinquishing certain claims to territory in Spanish Texas. Many persons in the United States were unhappy with the loss of territory, and with the renewal of the Mexican Revolution in September 1821, some American filibusterers sought to use the resulting chaos to reassert their land claims. Among the filibusterers was James Long, who was married to Wilkinson's niece Jane. Long consulted with Wilkinson on issues related to military campaigns along the Sabine River, and with Wilkinson's apparent support he launched a filibustering expedition and occupied Nacogdoches. Long proclaimed the "Long

Republic of Texas" with himself as president.[22] Unfortunately, the Long Republic was long in name only, and Spanish forces soon drove Long and his followers back into Louisiana. Undeterred, Long mounted another expedition but was ultimately captured by the Spanish in October 1821. Long was eventually imprisoned in Mexico City, where he was killed by a sentry of the new Mexican government in April 1822.

By the spring of 1822 Wilkinson decided that his future might be made in the chaos of the Mexican Revolution. Mexican nationalists were wrenching control of the country from Spain, and Wilkinson saw an opportunity for an American with long ties to the border region and familiarity with some of the issues that would be confronted by an evolving nation. He believed American commercial and government interests would need a representative to the new Mexican government and felt that he was ideally suited to fulfill that role. Furthermore, since American empresarios like Moses and Stephen Austin were seeking land grants from the new government to sponsor immigration into Mexican Texas, Wilkinson saw the possibility of becoming such an empresario himself, assuming he could obtain an endorsement from the new Mexican government.

Shortly after the death of six-year-old Theofannie, the sixty-five-year-old Wilkinson turned the management of his plantation over to his eldest son, Joseph Biddle Wilkinson, and departed for Mexico in April 1822. He left Celestine grieving for their daughter's death and responsible for the upbringing of their remaining two children, to live on whatever income Joseph could eke out of the plantation. Joseph would also be responsible for supporting Wilkinson in Mexico until such time as Wilkinson could establish himself in some form of commercial or government enterprise. While it may have been appropriate to leave Celestine and the children behind, not subjecting them to the climate, diseases, and revolutionary chaos that would be present in Mexico, Wilkinson's farewell was the last time he would see his children.

Wilkinson arrived in Mexico City in late April 1822 and soon introduced himself to Agustín de Iturbide, who had seized power the previous fall. Recalling the previous "reflections" that he had gratuitously crafted for his former Spanish paymasters, Wilkinson provided Iturbide and his cabinet with a series of "Observations" and "Reflections" on the establishment of Mexican-American trade and political relations.[23] Shortly after his arrival, Wilkinson attended the banquet that celebrated Iturbide's coronation as Emperor Augustin I. Unfortunately, the bankruptcy of the Mexican treasury and the instability of the Mexican government frustrated the establishment of any meaningful relationship. Iturbide abdicated his throne six months after his coronation and was replaced by a republican coalition that included future Mexican president Antonio López de Santa Anna.

While waiting for the establishment of a more stable Mexican government, Wilkinson commenced an outreach to the US government, in the hopes of being named its minister to Mexico. Unfortunately, President Monroe had no desire to place American interests in the hands of Wilkinson, and Monroe instead appointed Joel Poinsett, an experienced Latin American diplomat and South Carolina congressman, to be an unofficial representative.[24] When the Mexican Republic was officially established in 1825, Poinsett resigned his congressional seat and became the first US minister to Mexico. Poinsett, an amateur horticulturalist, "discovered" a Mexican plant known as the Christmas Eve flower, which became known in the United States as the poinsettia. He would go on to serve as secretary of war in the Van Buren administration.

As the Mexican republican government began to coalesce, Wilkinson again sought to establish himself as a source of information about and liaison to the United States for the new government. In July 1823 he presented the new Mexican congress with a Gilbert Stuart portrait of George Washington. He also represented American commercial interests in claims against the Mexican government and pursued land grants for himself. He even explored being a representative of the American Bible Society in distributing Bibles in historically Catholic Mexico.[25] None of these efforts resulted in economic success.[26]

Meanwhile, Wilkinson's health continued to deteriorate. He had started using laudanum heavily on the Montreal expedition in 1813, and by 1825 he may have become addicted to the substance. Over the intervening years he suffered from yellow fever, malaria, and recurring bouts of dysentery, which may have increased his reliance on the opiate. By late 1825 he was no longer able to ride a horse, and his health continued to deteriorate. On December 28, 1825, Wilkinson died in Mexico City at the age of sixty-eight, possibly from an overdose of laudanum. His body was brought to the home of Minister Poinsett and buried the following day in the Catholic cemetery of the Church of San Miguel, with a simple wooden cross as a marker.[27]

In 1872 the Grant administration made a belated attempt to have Wilkinson's remains moved to a more secure location. Secretary of War William Belknap proposed to send an American delegation to Mexico City to move Wilkinson's remains to the Mexican National Cemetery.[28] Unfortunately, the proposal was scrapped when it was learned that the cemetery of San Miguel had already been closed and that Wilkinson's unmarked remains had been placed in a common grave.

CONCLUSION

He was so ingrainedly venal, treacherous, and mendacious that nothing he
said or wrote can be accepted as true, and no sentiments which he at any
time professed can be accepted as those he really felt.
—Theodore Roosevelt, *Winning of the West*

Wilkinson, whose name has become synonymous with deviousness, and
whose reputation is beyond biographical rehabilitation.
—Russell F. Weigley, *History of the United States Army*

For the better part of forty years James Wilkinson maintained a pervasive presence in the military of the early republic. From his service at the beginning of the Revolution in 1775 through his forced retirement in 1815, Wilkinson served longer than most other military officers. Through luck, timing, and a pattern of scheming and character assassination against real and perceived rivals, Wilkinson served the longest term as commanding general of the US Army during the first fifty years of its existence. With virtually no meaningful combat experience and no history of independent command, Wilkinson was appointed to and allowed to remain in senior military positions by four successive presidents. Despite persistent rumors and convincing evidence of illicit Spanish connections that rendered him unworthy of an appointment as a government surveyor, Wilkinson commanded the army and was even simultaneously appointed a territorial governor during a period of increased national tensions with Spain. Even though his inability to lead and support troops in a peacetime environment resulted in the highest casualties ever suffered by the army in a single operation, he was subsequently chosen to command a wartime invasion, where he again failed his troops and suffered a humiliating defeat to a significantly inferior force. Given his proven failures of character, capabilities, and performance, why was Wilkinson repeatedly trusted, promoted, and protected throughout his long and checkered career?

One factor that cannot be discounted is Wilkinson's amazing ability to charm superiors. Wilkinson was obsequious in his communications with persons in authority, and many were unable to discern that his tone disguised his incompetence and, in many cases, both his betrayal of their trust and contempt for their leadership. While Spanish, French, and British officials with whom he came in contact certainly recognized Wilkinson's true nature and limited military worth, most of his American superiors were either unable or unwilling to make a critical and accurate assessment of Wilkinson's value to the American cause.

Each of the four American presidents who commanded Wilkinson failed to recognize his deficiencies or deliberately chose to ignore them. George Washington's failure to address Wilkinson's shortcomings was particularly acute because Washington had personal and direct knowledge of Wilkinson's limited Revolutionary War background. Washington knew that Wilkinson had never commanded troops in combat and knew of Wilkinson's unintended role in the exposure of the Conway Cabal, which required Wilkinson's resignation from the Board of War, from his general officer brevet position, and ultimately from the Continental Army. Washington also knew that as clothier-general, Wilkinson was more interested in social affairs than he was in addressing the supply needs of the army; he was dismissed from that position as well. As the first president under the Constitution, Washington was concerned with many pressing issues, both foreign and domestic, and he initially neglected the leadership of the army as an immediate concern. However, by late 1791, in light of the failed actions of Generals Harmar and St. Clair, Washington understood that the continuing Northwest Indian War required competent military leadership. It is inexplicable how Washington could then have concluded that Wilkinson's meager experience made him in any way fit to assume a major position in the army.

Washington compounded his failure when he refused to address Wilkinson's disloyalty to General Anthony Wayne. As commanding general of the Continental Army, Washington was familiar with the strife caused by fractious and competing military officers. By 1794 he knew of Wilkinson's growing disloyalty to Wayne and the rift that such disloyalty brought to the officer corps, but he did nothing to address it. Wilkinson's scheming and complaints against Wayne grew until Washington was forced to address the matter directly, but rather than relieve or court-martial Wilkinson, Washington seriously contemplated court-martialing Wayne as the response to Wilkinson's false charges.

When Wayne suddenly died in December 1796, Washington chose to ignore Wilkinson's pattern of disloyalty and left him in command of the army, despite his own awareness of an additional concern: that Wilkinson may have had an inappropriate relationship with Spain. Washington knew Wayne was actively investigating Wilkinson's relationship with Spain but failed to continue that investigation after Wayne's death. Though Washington dispatched Andrew Ellicott with a vague directive to gather information about said Spanish relationship, he failed to undertake any meaningful investigation into the possibility that his commanding general might be in the pay of a rival power. Furthermore, upon his departure from office in 1797, Washington apparently chose to not share any of these concerns with his successor, leaving John Adams to develop his own opinion of Wilkinson's worth.

Finally, as the commander of the army in 1798, Washington failed to address Wilkinson's continuing issues. When General Alexander Hamilton proposed Wilkinson's promotion to major general, Washington foolishly endorsed the proposal, not because Wilkinson had earned it but because he believed that the promotion would encourage Wilkinson's loyalty by feeding his ambition and soothing his vanity. Washington's failure was particularly egregious: by background and experience he should have known better and taken decisive action to address Wilkinson's treachery.

John Adams's refusal to address Wilkinson's failings can be explained more benignly. Not having a military background, Adams was not as attuned to issues relating to military affairs. Adams entered the presidency lacking meaningful knowledge of Wilkinson's disloyalty toward Wayne and the existing concerns regarding Wilkinson's relationship with Spain. Adams was particularly susceptible to Wilkinson's claim to being subjected to unsubstantiated calumnies by his many enemies. Adams's subsequent assurance to Wilkinson that he would not credit these allegations without proof guaranteed that no action would be taken to even gather such proof. Adams's last failure was his decision to support Wilkinson at his 1811 court-martial. Adams was under no obligation to provide favorable testimony for Wilkinson, and while the available evidence of Wilkinson's treachery with Spain during Adams's presidency was scant, by 1811 Daniel Clark's book and the successive congressional investigations had amassed a record that, at a minimum, should have given Adams pause about vouching for Wilkinson's loyalty. Unfortunately, Adams was apparently unwilling to conduct a true assessment of Wilkinson and continued to support him at the trial.

Jefferson's support of Wilkinson was the most devious and cynical of any of the presidential commanders. At first Jefferson seemed immune to Wilkinson's initial charm campaign. Wilkinson had avoided Jefferson's purge of Federalist officers, but Jefferson and War Secretary Dearborn appeared to understand Wilkinson's minimal worth to the army and the administration. Jefferson had deliberately snubbed Wilkinson by selecting Meriwether Lewis to advise him on the loyalty of the officer corps and the status of the army on the frontier. For the better part of Jefferson's first term in office, Wilkinson was kept away from Washington and the direct control of many army matters. But Jefferson was sufficiently concerned by Wilkinson's apparent improper relationship with Spain that he initially eliminated Wilkinson from consideration from several posts, including territorial governor and surveyor-general.

Despite the initial coolness of their relationship, Wilkinson's gradual rise in Jefferson's esteem was the direct result of Wilkinson skillfully playing Jefferson for a fool. Wilkinson first ingratiated himself by serving as one of the administration's representatives in the Louisiana Purchase, then exploited this role by secretly renewing his paid relationship with Spain. For a massive sum of money Wilkinson offered to compromise and destroy all of Jefferson's efforts to explore the newly acquired territory. Furthermore, Wilkinson offered to use his position and access to Jefferson to gather additional intelligence that would aid Spain in frustrating American settlement throughout the territory. Jefferson, completely unaware of Wilkinson's treachery with Spain, was fooled into thinking that Wilkinson would loyally serve as the governor of the Louisiana Territory, when in fact both Wilkinson and Burr intended to use the position to boost Burr's plan to separate the western territories and invade Spanish Mexico. When Jefferson finally admitted his suspicions about Wilkinson's true relationship with Burr in the summer of 1806, Wilkinson again fooled Jefferson into believing that he was opposed to Burr's plan and would loyally serve Jefferson in orchestrating Burr's demise.

In the fall of 1806 Wilkinson and Jefferson established an informal pact that would govern their relationship through the rest of Jefferson's administration. In return for providing Jefferson with any information he needed to convict Burr of treason, Jefferson would defend Wilkinson against any and all allegations regarding acceptance of a Spanish pension or an improper relationship with Burr. The bargain was dishonorable to both. Wilkinson's purchased testimony against Burr was unconvincing and nearly resulted in his own indictment for treason. Yet in repeated court proceedings he never wavered in delivering an altered story of Burr's perfidy and his own innocence. Despite Wilkinson's poor performance in court, Jefferson delivered his side of the bargain: he lied to Congress regarding his prior knowledge of Wilkinson's relationship with Spain, and then, when this mendacity failed to forestall a congressional investigation, he initiated a sham court of inquiry that was never intended to conduct a meaningful review of the evidence and was always intended to whitewash Wilkinson's role with Spain.

Jefferson's consistent refusal to consider the possibility of Wilkinson's illicit relationship with Spain left his successor, James Madison, in a quandary. Having no meaningful prior relationship with Wilkinson, Madison could have removed Wilkinson as part of his new administration. However, as he took office in 1809 Madison was preoccupied with the country's deteriorating relationship with Great Britain and was confronted with the fact that his mentor had sent Wilkinson to New Orleans to take charge of the army's largest peacetime deployment. Madison delegated the supervision of Wilkinson to his War Department secretary, who was particularly ill-equipped to provide meaningful supervision. The growing debacle at Terre aux Boeufs provided the excuse Madison needed to relieve Wilkinson of his command, but a series of renewed congressional investigations illustrated a larger problem: Jefferson's 1808 whitewash had failed to stifle the growing demands for Wilkinson's removal based on his relationship with Spain and Burr.

Though Madison was originally inclined to convene a court-martial only for Wilkinson's conduct regarding Terre aux Boeufs, Wilkinson saw the trial as a way to obtain a blanket exoneration for his twenty years of misconduct, even regarding charges that predated his return to federal service. As demonstrated in the 1808 court of inquiry, Wilkinson knew that he would be able to manipulate any military justice proceeding to produce a complete exoneration. Madison, too, realized that a trial aimed at reviewing all allegations of misconduct and producing a not guilty verdict would exonerate four presidents for their failure to conduct a meaningful review of Wilkinson's relationship with Spain. Madison may have found the process distasteful, but the trial in Frederick Town produced the result that both Madison and Wilkinson wanted.

Madison's final attempt to hold Wilkinson accountable for the disastrous Montreal campaign also failed, but not for a lack of trying. The military jury that acquitted Wilkinson in 1815 recognized that Madison and John Armstrong, his handpicked War Department secretary, were primarily responsible for the poor planning of the campaign and were equally culpable as Wilkinson for the campaign's failure. Armstrong's departure in disgrace from the War Department and Wilkinson's forthcoming removal from the army through the already-announced postwar downsizing made the purpose of the court-martial superfluous.

Wilkinson's longevity in command also displayed the inadequacy of congressional oversight. While a limited precedent had been established in 1792 regarding Congress's authority to conduct oversight hearings regarding failed military campaigns, that precedent remained uncertain as Congress repeatedly sought to address the possibility that the army's commanding general was a paid agent of Spain. Democratic-Republicans in general were hesitant to challenge Jefferson and Madison for their apparent inadequate supervision of Wilkinson, and partisan politics certainly contributed to this reticence. Many members of the House were clearly concerned about the question of its constitutional authority to conduct an inquiry into Wilkinson's conduct. Some believed Congress had no such authority, while others thought the body was limited to requesting the president to conduct an appropriate inquiry and report the results. The inadequacy of this process became clear in 1808 when John Randolph overcame the reticence of Jefferson loyalists and created a consensus in the House to at least raise questions regarding Wilkinson's relationship with Spain and Jefferson's knowledge of this relationship. Unfortunately, Randolph's attempt to address the matter was stymied by Jefferson's swift and mendacious response. Unwilling to subject Wilkinson to any kind of meaningful review, Jefferson convened a sham military court of inquiry to forestall any independent inquiry by the House and further rebuffed Randolph's concerns by falsely denying any knowledge of previous warnings regarding Wilkinson. The resulting whitewash court of inquiry was sufficient to quell any further congressional interest in the matter for the remainder of the Jefferson administration.

Congress was somewhat more successful when the issue arose again during the first years of the Madison administration. After Wilkinson led the army into horrendous casualties at Terre aux Boeufs, Congress debated the scope of its oversight authority. Recognizing the inadequacy of Jefferson's previous response, the House appointed four committees in two separate sessions of Congress to examine Wilkinson's failure at Terre aux Boeufs and his relationship with Spain and Burr. However, the House was poorly equipped to conduct fact-finding and was especially unable to pierce through Wilkinson's carefully constructed cover story and obfuscation tactics. One committee conducted a full review of the debacle at Terre aux Boeufs but could not reach a consensus on the assignment of fault. The other committee did an excellent postmortem on the 1808 court of inquiry whitewash and established that the Jefferson administration had allowed Wilkinson to steal the record of the proceeding, but it too could not reach a conclusion on accountability. The only result of these congressional actions was to place pressure on Madison to turn to the military justice process to address the repeatedly unresolved concerns.

It is hard to fathom why none of the four presidents wanted a meaningful inquiry to determine whether the commanding general of the army was on Spain's payroll. However, all were constrained by the fact that the early Republic did not have an effective way to conduct criminal or counterintelligence investigations into misconduct by senior officials. Federal law enforcement at the time was limited to customs inspectors, postal inspectors, and federal marshals, none of whom had the jurisdiction or the skill to even make such an inquiry. Furthermore, after the Revolution the nation had no foreign counterintelligence capability and would not even commence the development of this capability until the twentieth century. Finally, though the Articles of War provided a mechanism to conduct fact-finding proceedings, it would have been foolish to believe that its process could be credibly used to investigate the army's commander. Given this lack of investigative capability, Washington's half-hearted attempt to use Andrew Ellicott and Anthony Wayne to monitor Wilkinson's actions with his Spanish counterparts was at least an attempt to make an inquiry. Since neither Jefferson nor Madison wanted to know the truth, their use of compromised military justice proceedings was a cynical ploy to create the appearance of a meaningful inquiry when in truth none was desired.

Because the 1810 House hearing clearly demonstrated that the 1808 court of inquiry had been a sham, Madison realized that another military justice inquiry would require more subtlety in reaching its desired conclusion. Despite the need for the appearance of objectivity, Wilkinson was allowed to dictate the scope of the charges and selected jurors, many of whom would also serve as defense witnesses corroborating his own version of events. The same supine prosecutor who led the 1808 whitewash was chosen to lead the prosecution, and the result was an acquittal that provided a respite from three years of congressional scrutiny. While it is unlikely that any military justice inquiry would have been free from the taint of Wilkinson's interference, the 1811 court-martial was never intended to produce anything but an acquittal. The panel also concluded that none of the prior military justice or congressional proceedings had established Wilkinson's guilt.

An elaborately constructed cover story, buttressed by corroborating denials from his Spanish spymasters, withstood all scrutiny throughout Wilkinson's army career. Though many officials, such as Anthony Wayne, John Randolph, and Daniel Clark, had clear evidence of his improper relationship with Spain, none were sufficient to lead to a meaningful inquiry. In the final analysis Wilkinson was a reasonably successful spy, even if his espionage efforts produced little of true worth for his Spanish handlers. Wilkinson used his access to the highest levels of the federal government to provide military, political, and economic intelligence to a rival nation, and despite the compromise of his cash courier and his own business partner's rebuttal of his cover story, Wilkinson was able to maintain his cover and his position as commanding general of the army.

Ultimately, several factors can be seen as motivation for Wilkinson. As he stated when he rejoined the army in 1791, his goal was to seek "bread and fame." Throughout his post–Revolutionary War career Wilkinson was driven by greed into a treacherous relationship with Spain and numerous government contractors. Poor business judgment and an outlandish lifestyle guaranteed that he could never live on a government salary. His career was marked by consistent attempts to monetize his position and standing beyond the modest salary he would earn as the army's ranking general. Wilkinson repeatedly demonstrated that in return for bribes from Spanish authorities or government contractors he was willing to compromise his oath of office, his loyalty to his country, and any concern for the health and safety of its troops.

Similarly, Wilkinson was also driven by a need for greater personal recognition ("I pant for promotion") and ruthlessly attacked those who stood in his way. As an inexperienced staff officer at Saratoga, Wilkinson often claimed credit that properly belonged to others and assisted his superior, Horatio Gates, in denying proper credit to Benedict Arnold. Wilkinson's rapid and unwarranted promotion to general officer following the battle was ostentatiously flaunted in front of others and inspired an outcry by most of the senior officers in the Continental Line. When Wilkinson's subsequent unsuccessful attempt to establish a trading monopoly with Spain failed to catapult him to the top of the social and commercial order of Kentucky, his overinflated sense of military worth caused him to believe that he was the best qualified person to command the Legion of the United States, even though he had never commanded troops in combat. When another more qualified officer was chosen, Wilkinson engaged in a multiyear campaign to undermine his commander and compromise the success of a critical military campaign. In communications with presidents and War Department secretaries Wilkinson repeatedly overstated his accomplishments and bemoaned the constant slights he was forced to endure in the service of his nation.

Finally, aside from his relationship with his family, Wilkinson was incapable of loyalty to anyone, and he deliberately sought out ways to betray everyone he worked for, with, or near. Throughout his career Wilkinson betrayed friends and enemies alike, whenever an opportunity presented itself. He commenced his career of betrayals with Benedict Arnold, his first mentor, by assisting Gates in a series of attacks that denied Arnold proper credit for the Saratoga victory. When Washington reestablished Wilkinson's military career in 1791, Wilkinson betrayed him through his illicit relationship with Spain and by undermining Wayne's campaign against the Indians in the Northwest. Wilkinson's relationship with Andrew Ellicott and Thomas Freeman also demonstrated his insatiable need to betray one and all. When Ellicott asked for Wilkinson's advice on firing Freeman, Wilkinson "befriended" Ellicott by supporting Freeman's termination. Hiding this support to Ellicott, Wilkinson then hired Freeman and used Freeman's purchased loyalty to later attack Ellicott. Wilkinson then betrayed Freeman by urging the Spanish to intercept Freeman's Red River exploration. Later, unaware of this betrayal, Freeman gladly attacked Ellicott at Wilkinson's behest.

Wilkinson's greatest betrayal was of his final mentor, Thomas Jefferson. In return for Jefferson bringing Wilkinson into his inner circle of political appointees, Wilkinson reestablished his paid relationship with Spain, then used that relationship to betray each of the exploration parties that Jefferson dispatched to explore the lands gained through the Louisiana Purchase. Wilkinson knew of the importance that Jefferson placed on these explorations, but he also knew that their compromise was essential to his Spanish handlers. The compromise of three military expeditions, which might have resulted in an armed clash and American casualties, meant nothing to Wilkinson compared to the worth of his Spanish pension. Unaware of his betrayal to the Spanish, Jefferson expanded his trust in Wilkinson by appointing him governor of the Louisiana Territory; Wilkinson repaid this trust by entering a relationship with Aaron Burr, Jefferson's enemy, which was designed to embarrass Jefferson and possibly rend the western states and territories away from the United States. Wilkinson compounded this betrayal by subsequently betraying Burr as well, when the balance of competing loyalties had tipped in Jefferson's favor.

In the final analysis Wilkinson's tenure as the senior general in the post-Revolution army reflected a larger national pattern of neglect of military affairs. Though the cost of maintaining a military force comprised a significant portion of the young nation's budget, and repeated failures of leadership in war and peace had resulted in the loss of thousands of American lives, the leadership of the American army before the War of 1812 (apart from Anthony Wayne) was little more than a tool of opposing political factions. Washington, Adams, and Hamilton sought to populate the officer corps with avowed Federalists who would support the use of the army as a symbol of national strength. Jefferson and Madison believed a strong military was contrary to their small government principles and viewed the officer corps in the same way they viewed the judiciary: as a threat to their form of government. Their "chaste reformation" was designed to replace marginally qualified Federalist officers with equally marginal Democratic-Republicans.

The repeated hirings and purges of the officer corps during these four administrations resulted in the rise of a military leader who was without any meaningful military skill or moral compass and who could appear, chameleon-like, as the champion of whatever party was in power. Prior to the War of 1812 most senior officers were appointed based on the strength of their Revolutionary War records or their civilian political standing. Wilkinson, with a meager Revolutionary War record but significant political support in the West, was a natural selection under both of these limited criteria. Unfortunately, none of the Founding Fathers who used Wilkinson for their political ends recognized his inexhaustible capacity for treason and betrayal. Their failure of leadership was the ultimate cause of Wilkinson's rise and longevity as one of America's worst traitors.

NOTES

Introduction

1. Spanish officials documented Wilkinson's treachery and kept careful records of his oaths of allegiance, espionage communications, and pension payment history. However, fearing that such records would be damaging to Spanish interests and to Wilkinson's utility as a spy, these records were carefully stored in Spanish archives in Havana, Seville, and Madrid. The true nature of Wilkinson's treasonous relationship with Spain was only uncovered when American historians commenced research in the Spanish archives. In 1847 Charles Gayarre commenced the publication of his multivolume *History of Louisiana* and began the documentation of Wilkinson's treachery. Gayarre's work was then expanded on in the early twentieth century through the research in Spain and the publications of historians William R. Shepherd and Isaac Joslin Cox.

2. One of Wilkinson's biographers stated that in his treasonous relationship with Spain he never "betrayed any confidence placed in him by his government." Hay, "Some Reflections," 475. Such a conclusion ignores the fact that Wilkinson offered to use his position to gather intelligence for Spain from the president of the United States and other senior officials and knowingly compromised the safety of numerous federal explorations of the Louisiana Territory.

3. For this reason, citations to Wilkinson's memoirs in this work are included primarily for the purpose of demonstrating Wilkinson's stated feelings or observations. The author has sought to corroborate Wilkinson's representations of facts through alternative contemporaneous sources. Discrepancies between Wilkinson's versions of events and the contrary observations of other credible sources are noted throughout.

1. Young Doctor Wilkinson Goes to War

1. Wilkinson, *Memoirs*, 1:8.
2. Wilkinson, 1:12.
3. Bell, "Court-Martial of Dr. William Sheppard," 219. The founding of the school was their only collaborative effort. Morgan and Shippen detested one another and their feud followed them into their respective careers in the Continental Army.
4. Wilkinson, *Memoirs*, 1:13.
5. Wilkinson, 1:14.

6. Wilkinson, 1:14.

7. Hentz, "Unit History," 1–3.

8. Balch, *Papers,* 4–5.

9. Georgetown was created by an act of the Maryland General Assembly in 1751. From 1751 to 1776 it was part of Frederick County. Taggert, "Old Georgetown," 120.

10. Wilkinson, *Memoirs*, 1:16.

11. Wilkinson, 1:16.

12. Wilkinson, 1:29.

13. Wilkinson, 1:31.

14. Wilkinson, 1:34.

15. Wilkinson, 1:35.

16. Wilkinson, 1:36.

17. Wilkinson, 1:36.

18. In the fall of 1775 Washington dispatched forces under Brigadier General Richard Montgomery and Colonel Benedict Arnold to invade Canada and seize Quebec. Fleming, *1776,* 1–8.

19. Fleming, 218.

20. Wilkinson, *Memoirs*, 1:39.

21. Thomas was a veteran of the French and Indian War. A physician like Wilkinson, he preferred a line command instead of serving as a surgeon. When Arnold insisted on inoculating the American army against smallpox, Thomas objected to the practice of inoculations and overruled Arnold's orders. Shortly thereafter, Thomas contracted smallpox and died on June 2. Randall, *Benedict Arnold*, 231–32.

22. Wilkinson, *Memoirs*, 1:40.

23. Wilkinson, 1:44.

24. Wilkinson, 1:44.

25. Andro Linklater observes, "Wilkinson had confused theater with truth, a mistake that would in time become a habit." Linklater, *Artist in Treason*, 20.

26. Wilkinson, *Memoirs*, 1:48.

27. Wilkinson, 1:49.

28. Wilkinson, 1:44.

29. With Thomas's death from smallpox, Sullivan became the ranking general in Canada.

30. Wilkinson, *Memoirs,* 1:54–55.

31. Wilkinson, 1:62.

32. Wilkinson, 1:67.

33. Barbieri, "Infamous Skulkers."

34. Barbieri.

35. Wilkinson, *Memoirs,* 1:69.

36. Barbieri, "Infamous Skulkers."

37. Wilkinson, *Memoirs,* 1:69.

38. Ketchum, *Saratoga*, 400.

39. Martin, *Benedict Arnold*, 237.

40. Wilkinson, *Memoirs*, 1:73.

41. Wilkinson, 1:74–75. Congress eventually cleared Arnold of any allegation of theft. Martin, *Benedict Arnold*, 243.

42. Wilkinson, *Memoirs*, 1:75–76.

43. James Wilkinson to Richard Varick, August 5, 1776, in Coppet Autograph Collection; Morgan, *Naval Documents of the Revolution*, 6:61.

44. Wilkinson, *Memoirs*, 1:86.

45. Geppert and Paul, "Shot That Won," 298–99.

46. Wilkinson, *Memoirs,* 1:86.

47. See Kelly, *Valcour.*

48. Papas, *Renegade Revolutionary,* chap. 2.

49. Lee would later remark that Washington "was not fit to command a Sergeant's Guard." Chernow, *Washington*, 338.

50. Papas, *Renegade Revolutionary,* chap. 9.

51. Papas, chap. 9.

52. Fleming, *1776*, 378–79.

53. Wilkinson, *Memoirs*, 1:101.

54. Chernow, *Washington*, 267.

55. Wilkinson, *Memoirs*, 1:103.

56. Wilkinson, 1:108.

57. Wilkinson, 1:105.

58. McBurney, *Kidnapping the Enemy*, chap. 2.

59. Lee remained a prisoner of war for over fifteen months. During captivity he was entertained by senior British officers in New York and went on to advise them on how they could defeat the American rebels. At least one historian has suggested that this advice was treason. McBurney, *George Washington's Nemesis*. Washington and the Continental Congress were not aware of Lee's advice to the British, nor was Lee ever charged with treason. In April 1778 he was exchanged and returned to serve again as Washington's second in command. At the Battle of Monmouth in June 1778 he fought with Washington over the deployment of troops. Lee was court-martialed and convicted for disobeying orders, conducting a disorderly retreat, and acting disrespectfully toward Washington. He was suspended from the army for a year and eventually dismissed from the army by Congress.

60. McBurney, *Kidnapping the Enemy*, chap. 2.

61. Wilkinson, *Memoirs*, 1:126.

62. Chernow, *Washington*, 272.

63. Wilkinson, *Memoirs*, 1:126.

64. Wilkinson, 1:126.

65. Wilkinson, 1:128.

66. Nelson, *General Horatio Gates*, 76n34.

67. Washington had given Gates permission to travel to Philadelphia for health reasons

on December 23. George Washington to Horatio Gates, December 23, 1776, in Chase, *Papers of George Washington*, 418.

68. Fischer, *Washington's Crossing*, 254.

69. Chernow, *Alexander Hamilton*, 84–85.

70. Atkinson, *British Are Coming*, 547.

71. Wilkinson, *Memoirs*, 1:145.

72. See, e.g., Fischer, *Washington's Crossing*, 339; and Rogow, *Fatal Friendship*, 39n16.

73. Chernow, *Washington*, 283.

2. The "Military Genius" of the Northern Army

1. Wilkinson, *Memoirs*, 1:158.

2. Wilkinson, 1:160.

3. Hay, "Letters of Ann Biddle Wilkinson," 37.

4. Royal Shreve notes that in all fifteen hundred pages of the *Memoirs*, Wilkinson never mentions her name. Shreve, *Finished Scoundrel*, 57.

5. Ketchum, *Saratoga*, 75.

6. Weddle, *Compleat Victory*, 59.

7. Ketchum, *Saratoga*, 114.

8. Ketchum, 117.

9. Quoted in Weddle, *Compleat Victory*, 117.

10. Weddle, 168.

11. Ketchum, *Saratoga*, 336.

12. Wilkinson, *Memoirs*, 1:198.

13. Ketchum, *Saratoga*, 337.

14. William Howe to John Burgoyne, July 17, 1777, in Clinton Papers.

15. See "The Quill Letter," Clinton Papers.

16. Luzader, *Saratoga*, 370.

17. To improve morale and ease the integration of the militia and the Continental regulars, Gates banned flogging as a disciplinary tool. Linklater, *Artist in Treason*, 35.

18. Wilkinson, *Memoirs*, 1:303.

19. Wilkinson, 1:232.

20. Martin, *Benedict Arnold*, 371.

21. Benedict Arnold to Horatio Gates, September 22, 1777, in Wilkinson, *Memoirs*, 1:255.

22. Randall, *Benedict Arnold*, 355.

23. Wilkinson, *Memoirs*, 1:233.

24. Gale, *Meriwether Lewis*, chap. 9.

25. Ketchum, *Saratoga*, 357.

26. John Burgoyne to Henry Clinton, Albany, October 25, 1777, in Brumwell, *Turncoat*, chap. 3.

27. Compare, e.g., the mostly positive review of Arnold's battlefield performance in Martin's *Benedict Arnold*, with Nathaniel Philbrick's negative portrayal in *Valiant Ambition*.

28. In the three battles of the Revolution when Gates was in command, his headquarters were consistently established well behind the line and Gates repeatedly failed to exert any meaningful control over the troops engaged. At the Battles of Saratoga, Arnold's leadership was able to offset Gates's failure to command. At the Battle of Camden in August 1780, Gates established his headquarters far to the rear and, lacking Arnold's assistance, lost all control over the troops engaged, leading to one of the most significant American defeats of the Revolution. Stemple, *American Hannibal*, chap. 1.

29. Luzader, *Saratoga*, 206.

30. Wilkinson, *Memoirs*, 1:239.

31. Wilkinson, 1:237–38.

32. Wilkinson, 1:245–46.

33. Luzader, *Saratoga*, app. H.

34. Wilkinson, *Memoirs*, 1:254.

35. Ketchum, *Saratoga*, 387.

36. Benedict Arnold to Horatio Gates, September 23, 1777, in Wilkinson, *Memoirs*, 1:257.

37. James Wilkinson to Arthur St. Clair, September 21, 1777, quoted in Smith, *St. Clair Papers*, 1:442.

38. James Wilkinson to Arthur St. Clair, October 7, 1777, in Smith, 1:444.

39. Ketchum, *Saratoga*, 395.

40. Luzader, *Saratoga,* 282.

41. Ketchum, *Saratoga,* 389.

42. If Wilkinson's memoirs are to be believed, Learned's and Poor's brigades were deployed based on Wilkinson's personal direction and not as the result of his forwarding orders given to him by Gates. Wilkinson, *Memoirs*, 1:270–72.

43. Ketchum, *Saratoga*, 399.

44. Ketchum, 399–403.

45. Wilkinson, *Memoirs*, 1:272.

46. Wilkinson, 1:273.

47. Wilkinson, 1:271–73.

48. Wilkinson, 1:272.

49. See, e.g., Ketchum, *Saratoga,* 398–99.

50. Weddle, *Compleat Victory*, 317–18.

51. Horatio Gates to John Hancock, October 12, 1777, *Maryland Gazette* (Annapolis), October 30, 1777, 1.

52. Ketchum, *Saratoga*, 405.

53. Ketchum, 414–15; Wilkinson, *Memoirs*, 1:286–89.

54. Wilkinson, *Memoirs*, 1:286–89.

55. Wilkinson, 1:267.

56. Wilkinson, 1:274.

57. Wilkinson, 1:270–72.

58. Wilkinson, 1:271.

59. Wilkinson, 1:286–89.

60. Ketchum, *Saratoga,* 418–19.

61. Wilkinson, *Memoirs,* 1:302–3.

62. Wilkinson, 1:309–17.

63. Luzader, *Saratoga,* 326.

64. Wilkinson, *Memoirs,* 1:310–11.

65. *Hartford Courant,* October 28, 1777, 2.

66. See Jones, *Captives of Liberty.*

67. Ketchum, *Saratoga,* 429.

68. Wilkinson, *Memoirs,* 1:321.

69. Ketchum, *Saratoga,* 369.

70. See, e.g., Creasy, *Fifteen Decisive Battles,* 463.

71. Horatio Gates to John Hancock, October 18, 1777, quoted in Wilkinson, *Memoirs,* 1:324.

3. Wilkinson and the Conway Cabal

1. Wilkinson, *Memoirs,* 1:323.

2. Wilkinson, 1:331.

3. Wilkinson, 1:386.

4. Wilkinson, 1:373.

5. Lord Stirling to George Washington, November 3, 1777, in Grizzard and Hoth, *Papers of George Washington,* 110–11.

6. Hamilton viewed Gates as vain, cowardly, and inept. Chernow, *Alexander Hamilton,* 101–2.

7. Wilkinson, *Memoirs,* 1:270–72. Hamilton also engaged in a romantic detour on his return home from Albany. Following his meeting with Gates, Hamilton visited Philip Schuyler in Albany and was introduced to Schuyler's daughter, Hamilton's future wife, Eliza Schuyler. Chernow, *Alexander Hamilton,* 102–3.

8. Lender, *Cabal!,* 52.

9. Rossie, *Politics of Command,* 135–53.

10. George Washington to Thomas Conway, November 5, 1777, in Grizzard and Hoth, *Papers of George Washington,* 129–30.

11. Thomas Conway to George Washington, November 5, 1777, in Grizzard and Hoth, 130–31.

12. Wilkinson, *Memoirs,* 1:333.

13. Wilkinson, 1:336–38.

14. Response to a Report from the Board of War, November 6, 1777, in *JCC,* 9:870.

15. Wilkinson, *Memoirs,* 1:352.

16. Wilkinson, 1:340.

17. Jacobs, *Tarnished Warrior,* 48.

18. Thomas Mifflin to Horatio Gates, November 28, 1777, in Wilkinson, *Memoirs,* 1:374.

19. Horatio Gates to Thomas Conway, December 3, 1777, in Wilkinson, 1:374–76.

20. Wilkinson, 1:373.

21. Wilkinson, 1:384.

22. Wilkinson, 1:373.

23. Wilkinson, 1:373.

24. Wilkinson, 1:373.

25. Horatio Gates to George Washington, December 8, 1777, in Wilkinson, 1:395–96.

26. Congress officially appointed Wilkinson to this position on January 6, 1778. The *JCC* merely notes that Wilkinson was elected as secretary on this day. *JCC*, 10:24.

27. Resolution of Congress appointing Thomas Conway as inspector general and major general, December 13, 1777, in *JCC*, 9:1026.

28. Chernow, *Washington*, 316–17.

29. Thomas Conway to George Washington, January 10, 1778, in Lengel, *Papers of George Washington*, 13:195–96.

30. George Washington to Horatio Gates, January 4, 1778, in Lengel, 138–40.

31. Wilkinson, *Memoirs,* 1:382–83.

32. James Wilkinson to Thomas Conway, February 4, 1778, in Wilkinson, 1:383–84.

33. Hay and Werner, *Admirable Trumpeter*, 53.

34. Letter to George Washington from Certain General Officers, December 31, 1777, in Lengel, *Papers of George Washington*, 79–81.

35. Elbridge Gerry to George Washington, January 23, 1778, in Lengel, 218–20.

36. Horatio Gates to George Washington, January 23, 1778, in Wilkinson, *Memoirs*, 1:398–401.

37. The offending paragraph is in a letter reproduced in Wilkinson's memoirs. See Wilkinson, 1:398–401. Wilkinson claims to have been shown this document by Washington during their March 1778 dinner meeting at Valley Forge. See Horatio Gates to George Washington, January 23, 1778, in Lengel, *Papers of George Washington*, 319–22. Edward Lengel suggests that the paragraph directly implicating Wilkinson in forgery and treason was crossed out in the letter Gates sent to Washington. However, even if crossed out, the offending paragraph remained in the letter shown by Washington to Wilkinson. Wilkinson's memoirs describe the paragraph as being in the letter shown to him by Washington, which would clearly serve as a motivation for his subsequent second duel with Gates in September 1778. Wilkinson also mentions Gates's accusation of forgery in his March 28 letter to Washington. See James Wilkinson to George Washington, March 28, 1778, in Hoth, *Papers of George Washington*, 344–46.

38. George Washington to Horatio Gates, February 9, 1778, in Lengel, *Papers of George Washington*, 484–87.

39. Horatio Gates to George Washington, February 19, 1778, in Lengel, 590.

40. George Washington to Horatio Gates, February 24, 1778, in Wilkinson, *Memoirs*, 1:408.

41. Lender, *Cabal!*, 161.

42. Graydon, *Memories of a Life*, 319.

43. Fleming, *Washington's Secret War*, 329.

44. Taaffe, *Washington's Revolutionary War Generals*, chap. 4.
45. James Wilkinson to George Washington, March 28, 1778, in Hoth, *Papers of George Washington*, 344–46.
46. James Wilkinson to Horatio Gates, February 23, 1778, in Wilkinson, *Memoirs,* 1:385–86.
47. Horatio Gates to James Wilkinson, February 23, 1778, in Wilkinson, 1:386–87.
48. Wilkinson, 1:387.
49. See Schellhammer, "Duels of Honor."
50. Wilkinson, *Memoirs*, 1:388.
51. Wilkinson, 1:389–91.
52. Wilkinson, 1:410.
53. Wilkinson, 1:394.
54. Wilkinson, 1:409–10.
55. The *JCC* merely states that Congress received his letter of resignation, accepted it, and returned the letter as improper, to remain in the files. March 31, 1778, *JCC,* 10:297.
56. Wilkinson, *Memoirs*, 1:250.
57. Linklater, *Artist in Treason*, 58–59.
58. Buchanan, *Road to Guilford Courthouse,* 170.
59. See Head, *Crisis of Peace.*
60. Linklater, *Artist in Treason*, 63.
61. Wilkinson, *Memoirs*, 1:410.
62. Risch, *Supplying Washington's Army*, 278.
63. Risch, 276.
64. Linklater, *Artist in Treason,* 66.
65. Hay and Werner, *Admirable Trumpeter*, 49.
66. James Wilkinson to Samuel Huntington, March 27, 1781, in Jacobs, *Tarnished Warrior*, 66.

4. Agent 13 and the Spanish Conspiracy

1. Drury and Clavin, *Blood and Treasure*, 120–22.
2. Drury and Clavin, 189.
3. In the first US Census, taken in 1790, Kentucky reported a population of approximately seventy-four thousand free and enslaved persons. US Dept. of Commerce, "Historical Statistics," 28.
4. Shepherd, "Wilkinson and the Beginnings," 491–92.
5. Whitaker, "James Wilkinson's First Descent," 82.
6. Chalou, "James Wilkinson," 108.
7. Wilkinson, *Memoirs*, 2:109.
8. Shepherd, "Wilkinson and the Beginnings," 494.
9. Wilkinson's First Memorial to Spain, August 21, 1787, in Pontalba Papers.
10. Wilkinson Declaration of Allegiance to His Catholic Majesty, enclosure 6, August 22, 1787, in Pontalba Papers.

11. Hay and Werner, *Admirable Trumpeter*, 87. The wording of Wilkinson's oath is clearly of his own creation and significantly broader than the standard form that was usually required by Spanish officials. See Jacobs, *Tarnished Warrior*, 81, and the standard-form oath in Gayarre, *History of Louisiana*, 3:203.

12. Remini, "Andrew Jackson."

13. Wilkinson Declaration of Allegiance to His Catholic Majesty, enclosure 6, August 22, 1787, in Pontalba Papers; and Shepherd, "Wilkinson and the Beginnings," 499–500. Shepherd compares this promise to Spain with Wilkinson's later characterization of his actions in his memoirs: "But, that I have ever, in all my correspondence and intercourse with the Spanish government, conceded a title of the honour or interests of my own country, I most solemnly deny, in the face of God and man; and I have ample and undeniable testimony to shew that I omitted no occasion, to employ my ascendancy over the officers of Spanish Louisiana, to render them subservient to the interest, and accommodation of the United States." Wilkinson, *Memoirs*, 2:114–15.

14. Shepherd, "Wilkinson and the Beginnings," 501–2. Shepherd compares the language in Wilkinson's declaration with Wilkinson's later description: "The idea of alienating Kentucky from the United States, . . . would have been as absurd, as the idea of reducing them to the vassalage of Spain. Such a proposition would have been so vain and chimerical, that no man, whose interest it was, to preserve a consistency of character with the Spanish government, would have ventured to hazard it. Indeed, the monstrous extravagance of the thought, is too ludicrous for grave consideration, and could never have originated, with any person who understood the character, genius, and government of the people of the United States." Wilkinson, *Memoirs*, 2:113.

15. Shepherd, "Wilkinson and the Beginnings," 503.

16. Archivo de Indias, Legajo 2373.

17. Esteban Miro and Martin Navarro to Antonio Valdez, September 25, 1787, in Pontalba Papers; Shepherd, "Wilkinson and the Beginnings," 504.

18. Jacobs, *Beginning of the U.S. Army*, 79.

19. Harrison and Klotter, *New History of Kentucky*, 59–60.

20. Nancy Wilkinson to John Biddle, February 14, 1788, in Hay, "Letters of Ann Biddle Wilkinson," 39.

21. Esteban Miro to Antonio Valdes, June 15, 1788, quoted in Gayarre, *History of Louisiana*, 3:211–12.

22. Linklater, *Artist in Treason*, 91.

23. Linklater, 98.

24. Arthur St. Clair to Isaac Dunn, December 5, 1788, in Gayarre, *History of Louisiana*, 3:240. Wilkinson later transmitted a copy of St. Clair's message to Miro. See Esteban Miro to Antonio Valdez, April 11, 1789, Pontalba Papers.

25. Thomas Marshall to George Washington, February 12, 1789, in Twohig, *Papers of George Washington*, 1:291–98.

26. James Wilkinson to Esteban Miro, February 12, 1789, in Pontalba Papers; and Gayarre, *History of Louisiana*, 3:236–37.

27. Decision of the Council of State on Wilkinson's First Memorial, November 20, 1788, quoted in Shepherd, "Papers Bearing on James Wilkinson's Relations," 749.

28. Linklater, *Artist in Treason,* 99.

29. James Wilkinson to Esteban Miro, September 17, 1789, in Pontalba Papers; and quoted in Shepherd, "Papers Bearing on James Wilkinson's Relations," 751.

30. James Wilkinson to Esteban Miro, September 17, 1789, in Pontalba Papers; Shepherd, "Papers Bearing on James Wilkinson's Relations," 761.

31. James Wilkinson to Esteban Miro, September 17, 1789, in Pontalba Papers; and Shepherd, "Papers Bearing on James Wilkinson's Relations," 763.

32. James Wilkinson to Esteban Miro, September 18, 1789, in Pontalba Papers.

33. James Wilkinson to Esteban Miro, September 17, 1789, in Pontalba Papers; and Shepherd, "Papers Bearing on James Wilkinson's Relations," 764. Wilkinson describes Humphry Marshall as "a villain, without principles, very artful, and could be very troublesome." See Archivo de Indias, Legajo 2374.

34. Esteban Miro to James Wilkinson, September 18, 1789, in Pontalba Papers.

35. Linklater, *Artist in Treason*, 103.

36. James Wilkinson to Esteban Miro, January 11, 1790, quoted in Gayarre, *History of Louisiana,* 3:280.

37. Esteban Miro to James Wilkinson, April 30, 1790, quoted in Gayarre, 3:284.

38. Esteban Miro to Antonio Valdez, December 31, 1789, in Pontalba Papers.

39. Esteban Miro to Antonio Valdez, May 22, 1790, quoted in Gayarre, *History of Louisiana*, 3:286.

40. Kohn, *Eagle and Sword*, 70–71.

41. Winthrop Sargent to Arthur St. Clair, August 17, 1790, quoted in Calloway, *Victory with No Name,* 68.

42. Henry Knox to Josiah Harmar, September 30, 1790, in Knox Papers, New York Historical Society.

43. George Washington to Henry Knox, November 19, 1790, in Mastromarino, *Papers of George Washington*, 6:668–70.

44. "Court of Inquiry on General Harmar," September 24, 1791, in *American State Papers, Military Affairs,* 1:20–36.

45. James Wilkinson to Esteban Miro, December 17, 1790, in Archivo de Indias, Legajo 2374.

46. Nelson, "General Charles Scott," 232.

47. Cozzens, *Tecumseh and the Prophet*, 283–97.

48. James Wilkinson to Arthur St. Clair, August 24, 1791, in *American State Papers, Indian Affairs*, 1:133.

49. Henry Knox to Arthur St. Clair, September 29, 1791, in *American State Papers, Indian Affairs*, 1:182.

50. James Wilkinson to Henry Knox, August 26, 1791, in Washington Papers. See also George Washington to Henry Knox, September 22, 1791, in Mastromarino, *Papers of George Washington*, 8:556–58.

51. James Wilkinson to Peyton Short, December 28, 1791, quoted in Jacobs, *Tarnished Warrior*, 115.

52. Henry Innes to Thomas Jefferson, September 30, 1791, in Cullen, *Papers of Thomas Jefferson*, 22:175–77.

53. Humphry Marshall to George Washington, quoted in Shreve, *Finished Scoundrel,* 86.

54. George Washington to Senate, October 31, 1791, in Mastromarino, *Papers of George Washington*, 9:136–38.

55. James Wilkinson to Esteban Miro, Archivo de Indias, Legajos 2374, 2508.

56. Jacobs, *Tarnished Warrior*, 102.

57. Nelson, "General Charles Scott," 234.

58. Calloway, *Victory with No Name*, 108.

59. Calloway, 127.

5. Return to the Frontier Army

1. Sword, *President Washington's Indian War,* 201.

2. Chalou, "St. Clair's Defeat," 1:8.

3. Chalou, 1:10.

4. Calloway, *Victory with No Name,* 136.

5. "Report on the Causes of the Failure of the Expedition against the Indians, in 1791, under the Command of Major General St. Clair," May 8, 1792, in *American State Papers*, *Military Affairs*, 1:36–39.

6. Chalou, "St. Clair's Defeat," 1:17.

7. Wingate, "Military Professionalism," 6.

8. Sword, *President Washington's Indian War,* 82.

9. Sword, 145.

10. Calloway, *Victory with No Name,* 148.

11. Sword, *President Washington's Indian War,* 204.

12. James Wilkinson to Esteban Miro, November 4, 1791, in Archivo de Indias, Legajo 2374.

13. Hector de Carondolet to James Wilkinson, February 1, 1792, in Archivo de Indias, Legajo 2374.

14. Gaff, *Bayonets in the Wilderness,* 11–12.

15. Gaff, 15.

16. Gale, *Meriwether Lewis,* chap. 9.

17. Washington Memorandum on General Officers, March 9, 1792, and Jefferson Memorandum of a Meeting of the Heads of Executive Departments, March 1, 1792, both in Haggard and Mastromarino, *Papers of George Washington*, 10:74–79 and 10:69–73, respectively.

18. Stockwell, *Unlikely General,* 24.

19. Stockwell, 25; Gaff, *Bayonets in the Wilderness,* 32.

20. George Washington to US Senate, April 9, 1792, in Haggard and Mastromarino, *Papers of George Washington*, 10:236–40.

21. Gaff, *Bayonets in the Wilderness,* 86.

22. Coffman, *Portrait of the Old Army,* 7.

23. Anthony Wayne to Henry Knox, December 6, 1792, in Knopf, *Anthony Wayne,* 147.

24. Nagle, *History of Government Contracting,* 64.

25. Henry Knox to George Washington, July 21, 1792, in Haggard and Mastromarino, *Papers of George Washington*, 10:554–56.

26. Henry Knox to George Washington, August 5, 1792, in Haggard and Mastromarino, 10:615–22.

27. Anthony Wayne to Henry Knox, August 7, 1792, in Knopf, *Anthony Wayne,* 62.

28. George Washington to Henry Knox, August 13, 1792, in Haggard and Mastromarino, *Papers of George Washington*, 10:652–55.

29. Hay and Werner, *Admirable Trumpeter,* 137.

30. James Wilkinson to Hector de Carondelet, December 15, 1792, in Archivo de Indias, Legajo 2374.

31. James Wilkinson to Manuel Gayoso, December 21, 1792, in Archivo de Indias, Legajo 2374.

32. Gaff, *Bayonets in the Wilderness,* 214–16.

33. Gaff, 151.

34. James Wilkinson to Hector de Carondelet, December 15, 1794, in Archivo de Indias, Legajo 2374.

35. Linklater, *Artist in Treason,* 143.

36. Linklater, 144–46.

37. Jacobs, *Tarnished Warrior*, 148.

38. Hector de Carondelet to James Wilkinson, July 16, 1795, in Linklater, *Artist in Treason*, 152–53.

39. Hay and Werner, *Admirable Trumpeter,* 152.

40. Manuel Gayoso to Hector de Carondelet, June 18, 1795, in Cox, "Wilkinson's First Break," 49.

41. James Wilkinson to Hector de Carondelet, September 22, 1796, in Archivo de Indias, Legajo 2375.

42. Not to be confused with future secretary of war John Armstrong.

43. Kohn, "General Wilkinson's Vendetta," 364.

44. Gaff, *Bayonets in the Wilderness,* 181.

45. Hamilton, as secretary of the treasury, supported Wayne's interpretation of the contract. Alexander Hamilton to James Wilkinson, May 13, 1793, in Syrett, *Papers of Alexander Hamilton*, 14:448–49.

46. Gaff, *Bayonets in the Wilderness,* 181.

47. Linklater, *Artist in Treason,* 135.

48. Gaff, *Bayonets in the Wilderness,* 202.

49. Linklater, *Artist in Treason,* 135.

50. Henry Knox to Anthony Wayne, April 3, 1794, in Knopf, *Anthony Wayne,* 321.

51. Stockwell, *Unlikely General,* 246.

52. Linklater, *Artist in Treason,* 135.
53. James Wilkinson to Robert Elliot, April 15, 1794, in Wayne Papers, 34:13. See also, Rusche, "Treachery Within," 486; Stockwell, *Unlikely General,* 246.
54. James Wilkinson to Anthony Wayne, June 8, 1794, in Gratz Collection, 0250A.
55. Henry Knox to George Washington, June 25, 1794, in Hoth and Ebel, *Papers of George Washington,* 16:271–74.
56. Henry Knox to James Wilkinson, July 12, 1794, in Knox Papers, Massachusetts Historical Society, 35:165.
57. Hogeland, *Black Snake,* 315.
58. Gaff, *Bayonets in the Wilderness,* 240.
59. Hogeland, *Black Snake,* 324.
60. Henry Knox to Anthony Wayne, June 7, 1794, in Knopf, *Anthony Wayne,* 336.
61. Nelson, "General Charles Scott," 245.
62. Sword, *President Washington's Indian War,* 281–82.
63. Jacobs, *Tarnished Warrior,* 89.
64. See Chandler, *Jefferson Conspiracies*; Starrs and Gale, *Death of Meriwether Lewis*; and Gale, *Meriwether Lewis.*
65. Sword, *President Washington's Indian War,* 289.
66. Nelson, "General Charles Scott," 246.
67. Gaff, *Bayonets in the Wilderness,* 300.
68. Gaff, 303.
69. Gaff, 321–22.
70. See Cozzens, *Tecumseh and the Prophet.*
71. Anthony Wayne to Henry Knox, August 28, 1794, in Knopf, *Anthony Wayne,* 351.
72. James Wilkinson to John Brown, August 28, 1794, in James Wilkinson Papers, Chicago History Museum, 1:28.
73. George Washington to Edmond Randolph, October 6, 1794, in Hoth and Ebel, *Papers of George Washington,* 17:21–22.
74. Henry Knox to George Washington, December 4, 1794, in Hoth and Ebel, 17:233–34.
75. Henry Knox to Anthony Wayne, December 5, 1794, in Knopf, *Anthony Wayne,* 364–69.
76. Anthony Wayne to Henry Knox, January 29, 1795, in Knopf, 383.
77. Ten years later Joseph Hamilton Daviess, the US attorney for Kentucky, informed Jefferson that Wilkinson was an agent of Great Britain. Joseph Hamilton Daviess to Thomas Jefferson, April 21, 1806, in Jefferson Papers, Princeton University Library.
78. Rusche, "Treachery Within," 486.
79. Jacobs, *Tarnished Warrior,* 145.
80. Kohn, "General Wilkinson's Vendetta," 366–67.
81. Timothy Pickering to George Washington, February 20, 1795, in Hoth and Ebel, *Papers of George Washington,* 17:549–50.

82. Timothy Pickering to Anthony Wayne, April 15, 1795, in Knopf, *Anthony Wayne*, 407.

83. James Wilkinson to Thomas Power, November 11, 1795, in Wilkinson, *Memoirs*, 2: app. 40.

84. Timothy Pickering to Anthony Wayne, October 24, 1795, in Knopf, *Anthony Wayne*, 466.

85. Jacobs, *Tarnished Warrior*, 154.

86. Kohn, "General Wilkinson's Vendetta," 367.

87. James McHenry to Anthony Wayne, May 25, 1796, in Knopf, *Anthony Wayne*, 481.

88. James Wilkinson to Manuel Gayoso, September 22, 1796, in Report to the House of Representatives on Brigadier General James Wilkinson, May 1, 1810, in *American State Papers, Misc.*, 2:97–98.

89. One of the representatives he lobbied was Speaker of the House Jonathan Dayton. Kohn, *Eagle and Sword*, 183n36. Dayton later figured prominently with Wilkinson in the Burr Conspiracy.

90. James McHenry to Alexander Hamilton, July 4, 1796, in Syrett, *Papers of Alexander Hamilton*, 20:245.

91. Alexander Hamilton to James McHenry, July 15, 1796, in Syrett, 20:252–53.

92. James McHenry to Anthony Wayne, July 8, 1796, in Knopf, *Anthony Wayne*, 498.

93. Anthony Wayne to James McHenry, July 28, 1796, in Knopf, 506.

94. Anthony Wayne to James McHenry, July 8, 1796, in Knopf, 495.

95. Anthony Wayne to James McHenry, October 28, 1796, in Knopf, 536.

96. Charles Lee to James McHenry, November 20, 1796, in US War Department Papers.

97. Harrington, "Was General Anthony Wayne Murdered?"

98. James Wilkinson to John Adams, December 26, 1797, in Adams Papers.

6. Last Man Standing

1. Kohn, *Eagle and Sword*, 188.

2. Manuel Gayoso to Hector de Carondolet, June 18, 1795, quoted in Cox, "Wilkinson's First Break," 49.

3. Hector de Carondolet to James Wilkinson, April 20, 1797, quoted in Jacobs, *Tarnished Warrior*, 166.

4. Hector de Carondolet to Thomas Power, May 26, 1797, in *American State Papers, Misc.*, 2:102.

5. Thomas Power to Hector de Carondolet, December 5, 1797, in *American State Papers, Misc.*, 2:107–9.

6. Thomas Power to Hector de Carondolet, December 5, 1797, in *American State Papers, Misc.*, 2:109.

7. Deposition of Andrew Ellicott, May 22, 1808, in *American State Papers, Misc.*, 2:89.

8. Cox, "Wilkinson's First Break," 50.

9. Andrew Ellicott to Timothy Pickering, June 5, 1797, in *American State Papers, Misc.*, 1:710.

10. Ellicott's naivete regarding Wilkinson was on full display at Wilkinson's 1811 court-martial. Wilkinson rebutted the negative connotations of this report by showing that, on the same date as his report to Pickering, Ellicott sent a letter to Wilkinson and used Power as the courier for its delivery. He pointed out that Ellicott would not have communicated with him in this way if he saw Wilkinson as a traitor. See Andrew Ellicott to James Wilkinson, June 5, 1797, in Wilkinson, *Memoirs*, 2:168.

11. Wilkinson, 2:170–71.

12. Andrew Ellicott to Timothy Pickering, November 14, 1797, quoted in Linklater, *Artist in Treason,* 172.

13. James Wilkinson to John Adams, December 26, 1797, in Adams Papers.

14. John Adams to James Wilkinson, February 4, 1798, in Adams Papers.

15. Linklater, *Artist in Treason*, 175.

16. James Wilkinson to Manuel Gayoso, March 5, 1798, in Linklater, 175.

17. Andrew Ellicott to Timothy Pickering, November 8, 1798, in *American State Papers, Misc.*, 1:710.

18. Andrew Ellicott to Sarah Ellicott, January 10, 1799, in Matthews, *Andrew Ellicott*, 164.

19. Deposition of Thomas Freeman, August 20, 1811, in Wilkinson, *Memoirs*, 2:app32.

20. Deposition of Andrew Ellicott, May 22, 1808, in *American State Papers, Misc.*, 2:89.

21. Wilkinson, *Memoirs,* 2:176.

22. Andrew Ellicott to Timothy Pickering, November 8, 1798, in *American State Papers, Misc.*, 1:710.

23. Wilkinson, *Memoirs*, 2:app31.

24. Wilkinson, 2:178. At his court-martial Wilkinson showed evidence that Ellicott had stated in writing that he did not believe the charge. Wilkinson also alleged at the trial that the Gayoso-Power letter was a forgery.

25. Deposition of Andrew Ellicott, May 22, 1808, in *American State Papers, Misc.*, 2:89. Ellicott later complained that upon the completion of his surveying responsibilities he twice sought to brief Adams on his efforts and that Adams had refused to meet with him. Andrew Ellicott to James Madison, January 12, 1803, in Hackett et al., *Papers of James Madison*, 251–52.

26. Stinchcombe, "Diplomacy of the XYZ Affair," 598.

27. See, generally, Toll, *Six Frigates*.

28. John Adams to James McHenry, October 22, 1798, in Adams Papers.

29. Kohn, *Eagle and Sword*, 229.

30. Wilkinson, *Memoirs*, 1:435–36.

31. Alexander Hamilton to James Wilkinson, May 23, 1799, in Steiner, *Life and Correspondence of James McHenry*, 443.

32. Jacobs, *Tarnished Warrior*, 185–90.

33. Linklater, *Artist in Treason,* 189; Gayarre, *History of Louisiana*, 3:405; and Shreve, *Finished Scoundrel*, 105–6.

34. Wilkinson, *Memoirs*, 1:439.

35. Chernow, *Alexander Hamilton*, 529–33.

36. Wilkinson, *Memoirs,* 1:439.

37. "Notification of the Record & Qualities of General Wilkinson & Recommendations for His Promotion," in Brown Papers, no. 105.

38. James McHenry to Alexander Hamilton, June 27, 1799, in Syrett, *Papers of Alexander Hamilton*, 23:226.

39. Alexander Hamilton to George Washington, June 15, 1799, in Syrett, 23:191–92.

40. George Washington to Alexander Hamilton, June 25, 1799, in Syrett, 23:222–23.

41. Jacobs, *Beginning of the U.S. Army*, 236.

42. James Wilkinson to Alexander Hamilton, December 22, 1799, in Syrett, *Papers of Alexander Hamilton,* 24:117–19.

43. Hay and Werner, *Admirable Trumpeter,* 184.

44. McCullough, *John Adams,* 537.

45. James Wilkinson to Alexander Hamilton, July 28, 1800, in Syrett, *Papers of Alexander Hamilton,* 25:45–47.

46. Jacobs, *Beginning of the U.S. Army*, 241.

47. Linklater, *Artist in Treason,* 189.

48. James Wilkinson to Thomas Jefferson, May 22, 1800, in Oberg, *Papers of Thomas Jefferson*, 31:585.

49. Jacobs, *Tarnished Warrior*, 194.

50. Aaron Burr to James Wilkinson, October 10, 1800, in Wilkinson, *Memoirs*, 2:app64.

51. John Adams to Senate, February 4, 1801, in Adams Papers.

52. Crackel, *Mr. Jefferson's Army*, 38.

53. Thomas Jefferson to James Wilkinson, February 23, 1801, in Oberg, *Papers of Thomas Jefferson,* 33:54–55.

54. Linklater, *Artist in Treason,* 193.

55. Matthews, *Andrew Ellicott*, 205–6.

56. Thomas Jefferson to House of Representatives, January 20, 1808, in *Annals of Congress*, 10th Congress, 1st Session, 2726–28.

57. Linklater, *Artist in Treason,* 197.

58. Jacobs, *Tarnished Warrior*, 199.

59. Jacobs, *Beginning of the U.S. Army*, 252.

60. Thomas Jefferson to Nathaniel Macon, May 14, 1801, in Oberg, *Papers of Thomas Jefferson,* 34:109–10.

61. Jackson, "Jefferson, Meriwether Lewis," 92.

62. Fleming, *Duel*, 140.

63. Jacobs, *Beginning of the U.S. Army*, 254.

64. Wilkinson, *Memoirs*, 2:app126.

65. One French resident of Louisiana, knowing that Wilkinson's loyalty was for sale, recommended to French authorities in Paris that Wilkinson be brought into French service. See Hay and Werner, *Admirable Trumpeter,* 197.

66. Crackel, *Mr. Jefferson's Army*, 103.

67. Hay and Werner, *Admirable Trumpeter,* 210.

68. Cox, "General Wilkinson," 794–812.

69. Cox, 800.

70. According to the FBI, former FBI agent Robert Hanssen was paid $1.4 million for his espionage assistance to his KGB handlers (see https://www.fbi.gov/history /famous-cases/robert-hanssen). Similarly, Aldrich Ames, the CIA's most notorious Russian mole, was paid over $1.8 million for his treachery (see https://www.fbi.gov /history/famous-cases/aldrich-ames).

71. Linklater, *Artist in Treason,* 211.

72. Robinson, *Louisiana,* 2:337–38.

73. Cox, "General Wilkinson," 798.

74. Robinson, *Louisiana,* 2:343–44.

75. Robinson, 2:347.

76. Robinson, 2:346.

77. Robinson, 2:343.

78. Robinson, 2:341–42.

79. Robinson, 2:342–43.

80. Stroud, *Bitterroot,* 51.

81. Robinson, *Louisiana,* 2:342.

82. Jacobs, *Tarnished Warrior*, 102; Turnbow, *Hardened to Hickory,* 97.

83. James Wilkinson to Esteban Miro, May 2, 1790, in Archivo de Indias, Legajo 2374.

84. Stroud, *Bitterroot,* 92–93.

85. See, e.g., Matthews, *Pike*, 24.

86. See, e.g., Hollon, "Zebulon Montgomery Pike," 448.

87. Flores, *Southern Counterpart,* 323.

88. Montgomery, *Jefferson and the Gunmen*, 70.

89. Jacobs, *Beginning of the U.S. Army*, 320.

90. Flores, *Southern Counterpart,* 75.

91. Flores, 204–5.

92. Flores, 291–95.

93. Thomas Jefferson to Henry Dearborn, February 17, 1804, in McClure, *Papers of Thomas Jefferson*, 42:490–91.

94. Jacobs, *Tarnished Warrior,* 211.

95. James Wilkinson to Henry Dearborn, July 23, 1804, in Cox, "General Wilkinson," 800.

96. Stewart, *American Emperor,* 73.

97. Fleming, *Duel,* 359; Jacobs, *Tarnished Warrior*, 215; Sedgwick, *War of Two*, 357; Stewart, *American Emperor*, 73.

98. Melton, *Aaron Burr*, 69.

99. Thomas Jefferson to Samuel Smith, May 4, 1806, in Jefferson Papers, Princeton University Library.

100. Albert Gallatin to Thomas Jefferson, February 12, 1806, in Adams, *Writings of Albert Gallatin*, 1:290.

7. Wilkinson and the Burr Conspiracy

1. Abernethy, *Burr Conspiracy,* 23.

2. McCaleb, *Aaron Burr Conspiracy,* 68.

3. Aaron Burr to James Wilkinson, April 10, 1805, in Wilkinson, *Memoirs,* 2:app69.

4. Wilkinson, 2:305.

5. James Wilkinson to Thomas Jefferson, June 27, 1805, Jefferson Papers, Princeton University Library.

6. Bruff's testimony was from the October 1805 trial in Richmond. On November 23, 1807, Jefferson submitted the transcripts from all three Burr trials to the Senate and House. *American State Papers, Misc.,* 1:230.

7. Testimony of Major James Bruff, October 6, 1807, *American State Papers, Misc.,* 1:573.

8. Undated letter signed by seventeen officers to Thomas Jefferson, *American State Papers, Misc.,* 1:577–78.

9. Stoddard, *Autobiography Manuscript,* 81–82; Carter, *Territorial Papers of the United States,* 13:194. Stoddard eventually was a panel member and witness at Wilkinson's 1811 court-martial.

10. James Wilkinson to Henry Dearborn, September 8, 1805, in Carter, 13:204.

11. John B. Lucas to Albert Gallatin, February 13, 1806, in Carter, 13:444.

12. See, e.g., John B. Lucas to Albert Gallatin, February 13, 1806, in Carter, 13:444.

13. Memorial to the President by the Citizens of the Territory, December 27, 1805, in Carter, 13:329.

14. John B. Lucas to Albert Gallatin, February 13, 1806, in Carter, 13:444.

15. Wilkinson, *Burr's Conspiracy Exposed,* 17.

16. James Wilkinson to Henry Dearborn, September 8, 1806, in Bacon, *Report of the Committee,* 127.

17. See, e.g., Aaron Burr to James Wilkinson, December 12, 1805, in Wilkinson, *Memoirs,* 2:app84.

18. Abernethy, *Burr Conspiracy,* 39–40.

19. McCaleb, *Aaron Burr Conspiracy,* 62.

20. Joseph Hamilton Daviess to Thomas Jefferson, January 10, 1806, Jefferson Papers, Princeton University Library.

21. Lewis, *Burr Conspiracy,* 59–60.

22. Henry Dearborn to James Wilkinson, March 16, 1806, in Wilkinson, *Memoirs,* 2:app87.

23. Henry Dearborn to James Wilkinson, May 16, 1806, in Wilkinson, 2:app90.

24. See, e.g., James Wilkinson to Samuel Smith, June 17, 1806, in James Wilkinson to Samuel Smith (Extract), Jefferson Papers, Princeton University Library.

25. Samuel Smith to Thomas Jefferson, April 28, 1806, Jefferson Papers, Princeton University Library.

26. Thomas Jefferson to Samuel Smith, May 4, 1806, Jefferson Papers, Princeton University Library.

27. See, e.g., Samuel Smith to Thomas Jefferson, August 8, 1806, Jefferson Papers, Princeton University Library.

28. Jonathan Dayton to James Wilkinson, July 24, 1806, *American State Papers, Misc.*, 1:558.

29. Aaron Burr to James Wilkinson, July 25, 1806, Wilkinson, *Memoirs*, 2:315.

30. James Wilkinson to Henry Dearborn, September 8, 1806, Wilkinson, 2:app60.

31. Abernethy, *Burr Conspiracy*, 69.

32. Abernethy, 71.

33. James Wilkinson to John Smith, September 28, 1806, letter published in *Vermont Sentinel and Democrat*, January 3, 1808, 1.

34. James Wilkinson to John Adair, September 28, 1806, in Abernethy, *Burr Conspiracy*, 143.

35. Testimony of James Wilkinson, September 29, 1807, *American State Papers, Misc.*, 1:544.

36. Schwarz, *Forgotten Battlefield*, 16.

37. In the forthcoming twenty years Samuel Swartwout, along with his brothers John and Robert, figured prominently with Wilkinson, Burr, Jefferson, and Jackson. Samuel was a close New York friend and traveling companion of Burr. Following his involvement in the Burr Conspiracy, Samuel closely aligned himself with Jackson, and when Jackson was elected president was named customs collector for the port of New York. It was alleged that he embezzled over $1.2 million while he served there. At Burr's request, John Swartwout was appointed by Jefferson to be US marshal for the state of New York but he frustrated Jefferson's attempt to prosecute participants in a filibustering expedition against Spanish Latin America and was fired by Jefferson in 1806. Robert Swartwout was appointed a general in the War of 1812, and served as Wilkinson's incompetent quartermaster during the Montreal campaign of 1813, and was a witness against Wilkinson at Wilkinson's 1815 court-martial.

38. Aaron Burr to James Wilkinson, July 29, 1806, *American State Papers, Misc.*, 1:471. As a result of Wilkinson's alteration and decryption of the letter, its true authorship remains in dispute today. See, e.g., Kline, *Political Correspondence,* 2:984–86, for the hypothesis that Dayton was the true author of the letter. Theodore Crackel disputes this conclusion and remains convinced that Burr was the author. See Crackel, *Mr. Jefferson's Army*, 131n22. An example of the letter and the cypher code subsequently explained by Wilkinson can be found at Kerr, "Decryption Originalism," 920; and Melton, *Aaron Burr,* 121.

39. Quoted in Wheelan, *Jefferson's Vendetta,* chap. 9.

40. Deposition of Thomas Cushing, May 20, 1807, in Wilkinson, *Memoirs*, 2:app92.

41. James Wilkinson to Thomas Jefferson, October 20, 1806, in Wilkinson, 2:app95.

42. James Wilkinson to Thomas Jefferson, October 21, 1806, in Wilkinson, 2:app95.

43. Testimony of Lieutenant Colonel Thomas A. Smith, in Wilkinson, 2:app94.

44. Gideon Granger to Thomas Jefferson, October 16, 1806, in Abernethy, *Burr Conspiracy*, 185. See also Thomas Jefferson to Gideon Granger, March 9, 1814, in Looney,

Papers of Thomas Jefferson, 7:234–38; and Statement of Gideon Granger, October 16, 1806 in Henshaw, "Burr-Blennerhassett Documents," 9:10.

45. Thomas Jefferson's Notes on a Cabinet Meeting, October 22, 1806, Jefferson Papers, Princeton University Library.

46. Thomas Jefferson's Notes on a Cabinet Meeting, October 24, 1806, Jefferson Papers, Princeton University Library.

47. Thomas Jefferson's Notes on a Cabinet Meeting, October 25, 1806, Jefferson Papers, Princeton University Library.

48. James Wilkinson to Thomas Jefferson, November 12, 1806, Wilkinson, *Memoirs*, 2:app100.

49. James Wilkinson to Jose de Iturrigaray, December 17, 1806, in Shepherd, "Letter of James Wilkinson," 535.

50. Crackel, *Mr. Jefferson's Army*, 146.

51. Thomas Jefferson, Proclamation on Spanish Dominion Expedition, November 27, 1806, Jefferson Papers, Library of Congress.

52. Henry Dearborn to James Wilkinson, November 27, 1806, in Wilkinson, *Burr's Conspiracy Exposed*, 39.

53. Crackel, *Mr. Jefferson's Army*, 151.

54. James Wilkinson to Thomas Jefferson, November 12, 1806, Wilkinson, *Memoirs*, 2:app100.

55. Linklater, *Artist in Treason*, 259.

56. Thomas Jefferson to United States Congress, Message on Aaron Burr, January 22, 1807, Jefferson Papers, Library of Congress.

57. Lewis, *Burr Conspiracy*, 178.

58. Testimony of Major James Bruff, October 6, 1807, *American State Papers, Misc.*, 1:574–75.

59. John Smith to Thomas Jefferson, July 6, 1807, Jefferson Papers, Princeton University Library.

60. Vincente Folch to James Wilkinson, February 10, 1807, in Wilkinson ["Kentuckian"], *Plain Tale*, 19.

61. Abernethy, *Burr Conspiracy*, 263; Declaration of Thomas Power, May 16, 1807, in Wilkinson, *Memoirs*, 2:91.

62. Notes of the interrogation were taken by Madison, the author of the Fourth and Fifth Amendments to the Constitution. Report of Bollman's Communications, January 23, 1807, Madison Papers. Madison raised no objection when Jefferson subsequently sought to use the statement against Bollman at the Burr trial in violation of his promise of immunity.

63. Thomas Jefferson to Eric Bollman, January 25, 1807, Jefferson Papers, Princeton University Library.

64. Eric Bollman to Thomas Jefferson, January 26, 1807, Jefferson Papers, Princeton University Library.

65. Deposition of General James Wilkinson, December 26, 1806, *American State Papers, Misc.*, 1:469; and Newmyer, *Treason Trial*, 48.

66. *Ex Parte Bollman* and *Ex Parte Swartwout*, 8 U.S. 75 (1807), 132–33.

67. Abernethy, *Burr Conspiracy*, 232.

68. Newmyer, *Treason Trial*, 92.

69. Statement of Edmund Randolph, in Robertson, *Reports of the Trials*, 1:155.

70. John Randolph to Andrew Jackson, May 30, 1807, in Bruce, *John Randolph*, 301.

71. Cabell, "Trial of Aaron Burr," 77.

72. Washington Irving to James Paulding, June 22, 1807, in Irving, *Life and Letters*, 1:158.

73. James Wilkinson to Thomas Jefferson, June 17, 1807, Jefferson Papers, Princeton University Library.

74. Thomas Jefferson to James Wilkinson, June 21, 1807, Jefferson Papers, Princeton University Library.

75. Robertson, *Reports of the Trial*, 1:129.

76. Thomas Jefferson to George Hay, June 19, 1807, Jefferson Papers, Princeton University Library.

77. Thomas Jefferson to George Hay, June 19, 1807, Jefferson Papers, Princeton University Library.

78. Thomas Jefferson to George Hay, September 7, 1807, Jefferson Papers, Princeton University Library.

79. Newmyer, *Treason Trial*, 169.

80. Testimony of James Wilkinson, September 29, 1807, *American State Papers, Misc.*, 1:543.

81. Statement of Defense Attorney John Baker, September 29, 1807, *American State Papers, Misc.*, 1:544.

82. Testimony of James Bruff, October 6, 1807, *American State Papers, Misc.*, 1:575.

83. Testimony of James Wilkinson, October 8, 1809, *American State Papers, Misc.*, 1:580.

84. Abernethy, *Burr Conspiracy*, 256.

85. Record of Proceedings, October 19, 1807, *American State Papers, Misc.*, 1:610.

86. George Hay to Thomas Jefferson, October 15, 1807, Jefferson Papers, Princeton University Library. Clark did not testify at the hearing.

87. Bruce, *John Randolph*, 305.

88. James Wilkinson to Thomas Jefferson, September 13, 1807, Jefferson Papers, Princeton University Library.

89. James Wilkinson to Thomas Jefferson, September 15, 1807, Jefferson Papers, Princeton University Library.

90. Thomas Jefferson to James Wilkinson, September 20, 1807, Jefferson Papers, Princeton University Library.

91. Lewis, *Burr Conspiracy*, 331.

92. Statement of Samuel Swartwout, October 21, 1807, quoted in the *Evening Post* (New York City), October 29, 1807, 2.

93. Lewis, *Burr Conspiracy,* 332–36.

94. James Wilkinson to Samuel Smith, May 10, 1807, in Wilkinson Papers, University of Pittsburgh Library.

95. Bruce, *John Randolph,* 303–4.

96. Thomas Power to James Wilkinson, May 16, 1807, in Wilkinson, "Plain Tale," 21.

97. Deposition of Daniel W. Coxe, June 13, 1808, in Wilkinson, *Memoirs,* 2:app34.

98. Linklater, *Artist in Treason,* 277.

99. Wilkinson, *Memoirs,* 2:7.

100. James Wilkinson to John Randolph, December 24, 1807, in *Pittsburgh Weekly Gazette,* January 19, 1808, 3.

101. *Hartford Courant,* January 18, 1808, 3.

102. "Randolph . . . would have challenged anybody or anything, from Henry Clay to a field mouse, if the fancy happened to strike him." Lodge, *Daniel Webster,* 67. In 1825 Randolph and secretary of state Henry Clay fought a duel in which neither party was injured. Randolph was also fined by the House for beating a fellow congressman with a cane.

103. Motion by Rep. John Randolph to Introduce Documents Relating to General Wilkinson, December 31, 1807, *Annals of Congress,* 10th Congress, 1257.

104. Undated letter of Thomas Power, *Annals of Congress,* 1260.

105. Henry Dearborn to Henry Burbeck, January 2, 1808, *American State Papers, Misc.,* 1:706.

106. Daniel Clark to Thomas Power, January 2, 1808, in Ranzan and Hollis, *Hero of Fort Schuyler,* 261.

107. Statement of Delegate Daniel Clark, December 31, 1807, *Annals of Congress,* 10th Congress, 1261.

108. Statement of Delegate Daniel Clark, December 31, 1807, *American State Papers, Misc.,* 1:704.

109. Resolution of House of Representatives to Thomas Jefferson, January 13, 1808, *Annals of Congress,* 10th Congress, 1460.

110. Thomas Jefferson to House of Representatives, January 20, 1808, *Annals of Congress,* 10th Congress, 2726–28.

111. Thomas Jefferson to House of Representatives, February 4, 1808, Jefferson Papers, Princeton University Library.

112. Thomas Jefferson to House of Representatives, January 20, 1808, *Annals of Congress,* 10th Congress, 2726–28.

113. See, generally, Macomb, *Treatise on Martial Law.*

114. Henry Dearborn to Henry Burbeck, January 2, 1808, in *American State Papers, Misc.,* 1:706.

115. Winfield Scott noted that nearly all the officers appointed before 1808 were Wilkinson supporters. Scott, *Memoirs,* 1:36.

116. Dearborn's convening order, January 2, 1808, in Wilkinson, *Memoirs,* 2:10; and Henry Dearborn to Henry Burbeck, January 2, 1808, in *American State Papers, Misc.,* 1:706.

117. Thomas Jefferson to Thomas Randolph, January 26, 1808, Jefferson Papers, Princeton University Library.

118. "Court of Inquiry in the Case of Gen. Wilkinson," *Pittsburgh Weekly Gazette*, January 26, 1808, 3.

119. Deposition of Walter Jones, May 1, 1810, *American State Papers, Misc.*, 2:125.

120. As a result of the court's order the reporter for the *National Intelligencer* stopped taking notes. "Court of Inquiry in the Case of General Wilkinson," *National Intelligencer*, January 15, 1808, 3.

121. At least one witness later objected to the summary of his testimony printed in the press, claiming it was inaccurate. Robert T. Spence, *National Intelligencer*, March 16, 1808, 1.

122. "Court of Inquiry in the Case of General Wilkinson," Statement of James Wilkinson, *National Intelligencer*, January 20, 1808, 1.

123. Thomas Jefferson to House of Representatives, January 20, 1808, *Annals of Congress*, 10th Congress, 2726–28.

124. Statement of James Wilkinson before the Court of Inquiry, *National Intelligencer*, July 4, 1808, 3.

125. Andrew Ellicott to James Wilkinson, January 21, 1808, in Clark, *Proofs of the Corruption,* 69.

126. Andrew Ellicott to David Clark, January 14, 1808, in Clark, 148.

127. Deposition of Walter Jones, May 1, 1810, in *American State Papers, Misc.,* 2:125.

128. Deposition of Andrew Ellicott, May 22, 1808, in Wilkinson, *Memoirs,* 2:app28.

129. Harper's deposition of May 6 is one of the few statements taken for the court that was printed in full by the press. "Mr. R. G. Harper's Examination," *Aurora General Advertiser*, June 10, 1808, 2. Wilkinson's memoirs reproduce only a portion of the deposition. Wilkinson*, Memoirs,* 2:55–56.

130. Governor Folch's Declaration, February 18, 1808, Bacon, *Report of the Committee*, 47–50.

131. Vincente Folch to James Wilkinson, quoted in Cox, "Later Intrigues," 807–8. Spanish officials continued for many years to hinder attempts by American scholars and officials to obtain access to Spanish archives related to Louisiana and Florida. See Hill, *Descriptive Catalogue,* xxii.

132. Deposition of Walter Jones, May 1, 1810, *American State Papers, Misc.,* 2:125.

133. *National Intelligencer*, July 4, 1808, 3.

134. Wilkinson, *Memoirs,* 2:12.

8. Death of an Army on the Mississippi

1. Henry Dearborn to James Wilkinson, December 2, 1808, in *American State Papers, Military Affairs*, 1:272.

2. Cox, "West Florida Controversy," 234.

3. See, generally, Cox, "Pan-American Policy," 1:212–39.

4. Cox, 215.

5. James Wilkinson to Thomas Jefferson, October 1, 1808, in Jefferson Papers, Princeton University Library.

6. Cox, "Pan-American Policy," 222. Wilkinson was also reimbursed $1,099 by the War Department for the commercial costs of shipping these goods. Deposition of William Simmons, April 13, 1810, *American State Papers, Misc.*, 2:113–15.

7. Cox, "Pan-American Policy," 223.

8. Cox, 231.

9. Cox, 223–25.

10. Linklater, *Artist in Treason*, 284.

11. Crackel, *Mr. Jefferson's Army*, 177. Jefferson used the 1807 Insurrection Act to authorize federal military force to interdict smuggling into Canada.

12. Taylor, *Civil War of 1812*, 101.

13. Scott, *Memoirs*, 1:35–36.

14. Jacobs, *Beginning of the U.S. Army,* 274.

15. Crackel, *Mr. Jefferson's Army*, 176.

16. Coffman, *Portrait of the Old Army,* 40.

17. Jacobs, *Tarnished Warrior*, 247.

18. Henry Dearborn to James Wilkinson, December 2, 1808, in *American State Papers, Military Affairs*, 1:272.

19. Jacobs, *Beginning of the U.S. Army*, 274–76.

20. William Eustis to James Wilkinson, June 22, 1809, in Wilkinson, *Memoirs,* 2:391.

21. Captain Peter, a nine-year veteran of the army, resigned his commission the day his unit arrived at Terre aux Boeufs. Deposition of Captain George Peter, April 11, 1810, in *American State Papers, Military Affairs*, 1:282. Peter had been a loyal supporter of Wilkinson, but by the time of the movement to Terre aux Boeufs he had come to oppose him. Peter provided testimony to the House committee that investigated Terre aux Boeufs and was listed as a witness for the prosecution at the 1811 court-martial, but he died before the trial.

22. James Wilkinson to William Eustis, April 13, 1809, in Wilkinson, *Memoirs*, 2:344–46.

23. Deposition of James Morrison, January 16, 1811, in Wilkinson, 2:235.

24. Deposition of A. D. Abrahams, June 19, 1810, in Wilkinson, 2:app70.

25. James Morrison to James Wilkinson, July 28, 1809, in Wilkinson Papers, vol. 3, Chicago History Museum.

26. Maas, "Army's Disaster," 14.

27. James Morrison to James Wilkinson, July 28, 1809, in Wilkinson Papers, vol. 3, Chicago History Museum.

28. Morrison was paid $35,415 for the provisions from June to October 1809. Wilkinson, *Memoirs*, 2:510. War Department accountant William Simmons noted that Wilkinson did not contest any of the invoices. Deposition of William Simmons, January 12, 1811, Bacon, *Report of the Committee*, 179.

29. William Eustis to Representative Thomas Newton, April 4, 1810, *American State Papers, Military Affairs,* 1:275.

30. Colonel Alexander Parker of the Fifth Infantry Regiment was appointed to temporary command in New Orleans one month before Wilkinson arrived. Along with many other officers, Parker submitted his resignation shortly after the move to Terre aux Boeufs. James Wilkinson to William Eustis, July 5, 1809, in Wilkinson Papers, vol. 3, Chicago History Museum.

31. Wilkinson, *Memoirs,* 2:346–47.

32. Crackel, "Jefferson, Politics, and the Army," 28.

33. Wilkinson, *Memoirs,* 2:468.

34. Danisi, *Uncovering the Truth,* chap. 10.

35. Henry Dearborn to Thomas Jefferson, February 16, 1809, Jefferson Papers, Princeton University Library.

36. "Public Plunder," Library of Congress, 1809.

37. William Eustis to James Wilkinson, June 22, 1809, in Wilkinson, *Memoirs,* 2:391.

38. William Eustis to Oliver Spenser, August 10, 1809, Wilkinson Papers, vol. 3, Chicago History Museum; and Wilkinson, *Memoirs,* 2:451.

39. Wilkinson, 2:359.

40. Deposition of Colonel Alexander Parker, April 14, 1810, in *American State Papers, Military Affairs,* 1:284–86.

41. James Wilkinson to William Eustis, May 29, 1809, and James Wilkinson to William Eustis, June 5, 1809, in Wilkinson, *Memoirs,* 2:358–59 and 2:361–62, respectively.

42. Wilkinson, 2:363.

43. Gillette, *Army Medical Department,* chap. 6n55.

44. Weigley, *History,* 113.

45. James Wilkinson to William Eustis, April 13, 1809, in Wilkinson, *Memoirs,* 2:344.

46. Wilkinson, 2:471.

47. Wilkinson, 2:349.

48. Wilkinson, 2:350

49. Wilkinson, 2:351.

50. William Eustis to James Wilkinson, April 27, 1809, in Wilkinson, 2:368–70.

51. William Eustis to James Wilkinson, April 30, 1809, in Wilkinson, 2:375–76.

52. Shreve, *Finished Scoundrel,* 253.

53. Wilkinson, *Memoirs,* 2:368.

54. See, e.g., Adams, *History of the United States,* 131; Linklater, *Artist in Treason,* 285; and Jacobs, *Beginning of the U.S. Army,* 346.

55. Nets cost $2.50 apiece, the equivalent of half of a private's monthly pay.

56. Jacobs, *Beginning of the U.S. Army,* 348.

57. Jacobs, 348.

58. Deposition of Captain John Darrington, April 11, 1810, in *American State Papers, Military Affairs,* 1:283.

59. Deposition of Dr. Robert Dow, August 5, 1811, quoted in Danisi, *Uncovering the Truth,* chap. 12.

60. Testimony of Colonel H. V. Milton, [n.d.], in Wilkinson, *Memoirs,* 2:app58.

61. James Wilkinson to William Eustis, July 17, 1809, in Wilkinson Papers, vol. 3, Chicago History Museum.

62. Deposition of Captain John Darrington, April 11, 1810, in *American State Papers, Military Affairs,* 1:283.

63. William Eustis to James Wilkinson, June 22, 1809, in Wilkinson, *Memoirs,* 2:394.

64. Wilkinson, *Burr's Conspiracy Exposed,* 59.

65. David Porter to James Wilkinson, June 6, 1809, in Wilkinson, *Memoirs,* 2:app62.

66. *American State Papers, Military Affairs,* 1:253.

67. Jacobs, *Beginning of the U.S. Army,* 352.

9. The Rising Storm

1. Thomas Jefferson to James Madison, November 30, 1809, in Stagg, Cross, and Perdue, *Papers of James Madison,* 2:95–97.

2. John Wayles Eppes to James Madison, January 18, 1810, in Stagg, Cross, and Perdue, 2:189–90.

3. Bruce, *John Randolph of Roanoke,* 1:365.

4. Irving, *Knickerbocker's History of New York.*

5. Scott, *Memoirs,* 1:37.

6. Letter from nine officers to James Wilkinson, January 23, 1810, in *American State Papers, Military Affairs,* 1:295.

7. Wilkinson, *Memoirs,* 1:811–12.

8. Peskin, *Winfield Scott,* chap. 2.

9. Johnson, *Winfield Scott,* 17.

10. Mansfield, *Life of General Winfield Scott,* 27.

11. Danisi, *Uncovering the Truth,* chap. 10.

12. Meriwether Lewis to James Madison, September 16, 1809, in Rutland et al., *Papers of James Madison,* 1:380–81.

13. James Madison to Thomas Jefferson, October 30, 1809, in Stagg, Cross, and Perdue, *Papers of James Madison,* 2:48–49.

14. Ravenholt, "Triumph Then Despair," 366–79. Ravenholt speculates that Lewis contracted syphilis on the Pacific trip and was experiencing its growing debilitating effects in 1809.

15. See Chandler, *Jefferson Conspiracies*; Starrs and Gale, *Death of Meriwether Lewis*; and Gale, *Meriwether Lewis.*

16. Wilkinson, *Memoirs,* 2:15.

17. Statement of Rep. Joseph Pearson, March 21, 1810, in *Annals of Congress,* 11th Congress, 2nd Sess., 1606.

18. *Annals of Congress,* 11th Congress, 2nd Sess., 1735.

19. *Annals of Congress,* 11th Congress, 2nd Sess., 1730.

20. *Annals of Congress,* 11th Congress, 2nd Sess., 1731.

21. Deposition of Walter Jones, May 1, 1810, in *American State Papers, Misc.,* 2:125.

22. Clark, *Proofs of the Corruption,* 5–6.

23. Clark, 29.

24. Clark, 69–72.

25. Wilkinson, *Memoirs,* 2:app28.

26. Wilkinson, 2:12–13.

27. Clark, *Proofs of the Corruption,* 74.

28. Thomas Jefferson to House of Representatives, January 20, 1808, in *Annals of Congress,* 10th Congress, 2726–28.

29. Clark, *Proofs of the Corruption,* 148–49.

30. William Oliver Alan to Andrew Jackson, January 10, 1810, in Moser and MacPherson, *Papers of Andrew Jackson,* 2:228–29.

31. Andrew Jackson to Jenkin Whiteside, February 10, 1810, Moser and MacPherson, 2:230–32. While the editors of Jackson's papers state that there is no evidence that Jackson ever received the underlying Lacassange documents referred to by Allen, the documents were eventually provided to Madison.

32. *Annals of Congress,* 11th Congress, 2nd Sess., 1932.

33. Deposition of General James Wilkinson, April 24, 1810, in Newton Report, "Mortality in the Troops at New Orleans," Report No. 100, House of Representatives, 11th Congress, 2nd Sess., *American State Papers, Military Affairs,* 1:291–92.

34. *American State Papers, Military Affairs,* 1:268–95.

35. *American State Papers, Military Affairs,* 1:272.

36. Chalou, "St. Clair's Defeat," 138–39.

37. Deposition of William Simmons, April 13, 1810, in *American State Papers, Misc.,* 2:113–15.

38. Deposition of Captain George Peter, April 12, 1810, in *American State Papers, Misc.,* 2:115. Peter, a career army officer and original supporter of Wilkinson, became disillusioned and resigned shortly after their arrival at Terre aux Boeufs. Peter was scheduled to be a witness at Wilkinson's 1811 court-martial but died before the trial.

39. Deposition of Elisha Winters, April 16, 1810, in *American State Papers, Misc.,* 2:94–95.

40. Article 92, Articles of War 2 Stat. 359 (1806).

41. Deposition of Walter Jones, May 1, 1810, in *American State Papers, Misc.,* 2:124–26.

42. Deposition of Walter Jones, May 1, 1810, in *American State Papers, Misc.,* 2:124–26.

43. Deposition of John Smith, April 17, 1810, in *American State Papers, Misc.,* 2:115.

44. Report on Brigadier General James Wilkinson, May 1, 1810, in *American State Papers, Misc.,* 2:79.

45. Wilkinson, *Memoirs,* 2:17.

46. James Wilkinson to William Eustis, June 25, 1810, in Wilkinson Papers, vol. 3, Chicago History Museum; and Wilkinson, *Memoirs,* 2:app129.

47. Wilkinson, 2:app129.

48. William Eustis to James Madison, July 16, 1810, in Stagg, Cross, and Perdue, *Papers of James Madison,* 2:416–17.

49. James Madison to William Eustis, July 1810, in Stagg, Cross, and Perdue, 2:428–29.

50. Wilkinson, *Burr's Conspiracy Exposed.* Colvin probably ghost wrote the less vituperative portions of this work. A second anonymous pamphlet published at the same time, *A Brief Examination,* was also probably written by Wilkinson.

51. Wilkinson, *Memoirs,* 2:app130; and Bacon, *Report of the Committee,* 3.

52. Wilkinson, *Memoirs,* 2:app130.

53. Wilkinson, 2:18.

54. Statement of Representative Ezekiel Bacon, in *Annals of Congress,* House of Representatives, 11th Congress, 3rd Sess., 1030.

55. Bacon, *Report of the Committee,* 6.

56. *Annals of Congress,* House of Representatives, 11th Congress, 3rd Sess., 1033.

57. William Crawford to Speaker, House of Representatives, 1811, in Wilkinson Papers, vol. 3, Chicago History Museum; and Jacobs, *Tarnished Warrior,* 265.

58. James Wilkinson to James Madison, April 20, 1811, in Stagg, Cross, and Perdue, *Papers of James Madison,* 3:275–77.

59. Chalou, "James Wilkinson," 105.

60. James Wilkinson to Thomas Jefferson, January 21, 1811, in Looney, *Papers of Thomas Jeffersom,* 3:323–25.

61. Thomas Jefferson to James Wilkinson, March 10, 1811, in Looney, 3:440–41.

62. James Madison to Thomas Jefferson, April 1, 1811, in Stagg, Cross, and Perdue, *Papers of James Madison,* 3:238–40.

63. Thomas Jefferson to James Madison, April 7, 1811, in Stagg, Cross, and Perdue, 249–51.

64. Wilkinson, *Memoirs,* 2:28.

65. Wilkinson, 2:28.

66. Wilkinson, 2:24.

67. James Wilkinson to James Madison, April 20, 1811, in Stagg, Cross, and Perdue, *Papers of James Madison,* 3:275–77.

68. Wilkinson, *Memoirs,* 2:24.

69. Wilkinson, 2:24–25.

70. Wilkinson, 2:app131.

71. Wilkinson, 2:26.

72. Wilkinson, 2:app132.

10. Spy Trial in Frederick Town

1. Crocker, *Braddock's March,* 116.

2. See, generally, Macomb, *Treatise on Martial Law.*

3. Jacobs, *Tarnished Warrior,* 213.

4. Crackel, *Mr. Jefferson's Army,* 92.

5. Shreve, *Finished Scoundrel,* 229.

6. Crackel, *Mr. Jefferson's Army*, 116–18.

7. Ellery, *Memoirs of General Joseph Gardner Swift*, 42.

8. Jacobs, *Tarnished Warrior*, 200.

9. Hickey, "United States Army versus Long Hair," 470–71.

10. James Wilkinson to John Adams, September 12, 1804, and John Adams to James Wilkinson, November 16, 1804, both in Adams Papers.

11. John Adams to James Wilkinson, November 16, 1804, in Adams Papers.

12. Hickey, "United States Army versus Long Hair," 472.

13. "Biographical Sketch of Col. Thomas Butler," *Adams Sentinel*, November 27, 1805, 8.

14. Hickey, "United States Army versus Long Hair," 473.

15. Article 64 and Article 75, Articles of War.

16. Wilkinson, *Memoirs*, 2:app131.

17. Gansevoort had served under General Richard Montgomery during the 1775–76 invasion of Canada. In 1777 he successfully defended Fort Stanwix from the British assault by Colonel Barry St. Leger. On his way home from the Wilkinson court-martial, Gansevoort died from recurring health problems.

18. Williams, the grandnephew of Benjamin Franklin, had served as Franklin's secretary during Franklin's time in Paris during the Revolution. In 1814 Williams was elected to the House of Representatives from Philadelphia but died before he could take his seat.

19. Wilkinson, *Memoirs*, 2:app20.

20. Kingsbury also served as a juror and a character witness for Wilkinson at his 1815 court-martial.

21. Beall resigned his commission in August 1812, when he received orders transferring him to the Northern Department.

22. Porter went on to serve under Wilkinson during the 1813 St. Lawrence campaign. He was breveted a brigadier general, served again as both a juror and a character witness for Wilkinson at his 1815 court-martial, and survived the postwar elimination of officers.

23. Abimael Youngs Nicoll was, like Wilkinson, a doctor by training. Nicoll testified on Wilkinson's behalf at his 1815 court-martial, stating that he had the highest opinion of Wilkinson as a man of honor.

24. Swift served on the 1803 court-martial of "Long Hair" Butler. He received a brevet promotion to brigadier general in 1814, which he felt had been delayed because of his friendship with Wilkinson. Swift was also called as a witness at Wilkinson's 1815 court-martial, but refused to attend. Swift later resigned and began a civilian career as a civil engineer.

25. Macomb was not an attorney by background. His interest in military justice commenced when he served as the judge advocate at the 1803 court-martial in "Long Hair" Butler. During his career he published two well-respected treatises on military justice. While he refused to testify in person, he provided a written statement in support of Wilkinson at the 1815 court-martial.

26. Richards, *Memoir of Alexander Macomb*, 47. At Wilkinson's 1815 court-martial, Macomb provided the following characterization of Wilkinson: "I have always found him desireous of improving the army, a man of honour, a gentleman and a soldier; always willing to do that he expected from others, as far as it respected personal exposure, personal honour, and individual rights." Macomb Interrogatories, March 7, 1815, in Wilkinson, *Memoirs*, 3:183.

27. Macomb, *Treatise on Martial Law*, chap. 4, §2; and Article 71, Articles of War.

28. Burbeck was named the chief artillerist of the army in 1802. He went on to serve in noncombat roles during the War of 1812 and retired from the army in 1815.

29. Backus was killed at the Battle of Sackett's Harbor in 1813.

30. Stoddard was killed at the siege of Fort Meigs during the War of 1812. Armistead was the brother of Major George Armistead, who commanded Fort McHenry during the 1814 Battle of Baltimore. Walter Armistead's son, Lewis Addison Armistead, served as a Confederate general in the Civil War and was killed during Pickett's Charge in the Battle of Gettysburg in 1863.

31. Macomb, *Treatise on Martial Law*, §129.

32. Ellery, *Memoirs of General Joseph Gardner Swift*, 97. Swift dismissed the rumors of "unbecoming intimacy" that arose from these gatherings as "silly" and "ill natured."

33. Wilkinson, *Memoirs*, 2:26.

34. Wilkinson, *Burr's Conspiracy Exposed*.

35. When the Articles of War were first adopted by the Continental Congress in 1775, correspondence with the enemy was not listed as a capital offense. Following the discovery that Benjamin Church, the first surgeon general of the army, was communicating intelligence to the British, Washington recommended to the Continental Congress that the penalty for such correspondence be increased. A few weeks later the Continental Congress agreed to make such correspondence a capital offense. George Washington to John Hancock, October 5, 1775, in Chase, *Papers of George Washington,* 2:98–103.

36. Article 88, Articles of War.

37. Winthrop, *Military Law and Precedents*, 629–35. At his 1814 court-martial for the surrender of Detroit, General William Hull was charged with treason. In his closing argument Hull belatedly raised the issue that treason was not an offense under the Articles of War. The court rejected this argument as having been raised too late in the proceedings but acquitted Hull of the charge. Forbes, *Report of the Trial,* appendix 118.

38. Article II, Section 4 allows impeachment for treason, bribery, or other high crimes and misdemeanors.

39. Congress passed a law in 1789 addressing the bribery of customs officers, and the following year it passed the Crimes Act of 1790, which prohibits the bribing of judges.

40. Wilkinson, *Memoirs*, 2:35.

41. Following the Wilkinson trial, Jones went on to a successful legal career, both as an attorney for the government and as a private attorney. He argued before the Supreme Court in the landmark case *McCulloch v. Maryland.*

42. Tyler, *Memoir of Roger Brooke Taney*, 105.

43. In 1815 Thomas was appointed to the US Senate but died in a local epidemic before he could take his seat.

44. Macomb, *Treatise on Martial Law*, §93: "A lawyer is not recognized by a Court-Martial, though his presence is tolerated, as a friend to the prisoner, to assist him by advice in preparing questions for witnesses, in taking notes and shaping his defense."

45. Wiener, "Courts-Martial," 28.

46. US Army, *Army Lawyer*, 29.

47. Recreating the actions of the three-month trial is an interesting task. No complete record of the trial exists. Wiener, "Courts-Martial," 28. This account is recreated from partial transcripts of the court-martial that are maintained by the National Archives and Records Administration; by Heritage Frederick, the Frederick County Historical Society; vol. 2 of Wilkinson's memoirs; contemporaneous newspaper stories; and the memoirs and correspondence of trial participants.

48. Article 77, Articles of War.

49. Ellery, *Memoirs of General Joseph Gardner Swift*, 96.

50. Records of Heritage Frederick, Frederick County Historical Society.

51. James Madison to William Eustis, September 8, 1811, in Stagg, Cross, and Perdue, *Papers of James Madison*, 3:452–53. The War of 1812 commenced within a few months of the final act of the court-martial.

52. James Wilkinson to James Madison, October 9, 1811, in Stagg, Cross, and Perdue, *Papers of James Madison*, 3:481–82.

53. James Madison to James Wilkinson, October 12, 1811, in Stagg, Cross, and Perdue, 3:483–84.

54. William Eustis to James Madison, September 14, 1811, in Stagg, Cross, and Perdue, 3:461–64.

55. James Madison to William Eustis, September 15, 1811, in Stagg, Cross, and Perdue, 3:466.

56. William Eustis to James Madison, September 14, 1811, in Stagg, Cross, and Perdue, 3:461–64.

57. For example, Aaron Burr's daughter, Theodosia, was lost at sea on a similar coastal journey in 1812.

58. Article 74, Articles of War.

59. This was also reflected in military trial practice of the day. Macomb's treatise emphasizes the importance of live testimony in the assessment of witness credibility. See Macomb, *Treatise on Martial Law*, §77.

60. William Eustis to James Madison, September 14, 1811, in Stagg, Cross, and Perdue, *Papers of James Madison*, 3:461–64.

61. William Eustis to James Madison, September 11, 1811, in Stagg, Cross, and Perdue, 3:454–55.

62. James Madison to William Eustis, September 15, 1811, in Stagg, Cross, and Perdue, 3:466.

63. Macomb, *Treatise on Martial Law*, §80.

64. Ellery, *Memoirs of General Joseph Gardner Swift*, 97; and Jonathan Williams to James Madison, November 17, 1811, in Stagg et al., *Papers of James Madison*, 4:24–25.

65. "General Wilkinson's Trial," *Missouri Gazette and Public Advertiser*, February 2, 1812, 3.

66. "Trial of Gen. Wilkinson," *Pittsfield Sun*, December 21, 1811, 1.

67. Deposition of Andrew Ellicott, May 22, 1808, in *American State Papers, Misc.*, 2:89.

68. Answers to Interrogatories by Andrew Ellicott, May 22, 1808, in Wilkinson, *Memoirs*, 2:app38.

69. Wilkinson, 2:app31.

70. Wilkinson, 2:app32.

71. US Constitution, Article 1, Section 9, Clause 8 states: "No Title of Nobility shall be granted by the United States: And no Person holding any Office of Profit or Trust under them, shall, without the Consent of Congress, accept of any present, Emolument, Office, or Title, of any kind whatever, from any King, Prince or foreign State."

72. Jacobs, *Tarnished Warrior*, 270.

73. Cox, "General Wilkinson," 808.

74. See, generally, Daigler, *Spies, Patriots, and Traitors*.

75. See, generally, Schaeper, *Edward Bancroft*.

76. O'Toole, *Honorable Treachery*, 79.

77. Court-martial transcript, at 1849.

78. See, e.g., Wilkinson, *Memoirs*, 2:152.

79. John Adams to James Wilkinson, October 12, 1811, in Adams Papers.

80. Wilkinson, *Memoirs*, 2:565.

81. James Wilkinson to Peter Gansevoort, October 10, 1811, in Ranzan and Hollis, *Hero of Fort Schuyler*, loc. 4873.

82. Some eminent historians have contended that Taylor was merely subpoenaed to testify at the court-martial, but he never actually testified. See, e.g., Eisenhower, *Zachary Taylor*, 7; and Bauer, *Zachary Taylor*, 11. However, an examination of the trial transcript shows that Taylor was called as a witness by Wilkinson and testified on three separate days: October 31, November 2, and November 5.

83. Testimony of Lieutenant Colonel Thomas A. Smith, in Wilkinson, *Memoirs*, 2:app94.

84. Wilkinson, 2:573.

85. Wilkinson, 2:app70.

86. William Smith to James Wilkinson, June 22, 1807, in Durett Collection, box 1, folder 32.

87. US House Report, April 27, 1810, in *American State Papers, Military Affairs*, 1:268.

88. Chandler, *Jefferson Conspiracies*, 269; Shreve, *Finished Scoundrel*, 252.

89. Wilkinson, *Memoirs*, 2:363.

90. Shreve, *Finished Scoundrel*, 255; Coffman, *Portrait of the Old Army*, 287.

91. Former captain George Peter, who commanded a light artillery unit traveling to Terre aux Boeufs, provided much of the testimony to the 1810 and 1811 House

committees regarding the improper transportation of Wilkinson's gift of horses from Morrison. Peter resigned his commission shortly after arriving at Terre aux Boeufs. Unfortunately, Peter died shortly before the court-martial and his testimony was presented only through the records produced by the House committees.

92. LeRoy Opie to James Wilkinson, October 9, 1811, in Madison Papers, Library of Congress, ser. 1, General Correspondence, 1723–1859. Opie also testified on Wilkinson's behalf regarding the quality of the provisions provided by Morrison. See Wilkinson, *Memoirs*, 2:495.

93. James Wilkinson to James Madison, October 8, 1811, in Stagg, Cross, and Perdue, *Papers of James Madison,* 3:481–82.

94. James Madison to James Wilkinson, October 12, 1811, in Stagg, Cross, and Perdue, 3:483–84.

95. Wilkinson, *Memoirs,* 2:497.

96. Wilkinson, 2:500.

97. After the trial Simmons continued to serve as the War Department accountant until he was finally fired by Madison in July 1814. "Letter of James Madison to William Simmons, July 6, 1814," in *Vermont Journal,* July 25, 1814, 4.

98. "Wilkinson's Trial," *Hagerstown Gazette,* November 26, 1811, 3C.

99. Peter Gansevoort to James Madison, November 29, 1811, in Stagg et al., *Papers of James Madison*, 4:43. Gansevoort stated that he was looking for the appointment of "someone over whom the court can have a proper control."

100. Peter Gansevoort to Catherine Gansevoort, December 18, 1811, in Ranzan and Hollis, *Hero of Fort Schuyler,* 274.

101. *Pittsburgh Weekly Gazette,* January 17, 1812, 3.

102. Coffman, *Portrait of the Old Army,* 40.

103. William Eustis to James Madison, July 26, 1819, in Mattern et al., *Papers of James Madison,* 4:491–92.

104. William Crawford to James Madison, January 18, 1812, in Stagg et al., *Papers of James Madison,* 4:131–32.

105. Thomas Jefferson to James Monroe, January 11, 1812, in Looney, *Papers of Thomas Jefferson,* 4:412–13.

106. James Madison to Thomas Jefferson, February 7, 1812, in Stagg et al., *Papers of James Madison,* 4:168–70.

107. Wilkinson, *Memoirs,* 2:576.

11. Death of an Army on the St. Lawrence

1. Cozzens, *Tecumseh and the Prophet,* 293.

2. Thomas Jefferson to William Duane, August 4, 1812, in Looney, *Papers of Thomas Jefferson,* 5:293–94.

3. Hickey, *1812,* 26.

4. Elbridge Gerry to James Madison, May 19, 1812, in Stagg et al., *Papers of James Madison,* 4:397–99.

5. Hickey, *1812*, 31.

6. Morrison, "Henry-Crillon Affair of 1812," 216. Morrison states that Henry was a con artist and that the correspondence was purchased and paid for by Monroe and Madison before it was even read.

7. Hickey, *1812*, 34–36.

8. James Madison to Congress, June 1, 1812, in Stagg et al., *Papers of James Madison*, 4:432–39.

9. *Annals of Congress*, 12th Congress, 1634; and Senate, 12th Congress, 297.

10. James Wilkinson to James Madison, February 27, 1812, in Stagg et al., *Papers of James Madison*, 4:213–14.

11. Hay, "Some Reflections," 485n30.

12. "An Act for the Relief of James Wilkinson," *Vermont Gazette*, August 4, 1812, 1.

13. William Eustis to James Wilkinson, March 13, 1812, in Wilkinson, *Memoirs*, 1:469.

14. Wilkinson, 1:470–88.

15. William Eustis to James Wilkinson, April 9, 1812, in Wilkinson, 1:492.

16. James Wilkinson to William Eustis, April 11, 1812, in Wilkinson, 1:492–95.

17. William Eustis to James Wilkinson, April 15, 1812, in Wilkinson, 1:495.

18. William Eustis to James Wilkinson, June 19, 1812, in Wilkinson, 1:497.

19. Wilkinson, 1:498.

20. See Forbes, *Report of the Trial*.

21. Elting, *Amateurs to Arms*, 39.

22. Henry Dearborn to James Madison, August 15, 1812, in Stagg et al., *Papers of James Madison*, 5:157–58. Dearborn observed that "the moderate abilities I possess shall be exerted to their utmost stretch" and begged to delay offensive operations until the following spring.

23. Elting, *Amateurs to Arms*, 40.

24. Winfield Scott, who at the time served Dearborn as chief of staff, observed that "nature never designed him for *a great General*" (emphasis in original). Peskin, *Winfield Scott*, chap. 4.

25. Henry Dearborn to James Madison, December 13, 1812, in Stagg et al., *Papers of James Madison*, 5:503–5.

26. Jacobs describes him as a "piddling incompetent." See his *Beginning of the U.S. Army*, 383.

27. John Adams to Benjamin Waterhouse, September 15, 1812, in Adams Papers.

28. Head, *Crisis of Peace*, 150.

29. Henry Adams observed Armstrong's selection as follows: "In spite of Armstrong's services, abilities and experience, something in his character always created distrust. He had every advantage of education, social and political connection, ability and self-confidence; he was only fifty-four years old, which was the age of Monroe; but he suffered from the reputation of indolence and intrigue. So strong was the prejudice against him that he obtained only eighteen against fifteen votes in the Senate on his confirmation; and while the two senators from Virginia did not vote at all, the

two from Kentucky voted in the negative. Under such circumstances, nothing but military success of the first order could secure a fair field for Monroe's rival." Adams, *History of the United States*, 593. Jacobs describes Armstrong this way: "He was essentially a bustler, usually a meddler, and frequently a pedant. His egoism allowed him to think himself infallible, but he lacked the character to assume responsibility for his own mistakes, or those of his subordinates. He was gregarious, convivial, and ambitious; a rather skillful politician but a very mediocre general—one who thought less of military objectives than of safe political exits. Often a quibbler himself, he inspired fault-finding among others, much to his own injury and that of his generals." Jacobs, *Tarnished Warrior*, 291.

30. William Eustis to Willie Blount, October 21, 1812, in Moser and MacPherson, *Papers of Andrew Jackson*, 2:338n3.

31. Andrew Jackson to George Campbell, November 29, 1812, in Moser and MacPherson, 2:343.

32. James Wilkinson to Andrew Jackson, January 22, 1813, in Moser and MacPherson, 2:358.

33. James Wilkinson to James Monroe, February 9, 1813, quoted in Turnbow, *Hardened to Hickory*, 258.

34. Andrew Jackson to James Wilkinson, March 22, 1813, in Moser and MacPherson, *Papers of Andrew Jackson*, 2:396.

35. Turnbow, *Hardened to Hickory*, 415.

36. Wade Hampton to James Madison, November 10, 1812, in Stagg et al., *Papers of James Madison*, 5:448–49.

37. William Crawford to James Madison, March 3, 1813, in Kreider et al., *Papers of James Madison*, 6:79–80.

38. John Armstrong to James Wilkinson, February 16, 1813, in Wilkinson, *Memoirs*, 3:339–40.

39. "Occupation of Mobile," *Carlisle Herald*, June 11, 1813, 1.

40. James Wilkinson to Cayento Perez, April 12, 1813, in Wilkinson, *Memoirs*, 1:509–10.

41. Mauricio Zuniga to James Wilkinson, April 12, 1813, and Wilkinson to Zuniga, April 16, 1813, both in Wilkinson, *Memoirs*, 1:516–18.

42. Coker, "John Forbes & Co.," 61–97. Wilkinson's heirs attempted to perfect their title to the island in 1827 but their application was rejected by Congress, citing the fact that Wilkinson was not a Spanish citizen at the time of the transfer. See *American State Papers, Public Lands*, 5:498–99. Alternatively, Jacobs speculates that the Forbes "gift" to Wilkinson was meant to launder another payment from Spain. Jacobs, *Tarnished Warrior*, 280.

43. *Mississippi Free Trader*, September 29, 1813, 5. It is possible that the cause of young Wilkinson's death came from his participation in yet another filibuster against Spanish Mexico. Wilkinson was a member of the 1813 Gutierrez-Magee Expedition, which consisted of dissident Mexicans and former US Army officers. After some

initial success against Spanish officials in Texas, the expedition was virtually wiped out at the Battle of Medina in August 1813. Wilkinson was apparently wounded at the battle but was able to return to Dauphin Island before he died from his wounds in September 1813. Schwarz, *Forgotten Battlefield*, 126.

44. Lewis was a veteran of the Northern Army during the Battles of Saratoga. According to Wilkinson, Lewis had advised Gates to recall Arnold at the Battle of Freeman's Farm, stating, "he may by some rash act cause mischief." Gates then directed Wilkinson to recall Arnold. See Wilkinson, *Memoirs*, 1:245–46. Following Saratoga, Lewis married into the Livingston family and became active in New York politics. He defeated Aaron Burr to become governor of New York in 1804. See Barbuto, *New York's War of 1812*, 10. Lewis was commissioned a brigadier general in April 1812 and declined Madison's offer to serve as the secretary of war in early 1813. As a military leader he has been described as "a timid incompetent." See Elting, *Amateurs to Arms*, 138.

45. John Armstrong to James Wilkinson, March 10, 1813, in Wilkinson, *Memoirs*, 3:341.

46. James Wilkinson to John Armstrong, May 23, 1813, in Wilkinson, 3:341.

47. James Wilkinson to Morgan Lewis, July 6, 1813, in Wilkinson, 3:115–16.

48. John Armstrong to James Wilkinson, August 9, 1813, in *American State Papers, Military Affairs*, 1:465.

49. Graves, *Field of Glory*, 317.

50. James Wilkinson to John Armstrong, August 24, 1813, in Wilkinson, *Memoirs*, 3:app29.

51. James Wilkinson to John Armstrong, November 3, 1813, in Wilkinson, 3:app38.

52. John Armstrong to James Wilkinson, October 19, 1813, in *American State Papers, Military Affairs*, 1:471–72. Despite the late date, Wilkinson thought that he had time to conduct an offensive on the Niagara peninsula before commencing an assault on the St. Lawrence. Armstrong overruled him. Barbuto, *New York's War of 1812*, 158.

53. James Wilkinson to John Armstrong, September 16, 1813, in *American State Papers, Military Affairs*, 1:467. On September 20 Wilkinson wrote to Armstrong and complained about suffering the effects of his "Smelfungus." James Wilkinson to John Armstrong, September 20, 1813, in *American State Papers, Military Affairs*, 1:468–69.

54. Testimony of General Morgan Lewis, February 10, 1815, in Wilkinson, *Memoirs*, 3:353.

55. Graves, *Field of Glory*, 123.

56. Testimony of General Morgan Lewis, February 1, 1815, in Wilkinson, *Memoirs*, 3:134.

57. Graves, *Field of Glory*, 91.

58. Barbuto, *New York's War of 1812*, 162.

59. Graves, *Field of Glory*, 109.

60. Ellery, *Memoirs of General Joseph Gardner Swift*, 116.

61. Testimony of General John Boyd, February 10, 1815, in Wilkinson, *Memoirs*, 3:88.

62. Testimony of General John Boyd, February 6, 1815, in Wilkinson, 3:84–85.

63. Scott, *Memoirs,* 1:93–94.

64. Graves, *Field of Glory,* 254.

65. "Official Return of the Killed and Wounded of a Detachment of the Army of the U.S. Descending the St. Lawrence River," *Pittsfield Sun*, December 2, 1813, 3.

66. "Extract from the General Order of Gen. Wilkinson of the 13th November," *Tennessee State Gazette* (Nashville), January 4, 1814, 2.

67. James Wilkinson to Wade Hampton, November 12, 1813, in *American State Papers, Military Affairs*, 1:463.

68. As Wilkinson wrote, "The British commander, having failed to gain either of his objects, can lay no claim to the honors of the day." James Wilkinson to John Armstrong, November 16, 1813, in *American State Papers, Military Affairs*, 1:475.

69. Ellery, *Memoirs of General Joseph Gardner Swift,* 118–21.

70. Ellery, 122. Swift wisely chose not to report to Wilkinson the full details of his conversation with Armstrong. He only briefly stated that Armstrong had expressed dissatisfaction with both Wilkinson and Hampton. In February 1814 Swift received a brevet promotion to brigadier general. In his memoirs Swift stated that he believed he should have received the promotion in November 1813 but that Armstrong felt he was too close to Wilkinson. Ellery, *Memoirs of General Joseph Gardner Swift,* 127.

71. See Dr. William Ross to Inspector General, December 8, 1813, in Wilkinson, *Memoirs*, 3:app9.

72. Everest, *War of 1812,* 136.

73. Barbuto, *New York's War of 1812,* 171.

74. James Wilkinson to John Armstrong, December 7, 1813, in Wilkinson, *Memoirs*, 3:app43.

75. Wilkinson, 3:363–64.

76. James Wilkinson to John Armstrong, November 24, 1813, in *American State Papers, Military Affairs*, 1:480. Wilkinson renewed the request for Hampton's arrest two days later. James Wilkinson to John Armstrong, November 26, 1813, in Kreider et al., *Papers of James Madison,* 7:62–63.

77. Wilkinson, *Memoirs*, 3:app5.

78. Wade Hampton to John Armstrong, November 1, 1811, in Wilkinson Papers, vol. 4, Chicago History Museum.

79. John Armstrong to James Wilkinson, January 20, 1814, in Wilkinson, *Memoirs,* 3:app49.

80. Wilkinson, 3:352–53.

81. *American State Papers, Military Affairs*, 1:439.

82. Hay and Werner, *Admirable Trumpeter,* 323–24.

83. Graves, *Field of Glory,* 314.

84. John Armstrong to James Madison, February 21, 1814, in Kreider et al., *Papers of James Madison,* 7:318–19.

85. John Armstrong to James Wilkinson, March 24, 1814, in Wilkinson Papers, vol. 4, Chicago History Museum; and Wilkinson, *Memoirs*, 3:app50.

86. See, e.g., Wilkinson's objection to the appointment of a particular officer to serve as recorder for the court. James Wilkinson to John Armstrong, April 15, 1814, in Wilkinson Papers, vol. 4, Chicago History Museum.

87. James Madison to John Armstrong, May 17, 1814, in Kreider et al., *Papers of James Madison*, 7:487–89.

88. John Armstrong to James Wilkinson, May 23, 1813, in Wilkinson, *Memoirs*, 3:371.

89. Letter by William Simmons, *Vermont Watchman and State Journal*, July 28, 1814, 2.

90. John Armstrong to James Madison, June 29, 1814, in Kreider et al., *Papers of James Madison*, 7:591–94.

91. James Madison to William Simmons, July 6, 1814, in Kreider et al., 8:13.

92. *Pennsylvania Gazette*, June 1, 1814, 3.

93. James Madison to John Armstrong, August 13, 1813, in Kreider et al., *Papers of James Madison*, 8:98–101.

94. Armstrong, *Notices of the War of 1812*, 2:140.

95. Borneman, *1812*, 224.

96. James Madison, Memorandum of a Conversation with John Armstrong, August 29, 1814, in Kreider et al., *Papers of James Madison*, 8:153–56.

97. John Armstrong to James Madison, September 4, 1814, in Kreider et al., 8:178.

98. One of Wilkinson's strong supporters, Senator Samuel Smith, led the forces that defended Baltimore. See Cassell, *Merchant Congressman*, 198–209.

12. Court-Martialed Again, Acquitted Again, Dismissed at Last

1. Wilkinson, *Memoirs*, 3:234.

2. Wilkinson, 3:16–23.

3. Wilkinson, 3:6–7.

4. Wilkinson, 3:15.

5. D. Parker to James Wilkinson, November 31, 1814, in Wilkinson, 3:app52.

6. James Monroe to Evert Bancker, January 29, 1815, in NARA, RG 107.

7. Evert Bancker to James Monroe, February 7, 1815, in NARA, RG 107.

8. Deposition of Evert A. Bancker, January 24, 1815, in Wilkinson, *Memoirs*, 3:33–35.

9. Wilkinson, 3:40.

10. Wilkinson devoted an entire chapter of his memoirs to attacking Scott. Wilkinson, 1:796–821. Scott returned the favor in his own autobiography, setting forth numerous attacks on Wilkinson.

11. Scott, *Memoirs*, 1:100.

12. On January 26 Dearborn, president of the court, wrote to Madison and expressed his dismay about the delay caused by the failure of officers to respond to the summonses to testify. Henry Dearborn to James Madison, January 26, 1815, in Kreider et al., *Papers of James Madison*, 8:527–28.

13. Winfield Scott to Evert Bancker, January 25, 1815, in Wilkinson, Memoirs, 3:41.

14. Alexander Macomb to Evert Bancker, January 25, 1815, in Wilkinson, 3:41.

15. Adjutant General to James Wilkinson, January 23, 1815, in Wilkinson, 3:42.

16. Armstrong, *Notices of the War of 1812,* 2:211–12.

17. Ellery, *Memoirs of General Joseph Gardner Swift,* 116.

18. Testimony of Dr. W. M. Ross (n.d.), in Wilkinson, *Memoirs,* 3:110.

19. Wilkinson, 3:111.

20. Testimony of Colonel William King, February 3, 1815, in Wilkinson, 3:73.

21. Testimony of Colonel William King, February 4, 1815, in Wilkinson, 3:77.

22. Testimony of General Morgan Lewis, February 11, 1815, in Wilkinson, 3:129.

23. Armstrong's witnesses' statements, set forth in his 1840 memoirs but which were never presented at trial, recounted the fact that Wilkinson exhibited vulgar and obscene behavior on the date in question. See Armstrong, *Notices of the War of 1812,* 2:211–12. Swift's memoirs state that Wilkinson "sung and repeated stories, the only evil of which was that it was not of the dignified deportment to be expected from the commander-in-chief." See Ellery, *Memoirs of General Joseph Gardner Swift,* 116.

24. Testimony of General Morgan Lewis, February 8, 1815, in Wilkinson, *Memoirs,* 3:115–16.

25. Wilkinson, 3:20–21.

26. Wilkinson, 3:469–70.

27. Testimony of General Henry Dearborn, February 20, 1815, in Wilkinson, 3:197–98.

28. Wilkinson, 3:467.

29. Wilkinson, 3:app70.

30. Interrogatories of General Alexander Macomb, March 7, 1815, in Wilkinson, 3:165–84.

31. Wilkinson, 3:496.

32. Skelton, "High Army Leadership," 253–74.

33. James Monroe to James Madison, April 8, 1815, in Kreider et al., *Papers of James Madison,* 9:143–44.

34. James Madison to James Monroe, April 10, 1815, in Kreider et al., 150–51.

35. Alexander Dallas to Madison, April 9, 1815, in Kreider et al., 9:146–50.

36. Alexander Dallas to James Madison, March 13, 1815, in Kreider et al., 9:83.

37. James Monroe to James Madison, April 26, 1815, in Kreider et al., 9:213–15.

38. James Madison to James Monroe, May 2, 1815, in Kreider et al., 9:228–29.

39. Alexander Dallas to James Madison, April 12, 1815, in Kreider et al., 9:157–59.

40. From Alexander Dallas to James Madison, August 15, 1815, in Kreider et al., 9:533–34.

41. James Monroe to James Madison, June 3, 1815, in Kreider et al., 9:360–62.

13. Who Tells Your Story?

1. Wilkinson, *Memoirs,* 2:305.

2. Lewis, *Burr Conspiracy,* 432n100.

3. William Colvin to Thomas Jefferson, September 14, 1810, in Looney, *Papers of Thomas Jefferson,* 3:78–79.

4. US Constitution, Article II, Section 3, requires the president to "take care that the Laws be faithfully executed."

5. Thomas Jefferson to William Colvin, September 20, 1810, in Looney, *Papers of Thomas Jefferson*, 3:99–102.

6. Jefferson's words have often been used by the executive branch to support enhanced authorities in times of crisis, such as Lincoln did during the Civil War and George W. Bush did for the response to the 9/11 attacks.

7. William Colvin to Thomas Jefferson, February 4, 1811, in Looney, *Papers of Thomas Jefferson*, 3:359–60.

8. Willie Blount to Andrew Jackson, February 26, 1811, in Moser and MacPherson, *Papers of Andrew Jackson*, 2:259.

9. John Adams to Thomas McKean, July 30, 1815, in Adams Papers.

10. Thomas McKean to John Adams, November 20, 1815, in Adams Papers.

11. John Adams to Thomas McKean, November 26, 1815, in Adams Papers.

12. Cox, "Later Intrigues," 803.

13. Linklater, *Artist in Treason,* 319. Linklater speculates that because the writing is so bad, some of it must have been written by Wilkinson under the influence of laudanum.

14. Wilkinson's first biographer was not even able to confirm the fact of his second marriage. Shreve, *Finished Scoundrel,* 292.

15. "Wilkinson's Memoirs," *Raleigh Minerva*, July 4, 1814, 3.

16. January 27, 1816, Archives of Maryland Online, vol. 634, 222. Wilkinson converted this lifetime pension into a lump sum payment of $3,500. Hay and Werner, *Admirable Trumpeter,* 334.

17. "New Orleans," *Christian Messenger*, February 24, 1819, 3.

18. Hay, "General James Wilkinson," 419–20.

19. Jacobs, *Tarnished Warrior,* 325.

20. James Wilkinson to Solomon Van Rensselaer, January 16, 1821, in Linklater, *Artist in Treason,* 323.

21. "An Act for the Relief of James Wilkinson," *Weekly Raleigh Register,* June 23, 1820, 1.

22. Many early heroes of Texas lore, such as Jean Lafitte, Jim Bowie, and Ben Milam, were affiliated with Long's expedition. Jane Wilkinson, Long's wife, accompanied him and later claimed the title "Mother of Texas." She also claimed to have given birth to the first Anglo child born in Texas. See Henson, "Jane Herbert Wilkinson Long."

23. Hay, "General James Wilkinson," 427.

24. Hay, 425.

25. Hay, 433.

26. Hay, 433–34.

27. Hay, "Some Reflections," 494n45.

28. Journal of the Senate, December 5, 1872, 42nd Congress, 3rd Sess., 27. Belknap was an appropriate government official to save Wilkinson's remains. As War Department secretary, Belknap had engaged in his own form of government corruption. Enmeshed in a scandal regarding improper payments from government contractors, Belknap resigned in 1876 shortly before he was impeached by the House of Representatives.

BIBLIOGRAPHY

Archival Collections

Adams, John. Papers. Massachusetts Historical Society, Boston. https://founders.archives .gov.

Adjutant General. Records. National Archives and Records Administration, Washington, DC.

American State Papers. 38 vols. Executive and Congressional Records, 1789–1838. Library of Congress, Washington, DC. memory.loc.gov.

Annals of Congress, 10th Congress, 1st Session; 11th Congress, 2nd Session and 3rd Session; 12th Congress, 1st Session.

Archivo General de Indias. Library of Congress, Washington, DC.

Brown, John M. and Preston Brown. Papers. War Department Papers, 1784–1800. Roy Rosenzweig Center for History and New Media, George Mason University, Fairfax, Virginia.

Clinton, Sir Henry. Papers. William L. Clements Library, University of Michigan, Ann Arbor, Michigan. https://clements.umich.edu/exhibit/spy-letters-of-the-american-revo lution/secret-methods/quill-letter/.

Coppet, Andre de. Autograph Collection. Princeton University Library, Princeton, New Jersey.

Durett, Reuben. Collection of James Wilkinson Papers. University of Chicago Library, Chicago.

Gratz, Simon. Collection. Historical Society of Pennsylvania, Philadelphia.

Heritage Frederick. Frederick County Historical Society, Frederick, Maryland.

Jefferson, Thomas. Papers. Princeton University Library, Princeton, New Jersey. https:// founders.archives.gov.

Jefferson, Thomas. Papers, Series 1: General Correspondence 1651–1867, Manuscript /Mixed Material. Library of Congress, Washington, DC. https://www.loc.gov/item /mtjbib016205/.

Journals of the Continental Congress (*JCC*). 17 vols. Library of Congress, Washington, DC. www.loc.gov.

Knox, Henry. Papers, Gilder Lehman Collection. New York Historical Society, New York.

Knox, Henry. Papers. Massachusetts Historical Society, Boston.

Library of Congress. https://www.loc.gov/item/rbpe.22702700/.

Madison, James. Papers. Library of Congress, Washington, DC.

Madison, James. Papers. University of Virginia, Charlottesville, Virginia. https://founders .archives.gov.

Maryland State Archives. Annapolis, Maryland. http://aomol.msa.maryland.gov/.

National Archives and Records Administration (NARA). Records of the Secretary of War. Washington, DC.

Pontalba Papers, 1787–1791. Temple Bodley Collection. Filson Historical Society, Louisville, Kentucky.

Shepherd, William R. Papers. Library of Congress, Washington, DC.

War Department. Papers, 1784–1800. Roy Rosenzweig Center for History and New Media, George Mason University, Fairfax, Virginia.

Washington, George. Papers. General Correspondence, Series 4. Library of Congress, Washington, DC.

Wayne, Anthony. Papers. Historical Society of Pennsylvania, Philadelphia.

Wilkinson, James. Papers. Chicago History Museum, Chicago.

Wilkinson, James. Papers. Darlington Collection, Archives & Special Collections. University of Pittsburgh Library, Pittsburgh, Pennsylvania.

Published Works

Abernethy, Thomas Perkins. *The Burr Conspiracy*. New York: Oxford University Press, 1954.

Adams, Henry. *History of the United States during the Administrations of James Madison*. New York: Library of America, 1986.

———. ed. *The Writings of Albert Gallatin*. 3 vols. Philadelphia: J. P. Lippincott, 1879.

Armstrong, John. *Notices of the War of 1812*. 2 vols. New York: Wiley & Putnam, 1840.

Atkinson, Rick. *The British Are Coming: The War for America, Lexington to Princeton, 1775–1777*. New York: Henry Holt, 2019.

Bacon, Ezekiel. *Report of the Committee Appointed to Inquire into the Conduct of General Wilkinson*. Washington, DC: A. and G. Way, 1811.

Balch, Thomas, ed. *Papers Relating Chiefly to the Maryland Line during the Revolution*. Philadelphia: T. K. & P. G. Collins, 1857.

Barbieri, Michael. "Infamous Skulkers: The Shooting of Brigadier General Patrick Gordon." *Journal of the American Revolution* 11 (September 2013).

Barbuto, Richard V. *New York's War of 1812: Politics, Society and Combat*. Norman: University of Oklahoma Press, 2021.

Basset, John Spenser, ed. *Correspondence of Andrew Jackson*. 6 vols. Washington, DC: Carnegie Institution, 1926.

Bauer, K. Jack. *Zachary Taylor: Solider, Planter, Statesman of the Old Southwest*. Baton Rouge: Louisiana State University Press, 1985.

Bell, Whitfield J., Jr. "The Court-Martial of Dr. William Shippen, Jr., 1780." *Journal of the History of Medicine and Allied Sciences* 19, no. 3 (July 1964): 218–38.

Bell, William Gardner. *Commanding Generals and Chiefs of Staff, 1775–2013*. Washington, DC: US Army Center of Military History, 2013.

Borneman, Walter R. *1812: The War That Forged a Nation*. New York: HarperCollins, 2004.

Bruce, William Cabell. *John Randolph of Roanoke*. 2 vols. New York: G. P. Putnam's Sons, 1922.

Brumwell, Stephen. *Turncoat: Benedict Arnold and the Crisis of American Liberty*. New Haven, CT: Yale University Press, 2018.

Buchanan, John. *The Road to Guilford Courthouse: The American Revolution in the Carolinas*. New York: John Wiley & Sons, 1997.

Cabell, James Austin. "The Trial of Aaron Burr." *Proceedings of the New York State Bar Association* 23 (1900): 56–86.

Calloway, Colin G. *The Victory with No Name: The Native American Defeat of the First American Army*. New York: Oxford University Press, 2015.

Carp, E. Wayne. *To Starve the Army at Pleasure: Continental Army Administration and American Political Culture*. Chapel Hill: University of North Carolina Press, 1984.

Carter, Clarence Edwin. *Territorial Papers of the United States*. Vol. 13, *The Territory of Louisiana-Missouri, 1803–1806*. Washington, DC: Government Printing Office, 1948.

Cassell, Frank A. *Merchant Congressman of the Young Republic: Samuel Smith of Maryland, 1752–1839*. Madison: University of Wisconsin Press, 1971.

Chalou, Charles C. "James Wilkinson—The Spanish Connection 1810." In *Congress Investigates, 1792–1974*, Vol. 1, edited by Arthur Schlesinger Jr. and Roger Bruns, 105–243. New York: Chelsea House, 1975.

———. "St. Clair's Defeat." In *Congress Investigates: 1792–1974*, Vol. 1, edited by Arthur M. Schlesinger Jr. and Roger Bruns, 3–101. New York: Chelsea House, 1975.

Chandler, David Leon. *The Jefferson Conspiracies: A President's Role in the Assassination of Meriwether Lewis*. New York: William Morrow, 1994.

Chase, Philander D., ed. *The Papers of George Washington*. Vol. 2, *16 September 1775–31 December 1775*. Revolutionary War Series. Charlottesville: University of Virginia Press, 1987. https://founders.archives.gov.

———. *The Papers of George Washington*. Vol. 7, *21 October 1776–5 January 1777*. Revolutionary War Series. Charlottesville: University of Virginia Press, 1997. https://founders.archives.gov.

Chernow, Ron. *Alexander Hamilton*. New York: Penguin, 2004.

———. *Washington: A Life*. New York: Penguin, 2010.

Clark, Daniel. *Proofs of the Corruption of Gen. James Wilkinson, and His Connection with Aaron Burr*. Philadelphia: William Hall Jr. & George Pierie, 1809.

Coffman, Edward M. *A Portrait of the Old Army in Peacetime, 1794–1898*. New York: Oxford University Press, 1988.

Coker, William S., ed. "John Forbes & Co. and the War of 1812 in the Spanish

Borderlands." In *Hispanic American Essays in Honor of Max Leon Moorhead*, 61–97. Pensacola: Perdido Bay, 1979.

Cox, Isaac Joslin. "General Wilkinson and His Later Intrigues with the Spanish." *American Historical Review* 19, no. 4 (July 1914): 794–813.

———. "The Pan-American Policy of Jefferson and Wilkinson." *Mississippi Valley Historical Review* 1, no. 2 (September 1914): 212–39.

———. "The West Florida Controversy, 1798–1813: A Study in American Diplomacy." *The Albert Shaw Lectures in Diplomatic History, 1912.* Baltimore: Johns Hopkins University Press, 1918.

———. "Wilkinson's First Break with the Spaniards." *Proceedings of the Eighth Annual Meeting of the Ohio Historical Society*, 1915.

Cozzens, Peter. *Tecumseh and the Prophet: The Shawnee Brothers Who Defied a Nation.* New York: Alfred A. Knopf, 2020.

Crackel, Theodore J. "Jefferson, Politics, and the Army." *Journal of the Early Republic* 2, no. 1 (Spring 1982): 21–38.

———. *Mr. Jefferson's Army: Political and Social Reform of the Military Establishment, 1801–1809.* New York: New York University Press, 1987.

Creasy, Edward. *The Fifteen Decisive Battles of the World: From Marathon to Waterloo.* London: Richard Bentley, 1852.

Crocker, Thomas E. *Braddock's March: How the Man Sent to Seize a Continent Changed American History.* Yardley, PA: Westholme, 2009.

Cullen, Charles T., ed. *The Papers of Thomas Jefferson.* Vol. 22, *6 August 1791–31 December 1791.* Princeton, NJ: Princeton University Press, 1986. https://founders.archives.gov.

Daigler, Kenneth A. *Spies, Patriots, and Traitors: American Intelligence in the Revolutionary War.* Washington, DC: Georgetown University Press, 2014.

Danisi, Thomas C. *Uncovering the Truth about Meriwether Lewis.* Buffalo, NY: Prometheus, 2012.

Davis, William C. *The Rogue Republic: How Would-Be Patriots Waged the Shortest Revolution in American History.* Boston: Houghton Mifflin Harcourt, 2011.

Drury, Bob, and Tom Clavin, *Blood and Treasure: Daniel Boone and the Fight for America's First Frontier.* New York: St. Martin's, 2021.

Eisenhower, John S. D. *Agent of Destiny.* New York: Free Press, 1997.

———. *Zachary Taylor.* New York: Times Books, 2008.

Ellery, Harrison, ed. *Memoirs of General Joseph Gardner Swift.* Worchester, MA: F. S. Blanchard, 1890.

Ellis, Joseph. *American Sphinx: The Character of Thomas Jefferson.* New York: Vintage, 1996.

Elting, John R. *Amateurs to Arms: A Military History of the War of 1812.* Chapel Hill, NC: Algonquin, 1991.

Everest, Alan S. *The War of 1812 in the Champlain Valley.* Syracuse, NY: Syracuse University Press, 1981.

Fischer, David Hackett. *Washington's Crossing.* New York: Oxford University Press, 2004.

Fleming, Thomas. *Duel: Alexander Hamilton, Aaron Burr, and the Future of America*. New York: Basic, 1999.

———. *1776: Year of Illusions*. New York: W. W. Norton, 1975.

———. *Washington's Secret War: The Hidden History of Valley Forge*. Washington, DC: Smithsonian, 2005.

Flexner, James T. *The Traitor and the Spy: Benedict Arnold and John Andre*. Boston: Little Brown, 1953.

Flores, Dan L., ed. *Southern Counterpart to Lewis and Clark: The Freeman and Custis Expedition of 1806*. Norman: University of Oklahoma Press, 1984.

Forbes, James G. *Report of the Trial of Brigadier General William Hull, Commanding the Northwest Army of the United States*. New York: Eastburn, Kirk, 1814.

Gaff, Alan D. *Bayonets in the Wilderness: Anthony Wayne's Legion in the Old Northwest*. Norman: University of Oklahoma Press, 2004.

Gale, Kira. *Meriwether Lewis: The Assassination of an American Hero and the Silver Mines of Mexico*. Omaha: River Junction, 2015.

Gayarre, Charles. *History of Louisiana*. 4 vols. New York: William J. Widdleton, 1867.

Geppert, Cynthia, and Reid Paul. "The Shot That Won the Revolutionary War and Is Still Reverberating." *Federal Practitioner* 36, no. 7 (July 2019): 298–99.

Gillette, Mary C. *The Army Medical Department, 1775–1818*. Washington, DC: US Army Center of Military History, 1981.

Golway, Terry. *Washington's General: Nathaniel Greene and the Triumph of the American Revolution*. New York: Henry Holt, 2005.

Graves, David E. *Field of Glory: The Battle of Crysler's Farm, 1813*. Cap-Saint-Ignace, QC: Robin Brass Studio, 1999.

Graydon, Alexander. *Memories of a Life Chiefly Passed in Pennsylvania within the Last Sixty Years*. Harrisburg, PA: William Blackwood, 1811.

Grizzard, Frank E., Jr., and David R. Hoth, eds. *The Papers of George Washington*. Vol. 12, *26 October 1777–25 December 1777*. Revolutionary War Series. Charlottesville: University of Virginia Press, 1997. https://founders.archives.gov.

Hackett, Mary A., J. C. A. Stagg, Jeanne Kerr Cross, Susan Holbrook Perdue, and Ellen J. Barber, eds. *The Papers of James Madison*. Vol. 4, *8 October 1802–15 May 1803*. Secretary of State Series. Charlottesville: University of Virginia Press, 1998. https://founders.archives.gov.

Haggard, Robert F., and Mark A. Mastromarino, eds. *The Papers of George Washington*. Vol. 10, *1 March 1792–15 August 1792*. Presidential Papers Series. Charlottesville: University of Virginia Press, 2002. https://founders.archives.gov.

Harrington, Hugh T. "Was General Anthony Wayne Murdered?" *Journal of the American Revolution* 20 (August 2013).

Harrison, Lowell H., and James C. Klotter. *A New History of Kentucky*. Lexington: University Press of Kentucky, 1997.

Hay, Thomas Robson, ed. "General James Wilkinson—The Last Phase." *Louisiana Historical Quarterly* 19, no. 2 (April 1936): 407–35.

———. "Letters of Ann Biddle Wilkinson from Kentucky." *Pennsylvania Magazine of History and Biography* 56, no. 1 (1932): 33–55.

———. "Some Reflections on the Career of Gen. James Wilkinson." *Mississippi Valley Historical Review* 21, no. 4 (March 1935): 471–94.

Hay, Thomas Robson, and M. R. Werner. *The Admirable Trumpeter.* Cranbury, NJ: Scholar's Bookshelf, 1941.

Head, David. *A Crisis of Peace: George Washington, the Newburgh Conspiracy and the Fate of the American Revolution.* New York: Pegasus, 2019.

Henshaw, Lesley, "Burr-Blennerhassett Documents," *Quarterly Publication of the Historical and Philosophical Society of Ohio* 9 (January and April, 1914).

Henson, Margaret S. "Jane Herbert Wilkinson Long," *Texas State Historical Society*, https://tshaonline.org/handbook/online/articles/flo11.

Hentz, Tucker F. "Unit History of the Maryland and Virginia Rifle Regiment (1776–1781): Insights from the Service Record of Capt. Adamson Tannehill." Richmond: Virginia Historical Society, 2007.

Hickey, Donald R. "United States Army versus Long Hair: The Trials of Colonel Thomas Butler, 1801–1805." *Pennsylvania Magazine of History and Biography* 101, no. 4 (October 1977): 462–74.

———. *The War of 1812: A Forgotten Conflict.* Urbana: University of Illinois Press, 2012.

Hill, Roscoe R. *Descriptive Catalogue of the Documents Relating to the History of the United States in the Papeles Procedentes de Cuba Deposited in the Archivo General de Indias at Seville.* Washington, DC: Carnegie Institution, 1916.

Hogeland, William. *Black Snake: The Creation of the U.S. Army and the Invasion That Opened the West.* New York: Farrar, Straus, and Giroux, 2017.

Hollon, W. Eugene. "Zebulon Montgomery Pike and the Wilkinson-Burr Conspiracy." *Proceedings of the American Philosophical Society* 91, no. 5 (December 1947): 447–56.

Hoth, David R., ed. *The Papers of George Washington.* Vol. 14, *1 March 1778–30 April 1778.* Revolutionary War Series. Charlottesville: University of Virginia Press, 2004. https://founders.archives.gov.

Hoth, David R., and Carol S. Ebel, eds. *The Papers of George Washington.* Vol. 16, *1 May–30 September 1794.* Presidential Series. Charlottesville: University of Virginia Press, 2004. https://founders.archives.gov.

———. *The Papers of George Washington.* Vol. 17, *1 October 1794–31 March 1795.* Presidential Series. Charlottesville: University of Virginia Press, 2013. https://founders.archives.gov.

Irving, Pierre M., ed. *The Life and Letters of Washington Irving.* 4 vols. London: Richard Bentley, 1862.

Irving, Washington. *Diedrich Knickerbocker's History of New York.* New York: G. P. Putnam's Sons, 1892.

Isenberg, Nancy. *Fallen Founder: The Life of Aaron Burr.* New York: Viking, 2007.

Jackson, Donald. "Jefferson, Meriwether Lewis, and the Reduction of the United States Army." *Proceedings of the American Philosophical Society* 124, no. 2 (April 1980): 91–96.

Jacobs, James Ripley. *The Beginning of the U.S. Army, 1783–1812*. Westport: Greenwood, 1947.

———. *Tarnished Warrior: Major General James Wilkinson*. New York: MacMillan, 1938.

Johnson, David. *John Randolph of Roanoke*. Baton Rouge: Louisiana State University Press, 2012.

Johnson, Timothy D. *Winfield Scott: The Quest for Military Glory*. Lawrence: University Press of Kansas, 1998.

Jones, T. Cole. *Captives of Liberty: Prisoners of War and the Politics of Vengeance in the American Revolution*. Philadelphia: University of Pennsylvania Press, 2020.

Kelly, Jack. *Valcour: The 1776 Campaign That Saved the Cause of Liberty*. New York: St. Martin's, 2021.

Kerr, Orin, S. "Decryption Originalism: The Lessons of Burr." *Harvard Law Review* 134 (2021): 905–63.

Ketchum, Richard M. *Saratoga: Turning Point of America's Revolutionary War*. New York: Henry Holt, 1997.

Kline, Mary-Jo, ed. *Political Correspondence and Public Papers of Aaron Burr*. 2 vols. Princeton, NJ: Princeton University Press, 1983.

Knopf, Richard C., ed. *Anthony Wayne: A Name in Arms*. Pittsburgh, PA: University of Pittsburgh Press, 1960.

Kohn, Richard H. *Eagle and Sword: The Federalists and the Creation of the Military Establishment in America, 1783–1802*. New York: Free Press, 1975.

———. "General Wilkinson's Vendetta with General Wayne: Politics and Command in the American Army, 1791–1796." *Filson Club Historical Quarterly* 45, no. 4 (October 1971): 361–72.

Kreider, Angela, J. C. A. Stagg, Jeanne Kerr Cross, Anne Mandeville Colony, Mary Parke Johnson, and Wendy Ellen Perry, eds. *The Papers of James Madison*. Vol. 6, *8 February–24 October 1813*. Presidential Series. Charlottesville: University of Virginia Press, 2008. https://founders.archives.gov.

Kreider, Angela, J. C. A. Stagg, Mary Parke Johnson, Anne Mandeville Colony, and Katherine E. Harbury, eds. *The Papers of James Madison*. Vol. 7, *25 October 1813–30 June 1814*. Presidential Series. Charlottesville: University of Virginia Press, 2012. https://founders.archives.gov.

———. *The Papers of James Madison*. Vol. 8, *July 1814–18 February 1815*. Presidential Series. Charlottesville: University of Virginia Press, 2015. https://founders.archives.gov.

———. *The Papers of James Madison*. Vol. 9, *19 February 1815–12 October 1815*. Presidential Series. Charlottesville: University of Virginia Press, 2015. https://founders.archives.gov.

Leckie, Robert. *From Sea to Shining Sea: From the War of 1812 to the Mexican War, the Saga of America's Expansion*. New York: Harper Perennial, 1993.

Lender, Mark Edward. *Cabal! The Plot against General Washington.* Yardley, PA: West-holme, 2019.

Lengel, Edward G., ed. *The Papers of George Washington.* Vol. 13, *26 December 1777–28 February 1778.* Revolutionary War Series. Charlottesville: University of Virginia Press, 2003. https://founders.archives.gov.

Lewis, James E., Jr. *The Burr Conspiracy: Uncovering the Story of an Early American Crisis.* Princeton, NJ: Princeton University Press, 2017.

Linklater, Andro. *An Artist in Treason: The Extraordinary Double Life of General James Wilkinson.* New York: Walker, 2009.

Lodge, Henry Cabot. *Daniel Webster.* Boston: Houghton & Mifflin, 1898.

Looney, J. Jefferson, ed. *The Papers of Thomas Jefferson.* Vol. 3, *12 August 1810–17 June 1811.* Retirement Series. Princeton, NJ: Princeton University Press, 2006. https://founders.archives.gov.

———. *The Papers of Thomas Jefferson.* Vol. 4, *18 June 1811–30 April 1812.* Retirement Series. Princeton, NJ: Princeton University Press, 2007. https://founders.archives.gov.

———. *The Papers of Thomas Jefferson.* Vol. 5, *1 May 1812–10 March 1813.* Retirement Series. Princeton, NJ: Princeton University Press, 2008. https://founders.archives.gov.

———. *The Papers of Thomas Jefferson.* Vol. 7, *28 November 1813–30 September 1814.* Retirement Series. Princeton, NJ: Princeton University Press, 2010. https://founders.archives.gov.

Luzader, John F. *Saratoga: A Military History of the Decisive Campaign of the American Revolution.* El Dorado Hills, CA: Savas Beatie, 2008.

Maas, John R. "The Army's Disaster at Terre aux Boeufs, 1809." *Army History* 85 (Fall 2012): 6–25.

Macomb, Alexander. *A Treatise on Martial Law and Courts-Martial.* Charleston, SC: Military Philosophical Society, 1809.

Malone, Dumas. *Jefferson the President: Second Term, 1805–1809.* Boston: Little, Brown, 1974.

Mansfield, Edward D. *The Life of General Winfield Scott.* New York: A. S. Barnes, 1846.

Martin, James Kirby. *Benedict Arnold, Revolutionary War Hero: An American Warrior Reconsidered.* New York: New York University Press, 1997.

Martin, Joseph Plumb. *Memoir of a Revolutionary Soldier.* Hallowell, ME: Glazier, Masters, 2019; first published in 1830.

Mastromarino, Mark A., ed. *The Papers of George Washington.* Vol. 6, *1 July 1790–30 November 1790.* Presidential Series. Charlottesville: University of Virginia Press, 1996. https://founders.archives.gov.

———. *The Papers of George Washington.* Vol. 8, *22 March 1791–22 September 1791.* Presidential Series. Charlottesville: University of Virginia Press, 1999. https://founders.archives.gov.

———. *The Papers of George Washington.* Vol. 9, *23 September 1791–29 February 1792.* Presidential Series. Charlottesville: University of Virginia Press, 2000. https://founders.archives.gov.

Mattern, David B., J. C. A. Stagg, Mary Parke Johnson, and Anne Mandeville Colony, eds. *The Papers of James Madison.* Vol. 1, *4 March 1817–31 January 1820.* Retirement Series. Charlottesville: University of Virginia Press, 2009. https://founders.archives .gov.

Matthews, Catherine Van Courtland, ed. *Andrew Ellicott: His Life and Letters.* New York: Grafton, 1908.

Matthews, George R. *Zebulon Pike: Thomas Jefferson's Agent for Empire.* Santa Barbara, CA: Praeger, 2016.

McBurney, Christian M. *George Washington's Nemesis: The Outrageous Treason and Unfair Court-Martial of Major General Charles Lee during the Revolutionary War.* El Dorado Hills, CA: Savas Beatie, 2020.

———. *Kidnapping the Enemy: The Special Operations to Capture General Charles Lee & Richard Prescott.* Yardley, PA: Westholme, 2014.

McCaleb, Walther Flavius. *The Aaron Burr Conspiracy.* New York: Dodd, Meade, 1903.

McClure, James P., ed. *The Papers of Thomas Jefferson.* Vol. 42, *16 November 1803–10 March 1804.* Princeton, NJ: Princeton University Press, 2016. https://founders.archives.gov.

McCullough, David. *John Adams.* New York: Simon & Schuster, 2001.

McMaster, John Bach. *A History of the People of the United States, from the Revolution to the Civil War.* 5 vols. New York: D. Appleton, 1884.

Melton, Buckner F., Jr. *Aaron Burr: Conspiracy to Treason.* New York: John Wiley & Sons, 2002.

Montgomery, M. R. *Jefferson and the Gunmen: How the West Was Almost Lost.* New York: Crown, 2000.

Morgan, William James, ed. *Naval Documents of the Revolution.* 13 vols. Washington, DC: Director of Naval History, 1972.

Morrison, Samuel Eliot. "The Henry-Crillon Affair of 1812." *Proceedings of the Massachusetts Historical Society* 69 (October 1947–May 1950): 207–31.

Moser, Harold D., and Sharon MacPherson, eds. *The Papers of Andrew Jackson.* 17 vols. Knoxville: University of Tennessee Press, 1984.

Nagle, James F. *A History of Government Contracting.* Washington, DC: George Washington University Press, 1992.

Narrett, David E. "Geopolitics and Intrigue: James Wilkinson, the Spanish Borderlands, and Mexican Independence." *William and Mary Quarterly* 69, no. 1 (January 2012): 101–46.

Nelson, Paul David. "General Charles Scott, the Kentucky Mounted Volunteers, and the Northwest Indian Wars, 1784–1794." *Journal of the Early Republic* 6, no. 3 (Autumn 1986): 219–51.

———. *General Horatio Gates.* Baton Rouge: Louisiana State University Press, 1976.

Newmyer, R. Kent. *The Treason Trial of Aaron Burr: Law, Politics, and the Character Wars of the New Nation.* New York: Cambridge University Press, 2012.

Oberg, Barbara B., ed. *The Papers of Thomas Jefferson.* Vol. 31, *1 February 1799–31 May 1800.* Princeton, NJ: Princeton University Press, 2004. https://founders.archives.gov.

———. *The Papers of Thomas Jefferson*. Vol. 33, *17 February–30 April 1801*. Princeton, NJ: Princeton University Press, 2006. https://founders.archives.gov.

———. *The Papers of Thomas Jefferson*. Vol. 34, *1 May–31 July 1801*. Princeton, NJ: Princeton University Press, 2006. https://founders.archives.gov.

O'Toole, G. J. *Honorable Treachery: A History of U.S. Intelligence, Espionage, and Covert Action from the American Revolution to the CIA*. New York: Atlantic Monthly, 1991.

Papas, Phillip. *Renegade Revolutionary: The Life of General Charles Lee*. New York: New York University Press, 2014.

Peskin, Allan. *Winfield Scott and the Profession of Arms*. Kent, OH: Kent State University Press, 2003.

Philbrick, Nathaniel. *Valiant Ambition: George Washington, Benedict Arnold, and the Fate of the American Revolution*. New York: Viking, 2016.

Randall, Willard Sterne. *Benedict Arnold: Patriot and Traitor*. New York: William Morrow, 1990.

Ranzan, David, and Matthew J. Hollis, eds. *Hero of Fort Schuyler: Selected Revolutionary War Correspondence of Brigadier General Peter Gansevoort, Jr.* Jefferson, NC: McFarland, 2014. Kindle.

Ravenholt, Reimert T. "Triumph Then Despair: The Tragic Death of Meriwether Lewis." *Epidemiology* 5, no. 3 (May 1994): 366–79.

Remini, Robert V. "Andrew Jackson Takes an Oath of Allegiance to Spain." *Tennessee Historical Quarterly* 54, no. 1 (Spring 1995): 2–15.

Richards, George R., ed. *Memoir of Alexander Macomb, the Major General Commanding the Army of the United States*. New York: McElrath, Bangs, 1833.

Risch, Erna. *Supplying Washington's Army*. Washington, DC: US Army Center of Military History, 1981.

Robertson, David. *Reports of the Trials of Aaron Burr for Treason*. 2 vols. Philadelphia: Hopkins & Earle, 1808.

Robinson, James A., ed. *Louisiana under the Rule of Spain, France, and the United States, 1785–1807*. 2 vols. Cleveland: Arthur H. Clark, 1911.

Rogow, Arnold A. *A Fatal Friendship: Alexander Hamilton and Aaron Burr*. New York: Hill & Wang, 1998.

Roosevelt, Theodore. *The Winning of the West: From the Alleghenies to the Mississippi*. 4 vols. New York: Current Issues, 1905.

Rossie, Jonathan Gregory. *The Politics of Command in the American Revolution*. Syracuse, NY: Syracuse University Press, 1975.

Rusche, Timothy M. "Treachery within the United States Army." *Pennsylvania History: A Journal of Mid-Atlantic Studies* 64, no. 4 (Autumn 1998): 478–91.

Rutland, Robert A., Thomas A. Mason, Robert J. Brugger, Susannah H. Jones, Jeanne K. Sisson, and Fredrika J. Teute, eds. *The Papers of James Madison*. Vol. 1, *1 March–30 September 1809*. Presidential Series. Charlottesville: University of Virginia Press, 1984. https://founders.archives.gov.

Schaeper, Thomas J. *Edward Bancroft: Scientist, Author, Spy*. New Haven, CT: Yale University Press, 2011.

Schecter, Barnet. *The Battle for New York: The City at the Heart of the American Revolution.* New York: Walker, 2002.

Schellhammer, Michael. "Duels of Honor." *Journal of the American Revolution* 7 (August 2014).

Schwarz, Ted. *Forgotten Battlefield of the First Texas Revolution: The Battle of Medina, August 18, 1813*, Fort Worth: Eakin Press, 1985.

Scott, Winfield. *Memoirs of Lieutenant General Winfield Scott.* 2 vols. New York: Sheldon, 1864.

Sedgwick, John. *War of Two: Alexander Hamilton, Aaron Burr, and the Duel That Stunned the Nation.* New York: Berkley, 2015.

Shepherd, William R. "A Letter of James Wilkinson, 1806." *American Historical Review* 9, no. 3 (April 1904): 533–37.

———. "Papers Bearing on James Wilkinson's Relations with Spain, 1787–1816." *American Historical Review* 9, no. 4 (July 1904): 748–66.

———. "Wilkinson and the Beginnings of the Spanish Conspiracy." *American Historical Review* 9, no. 3 (April 1904): 490–506.

Shreve, Royal Ornan. *The Finished Scoundrel.* Indianapolis, IN: Bobbs-Merrill, 1933.

Skelton, William B. "High Army Leadership in the Era of the War of 1812: The Making and Remaking of the Officer Corps." *William and Mary Quarterly* 51, no. 2 (April 1994): 253–74.

Smith, William Henry, ed. *The St. Clair Papers, The Life and Public Services of Arthur St. Clair.* 2 vols. Cincinnati: Robert Clarke, 1882.

Snow, Dean. *1777: Tipping Point at Saratoga.* New York: Oxford University Press, 2016.

Stagg, J. C. A., Jeanne Kerr Cross, and Susan Holbrook Perdue, eds. *The Papers of James Madison.* Vol. 2, *1 October 1809–2 November 1810.* Presidential Series. Charlottesville: University of Virginia Press, 1992. https://founders.archives.gov.

———. *The Papers of James Madison.* Vol. 3, *3 November 1810–4 November 1811.* Presidential Series. Charlottesville: University of Virginia Press, 1996. https://founders.archives.gov.

Stagg, J. C. A., Jeanne Kerr Cross, Jewel L. Spangler, Ellen J. Barber, Martha J. King, Anne Mandeville Colon, and Susan Holbrook Perdue, eds. *The Papers of James Madison.* Vol. 4, *5 November 5–9 July 1812, and Supplement March 5, 1809–October 19, 1811.* Presidential Series. Charlottesville: University of Virginia Press, 1996. https://founders.archives.gov.

Stagg, J. C. A., Martha J. King, Ellen J. Barber, Anne Mandeville Colony, Angela Kreider, and Jewel L. Spangler, eds. *The Papers of James Madison.* Vol. 5, *10 July 1812–7 February 1813.* Presidential Series. Charlottesville: University of Virginia Press, 2004. https://founders.archives.gov.

Starrs, James E., and Kira Gale. *The Death of Meriwether Lewis: A Historic Crime Scene Investigation.* 2nd ed. Omaha: River Junction, 2012.

Steiner, Bernard C., ed. *The Life and Correspondence of James McHenry, Secretary of War under Washington and Adams.* Cleveland: Burrows Brothers, 1907.

Stemple, Jim. *American Hannibal: The Extraordinary Account of Revolutionary War Hero Daniel Morgan at the Battle of Cowpens.* Tucson, AZ: Penmore, 2017.

Stewart, David O. *American Emperor*. New York: Simon and Schuster, 2011.

Stinchcombe, William. "The Diplomacy of the XYZ Affair." *William and Mary Quarterly* 34, no. 4 (October 1977): 590–615.

Stockwell, Mary. *Unlikely General: "Mad" Anthony Wayne and the Battle for America*. New Haven, CT: Yale University Press, 2018.

Stoddard, Robert A., ed. *The Autobiography Manuscript of Major Amos Stoddard*. San Diego: Robert Stoddard, 2016.

Stroud, Patricia Tyson. *Bitterroot: The Life and Death of Meriwether Lewis*. Philadelphia: University of Pennsylvania Press, 2018.

Sword, Wiley. *President Washington's Indian War: The Struggle for the Old Northwest, 1790–1795*. Norman: University of Oklahoma Press, 1985.

Syrett, Harold C., ed. *The Papers of Alexander Hamilton*. Vol. 14, *February 1793–June 1793*. New York: Columbia University Press, 1969. https://founders.archives.gov.

———. *The Papers of Alexander Hamilton*. Vol. 20, *January 1796–March 1797*. New York: Columbia University Press, 1974. https://founders.archives.gov.

———. *The Papers of Alexander Hamilton*. Vol. 23, *April 1799–October 1799*. New York: Columbia University Press, 1976. https://founders.archives.gov.

———. *The Papers of Alexander Hamilton*. Vol. 24, *November 1799–June 1800*. New York: Columbia University Press, 1976. https://founders.archives.gov.

———. *The Papers of Alexander Hamilton*. Vol. 25, *July 1800–April 1802*. New York: Columbia University Press, 1977. https://founders.archives.gov.

Taafe, Stephen R. *Washington's Revolutionary War Generals*. Norman: University of Oklahoma Press, 2019.

Taggert, Hugh T. "Old Georgetown." *Records of the Columbia Historical Society* 11 (1908): 120–224.

Taylor, Alan. *The Civil War of 1812*. New York: Alfred A. Knopf, 2010.

Toll, Ian. *Six Frigates: The Epic History of the Founding of the U.S. Navy*. New York: W. W. Norton, 2006.

Trogden, Jo Ann. *The Unknown Travels and Dubious Pursuits of William Clark*. Columbia: University of Missouri Press, 2015.

Turnbow, Tony L. *Hardened to Hickory: The Missing Chapter in Andrew Jackson's Life*. Self-published, 2018.

Twohig, Dorothy, ed. *The Papers of George Washington*. Vol. 1, *24 September 1788–31 March 1789*. Presidential Series. Charlottesville: University of Virginia Press, 1987. https://founders.archives.gov.

Tyler, Samuel. *Memoir of Roger Brooke Taney, LL.D, Chief Justice of the Supreme Court of the United States*. Baltimore: John Murphy, 1872.

US Army. *The Army Lawyer: A History of the Judge Advocate General's Corps, 1775–1975*. Washington, DC: Government Printing Office, 1975.

US Department of Commerce. "Historical Statistics of the United States, Colonial Times to 1970." Washington, DC: Bureau of the Census, 1976.

Watson, Thomas E. *The Life and Times of Thomas Jefferson*. New York: D. Appleton, 1903.

Weddle, Kevin J. *The Compleat Victory: Saratoga and the American Revolution.* New York: Oxford University Press, 2021.

Weigley, Russell F. *History of the United States Army.* New York: McMillan, 1967.

Wheelan, Joseph. *Jefferson's Vendetta: The Pursuit of Aaron Burr and the Judiciary.* New York: Carroll & Graff, 2005.

Whitaker, Arthur P. "James Wilkinson's First Descent to New Orleans in 1787." *Hispanic American Historical Review* 8, no. 1 (February 1928): 82–97.

Wiener, Frederick Bernays. "Courts-Martial and the Bill of Rights: The Original Practice." *Harvard Law Review* 72, no. 1 (1958): 1–49.

Wilkinson, James. *A Brief Examination of Testimony to Vindicate the Character of General James Wilkinson against the Imputation of a Sinister Connection with the Spanish Government for Purposes Hostile to His Own Country.* Washington, DC: W. Cooper, 1811.

———. *Burr's Conspiracy Exposed and General Wilkinson Vindicated against the Slander of His Enemies on That Important Occasion.* Washington, DC, 1811.

———. *Memoirs of My Own Times.* 3 vols. Philadelphia: Abraham Small, 1816.

———. [pseud. "Kentuckian"]. *A Plain Tale Supported by Authentic Documents, Justifying the Character of General Wilkinson.* New York: 1807.

Wingate, Christopher W. "Military Professionalism in the Early American Officer Corps, 1789–1796." Master's thesis, US Army Command and General Staff College, 2013.

Winthrop, William, *Military Law and Precedents*, Washington, DC: Government Printing Office, 1920.

Wohl, Michael, "Not Yet Saint nor Sinner: A Further Note on Daniel Clark." *Louisiana History: The Journal of the Louisiana Historical Association* 23, no. 2 (Spring 1983): 195–205.

Zambone, Albert Louis, *Daniel Morgan: A Revolutionary Life.* Yardley: Westholme Publishing, 2018.

Newspapers Cited

The Adams Sentinel (Gettysburg, PA)
Aurora General Advertiser (Philadelphia)
Carlisle (PA) Herald
Christian Messenger (Middlebury, VT)
Colvin's Weekly Register (Washington, DC)
The Evening Post (New York City)
Hagerstown (MD) Gazette
Hartford (CT) Courant
Maryland Gazette (Annapolis, MD)
Mississippi Free Trader (Natchez, MS)
Missouri Gazette and Public Advertiser (St. Louis, MO)
The Monitor (Washington, DC)
National Intelligencer and Washington Advertiser (Washington, DC)
Pennsylvania Gazette (Philadelphia)

Pittsburgh (PA) Weekly Gazette
The Pittsfield (MA) Sun
The Raleigh (NC) Minerva
Tennessee State Gazette (Nashville, TN)
Vermont Gazette (Bennington, VT)
The Vermont Journal (Windsor, VT)
The Vermont Sentinel and Democrat (Burlington, VT)
Vermont Watchman and State Journal (Montpelier, VT)
Weekly Raleigh (NC) Register

INDEX

ABOUT THE AUTHOR

Howard W. Cox is a former trial attorney in the US Army's Judge Advocate General's Corps, a former staff counsel of the Senate Permanent Subcommittee on Investigations, a former federal prosecutor, and the assistant inspector general for investigations at the CIA. He holds an AB in history from Seton Hall University and a JD from Georgetown University Law Center.